D0082426

BLOND'S MULTISTATE

by
NEIL C. BLOND, Esq.

fourth edition
revised with
the assistance of
ELYSE ECHTMAN

**SULZBURGER & GRAHAM
PUBLISHING, Ltd.
NEW YORK**

(800) 366-7086

Also Available in this Series:

Blond's Torts
Blond's Evidence
Blond's Property
Blond's Contracts
Blond's Income Tax
Blond's Family Law
Blond's Corporations
Blond's Criminal Law
Blond's Corporate Tax
Blond's Civil Procedure
Blond's International Law
Blond's Criminal Procedure
Blond's Administrative Law
Blond's Constitutional Law
Blond's Multistate Questions

Copyright 1992 © Sulzburger & Graham Publishing, Ltd.

All rights reserved - No part of this book may be reproduced by any electronic or other means without written permission from the publisher.

ISBN 0-945-819-17-X

Printed in The United States of America

TABLE OF CONTENTS

CONSTITUTIONAL LAW CONTENTS

CONSTITUTIONAL LAW QUESTIONS

Questions 1-2 are based upon the following fact situation.

The federal government enacted a $100 tax on all persons running in a marathon sanctioned by a national athletic organization. The law specified that all monies raised by the marathon tax would be used to build a New Mexico shelter for homeless persons.

1.   Which of the following people have the best chance of asserting a successful challenge to the statute?

    (A)   a running shoe company

    (B)   the city of New York because, although home of the country's largest homeless population, the city has not received federal money for the homeless

    (C)   a woman registered for the Honolulu Marathon

    (D)   the American Heart Association

2.   Should the statute be declared constitutional?

    (A)   Yes, if it is related to the public interest.

    (B)   Yes, because society has an interest in helping poor persons.

    (C)   No, because the distribution is not apportioned equally among the states.

    (D)   No, because the tax is unrelated to its use.

3.   Reagan's will contained the following clause:
"To honor the people of my favorite country, I hearby request that royalties from my movie *Bedtime for Bonzo* be used to establish an elementary school for the children of citizens of Grenada. The school shall stress the culture and values of the United States and Grenada, and admission shall be limited to Grenadian Americans."
The Bernard Coard School was established with the *Bonzo* proceeds. A constitutional challenge should be based upon the

    (A)   Equal Protection Clause

    (B)   Privileges and Immunities Clause

    (C)   Fourteenth Amendment

    (D)   all of the above

GO ON TO THE NEXT PAGE

4.   The Federal Hazardous Waste Act of 1987 contained the clause "All disposal of Lithium 235 must be preceded by the rendering of the element inert by combining it with Au isotopes. Li Au compound may only be shipped by rail in lead-reinforced containers." The federal standard was prohibitively expensive compared to the methods previously used by Lithium Chemical, a company incorporated and doing business in the state of Nevada. Lithium Chemical developed and patented Lithium 235 and was the only company producing it.

   In 1988, the state of Nevada passed a statute that "Lithium 235 may be disposed of only after being rendered inert by combining it with Au or Pb isotopes."

   The Nevada statute will be found unconstitutional

(A)   because it interferes with powers delegated to the federal government

(B)   because it constitutes state interference with interstate commerce

(C)   because of the Supremacy Clause

(D)   unless the state can prove the added cost of the federal standards are not justified

Questions 5-7 are based upon the following fact situation.

   Alice and Bob were seniors at Midwood High School, Brooklyn, New York. On September 1, 1987, Bob was suspended from Midwood High for a period of three days for violating a school rule that provided: "All students must wear shoes at all times except during designated physical education courses. Violators of this rule shall be punished by an automatic three-day suspension."

   Bob demanded a formal hearing after explaining to the principal that he walked without shoes for medical reasons. Bob's request for a hearing was denied.

   On October 1, 1987, Alice used profane language after Ms. Jones, Alice's homeroom teacher, scolded Alice for being late. Ms. Jones reacted with a brief, but obscene, response. Later that day, Alice was suspended from school for one week. Her request for a hearing was denied.

   Ms. Jones received the following memo on November 1, 1987: "Your contract will not be renewed when it expires."

   After inquiring as to the reason why her contract would not be renewed, Ms. Jones was told, "You used obscene language before your students and you told the *Daily Brooklyn Eagle* our dress codes are 'archaic.'"

   On December 1, Bob received a letter in the mail that stated, "For failure to maintain the requisite 2.0 average, you are hereby expelled from Midwood High School. We wish you the best of luck in your future career." Bob's demands for a hearing were refused.

5.   Which of the following statements most accurately describes the September 1 suspension?

(A)   Bob was unlawfully deprived of property and liberty guaranteed by the Fourteenth Amendment.

(B)   The suspension violated Bob's due process rights.

(C)   The school rule should be found a violation of the students' due process rights.

(D)   The suspension was lawful and proper.

6.   Which of the following statements is best?

(A)   Alice's suspension violated her rights to due process and free speech.

(B)   A formal evidentiary hearing is required before a student may be temporarily suspended from a public school.

(C)   A formal evidentiary hearing is not required before a student may be temporarily suspended from a public school.

(D)   Alice's suspension did not violate her due process or First Amendment rights.

7.   Four statements below are numbered (1), (2), (3), and (4). Select the correct choice: (A), (B), (C), or (D) based on the following statements.

(1)   Ms. Jones's conversation with the *Brooklyn Eagle* was protected under the First Amendment.

(2)   The dismissal of December 1 was proper without any prior evidentiary hearing.

(3)   The nonrenewal of Ms. Jones's contract will be ruled proper only if the decision was based on the obscene language charge.

(4)   A formal evidentiary hearing is required for the dismissal of a student for academic deficiencies.

(A)   Only (1) and (3) are correct.

(B)   Only (2) and (4) are correct.

(C)   Only (1), (2) and (3) are correct.

(D)   Only (4) is correct.

8.   Sharon Waybak, principal of Fulton High School, instituted a plan that would, according to Sharon, "help students reach their ultimate potential." She sectioned off a portion of the auditorium for students to voluntarily pray, and next to each chair was a short prayer that students could recite. A group of seniors calling themselves The Order protested. One of the student's parents, Glen Jacksonville, hired a lawyer to enjoin the voluntary prayer. As a plaintiff, Glen Jacksonville is most likely to

(A)   succeed, since the primary effect of the plan advances religion

(B)   succeed, since the plan violates the Establishment

GO ON TO THE NEXT PAGE

Clause of the First
Amendment

(C)   not succeed, since the prayer
      is voluntary

(D)   not succeed, since the prayer
      would not take place inside a
      classroom.

9.   In New York State there are 13,500
     dairy farmers and about 947,000
     cows, mostly black-and-white
     Holsteins. New York is the third
     largest producer of milk in the
     United States, behind California and
     Wisconsin, and is the largest
     producer of several cheeses.
         Citing "destructive
     competition in counties already
     served," the state of New York
     enacted a statute placing a
     moratorium on permits to sell milk in
     the five counties that compose the
     city of New York. On the law's
     effective date, December 1, 1933,
     eight companies owned permits and
     all eight were companies domiciled
     within the state of New York. In
     1987, Penn Farms, a milk producer
     based in East Straudsberg,
     Pennsylvania, challenged the
     constitutionality of the New York
     Milk Rule. Penn Farms provided
     evidence that the average cost of
     milk in New York City was $2.48 per
     gallon, whereas $1.98 was the average
     price per gallon outside the New
     York area.
         New York argued that the
     laws were still necessary to prevent
     ruinous competition and that
     neighboring states had similar
     protection laws. New Jersey bars
     distributors from selling milk below

cost and requires two weeks notice
when a retailer changes suppliers.
Connecticut requires out-of-state
milk to be inspected on the farm.
    Penn Farms should assert a
constitutional challenge based upon
the

(A)   Equal Protection Clause of
      the Fourteenth Amendment

(B)   Commerce Clause

(C)   Privileges and Immunities
      Clause of Article III, Section
      2

(D)   Due Process Clause

10. Hart-Rice Publishers founded
     Newsmonth, a glossy news magazine,
     in January 1989. *Newsmonth* was an
     overnight sensation in the six cities in
     which it was test-marketed. Hart-
     Rice employed salespersons dressed
     as clowns who selected homes at
     random and sang loud songs about
     the virtues of *Newsmonth* before
     offering a half-price subscription.
     Pikesville, Maryland, a test-market
     city, passed an ordinance protecting
     the privacy of homeowners against
     the clowns. Hart-Rice challenged the
     constitutionality of the Pikesville
     statute. Clayton, Mississippi, passed
     a law taxing magazines with
     circulations of more than 2,000,000.
     Newsmonth would have been taxed
     under the statute and Hart-Rice
     challenged the Clayton law.
     Newsmonth published an article
     about Los Angeles Mayor Tom
     Bradley by investigative reporter
     Susie Spielberg. Bradley demanded
     space in *Newsmonth* to respond to

the highly critical article, citing a California statute that gives candidates a right to equal space to reply to criticism by a periodical. Hart-Rice challenged the constitutionality of the California statute.

Hart-Rice will succeed in its First Amendment challenge of which of the following statutes?

(A)   the Clayton and California statutes

(B)   the Clayton and Pikesville statutes

(C)   the California and Pikesville statutes

(D)   the Pikesville statute

11.   A difficult and hard-fought campaign for mayor of Cincinnati pitted Democrat Don Decent against Republican Ron Recent. Both men had served as public servants for many years and had been longtime adversaries.

Radio station WKRP and *The Cincinnati Enquirer*, the city's only newspaper, both endorsed Decent. Recent demanded equal time and space to rebut the *Enquirer's* editorials. Recent's demands were refused, whereupon Recent asserted an action based upon an Ohio statute that provided, "The media must provide a candidate the right to an equal reply to criticism and attacks on his record."

An Ohio court ruled in favor of Recent, whereupon an appeal was filed by WKRP. Will the appeal prevail?

(A)   Yes, if appellant asserts a constitutional challenge based upon the First Amendment.

(B)   Yes, if appellant asserts a constitutional challenge based upon the First Amendment as made applicable by the Fourteenth Amendment.

(C)   No, because the state statute is not constitutionally valid.

(D)   No, appellant will not prevail.

Questions 12-13 are based upon the following fact situation.

In 1987, Congress passed a sweeping new immigration law providing, in part, that all employers must file proof of citizenship for every new employee. The state of Florida enacted the following statute:

"All voters in the state of Florida must fill out a new registration form before voting in the 1987 elections. Such form shall be accompanied by proof of United States citizenship and birth place for all persons not born in the United States."

Maryanne Aliza Odio Stauberino, a candidate for mayor of Miami, challenged the constitutionality of the Florida statute in Federal District Court. Stauberino depended heavily on votes from Miami's Cuban and Russian-Jewish communities, who would have difficulty obtaining documents from Cuba and the Soviet Union. Grover Cement, counsel to the state of Florida, challenged the court's jurisdiction.

GO ON TO THE NEXT PAGE

12.   Should a federal court hear the case?

(A)   Yes, the court should hear the case on its merits.

(B)   The court should not hear the case until it has been tested in the state courts, because of the Abstention Doctrine.

(C)   The court should not hear the case, because the case involves a nonjustifiable political question.

(D)   The court should not hear the case, because of the Preemption Doctrine.

13.   Of the following, which will be most helpful to Stauberino's case?

(A)   The 1965 Voting Rights Act outlawing literacy tests.

(B)   The Due Process Clause.

(C)   The Equal Protection Clause of the Fourteenth Amendment.

(D)   The state requirement is merely a political action without an inherent reason.

14.   Reacting to high unemployment in the Youngstown area, and worries about the nation's future, the state of Ohio enacted the following statute:
"Since our nation's steelmaking capacity has decreased in alarming proportions over the past two decades; since steel is necessary for our nation's defense industry; and since relying on foreign steel is a threat to American security, starting January 1, 1988, any construction projects over $250,000 receiving any form of state or local aid must use steel produced in Ohio."
Sharon Steel Corp., a company incorporated in the state of Pennsylvania, and Tokyo Steel, a Japanese corporation, asserted actions challenging the constitutionality of the Ohio statute.
The state of Ohio, in its defense, asserted:

(1)   the statute does not discriminate against interstate commerce;

(2)   the statute concerns an issue on which the court should not rule, because it inherently requires uniform national regulation;

(3)   the burden on interstate commerce is outweighed by the state interest; and

(4)   the statute provides for conservation of local resources

Assume the court accepted all four of the state's arguments. Which of these arguments will advance the state of Ohio's position?

(A)   1 and 3

(B)   2 and 4

(C)   1, 2, and 3

(D)   1, 2, 3, and 4

15.   Oliver South was a brilliant and respected officer in the United States Marines. South, a 1967 graduate of West Point, served in Vietnam, where he saw much combat, was awarded six medals, and was promoted to captain. South was eventually promoted to Colonel while working in the Pentagon. He was a tactical adviser during the attempted rescue of American hostages from Iran in 1979 and for the U.S. Marine Base in Beirut in 1983.

During the 1980s, South acted as a liaison between the White House, the U.S. Marines, and several foreign governments. It was later revealed that South had violated U.S. law by trading arms with hostile powers and diverting the profits to Vanunu, a Pacific island to which aid was prohibited by U.S. law. Despite the fact that South had received orders from his superior, General Richard Threecord, South was asked to resign his position.

All U.S. armed forces personnel, veterans, and their families have shopping privileges at special stores that sell goods at below market prices. South was denied shopping privileges at the stores because of the Vanunu affair. A federal statute provided that the stores be closed to servicemen and officers dismissed from the service. South asserted an action in a federal district court challenging the constitutionality of the denial of his shopping rights, alleging, *inter alia*, that he followed orders given by his military superior and hence the military should not violate his employment contract. The government's most persuasive argument in defending its actions would be to assert that

(A)   South had prior notice because the armed forces often revoked shopping privileges

(B)   South had been awarded due process

(C)   implied in South's employment agreement with the U.S. Marines was a condition that South not violate the laws of the United States

(D)   one may not violate the laws of the United States even if ordered to do so by a military superior

16.   On January 15, 1986, Congress passed the "Surplus Federal Property Statute," which ordered the General Services Administration to dispose of excess federal property. The bill provided that half the property be given to charities operating "within the public interest." The General Services Administration decided shortly thereafter to donate the Old Customs House in lower Manhattan to the New York Holocaust Survivors Association to be used as a museum for the Holocaust. The General Services Administration reversed its decision on September 1, 1987, deciding to donate the building to the Richard Nixon Society, a group formed to honor the former

GO ON TO THE NEXT PAGE

President. A suit was filed alleging, *inter alia*, that the building's use would not be considered "within the public interest" if it were to be donated to the Richard Nixon Society. Which of the following parties would most likely have standing to challenge the General Services Administration?

(A)   a taxpayer residing in Manhattan

(B)   the Manhattan Borough President

(C)   a survivor of the Treblinka concentration camp residing in Long Island

(D)   the New York Holocaust Survivors Association

17.   Believer, a devout member of the Church of Sun Myung Bakker, lived in a church commune. He spent fourteen hours a day selling flowers and Tammy Bakker record albums for the church. The church maintained a very complex philosophy enumerated on ten holy records and six holy videos. The flip side of the fourth record declares, "It is a sin to thwart the will of God by providing medical treatment. Only God may decide who shall live and who shall die, who shall be sick and who shall be well. Sometimes one must die to atone for his sins; healing such a person will prevent such atonement and condemn that person to hell." Believer's six-year-old son, Believer Jr., was born with a defective heart. Before his fourth birthday, he was hours away from

death. A boy with the exact blood type as Believer Jr. died in a car accident, and his heart was offered to Believer Jr., but Believer Sr. refused to allow the operation. Dr. DeFreeze, Believer Jr.'s physician, and the Human Heart Institute asserted an action to compel the operation. Upon which of the following issues will the outcome of the case depend?

(A)   The Free Exercise Clause of the First Amendment as made applicable by the Fourteenth Amendment.

(B)   The fact that the five-year survival rate for heart transplant patients is less than fifty percent.

(C)   Whether or not medical treatment of Believer Jr. will save his life.

(D)   Whether current medical knowledge is in conformity with Dr. DeFreeze's decision to perform the transplant.

18.   The state of Iowa enacted the following statute:
    "(a) No milk may be sold within the state of Iowa unless such milk is pasteurized in a plant regularly inspected by the Iowa Department of Agriculture; (b) firm may dispose the wastes from milk pasteurized in a state other than Iowa within the state of Iowa; (c) milk may not be sold in the state of Iowa more than three days after it has been pasteurized; and (d) milk may not be sold in the state of Iowa

unless its fat content is clearly stated on the label."

The Iowa Department of Agriculture refused to send inspectors further than one hour from Des Moines due to budgetary considerations.

Kansas Milk, a company incorporated in the state of Kansas with its principal offices and plants in Lawrence, Kansas, challenged the constitutionality of section (a). Iowa Toxic, a company who owned a dump in Des Moines used by milk producers, asserted an action on constitutional grounds against section (b) of the statute. The most likely outcome will be that

(A) neither Kansas Milk nor Iowa Toxic will prevail, because a state has the right to protect the health, morals, and welfare of its citizens

(B) only one of the challenges will be successful, and the court will rule in favor of the challenge by relying on the Privileges and Immunities Clause of Article IV, Section II as the strongest constitutional challenge

(C) only one of the challenges will be successful, and the court will rule in favor of the challenge by relying on the Equal Protection Clause of the Fourteenth Amendment as the strongest constitutional challenge

(D) both challenges will succeed and in both cases the court will rule that the Commerce Clause was the most persuasive challenge

19. Hilary, a homeless woman who lived on the streets of Maricopa, a county in Arizona, was caught in a revolving door as she attempted to enter a local bank. She fell and broke her hip and left arm. An ambulance arrived and transported Hilary to the public hospital in Maricopa. When she arrived, she told the admitting staff that she used to live in Los Angeles but just last month someone handed her a bus ticket to Maricopa. Hilary was refused admission to the hospital based on an Arizona statute stating that in order for an indigent to receive free medical treatment at a public hospital, the indigent must be a resident of the county for the preceding twelve months. In an action challenging the constitutionality of the statute, a court would declare it

(A) unconstitutional, as violative of the right to free medical treatment

(B) unconstitutional, as violative of the Equal Protection Clause

(C) constitutional, since the statute is within the state's police power

GO ON TO THE NEXT PAGE

(D) constitutional, since the statute promotes a compelling state interest

20. Keystone Medical, a company incorporated in the state of Pennsylvania, marketed a patented condom coated with an anti-viral fluid under the trade name NoAIDS. The condoms were thoroughly tested by the FDA and approved as an effective AIDS virus killer. NoAIDS was available only with a prescription from a licensed physician. A so-called Jim and Tammy Bakker No-condom Law, prohibiting the use of contraceptives by married persons, was passed after the TV evangelists convinced many that the availability of NoAIDS would lead to sexual immorality. Which of the following choices is most correct?

(A) The law will be held constitutional as promoting the general welfare.

(B) The law will be held unconstitutional as a violation of privacy if challenged by a NoAIDS user.

(C) The law will be held unconstitutional as a deprivation of property if challenged by the manufacturers of NoAIDS.

(D) The law will be held unconstitutional if a doctor asserts a third-party suit because he cannot prescribe NoAIDS.

Questions 21-22 are based upon the following fact situation.

The city of San Diego passed the following statute:
"Aliens may not reside within 500 yards of Balboa Park. Violation of this statute shall be punishable by eviction, imprisonment, and fine."
Anne, an alien and vice-president of Pemex, Mexico's oil monopoly, purchased an apartment overlooking the park.

21. If prosecuted for violating the statute, Anne's best constitutional challenge will be based upon

(A) the Privileges and Immunities Clause

(B) the Commerce Clause

(C) the Equal Protection Clause

(D) the Fourteenth Amendment

22. The statute will be ruled constitutional if

(A) the state can prove the statute is supported by a compelling state interest

(B) Anne cannot prove the statute is not supported by a compelling state interest

(C) the state can prove the statute was a valid exercise of the reserved powers under the Tenth Amendment

(D) the state can prove the applicability of Article IV, Section II

23. Krishna was arrested for handing out religious literature on public streets. Krishna's best constitutional defense for his actions will be based on

    (A) First Amendment rights

    (B) freedom of press

    (C) freedom of speech

    (D) equal protection

Questions 24-25 are based upon the following fact situation.

Adolescent, a fifteen-year-old boy, was angry at Dorothy because she insulted Adolescent's dog. Adolescent called Dorothy and made lewd and indecent remarks about her anatomy. Dorothy proceeded to call the police, who took Adolescent into custody without notifying his parents. A petition was filed in the state court, but not served on Adolescent's parents, alleging that Adolescent was a delinquent minor. Neither Adolescent's parents nor Dorothy were present at a hearing. No decision was reached at the hearing and no one was sworn, nor were records kept. A second hearing was held, again without Dorothy's presence. Adolescent was adjudged to be a juvenile delinquent and was committed "to a state vocational school until his twenty-first birthday, unless discharged earlier by the law." State law did not provide for an appeal. The state criminal code provided a maximum punishment for adults making lewd and obscene phone calls of "a fine of no more than $500 or imprisonment for no

more than thirty days, or both." Adolescent filed a writ of habeas corpus.

24. Which of the following choices is best?

    (A) A writ of habeas corpus is not applicable to the instant fact situation.

    (B) Adolescent's best argument will be that he was denied a right to the transcripts.

    (C) Adolescent's best argument will be to assert his right of appellate review.

    (D) Adolescent is not constitutionally assured all the rights that would be due him had he been an adult.

25. Which of the following constitutional rights were violated?

    (A) privilege against self-incrimination

    (B) right to counsel and notice of charges

    (C) right to confrontation and cross-examination

    (D) all of the above

26. On July 20, 1987, the flags of several countries were lowered on oil tankers in the Persian Gulf. United States flags were raised on these same vessels. John Tunney, a

GO ON TO THE NEXT PAGE

spokesperson for the U.S. State Department, announced that the tankers were being protected by American warships and that any interference with such vessels would constitute an act of war. Tunny said that the Iran-Iraq War could threaten U.S. national security by disrupting the shipment of oil through the Persian Gulf, and the United States was, therefore, forced into protecting its interests.

On September 1, 1987, a federal grand jury was convened to investigate Robert Ludlum, Deputy Secretary of State for Near Eastern Affairs. The investigation sought to determine the veracity of press reports that Ludlum masterminded a plan to convince the President to protect the Persian Gulf after receiving a $7,000,000 bribe from the Quawate Oil Company (QOCO).

Ludlum testified that he had, indeed, strongly recommended defense of the Gulf and had so convinced the President, who had been leaning against implementing the operation prior to meeting with Ludlum.

On September 15, the grand jury returned a criminal indictment against Ludlum and two White House aides for perjury, bribery, and conspiracy. A written request was forwarded to the President for notes taken during meetings with the persons indicted. The President sought to avoid complying with the request and asked his counsel whether he could be forced to comply with the request. The President's counsel should advise the President that

(A)   the President may avoid complying with the request by asserting executive privilege

(B)   Presidential aides share executive immunity and, therefore, the request need not be granted

(C)   the President must grant the request because of the nature of the indictment

(D)   the President should grant the request despite the presumption of privilege because military, diplomatic, and sensitive national secrets are given great deference

Questions 27-28 are based upon the following fact situation.

Bergman was arrested as part of a well-publicized series of arrests, dubbed by the press as the "Jamaica Bay Cocaine Cruise." Bergman operated passenger cruises between Sea Gate Beach and Rockaway Beach. He was put in prison, charged with smuggling cocaine and other drugs in the vessel's hull.

Bergman owned a seventy-foot personal yacht called the Rutheshy. He kept the yacht docked in Bayswater Marina, which was owned by Genuth. Genuth was responsible for protecting the boat and had permission to go on board to perform certain routine maintenance. Bergman and Genuth had an understanding that Oscar, Genuth's partner, could also go on board the yacht.

Hudson Austin, a retired general with big feet and a narcotics agent in the Bayswater police force, also docked a boat at Bayswater Marina. Austin walked along a pier with a pet dog he called Katz. Katz was trained to detect the smell of cocaine.

Katz went crazy upon passing the Rutheshy, barking and jumping with such intensity that Austin was almost knocked off his big feet. Austin asked Genuth if he could search the boat. Genuth assented. The search revealed large quantities of marijuana, cocaine, heroin, and patchkez.

27. In a trial before Judge Nosson of the state of Kol Towra Court of Common Pleas, what effect will Genuth's consent have?

    (A) The consent will be a valid waiver of Bergman's Fourth Amendment rights.

    (B) The consent will not be a valid waiver of Bergman's Fourth Amendment rights.

    (C) The Fourth Amendment is not applicable to the instant case because defendant's rights are not encompassed by the Fourteenth Amendment.

    (D) Austin may assume Genuth's rights.

28. Does defendant have standing to challenge the search?

    (A) No, because he was incarcerated at the time of the search.

    (B) No, because Austin had valid cause.

    (C) Yes, because he had a valid interest in Rutheshy.

    (D) Yes, because Austin did not have valid cause.

29. Which of the following government practices will NOT survive a constitutional challenge based on the establishment clause?

    (A) The federal government provided a church-related hospital with $2,000,000 to renovate a charity ward.

    (B) The federal government provided a church-related university with $2,000,000 to study the reproduction of tse-tse flies.

    (C) The federal government provided a church-related elementary school with $2,000,000 to hire mathematics teachers.

    (D) The federal government provided a church-related university with $2,000,000 to hire mathematics teachers.

30. Georgio construction company, a private corporation based in the state of Orange with offices in Orange and New York, was in the business of developing luxury condominiums in undeveloped areas near large cities. The company had recently purchased 500 acres of land north of the state's largest city. Before Georgio began

GO ON TO THE NEXT PAGE

construction, the state of Orange enacted a statute requiring, in part, that a certain percentage of the land surrounding its cities must be used as state recreational facilities. The state court ordered possession, after a hearing, of the 500 acres of land, subject to compensation that would be awarded for damages. Georgio sued to enjoin the sale. The best argument for upholding the court-ordered possession is:

(A) The power of eminent domain does not require that payment be made prior to condemnation of the property.

(B) The power of eminent domain may only be delegated to a private enterprise for a publicly related use or activity.

(C) There has been no violation of substantive due process.

(D) It is in the public interest to have parks surrounding cities.

31. Under the Enabling Clause of the Fourteenth Amendment, a state would most likely be able to regulate

(A) a state official from discriminating against an African-American

(B) a private individual from discriminating against a woman

(C) a federal official from discriminating against an elderly person

(D) a federal official from discriminating against a state official

32. Hilary maintains a religious belief that the firstborn daughter of every woman should be sacrificed to God. Her belief is that the baby should be sacrificed by tossing it off a high suspension bridge. May Hilary be successfully prosecuted?

(A) No, if she asserts her constitutional freedom of religion.

(B) Yes, because religious beliefs are not absolutely protected.

(C) No, because the court should balance the burden of an individual's belief against the state's interest.

(D) No, because a third party is involved.

33. A state statute provided, "Any male having had sexual intercourse with a woman below the age of sixteen shall be found guilty of statutory rape, regardless of whether the woman consented."

Bob, charged with statutory rape, challenged the constitutionality of the statute, claiming it violated the due process of males. The court should rule the statute

(A) valid, if the law is substantially related to an

important government
interest of preventing teenage
pregnancy

(B)   valid, if the law accomplishes
the compelling state interest
of preventing teenage
pregnancy

(C)   not valid, because it
distinguishes between two
classes

(D)   not valid, if the objective may
be accomplished in another
manner

34.   A state statute provided, "No alien
may serve as a teacher in the public
school system." The statute will
survive a constitutional challenge
invoking the Equal Protection Clause
if the state can prove the statute

(A)   has a rational basis

(B)   is related to a governmental
interest

(C)   is necessary to promote a
compelling state interest

(D)   is merely de jure
discrimination

35.   Which of the following rights
guaranteed by the Bill of Rights
MUST also be respected by the
states?

(A)   the Second Amendment right
to bear arms

(B)   the Seventh Amendment right
to a jury in civil cases

(C)   the Sixth Amendment right to
a speedy and public trial by
an impartial jury

(D)   the Grand Jury Clause of the
Fifth Amendment

36.   Suzie Tan, a Japanese-American,
moved into the upper-class town of
Grapetown with her husband and two
kids. After residing in the town for
two months, Suzie befriended Lilly
Rich, who recently joined the
Grapetown Golf Club with her
husband, Tom. Suzie and her
husband went to the golf club one
week later to check out the facilities
and to ask about membership. When
they met Joe Means, the owner, he
refused to accept their application
and suggested that they join
Golftown, another private golf club
on the other side of town. The Tans
brought suit against Joe Means and
the Grapetown Golf Club, claiming
that denial of membership to
Japanese violated their equal
protection rights.
       Which of the following
statements is best?

(A)   Plaintiffs will win, because
discrimination based on
national origin violates the
Fourteenth Amendment.

(B)   Plaintiffs will win, if they can
prove that other Japanese
have been discriminated
against by the club.

GO ON TO THE NEXT PAGE

(C)   Joe Means and the club will win, because its denial of membership to Japanese lacks the requisite "state action."

(D)   Joe Means and the club will prevail, because the Tans lack standing to assert the rights of discrimination against the Japanese as a group.

37.   Sandra, a black tenant at the Lawrence Tides apartment complex signed a two-year lease on a one-bedroom unit on the third floor. She told her friend Jackie, who was also a black woman, that the apartment next door, 2J, was vacant. Jackie looked at the apartment, but the manager told her it had been rented to Mr. and Mrs. Jones, a white couple. David, a neighbor of Sandra, had been living in the complex for six years. Sandra and David both asserted actions against the manager alleging that the manager discriminated against blacks. The manager moved to dismiss the action. Which of the following choices is most correct?

(A)   Only Sandra's action will be judged on its merits.

(B)   Only David's action will be judged on its merits.

(C)   Neither Sandra's nor David's action will be judged on its merits.

(D)   Both Sandra's and David's actions will be judged on their merits.

38.   A state enacted a statute that provided, "Children of undocumented aliens will be admitted to public schools only after children of resident aliens and citizens have been admitted and the school board has determined that space is available." Which of the following tests will be applied to determine if the clause will survive a constitutional challenge based on the Equal Protection Clause?

(A)   Does the statute have any conceivable basis?

(B)   Is the statute related to any governmental objective?

(C)   Does the statute assist the public in a substantial manner?

(D)   Is the classification necessary to promote a compelling state interest?

39.   While searching a house, the police found equipment used to counterfeit currency. The police conducted the search without a warrant. Defendant, who admits owning the equipment, is charged with counterfeiting U.S. currency.

If Defendant objects to admission of the equipment into evidence, which of the following statements is NOT correct?

(A)   Defendant will have standing to raise a Fourth Amendment claim if he owned the place searched.

(B) Defendant will have standing to raise a Fourth Amendment claim if he had a right to possession of the place searched.

(C) Defendant will have standing to raise a Fourth Amendment claim if the place searched was in fact his home, whether or not he had a right to possess it.

(D) Defendant will have standing to raise a Fourth Amendment claim if the equipment did, in fact, belong to him.

40. On December 19, 1989, Harry X was arrested for forging two bank notes and attempting to cash them at the local savings bank. The following day, Harry appeared at a preliminary hearing to determine probable cause to detain. That afternoon, the local deputy asked Harry to submit three handwriting samples. One week later, Harry appeared at a preliminary hearing in the local courthouse to determine probable cause to prosecute. One month later, Harry appeared at a post-conviction hearing. At which of the following stages of prosecution did Harry have a right to counsel?

(A) At the preliminary hearing to determine probable cause to detain.

(B) At the taking of the handwriting samples.

(C) At the preliminary hearings to determine probable cause to prosecute.

(D) At the post-conviction hearing.

41. The state of Scenic seeks to enact a statute to limit or substantially reduce the number of advertising billboards alongside its highways. In order to survive a challenge based upon the First Amendment, the statute should

(A) further an important government interest unrelated to the message communicated by the billboard

(B) be narrowly drawn

(C) leave alternate channels of communication open

(D) all of the above

42. Brooke challenged a state statute prohibiting the sale of contraceptives to persons below the age of sixteen. Brooke argued that her right to privacy had been violated. The court should

(A) apply the test requiring a showing of a compelling state interest, because age is a suspect class

(B) apply the test requiring a showing of a compelling state interest, because privacy is a fundamental right

GO ON TO THE NEXT PAGE

(C)   apply the rational basis test

(D)   rule the statute is valid

43.   Federal law provides employees of foreign embassies and consulates with diplomatic immunity. Under the law, the employees are immune from prosecution for parking tickets.
       Vladamir, a junior diplomat employed by an embassy located in Fed Up City, was arrested and incarcerated, pursuant to a city statute which provided that diplomats may be prosecuted for constant disregard of the law. Vladamir was arrested as a traffic scofflaw after accumulating 2,000 traffic summonses. If Vladamir attacks the constitutionality of the Fed Up City statute, his best argument will be based upon

(A)   the Due Process Clause

(B)   the Equal Protection Clause

(C)   the Privileges and Immunity Clause

(D)   the Supremacy Clause

44.   The state of Mott enacted a new voter registration act. The act required a voter to be a resident of the state of Mott for one year and a resident of the county where the election would take place for three months prior to voting. The state argued that the time periods encouraged voters to know about the candidates and issues in their counties prior to voting. The statute, if challenged, would be found to

(A)   further the state's objectives and thus be legitimate legislation

(B)   not infringe upon any fundamental right

(C)   violate the right to vote and the right to travel

(D)   violate the right to travel only

45.   The Mott legislature also passed a bill that provided, "An election shall be held on the first Tuesday in March of odd-numbered years. Only persons owning stores within the state of Mott may participate in such elections. Persons owning more than one store may cast one ballot for each store owned." R.K. Dutch, owner of a store in Mott, challenged the constitutionality of the statute because it allowed some store owners more than one vote. Libby Swimmer, a forensic pathologist, challenged the statute on the grounds that persons not owning stores were not permitted to vote. Which of the following choices is most correct?

(A)   Dutch will prevail but Swimmer will not.

(B)   Swimmer will prevail but Dutch will not.

(C)   Both Dutch and Swimmer will prevail.

(D)   Neither Dutch nor Swimmer will prevail.

46. The state of Worry enacted a statute that provided, "The transport of nuclear waste through the state of Worry shall be absolutely prohibited." The federal government regularly transports nuclear waste through the state of Worry. In an action challenging the constitutionality of the Worry statute, the federal government will most likely prevail by asserting that the statute violates the

    (A) Obligation of Contracts Clause

    (B) Due Process Clause

    (C) Supremacy Clause

    (D) Equal Protection Clause

47. An aide to Congressman Krook walked across the floor of the House to Congressman Stu Lee, and whispered in Lee's ear, "Vote for those pork barrels to be sent to my district, and I'll give your son ten percent of all the barrels." The aide did not know that Lee happened to be wired with a tape recorder, as part of another investigation.
    Charged with attempted bribery, the aide asserted the Speech and Debate Clause as a defense. May this defense be invoked by an aide?

    (A) Yes, because an aide to a congressman may assume the defense.

    (B) Yes, because the act occurred on the floor of the House.

    (C) No, because an aide to a congressman does not assume the Speech and Debate Clause defense.

    (D) No, because the taking of a bribe is not in the regular course of business.

Questions 48-49 are based upon the following fact situation.

Congress enacted a law, over a veto by President Mario Cuomo, appropriating two billion dollars to help assist the Rebels, a small faction seeking the overthrow of communist leader Manooagah and the installation of a democratic government. Congress also appropriated one billion dollars to U.S. troops fighting there. In defiance, Cuomo ordered Secretary of Defense Billy Graham not to spend the funds.

48. An action asserted against Cuomo and Graham by which of the following persons will be judged on the merits of the case?

    (A) A U.S. citizen that paid $2,000,000 in income taxes over a three-year period.

    (B) A Rebel soldier.

    (C) A U.S. soldier fighting in the communist country.

    (D) A U.S. tank manufacturer who, under the appropriation, was to supply the Rebels with tanks.

GO ON TO THE NEXT PAGE

49.   The best constitutional argument against Cuomo's and Graham's actions is that

    (A)   the power of Congress to appropriate money includes the power to ensure the money is used as ordered

    (B)   the president cannot declare war

    (C)   the president may not withhold the funds, because Congress has overridden his veto

    (D)   the legislative branch has the express power to disburse government revenue

50.   Congress enacted the following statute: "Persons above the age of seventeen may marry without parental permission. Persons seventeen years of age or less must obtain permission of their parents in order to marry." Andrew and Dorothy, both age sixteen, will be prevented from marrying under the statute despite their constitutional challenge if

    (A)   either Andrew or Dorothy is serving in the U.S. Navy

    (B)   either Andrew or Dorothy is a federal employee

    (C)   Andrew and Dorothy intend to marry on the steps of the United States Capitol

    (D)   either Andrew or Dorothy was previously granted a divorce by a federal judge

51.   Which of the following plaintiffs will not be judged as a member of a suspect class?

    (A)   Alex, a resident alien who challenges a state statute that gives preference to U.S. citizens in state hiring.

    (B)   Cynthia, who challenges a state statute that allows only men to be hired by the state police.

    (C)   Hispanic, who challenges a statute that provides, "Citizens must be fluent in English to obtain a driver's license." Hispanic argues that the law discriminates against him on the basis of race.

    (D)   Scientist, who challenges a state statute that prohibits foreign-born citizens from working on defense research.

52.   Puff was arrested and charged with violating a state statute that provided that "One may neither smoke nor carry a lit cigar or pipe in an elevator." Puff challenged the constitutionality of the state statute on the grounds that it violated his right of free exercise of religion. Puff was a member of a religion that required its members to smoke in elevators as a means of achieving higher levels of consciousness.

Which of the following choices may not be considered by a court in determining Puff's challenge to the constitutionality of the statute?

(A) whether Puff's beliefs were reasonable

(B) whether Puff smoked in other restricted areas

(C) whether the religion actually required smoking in elevators

(D) whether Puff is sincere in his beliefs

53. The National Association of Left-Handed Persons (NALHP) asserted an action in federal district court, alleging state discrimination against left-handed persons. The action alleges that desks in public schools were designed for students who write with their right hands and caused discomfort to left-handed persons. The suit further alleges that the handwriting of left-handed persons was adversely affected by the desks, causing lower grades and resulting in lower economic achievement.
If the state moves to dismiss the case,

(A) the motion should be granted, because left-handed persons are not a suspect class

(B) the motion should be granted, because the plaintiff does not have standing

(C) the motion should not be granted, because a real and actual injury has been incurred

(D) the motion should not be granted

Questions 54-57 are based upon the following fact situation.

Congress enacted the Federal Aid to Education Act, which provided, "Federal transportation funds may be used to transport students to and from public, private, and parochial schools. Gymnasiums and other physical education facilities at public, private, and parochial schools may be built with federal assistance. The federal government will pay one-half of health insurance premiums provided to teachers in public, private, or parochial schools, only if the teacher is not involved in the teaching of religion."

54. Troublemaker, an ordinary citizen who always mails the I.R.S. its check by April 15, challenged the Federal Aid to Education Act. Will the case be decided on its merits?

(A) Yes, because a taxpayer may challenge any federal allocation of funds.

(B) Yes, because Troublemaker has alleged a violation of specific constitutional limitations of the exercise of congressional spending power.

(C) No, because Troublemaker has not suffered injuries

GO ON TO THE NEXT PAGE

different from the general public.

(D)   No, because Troublemaker is too remote from the application of the challenged statute.

55.   Assuming that the case is decided on its merits, will Troublemaker prevail in his challenge of the clause providing aid for construction of physical education facilities?

(A)   Yes, because the federal government may not provide aid to an organization whose purpose is to teach religion.

(B)   Yes, because the clause creates an excessive entanglement between religion and state.

(C)   No, because the construction will not aid religion in any way.

(D)   No, because aid provided for use by an institution is not assumed to be aid to the institution's teachings.

56.   Assuming the case is decided on its merits, will Troublemaker prevail in his challenge of the clause providing funds for transporting students to parochial schools?

(A)   Yes, because the federal government may not provide aid to an organization whose purpose is to teach religion.

(B)   Yes, because the clause creates an excessive entanglement between religion and state.

(C)   No, because the transportation will not aid religion in any way.

(D)   No, because the transportation is sufficiently secular.

57.   Assuming the case is decided on its merits, will Troublemaker prevail in his challenge of the clause providing for subsidizing teachers' insurance premiums?

(A)   Yes, because enforcing the conditions of the clause would constitute an excessive entanglement with religion.

(B)   Yes, because the government may not assist a religious institution in any manner.

(C)   No, because the funding will not aid religion.

(D)   No, because the teaching is secular.

Questions 58-59 are based upon the following fact situation.

The University Association, located in the state of Malka, is an organization of private citizens formed as an open forum for discussion of social issues. The association is headquartered in a plush downtown building, where it often sponsors speakers and forums. The downtown headquarters include several lounges and a restaurant. Obtaining membership in the University Association is a long and arduous process. Most people feel the effort expended to obtain membership is a small price to pay because the "powerful" gather in the association and many important contacts are made. The association has neither blacks nor women among its members.

Several association members were employees and elected officials of the state of Malka, because the state felt that in order to advance the state's interests it was important for state officials to maintain contact with Malka's "elite."

An action was asserted in a federal district court, seeking to enjoin the state of Malka from payments of dues to the University Association.

58.   Which of the following arguments will best support the plaintiff's suit?

   (A)   Race and gender are suspect classes.

   (B)   The state of Malka is promoting discrimination by paying dues to the University Association.

   (C)   The state is providing the association with tacit approval.

   (D)   The state has violated the Equal Protection Clause of the Fourteenth Amendment.

59.   If the court's jurisdiction is challenged, will the federal district court have proper jurisdiction?

   (A)   Yes, because interstate commerce is indirectly affected.

   (B)   Yes, because a federal claim is being presented.

   (C)   No, unless all possible state remedies have been exhausted.

   (D)   No, because a federal court does not have jurisdiction over a local club.

60.   Freedom is a cult advocating the violent overthrow of the United States government. A state statute made it a crime for any member of Freedom to teach in a state school.

   Bomber, a member of Freedom and a licensed teacher, seeks to challenge the statute on constitutional grounds. Freedom should argue that the statute

   (A)   violates his First Amendment right of association

   (B)   is a bill of attainder

   (C)   is an unlawful impairment of contract

   (D)   is an *ex post facto* law

61.   Novada, a state out west, enacted a statute in the summer of 1988 that prohibited the showing of obscene films in public areas. Larry Stud owned the One Stop Motel on Route 10 in Novada. Stud advertised that

GO ON TO THE NEXT PAGE

his motel had televisions that show adult movies in each room. Stud is arrested and convicted for violating the statute. On appeal, Stud's conviction most probably will be

(A)   sustained, because the statute is a reasonable police power measure

(B)   sustained, because the adult movies will be shown in public areas

(C)   overturned, because the statute is inapplicable to motel visitors

(D)   overturned, because the statute violates the First and Fourteenth Amendments

62.   Warren was arrested and given his Miranda warnings. Warren asked for an attorney and was told that counsel would be appointed. While Warren was posing for a "mug shot" and before counsel arrived, Warren said, "I wish I could change my face, because I am the killer."

Should Warren's motion to suppress the statement be granted?

(A)   Yes, because he requested counsel.

(B)   Yes, because the taking of photographs is a stage of the proceedings requiring that counsel be present.

(C)   No, because the taking of photographs is not a crucial stage of the proceedings requiring counsel.

(D)   No, because the statements were voluntary.

63.   Metropolis State officials were convinced the state had not received its proper share of revenue from the federal government. Metropolis State filed suit in a federal court. Which of the following choices is best?

(A)   A state may not sue for share of revenues.

(B)   A state may sue the United States when monetary obligations have not been fulfilled.

(C)   A state may sue the United States only if the United States consents.

(D)   A state may not sue the United States.

64.   Which of the following forms of government aid will violate the Establishment Clause?

(A)   The state provides the same mathematics textbook, without charge, to students at private and public schools.

(B)   The state provides free transportation to and from school for students at public and private schools.

(C)   The state provides free lunches for students at all private schools.

(D)   The state provides free transportation for school field trips.

Questions 65-66 are based upon the following fact situation.

Leaker was a state senator and chairman of the Water Commission for the state of Drip. The federal government prosecuted Leaker because the Drip Water Commission pumped water from a well that did not meet environmental standards. Leaker moved to dismiss the case, claiming that his actions were in the course of state senate business and that therefore he could not be prosecuted.

65.   Leaker should assert which of the following arguments?

(A)   Leaker is entitled to legislative immunity.

(B)   The states may delegate local governments to determine environmental standards.

(C)   Under the federalism doctrine, federal law may not be imposed upon state senators acting within the scope of state business.

(D)   The state of Drip should be prosecuted, not Leaker.

66.   The federal government should assert which of the following arguments?

(A)   The flow of water affects interstate commerce.

(B)   State senators are liable for willful misconduct.

(C)   Preferential treatment for legislators would be a violation of equal protection to the ordinary citizen.

(D)   Enforcing environmental standards is not a significant interference with state government.

67.   A state statute requires all tailors to obtain a license. The state only grants licenses to tailors who have served as apprentices to tailors located in the state, who have resided in the state for one year, and who are United States citizens.
        If an appropriate challenge is raised against the requirement that tailors must be trained by in-state tailors, will the clause be ruled constitutional?

(A)   Yes, as valid economic protection.

(B)   Yes, because a state may protect the welfare of its citizens.

(C)   No, because it violates the Privileges and Immunity Clause of the Fourteenth Amendment.

(D)   No, because it violates the Equal Protection Clause of the Fourteenth Amendment.

GO ON TO THE NEXT PAGE

68.   Congress enacted a statute requiring that all constitutional challenges against state statutes be screened by a judicial committee before proceeding to the usual courts.

Rhonda asserted an action to declare a certain state statute unconstitutional. She then filed a suit challenging the new congressional act. The statute forcing the judicial review is

(A)   unconstitutional, because it denies the right to a trial by jury

(B)   constitutional, if a compelling need is satisfied by the statute

(C)   constitutional, because Congress has the option to decide the mechanics of appellate jurisdiction

(D)   unconstitutional, as a violation of the Due Process Clause

69.   The state of New Hope enacted a statute prohibiting the disposal of nuclear waste within the state. Mr. Lewis is the owner of a company that is engaged in disposal of nuclear waste. Many out of state firms have contracted with Lewis to dispose of their nuclear waste in New Hope. The state statute does not conflict with any federal laws. Assuming Lewis has standing, his best argument to challenge the state statute would be the

(A)   Equal Protection Clause

(B)   Due Process Clause

(C)   Contracts Clause

(D)   Commerce Clause

70.   If an appropriate challenge against the state licensing procedure for plumbers is raised in a federal court, will the case be dismissed for lack of proper jurisdiction?

(A)   Yes, because of lack of diversity.

(B)   Yes, because a state statute is in question.

(C)   No, because a state may not rule on its own laws.

(D)   No, because the challenge involves a federal question.

71.   In which of the following cases will Defendant fail in arguing that the state has passed an *ex post facto* law?

(A)   Defendant is charged with possession of marijuana. Marijuana possession had been legal on the date Defendant was alleged to possess it, but it has since been legislated as a controlled substance.

(B)   The maximum sentence for possession of marijuana was increased from 60 days to one year while Defendant awaited trial for the same charge. After being convicted for possession of marijuana,

Defendant was sentenced to six months in prison.

(C) While Defendant awaited trial, the state legislature changed the burden required to prove possession with intent to sell from "beyond a reasonable doubt" to "clear and convincing." Defendant is convicted.

(D) While Defendant awaited trial, the statute under which he was charged was struck down as having overly vague procedural aspects. A new, similar statute was enacted. Defendant was convicted under the new statute.

72. Kim Ell asserted an action in a federal court against M.D. Grizly, a veterinarian employed by the National Park System. Ell alleged that Grizly was negligent in sedating a bear. The bear, known to be violent, escaped and mauled Kim Ell while she was visiting Jellystone National Park.

   Grizly motioned to dismiss the case due to improper jurisdiction. The court should rule jurisdiction is

(A) proper, because the alleged injury and negligence occurred on federal property

(B) proper, because Grizly was an officer of the federal government, and the federal government may be liable in the case

(C) not proper, because no diversity has been shown

(D) not proper, because the defendant has objected to jurisdiction

Questions 73-74 are based upon the following fact situation.

   Abandoned was an illegitimate son of Abandoner. Abandoned felt love for his father and tried to befriend him on many occasions, but Abandoner refused to admit Abandoned was his son. Abandoned purchased a life insurance policy on his father's life.

   Abandoner died and the insurance company refused to pay Abandoned, citing a state law that provided, "An unacknowledged, illegitimate child is not considered a child for legal purposes." Since Abandoner was not legally related to Abandoned, Abandoned did not have an insurable interest and could not recover.

73. If Abandoned challenges the state law, his best argument will be that

(A) he has been deprived of property

(B) the law violates the Obligation of Contracts Clause

(C) there is no reason to discriminate against illegitimate children, and therefore the law violates the Equal Protection Clause

GO ON TO THE NEXT PAGE

(D)   he has been deprived of property without due process

74.   The most persuasive defense the state could offer would be

(A)   that the law is rational and nondiscriminatory

(B)   that the law defines family relationships

(C)   that promotion of family life and encouraging paternity forms a rational basis for the law

(D)   that the law is not invidiously discriminating

75.   Under which of the following circumstances will a search withstand a Fourth Amendment challenge?

(A)   Officer Zealous obtains a warrant to search 383 Kling Street for obscene magazines. The structure is a duplex. Zealous searches the entire structure.

(B)   Officer Zealous obtains a warrant to search 605 Reads Lane for narcotics and other unknown evidence related to narcotics.

(C)   Officer Zealous obtains a warrant based on the reckless, intentional, and materially false statement by an affiant.

(D)   Officer Zealous obtains a warrant to search the home of a person who is not a suspect. Zealous had no reason to believe that evidence of a crime was present.

Questions 76-77 are based upon the following fact situation.

Cleaver was employed for seven years by the city of Metropolis's Department of Sanitation. One day, he received a notice stating, "You are hereby notified that effective six weeks from now, your services will no longer be needed." Cleaver was not given a reason for his dismissal or an opportunity to appeal the decision. An applicable state statute provides, "A municipal employee may be dismissed without cause." Cleaver's employment contract was silent as to this matter.

76.   If Cleaver asserts an action against Metropolis to force them to provide a reason for his termination, which of the following choices will be Cleaver's most persuasive argument?

(A)   He purchased a new car, assuming an obligation to make payments in reliance of his employment contract.

(B)   His work is as satisfactory as workers not terminated.

(C)   He was the only Sanitation Department employee terminated.

(D)   The city of Metropolis has enjoyed budget surpluses in recent years.

77. Which of the following choices will be Metropolis's most persuasive argument?

    (A) The city found a more efficient employee to replace Cleaver.

    (B) Cleaver was a slob.

    (C) Cleaver's contract was not breached.

    (D) Cleaver was absent more than twice as often as the average city worker.

78. The state of Oz enacted a statute that provided that family recipients of aid to families with dependent children would receive financial assistance based on a scale that would be used to determine each family's standard of need. A maximum grant would be $450 per family. Harry and Jane Doe brought suit to enjoin application of the statute on the ground that it violated the Equal Protection Clause. Harry and Jane had five children. They claimed that their neighbors, the Cats, were receiving the same amount of money with only three kids. A court would most likely rule that the statute

    (A) violates the Equal Protection Clause on its face

    (B) requires strict scrutiny to determine if there is a violation

    (C) violates the Equal Protection Clause only if the law is determined to be imperfect

    (D) does not violate the Equal Protection Clause

79. Claiming his fair process was violated, plaintiff challenged a state action. In which of the following situations will the court dismiss the case because Plaintiff's "property," as defined by the Supreme Court, was not taken?

    (A) Plaintiff alleges he was unfairly denied welfare benefits.

    (B) Plaintiff alleges he was unfairly denied public education.

    (C) Plaintiff alleges he was drafted into the army without a proper hearing, damaging his reputation.

    (D) Plaintiff alleges he was terminated from his job with the local Department of Sanitation without cause.

Questions 80-81 are based upon the following fact situation.

General Goof was subpoenaed to testify before a congressional committee investigating the loss of a military satellite aboard the space shuttle during the tragic explosion. Goof refused to answer certain questions. Congress ordered a Florida district

GO ON TO THE NEXT PAGE

attorney to prosecute Goof for contempt. The district attorney refused.

80.   May the district attorney refuse to prosecute Goof?

    (A)   Yes, because a general is not accountable for judgment decisions.

    (B)   Yes, because the district attorney's duties are executive actions.

    (C)   No, because the district attorney must act as directed.

    (D)   No, because one who violates the law must be prosecuted.

81.   If Goof is prosecuted for refusing to answer questions, which of the following choices, if proved, will best help Goof's case?

    (A)   The space shuttle was funded by the state of Florida and by private corporations.

    (B)   The questions were not related to legislative matters.

    (C)   Goof has only limited and trivial knowledge of the shuttle.

    (D)   All space shuttle decisions were ultimately approved by civilian authorities.

82.   Nexol, a pharmaceutical company, manufactured a new pill that was supposed to relieve headaches within five minutes. The pill was called "Nohed." The Federal Food and Drug Administration, however, announced that the drug caused side effects such as vomiting and foot aches. As a result, Congress enacted legislation prohibiting shipment of Nohed across state lines. The legislation is most likely

    (A)   unconstitutional as a violation of due process

    (B)   unconstitutional as a deprivation of Nexol's property right

    (C)   constitutional as within the state's police power

    (D)   constitutional, because Congress has the power to regulate interstate commerce

Questions 83-84 are based upon the following fact situation.

    Congress enacted the National Acid Rain Act in response to sulfur rain pollution of northeastern lakes and streams. The act established a ten-person "advisory committee" to monitor testing and new technology, recommend enforcement, and prosecute those who violate standards. The Department of the Interior and Congress were empowered to appoint members of the commission.

    Sulferspewer, owner of Altoona Chemical Works, was prosecuted by the advisory committee.

83.   Which of the following facts will be most persuasive in favor of Sulfurspewer's defense that the

National Acid Rain Act is unconstitutional?

(A)   Sulfurspewer was denied equal protection because the commission has discretion on whom to prosecute.

(B)   Sulfurspewer was not involved in interstate commerce and, therefore, was not under the commission's jurisdiction.

(C)   The commission is powerless because members were appointed by others besides the Department of the Interior.

(D)   The executive branch may not enforce legislation enacted by Congress.

84.   What will be the proper ruling regarding the constitutionality of the National Acid Rain Act?

(A)   The advisory committee is null and void.

(B)   The advisory committee may prosecute those deemed to have violated environmental standards.

(C)   The committee may make recommendations to the legislative branch.

(D)   The committee members must be appointed by the Department of the Interior.

85.   The state of Prude enacted a statute restricting the sale of magazines showing partially clothed women to persons below the age of eighteen. Innocent, a fifteen-year-old boy, challenged the statute after he was not allowed to purchase *National Geographic Magazine*. Which of the following choices is NOT correct?

(A)   Regulation of speech must accomplish a compelling government interest.

(B)   Material sexually explicit but not obscene may be zoned away from residential areas.

(C)   Material considered obscene for children will be considered obscene for adults.

(D)   Material deemed to be obscene may be read but not sold.

86.   The town of Skeed was a popular ski resort area for twenty-five years. Local residents, however, claimed that visitors during the winter months turned Skeed into a college party town. A local ordinance was passed in 1989 prohibiting any skiing in Skeed and further prohibited the sale of skis within the town. Snowline, a manufacturer of skis, sought to enjoin application of the ordinance. The town of Skeed's weakest defense to keep the ordinance would be

(A)   Snowline's case is moot

(B)   the case is not ripe

GO ON TO THE NEXT PAGE

(C)   there is no case or
controversy

(D)   Snowline lacks standing

87.   With respect to administrative
searches, which of the following
statements is NOT correct?

(A)   A warrant is not required for
searches of businesses in
highly regulated industries.

(B)   Administrative inspections are
an exception to the warrant
requirement; inspectors do
not require a warrant.

(C)   A warrant is not required for
the seizure of spoiled or
contaminated food.

(D)   A search of a passenger
boarding an airline does not
require a warrant.

88.   Defendant was tried and convicted of
third-degree larceny, a misdemeanor,
for stealing a magazine. Which of
the following choices did NOT
violate Defendant's Sixth and
Fourteenth Amendment rights to a
fair trial?

(A)   Defendant was forced to
appear in prison clothing
during the trial.

(B)   The judge presiding over
Defendant's case was not a
lawyer.

(C)   During the trial, the arresting
officer ate three meals with
members of the jury.

(D)   The judge owned a newsstand
and often had magazines
stolen.

89.   At which of the following stages of
prosecution will a defendant NOT
have the right to counsel?

(A)   investigative (or pre-charge)
lineups

(B)   post-charge lineups

(C)   custodial police interrogation

(D)   non-custodial post indictment
interrogation

90.   In which of the following choices will
the defendant be UNABLE to
invoke the Fourteenth Amendment
and force the state to honor a federal
right?

(A)   Yankee Freed's house was
condemned by the state to
make room for a new baseball
stadium. Yankee argues that
his property was taken
without just compensation, in
violation of the Fifth
Amendment.

(B)   Bick was arrested for ice-
skating with a pen in his
skates. The judge imposed
$500,000 bail. Bick argues
that his right against excessive
bail has been violated.

(C) Roz Nah kept a small arsenal of semi-automatic weapons to protect her house filled with Hershey bars. Nah challenged a state statute prohibiting citizens from owning any type of firearms.

(D) Warsaw left work for two weeks without permission in order to demonstrate with the Support Kaddafi's Line of Death Society. The state refused to apply the First Amendment to local law.

Questions 91-92 are based upon the following fact situation.

Congress enacted some very specific banking laws in instituting the Congressional Banking Act (CBA). The CBA applied to every commercial bank in the United States. The legislation was enacted to assure fair banking practices to the public.

91. If the constitutionality of the CBA is challenged, which of the following provisions should be advanced to justify the statute?

(A) taxing and spending for general welfare

(B) the Contract Clause

(C) the Commerce Clause

(D) the Equal Protection Clause of the Fourteenth Amendment

92. If the constitutionality of the CBA is challenged by a church that claims that under the regulations it will not be able to secure a loan to build a new school, the federal government must prove which of the following choices in order to uphold the CBA?

(A) The CBA helps uphold a state interest.

(B) The CBA benefits a majority of the public.

(C) The CBA protects a compelling government interest.

(D) Establishment of banking laws is exclusively the domain of the federal government.

Questions 93-95 are based upon the following fact situation.

A federal statute provides that any state not enforcing certain educational standards among public high schools will be denied federal aid for secondary education. The state of Ignorance did not comply with the standards, and federal funding was eliminated.

93. Which of the following persons is most likely to obtain a judicial determination if he challenges the constitutionality of the federal statute?

(A) a taxpayer living in the state of Ignorance

GO ON TO THE NEXT PAGE

(B)   a student at a state of Ignorance public high school

(C)   a teacher laid off because of the cuts in federal aid

(D)   a high school principal worried about the education of his students

94.   The federal government should argue that the statute is constitutional because

(A)   the standards will ensure that federal money spent on education will be properly used

(B)   the vast majority of people in the state of Ignorance and in the United States support the statute

(C)   the federal government may regulate the education of its citizens

(D)   the state of Ignorance gave the federal government an implied right to regulate education by accepting federal aid

95.   Will a court be likely to rule the federal statute constitutional?

(A)   No, because it is an unlawful intrusion of a right reserved to the states.

(B)   No, because of the Fourteenth Amendment.

(C)   No, because of the Privileges and Immunities Clause.

(D)   Yes.

Questions 96-98 are based upon the following fact situation.

Suzy Stripper protested in front of the Metropolis Church on Sunday morning. Stripper, upset about church support for anti-pornography legislation proposed by the City Council, screamed as loud as she could, "Kill all ministers afraid to look at skin."

A large audience gathered to watch Suzy, who had received much media attention. Suzy was arrested and charged with violating a local statute that provides, "No speechmaking or protesting shall be permitted within seventy-five feet of a church on Sunday mornings."

96.   If Suzy challenges the constitutionality of the statute, which of the following choices is best?

(A)   The city must prove the statute's enactment had a rational basis.

(B)   The city must prove the statute was enacted to satisfy a compelling need and no less restrictive means of satisfying this need were available.

(C)   Suzy must prove the statute was not enacted with a rational basis.

(D)   Suzy must prove that the statute was enacted without a compelling need or that a less restricting means was available.

97.   Which of the following persons may also challenge the statute?

    (A)   An owner of a movie theater that shows pornographic movies.

    (B)   The city councilman who led the opposition to the statute.

    (C)   An anti-pornography organizer who wanted to demonstrate on a Sunday morning.

    (D)   A person who owned a home on the same street as the church.

98.   Should the statute be ruled constitutional?

    (A)   Yes, because speech may be prohibited on Sundays.

    (B)   Yes, because at certain times and places the First Amendment right to free speech may be limited.

    (C)   No, because of the First Amendment right to free speech.

    (D)   No, because the statute assists a religion.

99.   In November of 1987, the town of Luxville decided to attract more rich people to the area, so it leased a sizable portion of Lux Lake to a successful company in order to build a yacht house and club, complete with marina, restaurant, and health club. The new private club would be called "The Lux-Rich Club" and would be owned by the Doves, who were also the owners of the company that was granted the lease to build the club. The Narrows, residents of Luxville who could not afford the high membership rates, brought an action against the Lux-Rich Club two months after the club began operating. Mr. Narrows claimed that the club discriminated against the poor in violation of the Equal Protection Clause. Which of the following statements is most accurate?

    (A)   The club will prevail, because the deprivation is not substantial enough to trigger the Equal Protection Clause.

    (B)   The club will win, because de facto discrimination against the poor has not been held to violate equal protection.

    (C)   Narrows will win, because discrimination against the poor violates the equal protection clause.

    (D)   Narrows will win because there is "state action" involved.

Questions 100-101 are based upon the following fact situation.

GO ON TO THE NEXT PAGE

Arayan High School is a religious school that limits its enrollment to "white, third-generation Americans." The school is accredited by the state of Barf. The state sets accreditation standards and inspects religious, private, and public schools.

Free transportation to all accredited schools is provided by the state of Barf.

100. Which of the following choices is the best argument in a suit to end free bus service for the students of Arayan High School?

(A)   There is no constitutional right to free bus service.

(B)   Barf is aiding a religion.

(C)   Discrimination of any kind is forbidden by the federal constitution.

(D)   Barf is furthering segregation by providing bus service to Arayan High.

101. Which of the following choices is the best argument in favor of Arayan High in the above suit?

(A)   A school's selection process is not subject to review.

(B)   Religious education is a constitutional right.

(C)   Bus transportation is secular and nonpolitical.

(D)   A state may not regulate the philosophy of private schools.

102. The state of Lincoln passed a statute that was identical to a federal law. The statute provided that aliens are ineligible for welfare benefits. Doran, a resident alien, challenged both statutes. Doran will most likely prevail against

(A)   both Lincoln and the federal government

(B)   Lincoln only

(C)   the federal government only

(D)   neither Lincoln nor the federal government

103. Acting on a hunch, a police officer barged into Snorter's house by opening an unlocked door. Snorter was immediately given his Miranda warnings and placed under arrest. "Go easy on me. I'll tell you where the loot is," Snorter said. He told the police to look under his bed. The police found a box full of stolen jewels. Snorter was prosecuted for burglary. At the trial, Snorter moved to exclude the jewels from the evidence. Which of the following arguments will provide the most support for Snorter's motion?

(A)   The statements were fruits of an unlawful search.

(B)   Snorter was tricked into making the statements.

(C)   Snorter must be treated leniently as part of the agreement.

(D)   The Miranda warnings were not timely.

104.   Crazy, a minister in the Church of Polygamy, had seven wives. The church preached that every man must serve God by taking at least six wives.

Crazy was arrested and charged with polygamy. Crazy made a motion to dismiss the case. Should the motion be granted?

(A)   Yes, because conviction of Crazy would violate his freedom of religion.

(B)   Yes, because the Church of Polygamy's beliefs are honest and reasonable.

(C)   No, because sincere religious beliefs are not a defense to polygamy.

(D)   No, because a belief in polygamy is by definition not a religion.

105.   Kisco Drive Corporation (KDC) breeds exotic birds. The birds are transported across the United States by trucks that are both company owned and operated. A state government passed legislation prohibiting the use of trucks with more than one trailer on interstate highways elevated more than 4,000 feet above sea level. KDC operated ten such trucks.

KDC asserted a constitutional challenge to the statute based on the Fourteenth Amendment clause that

provides, "No state shall make or enforce any law which shall abridge the privilege or immunities of citizens of the United States."

Which of the following choices is most correct?

(A)   The state will prevail by showing a rational basis for the statute.

(B)   KDC's action will be dismissed before being heard on its merits.

(C)   KDC will prevail, because the state has unlawfully interfered with interstate commerce.

(D)   KDC will prevail, because the state has unlawfully interfered with the right to interstate level.

106.   The city of Metropolis signed an agreement with General Contractor to build a junior high school. The city suffered a slight fiscal deficit before construction began.

Metropolis repealed a statute that formed the basis of the agreement, thereby canceling the agreement so that it could save money. General Contractor asserted an action to enforce the agreement. Should the court rule that the Metropolis statute canceling the agreement is valid?

(A)   Yes, because a municipality may repeal its own laws.

GO ON TO THE NEXT PAGE

(B)   Yes, because the contract was revoked due to necessity.

(C)   No, because it violates the constitutional prohibition against the impairment of contracts.

(D)   No, because of the power to spend and the General Welfare Clause.

Questions 107-108 are based upon the following fact situation.

The state of Landlock enacted a statute that provided, "All drivers licensed after May 1, 1986, will receive an 'In-State License' valid for driving only within the state of Landlock. Drivers will be granted an unrestricted driver's license after attending a six-hour class educating them on safety measures necessary for long trips." The minimum age required for any type of driving license in the state of Landlock is seventeen.

107.   Dragster, a fourteen-year-old resident of the state of Landlock, asserted an action in a federal district court challenging the constitutionality of the act. Which of the following choices present the best reason for dismissing Dragster's action?

(A)   A fourteen-year-old may not challenge the constitutionality of a state statute.

(B)   No federal question is presented.

(C)   The suit presents a nonjusticiable question.

(D)   The suit is not ripe.

108.   Assume for this question only that the constitutional challenge will be judged on its merits. The burden of persuasion will be on the

(A)   state, because a fundamental right is affected

(B)   state, because the suit involves a federal question

(C)   party challenging the statute, because the law provided for the presumption that a state statute is constitutional

(D)   party challenging the statute, because the issue involves public safety

Questions 109-110 are based upon the following fact situation.

Congress enacted a statute that provided, "The federal courts are prohibited from issuing any order with respect to the First Amendment."

109.   If the statute is challenged, which of the following arguments will best support the statute's constitutionality?

(A)   Regulation of the environment is within the jurisdiction of the federal government.

(B)   The First Amendment affects interstate commerce.

(C)   Article III provides that Congress may restrict the jurisdiction of federal courts.

(D)   Congress has exclusive power over the First Amendment.

110.   Which of the following arguments will best support the challenge to the statute's constitutionality?

(A)   Congress may not limit the jurisdiction of a federal court.

(B)   Congress may not endanger the rights of its citizens by altering the minimum requirements of the Bill of Rights.

(C)   The statute violates the Privileges and Immunities Clause of the Fourteenth Amendment.

(D)   The statute unfairly discriminates against state judicial systems.

Questions 111-113 are based upon the following fact situation.

The state of Hersey enacted a statute that provided, "Every corporation doing business in the state of Hersey must first give preference to citizens of the state and then to United States' citizens when hiring employees."

111.   Which of the following choices would be most relevant to a challenge of the statute based on the Supremacy Clause?

(A)   The economic conditions prevalent at the time.

(B)   The number of illegal aliens residing in Hersey.

(C)   The treaties and immigration laws of the United States.

(D)   The number of unskilled resident aliens in the United States.

112.   Which of the following choices LEAST supports the statute's constitutionality?

(A)   The statute will help assure that a stable supply of workers exists in the state of Hersey.

(B)   The statute will help assure that the state of Hersey will have a quality work force.

(C)   The statute will help assure that the workers in the state of Hersey are dedicated to their employers.

(D)   The statute will help assure that citizens of Hersey will be protected from competition for jobs.

113.   Assume for this question only that the Supreme Court of the state of Hersey rules the statute unconstitutional as a violation of the privileges and immunities clause of the Fourteenth Amendment to the United States Constitution and the Equal Protection Clause of the Hersey Constitution. If the state of

GO ON TO THE NEXT PAGE

Hersey attempts to test the statute before the United States Supreme Court,

(A)   the statute should be reviewed by *certiorari* only

(B)   the statute should be reviewed by *certiorari* or appeal

(C)   the statute should be reviewed by appeal only

(D)   the statute should not be reviewed

114.   A statute in the state of Penciltown provided that "whenever the Secretary of Commerce shall determine that commercial mail sent to residents of the State is inappropriate for minors, the Secretary shall have the power to prohibit such mailing." A video store called Viewers Inc. in Penciltown sent brochures of its stock to local residents, and many of its movies were in the adult film category. Viewers Inc. instituted an action in State court after the Secretary of Commerce attempted to stop the mailing of Viewers Inc.'s brochures containing photos of scenes in the adult films. Penciltown's highest court affirmed the lower courts, holding that the statute was unconstitutional. If the U.S. Supreme Court reviews the case, it will reach that court

(A)   under the doctrine of adequate and independent state grounds

(B)   by appeal

(C)   by *certiorari*

(D)   as a matter of right

115.   Which of the following persons may issue a valid search warrant without violating the Fourth Amendment right against search and seizure?

(A)   a state attorney general

(B)   a United States Attorney General

(C)   a clerk of court

(D)   a magistrate who is compensated only for each warrant issued

116.   Itzal, outraged at Mayor Bradley's support of the sale of pretzels on city streets, demonstrated in front of City Hall. Itzal chanted, "Bradley, you liar, I'll set your rear on fire." While being handcuffed and arrested by police, Itzal shouted several offensive obscenities. A state statute provided, "One may not utter obscene or highly offensive language in public." If prosecuted for violating this statute, which of the following choices should Itzal advance?

(A)   The statute advances religion and, therefore, violates the Due Process Clause.

(B)   The statute is vague and, therefore, violates the Due Process Clause.

(C) Itzal's arrest denied him equal protection guaranteed by the Fourteenth Amendment.

(D) Itzal's arrest denied him freedom of speech guaranteed by the Fourteenth Amendment.

117. President Bush announced that an army would be sent to Nicargo, a small communist country in South America, for joint training exercises with Nicargo Military Forces. One week later, Congress enacted a statute prohibiting the U.S. armed forces from interference with the Nicargo Army in Nicargo unless Congress has received notice of such intention to take action at least 90 days prior to the commencement of the training exercises. This statute is most likely

(A) unconstitutional, because of Bush's authority to execute the laws of the United States

(B) unconstitutional, because of Bush's authority as Commander-in-Chief of the armed forces

(C) constitutional, because of congressional power under the War Powers Act

(D) constitutional, because of congressional power to raise and support the armed forces

118. An annual ceremony is held to inaugurate new members of the State Highway Patrol. All candidates are required to swear or affirm that they will "use every measure at their means to uphold, defend, and enforce the constitutions of the state and federal governments."

Candidates must also swear or affirm that they "do not support the overthrow of the United States government by illegal means and will help defend the country from any individual or organization that seeks to do so."

Anarchist was not hired as a State Highway patrolman, because he refused to take the required oath. He filed suit in a federal court, challenging the statute.

Which of the following arguments best supports the constitutionality of the statute?

(A) Law enforcement employees are subject to a higher degree of scrutiny than ordinary citizens.

(B) The oath merely affirms a commitment to abide by the law.

(C) The Fourteenth Amendment allows a state to set conditions of employment.

(D) The government has a compelling right to assume the loyalty of its employees.

119. The city of Coral Gables passed a law providing for thirty days of

GO ON TO THE NEXT PAGE

incarceration for "vagrancy." The statute defined vagrancy as "rogues, vagabonds, and lewd, wanton, and lascivious persons. A person wandering from place to place or loitering without any lawful purpose or object is a vagrant." Homeless was arrested and charged with vagrancy after spending three nights in a Coral Gables bus depot.

If Homeless decides to attack the constitutionality of the Coral Gables vagrancy statute, which of the following arguments will help his case most?

(A)   The ordinance is overly broad.

(B)   The ordinance is void because it violates freedom of movement.

(C)   The First and Fourteenth Amendments guarantee expression of oneself by this choice of lifestyle.

(D)   The ordinance is a prior restraint.

120.   Jefferson, age sixteen, asserted an action in a federal court, challenging the state driving statute. The statute provided that, "Any citizen eighteen years of age or older may apply for a driver's license." Jefferson alleged that the law discriminated against him based on his age. Jefferson further alleged that the law had no rational basis, nor did it achieve any compelling state interest. The case was finally heard by the district court, two years after Jefferson filed his complaint. The court should

(A)   rule that the statute is unconstitutional

(B)   rule that the statute is constitutional as a valid exercise of state police action

(C)   rule the statute is constitutional as a valid exercise for the public welfare

(D)   dismiss the case, because of the prohibition against advisory opinions

121.   A federal statute required members of the United States Army holding the rank of Captain or higher to retire upon reaching the age of sixty-five. The statute provides further that members of the armed forces holding the rank of Lieutenant or lower must retire upon reaching the age of sixty.

Lieutenant Sanders, a sixty-year-old officer in the U.S. Army, asserted an action challenging the statute's constitutionality. Sander's best argument is that the law

(A)   deprives him of property

(B)   deprives him of a privilege or immunity

(C)   is an invidious discrimination on the basis of age, violating the Fifth Amendment

(D)   is a usurpation of local power

122.   The Federal government appointed Major General Sean Benham of the Army's Judge Advocate Corps to

judge disputes between the United States government and citizens of Grenada. The Grenadians submitted claims demanding compensation for damages inflicted by the U.S. Army.

In 1986, Benham's work with Grenadians was completed; he was removed from office and reassigned to another branch of the Army.

Benham filed suit against the U.S. government, claiming that a federal judge may not be removed from office while exhibiting good behavior. Will Benham prevail?

(A)   Yes, if he can show damages.

(B)   Yes, because his constitutional rights were violated.

(C)   No, because the position was eliminated.

(D)   No, because Benham's position was not covered by Article III.

123.   The state of Coed enacted a statute authorizing school districts to charge a fee for school bus service. The Kraus family refused to agree to a busing fee, since their daughter, Lisa Kraus, had no alternative but to take the bus or walk four and a half miles each way. The Kraus family claimed that the fee violated the Equal Protection Clause by placing an obstacle in the path of Lisa's education. In reviewing the state statute, the United States Supreme Court would

(A)   apply strict scrutiny because education is a fundamental right

(B)   apply the rational basis test and determine that the statute violates the Equal Protection Clause

(C)   apply the rational basis test and determine that the statute does not violate the Equal Protection Clause

(D)   apply strict scrutiny because the statute interferes with interstate commerce

124.   The state of Glut suffered economic problems due to a decline in the price of oil. In an effort to stimulate its local economy and balance the state budget, the Glut State Legislature enacted a ten dollar tax on every barrel of American oil produced out of state. The statute would be attacked best by relying on which of the following constitutional provisions?

(A)   equal protection

(B)   due process

(C)   Commerce Clause

(D)   privileges and immunities

125.   Sidney was stopped by Cheskie, a police officer, after passing a red light. Cheskie noticed that Sidney's speech was slurred and placed him

GO ON TO THE NEXT PAGE

under arrest for drunk driving. Sidney was searched and six grams of cocaine were found in his pocket.

Charged with possession of cocaine, Sidney objected to the introduction of the cocaine into evidence. Sidney's objection should be

(A) sustained, because Cheskie had no reason to search Sidney

(B) sustained, because Cheskie was not in fear

(C) overruled, because the search was incident to a valid arrest

(D) overruled, because a law officer may act on a reasonable suspicion

126. A state law provided, "No truck may operate on a state highway with more than one trailer." Doubler Decker Lines, operating a trucking company that uses many tandem trailers, challenged the statute. Which of the following choices provides the best basis for a constitutional challenge?

(A) the Equal Protection Clause of the Fourteenth Amendment

(B) the difficulty of enforcement will violate the rights of some

(C) the Due Process Clause of the Fourteenth Amendment

(D) the Commerce Clause

127. Steve Smith, a private in the United States Army, went home for a thirty-six-hour leave. While on leave, Smith burglarized six of his neighbors' homes. When he returned to his base, Smith was court-martialed. How should a court rule, if Smith asserts a constitutional challenge to the court-martial's jurisdiction?

(A) Dismiss the action, because a court-martial's jurisdiction is limited to military justice.

(B) Dismiss the action, because the crime was not service-connected.

(C) Overrule the challenge, because Smith was a member of the U.S. armed forces.

(D) Overrule the challenge if the act occurred during a period of war or natural emergency.

128. A state statute provided that "all women must take a leave of absence from their work during the last trimester of pregnancy." Joan was a driver for Texas Trucking. Joan became pregnant and asserted an action in federal court challenging the constitutionality of the state statute. By the time Joan's case came to trial, Joan had already given birth to twin girls whom she named Deborah and Susan.

The state moved to dismiss Joan's case. The court should

(A) hear the case on its merits because pregnancy lasts only nine months and Joan may become pregnant again

(B)   hear the case on its merits, if Joan signs an affidavit stating that she intends to have more children

(C)   dismiss the case as moot

(D)   dismiss the case, because the court can only offer an advisory opinion

129.   The Fort Hamilton Police Department had expended thousands of man-hours trying to solve the "Case of the Knifing Furriers," but had little solid information. Twenty fur hats had been robbed over a two-year period on Thirteenth Avenue, the town's main street. The assailants, one of average height and the other of much shorter height, often struck late at night, flashing knives and warning persons that they would be hurt if they did not volunteer their fur hats. Wineburger had been a suspect, but he refused to testify before a grand jury that served him with a subpoena. After Wineburger was granted use immunity, he testified, "I stole the hats with Shaye, my five-foot-tall friend." In exchange for a promise of leniency, Shaye testified, "I robbed the hats with Wineburger, but it was all Wineburger's idea."

Wineburger was indicted for armed robbery. At his trial, Wineburger objected to Shaye's testimony. The trial judge should rule this testimony

(A)   admissible, because the testimony was relevant and voluntary

(B)   admissible, because the use immunity applies only to Wineburger's own testimony

(C)   not admissible, because the offer of leniency to Shaye provides him with a motive to be less than truthful

(D)   not admissible, because Shaye's testimony was acquired as a result of Wineburger's testimony under use immunity

130.   Industrialist owned a die-stamping factory. Addict lived with seventy of Industrialist's employees in a dormitory complex adjacent to Industrialist's factory. The employees were supplied with subsidized housing as a fringe benefit of working for Industrialist. An employee informed Industrialist that Addict was selling cocaine to the employees. Industrialist invited a passing police officer into the dormitory and told him to search Addict's room. The search revealed cocaine and other controlled substances.

Should the court sustain a motion set forth by Addict to prevent introduction of the cocaine into evidence?

(A)   Yes, because possession of cocaine is not the same as the selling of cocaine.

GO ON TO THE NEXT PAGE

(B)   Yes, because Addict had a right to privacy that was violated without sufficient cause.

(C)   No, because the police officer had probable cause to conduct the search.

(D)   No, because the dormitory was under Industrialist's control.

131.   Larry Drunk, a citizen of the state of Scotch, was charged and found guilty of violating a state statute making it a felony for anyone to sell alcoholic drinks to a female under the age of twelve. Larry attacked the statute claiming that it violated his constitutional rights. The court would hold the statute

(A)   constitutional as a reasonable state regulation

(B)   constitutional, because gender is not a suspect class

(C)   unconstitutional, because gender is a suspect class

(D)   unconstitutional, because the statute treats males and females differently without adequate justification

132.   Cultist was arrested for driving forty miles an hour above the posted speed limit. Cultist challenged the constitutionality of the state statute establishing speed limits, on the grounds that it violated his right of free exercise of religion. Cultist belonged to a religious group called the Indyfivehundreds. The group's members believed that they should serve God by driving ninety miles per hour on alternate Tuesday mornings.

Which of the following choices may NOT be considered by a court determining Cultist's challenge to the constitutionality of the state speed regulations?

(A)   Whether Cultist was required by his religion to exceed the speed limit.

(B)   Whether Cultist is sincere in his beliefs.

(C)   Whether Cultist's religious beliefs are reasonable.

(D)   Whether Cultist was considered a member of the Indyfivehundreds.

133.   The town of Hempstead passed an ordinance that provided, "One may not address a public gathering with language that stirs the public to anger or invites dispute."

Three days after the ordinance was passed, Burntout addressed a gathering of several thousand people protesting a citywide crackdown on motorists driving with one headlight in operation. "We should eliminate those who discriminate against owners of one-headlight cars," said Burntout, in an impassioned cry. The crowd responded by rhythmically chanting, "Burntout, Burntout."

If prosecuted under the town of Hempstead ordinance, which of the following arguments will help Burntout's case most?

(A) The First and Fourteenth Amendments' guarantee of the right of association.

(B) The ordinance is a form of prior restraint.

(C) The public's speech may not be regulated.

(D) The ordinance is an overly broad regulation of speech.

134. The federal government enacted legislation that made 6,000,000 acres of federally owned land into forest preserves. Hunting and harvesting timber are prohibited in forest preserves. Will a court find this legislation constitutional?

(A) Yes, because forest preserves are important to the public's welfare.

(B) Yes, because Congress may regulate federally owned property.

(C) No, because the federal government has usurped local authority.

(D) No, because the right to harvest timber is protected by the United States Constitution.

135. A state statute provides that all private and public schools accredited by the state may receive textbooks on secular subjects that will be paid for by state funds. The High School for Racists, an accredited private school, admits only Caucasian students. In a constitutional challenge to the admissions policy of the High School for Racists, which of the following choices will best support the challenge?

(A) Government funds may not be used to support racism because it is against public policy.

(B) The state is obligated by the Constitution to prevent racism.

(C) The state's involvement in school regulation and support mandates invoking the Equal Protection Clause of the Fourteenth Amendment to the U.S. Constitution.

(D) By accepting state accreditation, a school impliedly warrants it will not discriminate on the basis of race.

136. The state of Angels enacted a statute that provided, "no person may use offensive, insulting, or obscene language in a public area." Lender saw Loaner passing on the opposite side of a wide street. Lender shouted at Loaner, "You cheap, stupid, idiot, liar. You owe me

GO ON TO THE NEXT PAGE

money and your wife wears pink underwear. I hope you drop dead of a heart attack, mooseface."

If prosecuted under the above statute, can Lender be convicted?

(A)   Yes.

(B)   No, because the statute should be held void for violating the freedom of speech clause of the First and Fourteenth Amendments.

(C)   No, because Lender's words to Loaner would not invoke liability under the statute.

(D)   No, because the statute will be held void because it is too vague.

137.   The Hillside Mall was a shopping center complex privately owned by Lou Deed, Inc., which leased retail store space to private retailers. Michael Rabbit, a student at Hillside High School, was president of a school club called The Animal Savers. The club planned to distribute pamphlets at the Hillside Mall on a Saturday afternoon. The literature explained how animals are slaughtered and offered alternatives to purchasing products made from animal skins. When the club members began distributing the pamphlets, the Hillside Mall management insisted that they leave the premises immediately. Subsequently, the students brought suit in federal court seeking an injunction against prohibiting distribution of the material inside the mall. The students will

(A)   prevail, because their activity amounts to free speech that is protected by the First and Fourteenth Amendments

(B)   prevail, because it is in the public interest to learn about the ideas of others

(C)   not prevail, because the mall is private property

(D)   not prevail, because the common law nuisance doctrine will govern the activity

138.   Dorothy, a mother of six children supported by public assistance, asserted an action in federal court against the state, seeking to compel the state to prosecute her former husband for nonpayment of child support.

Which of the following choices is most correct?

(A)   Dorothy should prevail because Dorothy has suffered an injury in fact.

(B)   Dorothy should prevail, because a citizen may force the state to bring an action when that citizen has been victimized.

(C)   Dorothy should not prevail, because she does not have a stake in the outcome.

(D)   Dorothy should not prevail, because she is receiving public assistance in place of child support.

139. A state statute provided, "No airline may discriminate in its hiring on the basis of race, religion, creed, or color." The statute was challenged on constitutional grounds by Intra-State Airlines, an airline engaged in flying within the state, and Inter-State Airlines, an airline servicing several states. Which of the following choices is correct?

(A)   Only Intra-State Airlines will prevail.

(B)   Only Inter-State Airlines will prevail.

(C)   Both will prevail.

(D)   Neither will prevail.

140. Stallone challenged the constitutionality of the statute requiring registration for the draft. Stallone argued that the statute violated the Equal Protection Clause because it required only males to register. The court should rule the statute

(A)   valid, if it accomplishes a compelling state interest

(B)   valid, if it is substantially related to an important government interest

(C)   not valid, because women can serve in support roles

(D)   not valid, if the same objective could be

accomplished in another manner

Questions 141-142 are based upon the following fact situation.

A state statute provided, "Any alien doing business within the state must pay an excise tax of 0.05% of gross revenue." Charles Prince, a citizen of the United Kingdom and manufacturer of Polo Equipment, challenged the statute in federal court.

141. Prince's most persuasive argument will be that

(A)   the Commerce Clause will prevent a state from limiting the rights of aliens

(B)   the statute is unconstitutional because it violates Prince's right to equal protection

(C)   the statute is unconstitutional because it violates the Obligation of Contracts Clause

(D)   the statute constituted an unlawful "taking"

142. The state motioned to dismiss the case. Should the judge dismiss the action?

(A)   Yes, because an alien does not enjoy the same rights as a U.S. citizen.

GO ON TO THE NEXT PAGE

(B)   No, because Prince owned
the factory before the statute
was enacted.

(C)   Yes, because a state may
decide who may own a large
in-state business.

(D)   No, because the suit raises a
federal question.

143.   The county of Skim passed an
ordinance providing that all dairy
products sold in Skim County must
be inspected by a licensed local
inspector. The local inspectors were
unauthorized to inspect dairy
products from plants outside of Skim.
            Which of the following would
have the best standing to challenge
the constitutionality of the
ordinance?

(A)   A county of Skim licensed
inspector.

(B)   A county of Skim dairy
producer.

(C)   A resident-consumer of Skim
County.

(D)   A milk producer from a
neighboring county.

144.   Which of the following constitutional
provisions are applicable to aliens?

I.   the Fifth Amendment
prohibition against
compulsory self-incrimination

II.   the Privileges and Immunities
Clause

III.   the Fourth Amendment
guarantee against
unwarranted searches and
seizures

IV.   the Due Process Clause of
the Fourteenth Amendment

(A)   I, III and IV

(B)   III only

(C)   I and III

(D)   II and IV

Questions 145-146 are based upon the
following fact situation.

A federal statute provides that any
state not enforcing certain civil rights
standards among public schools will be
denied federal aid for education. The state
of Segregate did not comply with the
standards, and federal funding was
eliminated.

145.   Which of the following persons is
most likely to obtain a judicial
determination if he challenges the
constitutionality of the federal
statute?

(A)   a teacher laid off because of
the cuts in federal aid

(B)   a student at a state of
Segregate public high school

(C)   a school principal worried
about the education of his
students

(D)   a taxpayer living in the state
of Segregate

146. The federal government should argue that the statute is constitutional because

    (A) the vast majority of people in the state of Segregate and in the United States support the statute

    (B) the standards will ensure that federal money spent on education will be properly used

    (C) the state of Segregate gave the federal government an implied right to regulate its education by accepting federal aid

    (D) the federal government may regulate the education of its citizens

147. Will a court be likely to rule the federal statute constitutional?

    (A) Yes.

    (B) No, because it is an unlawful intrusion of a right reserved for the states.

    (C) No, because of the Privileges and Immunities Clause.

    (D) No, because of the Fourteenth Amendment.

148. Federal law provides employees of foreign embassies and consulates with "diplomatic immunity." Under the law, employees are immune from prosecution for any offense.

    Julio, employed by an embassy located in Dodge City, was arrested and incarcerated, pursuant to a city statute that provides, "Diplomats may be prosecuted for constant disregard of the law." Julio was arrested after repeatedly shooting the lights out at local bars. If Julio attacks the constitutionality of the Dodge City statute, his best argument will be based upon

    (A) the Due Process Clause

    (B) the Supremacy Clause

    (C) the Privileges and Immunities Clause

    (D) the Equal Protection Clause

Questions 149-150 are based upon the following fact situation.

Bert was an illegitimate son of Ernie. Ernie died intestate, leaving a substantial estate. A local statute provided, "An unacknowledged, illegitimate son is not considered a son for the purpose of inheritance."

149. If Bert challenges the state law, his best argument will be that

    (A) the law violates the obligation of the Contracts Clause

    (B) he has been deprived of property without due process

GO ON TO THE NEXT PAGE

(C)   there is no reason to discriminate against illegitimate children, and therefore, the law violates the Equal Protection Clause

(D)   no state objective has been achieved

150.   The most persuasive defense the state could offer would be

(A)   that the state seeks to define family relationship

(B)   that promotion of family life and encouraging paternity form a rational basis for the law

(C)   that the law is rational and non-discriminatory

(D)   that the law is not invidiously discriminating

Questions 151-153 are based upon the following fact situation.

Duke wanted to protest against the Louisville basketball team. Duke stood on the steps of Louisville City Hall and charged, "You are cheaters, You give your players growth hormones."

Duke was arrested and charged with unlawfully demonstrating pursuant to a statute that provides, "No person may demonstrate or loiter on the City Hall steps between the hours of 7 and 9 a.m. and 4 and 6 p.m."

151.   If Duke challenges the constitutionality of the statute, which

of the following choices is most correct?

(A)   The city must prove that the statute was enacted to satisfy a compelling need and no less restrictive means of satisfying this need were available.

(B)   Duke must prove the statute was enacted without a compelling need or that a less restricting means was available.

(C)   Duke must prove that the statute was not enacted with a rational basis.

(D)   The city must prove that the statute's enactment had a rational basis.

152.   Which of the following persons may also challenge the statute?

(A)   a person who owned a home on the same street as City Hall

(B)   an anti-abortion organizer who wanted to demonstrate on the steps

(C)   the city councilman who led the opposition to the statute

(D)   an owner of a professional basketball team

153.   Should the statute be ruled constitutional?

(A)   No, because of the First Amendment right to free speech.

(B)   Yes, because at certain times and in certain places the First Amendment right to free speech may be limited.

(C)   No, because the statute assists a religion.

(D)   Yes, because speech may be prohibited in front of a public building.

Questions 154-157 are based upon the following fact situation.

Congress allocated $17,000,000 as part of the annual budget for construction of a new building for a church-sponsored medical school. The budget also provided that salaries of private high school teachers may be subsidized, as well as transportation of students to and from those schools. Suzanne, a taxpayer, challenged the above budget clause.

154.   Will the case be decided on its merits?

(A)   No, because Suzanne has not suffered injuries different from the general public.

(B)   Yes, because a taxpayer may challenge any federal allocation of funds.

(C)   Yes, because Suzanne has alleged a violation of specific constitutional limitations on

the exercise of congressional spending power.

(D)   No, because Suzanne is too remote from the application of the challenged statute.

155.   Assuming that the case is decided on its merits, will Suzanne prevail in her challenge of the clause providing aid for construction of the medical school?

(A)   Yes, because the federal government may not provide aid to an organization whose purpose is to teach religion.

(B)   No, because the construction will not aid religion in any way.

(C)   No, because aid provided for one use by an institution is not assumed to be aid for the institution's teachings.

(D)   Yes, because the clause creates an excessive entanglement between religion and state.

156.   Assuming the case is decided on its merits, will Suzanne prevail in her challenge of the clause providing funds for transporting students to parochial schools?

(A)   No, because the transportation will not aid religion in any way.

GO ON TO THE NEXT PAGE

(B)   No, because transportation is sufficiently secular.

(C)   Yes, because the clause creates an excessive entanglement between religion and state.

(D)   Yes, because the federal government may not provide aid to an organization whose purpose it is to teach religion.

157.   Assuming the case is decided on its merits, will Suzanne prevail in her challenge of the clause providing for subsidizing of teacher's salaries?

(A)   No, because the teaching is secular.

(B)   Yes, because enforcing the conditions of the clause would constitute an excessive entanglement with religion.

(C)   No, because the funding will not aid religion.

(D)   Yes, because the government may not assist a religious institution in any manner.

158.   Beverly Hills, California, passed a tough zoning law, allegedly to exclude low-income residents. Residents from neighboring Hollywood brought suit, claiming its taxes had increased since the Beverly Hills zoning law forced Hollywood to build more low-income housing to make up for the extra demand. A group of Westward residents, who had never resided in Beverly Hills, joined the suit claiming they would have settled in luxurious Beverly Hills if housing had been more affordable. The Westward residents, however, could not show that they would have purchased a home "but for" the zoning law. Which statement is best?

(A)   The Hollywood citizens have standing.

(B)   The Westward citizens have standing.

(C)   Both the Hollywood citizens and the Westwood citizens have standing.

(D)   Neither Hollywood nor Westward citizens have standing as third parties.

159.   Linda made a decision to have an abortion in the state of Carsdale, where she resides. When the state refused to provide governmental Medicaid funding for the abortion, Linda brought suit claiming it was her constitutional right. The court deciding the case will rule

(A)   the government must fund only medically necessary abortions

(B)   the government may refuse to fund abortions, whether or not they are medically necessary to the health of the mother

(C)   the government must fund all abortions, as long as the mother cannot pay

(D) the government may refuse to fund abortions, but Linda is guaranteed access to public hospitals and abortion counseling at public clinics.

160. The federal government enacted a statute requiring that all gasoline sold be listed by grade based on the gasoline's octane level. The best argument to thwart a constitutional challenge to this statute is that

 (A) the health and safety of the public is at stake

 (B) the sale of gasoline affects interstate commerce

 (C) the law supports the country's general welfare

 (D) gasoline is a necessity

Questions 161-162 are based upon the following fact situation.

The Plantain Growers Association, located in the state of Castries, is an organization of private citizens formed as an open forum for discussion of social issues. The association often sponsors speakers and forums. The headquarters include several lounges and a restaurant. Obtaining membership in the association is a long and arduous process. Most people feel the effort expended to obtain membership is worthwhile, because the "powerful" gather in the Association and many important contacts are made. The association has neither blacks nor women among its members.

Several association members were employees of the state of Castries, because the state felt that in order to advance its interests it was important for state officials to maintain contact with Castries "elite."

An action was asserted in a federal district court, seeking to enjoin the state of Castries from payments of dues to the association.

161. Which of the following arguments will best support the plaintiff's suit?

 (A) The state has violated the Equal Protection Clause of the Fourteenth Amendment.

 (B) The state is providing the association with tacit approval.

 (C) The state of Castries is promoting discrimination by paying dues to the association.

 (D) Race and gender are suspect classes.

162. If the court's jurisdiction is challenged, will the federal district court have proper jurisdiction?

 (A) No, unless all possible state remedies have been exhausted.

 (B) Yes, because a federal claim is being presented.

 (C) Yes, because interstate commerce is indirectly affected.

GO ON TO THE NEXT PAGE

(D)   No, because a federal court does not have jurisdiction over a local club.

Questions 163-166 are based upon the following fact situation.

A state statute requires all taxi drivers to obtain a license. The state only grants licenses to those who have driven for an in-state fleet for six months, who have resided in the state for one year, and who are United States citizens.

163.   If appropriate challenge is raised against the requirement that drivers must have driven for an in-state fleet, will the clause be ruled constitutional?

(A)   No, because it will burden interstate commerce.

(B)   Yes, because the state does not know the quality of drivers in other states.

(C)   No, because it violates the Privileges and Immunity Clause of the Fourteenth Amendment.

(D)   Yes, because a profession may be regulated.

164.   If an appropriate challenge is raised against the clause requiring one-year state residency, will the clause be ruled constitutional?

(A)   No, because it violates the Privileges and Immunity Clause of the Fourteenth Amendment.

(B)   Yes, because a state may protect the welfare of its citizens.

(C)   No, because it violates the Equal Protection Clause of the Fourteenth Amendment.

(D)   Yes, as valid economic protection.

165.   If an appropriate challenge is raised against the requirement that drivers must be U.S. citizens, the strongest ground on which to invalidate the clause will be

(A)   interstate commerce

(B)   equal protection

(C)   privileges and immunities

(D)   due process

166.   If an appropriate challenge against the state licensing procedure is raised in a federal court, will the case be dismissed for lack of proper jurisdiction?

(A)   Yes, because a state statute is in question.

(B)   Yes, because of a lack of diversity.

(C)   No, because the challenge involves a federal question.

(D)   No, because a state may not rule on its own laws.

Questions 167-168 are based upon the following fact situation.

Idid Slipbuck was forced to testify before a congressional committee investigating the disappearance of $2,000,000 in government funds. Slipbuck refused to answer certain questions. Congress ordered a Kansas district attorney to prosecute Slipbuck for contempt. He refused.

167. May the district attorney refuse to prosecute Slipbuck?

(A) No, because the district attorney must act as directed.

(B) Yes, the district attorney's duties are executive actions.

(C) Yes, because Slipbuck is not accountable.

(D) No, because one who violates the law must be prosecuted.

168. If Slipbuck is prosecuted for refusing to answer questions, which of the following choices, if proved, will best help Slipbuck's case?

(A) The missing funds came from the state of Kansas and private corporations.

(B) All of Slipbuck's decisions were ultimately approved by civilian authorities.

(C) Slipbuck has only limited and trivial knowledge.

(D) The questions were not related to legislative matters.

Questions 169-170 are based upon the following fact situation.

Congress enacted the National Air Pollution Act. The act established an advisory committee to monitor testing and prosecute those who violate standards. The Department of the Interior and Congress were empowered to appoint members to the commission.

Polluter, owner of a coal-burning plant, was prosecuted by the advisory committee.

169. Which of the following facts will be most persuasive in favor of Polluter's defense that the National Air Pollution Act is unconstitutional?

(A) Polluter was not involved in interstate commerce and, therefore, was not under the commission's jurisdiction.

(B) The executive branch may not enforce legislation enacted by Congress.

(C) The commission is powerless because members were appointed by other agencies than the Department of the Interior.

(D) Polluter was denied equal protection because the commission has discretion on whom to prosecute.

GO ON TO THE NEXT PAGE

170. What will be the proper ruling regarding the constitutionality of the National Air Pollution Act?

    (A) The committee may make recommendations to the legislative branch.

    (B) The committee members must be appointed by the Department of the Interior.

    (C) The advisory committee may prosecute those deemed to have violated environmental standards.

    (D) The advisory committee is null and void.

171. Reck and Less, two members of the executive branch, were old political enemies of Representative Pure. After Reck and Less heard Representative Pure give a speech on the House floor, to harass him they initiated a criminal suit relating to the legislative action he proposed. Representative Pure might

    (A) just grin and bear it, since political feuds are as old as politics

    (B) use a writ of *habeas corpus*

    (C) invoke the Establishment Clause

    (D) invoke the Speech and Debate Clause

172. The state of Metro enacted a statute that imposed a tax on out-of-state insurance companies doing business in the state of Metro which was 20 percent higher than the tax imposed on in-state insurance companies. The strongest argument for an out-of-state company to make in challenging the statute would be

    (A) that it is void as against public policy and is not in the public interest

    (B) that it violates the Commerce Clause

    (C) that it violates the Equal Protection Clause

    (D) that it violates the Due Process Clause of the Fifth Amendment

Questions 173-174 are based upon the following fact situation.

The federal government fined Harvey, director of the State Motor Vehicle Fleet, because several cars and trucks did not meet federal standards. Harvey moved to dismiss the case, claiming that his actions were in the course of state senate business and that, therefore, he may not be prosecuted.

173. Harvey should assert which of the following arguments?

    (A) The states may delegate local governments to determine environmental standards.

    (B) The state should be prosecuted, not Harvey.

(C) Under the federalism doctrine, federal law may not be imposed upon state senators acting within the scope of state business.

(D) Harvey is entitled to legislative immunity.

174. The federal government should assert which of the following arguments?

(A) Preferential treatment for legislators would be a violation of equal protection to the ordinary citizen.

(B) State senators are liable for willful misconduct.

(C) Enforcing environmental standards is not a significant interference with state government.

(D) Regulation of trucks affects interstate commerce.

CONSTITUTIONAL LAW ANSWERS

1. (C)   To have standing, one must have a significant stake in the outcome of the controversy. This requirement is met if the litigant has suffered an "injury in fact." Federal taxpayers, such as the woman in (C), have standing if they establish that the tax imposed was enacted under Congress's taxing and spending powers and that the tax exceeds some specific limitation on the taxing and spending powers.

    The other choices are less likely to be successful because each would have difficulty proving injury in fact.

2. (B)   Article I, Section 8 declares that Congress may spend to "provide for the common defense and general welfare." Congress's spending power is for any public purpose. A tax will usually be upheld if it bears some reasonable relationship to revenue production.

3. (D)   By limiting admission to only Grenadian Americans, the school has discriminated based on nationality in violation of the Fourteenth Amendment, which includes the Equal Protection Clause and the Privileges and Immunities Clause. The U.S. Supreme Court has held that federal legislation prohibiting discrimination in private education is a valid exercise of federal legislative power [See *Runyon v. McCrary*, 96 S.Ct. 2586 (1976)].

4. (C)   The Supremacy Clause invalidates state or local laws that conflict with a federal statute.

    (A) and (B) may also be correct but, when given the choice on the Multistate Exam, choose a legal theory over an explanation of the facts.

5. (D)   The Supreme Court has defined a suspension of ten days or less to be a "short suspension" [*Gross v. Lopez*, 419 U.S. 505 (1975)]. The Court held that no formal evidentiary hearing is required for a short suspension; due process is satisfied with notice of charges and opportunity to explain. Note: The Court in Gross ruled that there is a property interest in public education when school attendance is required.

6. (D)   The rule stated in the previous explanation applies.

    (B) and (C) are not correct, because neither includes reference to the "10-day short suspension" rule set in *Gross v. Lopez*.

7.   (C)   Ms. Jones's conversation with the *Brooklyn Eagle* was protected by the First Amendment but her obscene language before her students was not protected. Her dismissal, therefore, could only have been based on the obscene language charge.

(4) is false because a prior hearing for academic dismissal is not required as long as the student is adequately informed of the deficiency and allowed an opportunity to respond [*Board of Curators v. Horowitz*, 1435 U.S. 78 (1978)].

8.   (B)   The voluntary prayer that takes place inside the school building violates the Establishment Clause of the First Amendment.

(A) is too general. See *Abington School District v. Schempp*, 374 U.S. 203 (1963).

9.   (B)   Congress may regulate activities, whether carried out in one or several states, if the activities have an appreciable effect on interstate commerce. A state may regulate local aspects of interstate commerce if (1) Congress has not exercised its power; *and* (2) the burden on interstate commerce is slight; *and* (3) the regulation does not discriminate against out-of-state competitors; *and* (4) the local interest is substantial and reasonable.

The Commerce Clause would be the best grounds to challenge the New York statute.

10.   (A)   In *Breard v. Alexandria*, 341 U.S. 622 (1951), the Court held that door-to-door sellers of magazines may be subjected to general regulations protecting the privacy of householders against unwanted solicitors. In *Grosjean v. American Press Co.*, 297 U.S. 233 (1936), the court held that a Louisiana tax on newspapers above a certain circulation violated the First Amendment: "The tax . . . is bad not because it takes money . . . it is seen to be a deliberate and calculated device in the guise of a tax to limit the circulation of information."

The Supreme Court has held that a Florida statute that granted a political candidate a right to equal space to reply to criticism and attacks on his record by a newspaper violated the guarantees of a free press [*Miami Herald Publishing Co. v. Tornillo*, 418 U.S. 241 (1974)].

11.   (D)   In *Miami Herald Publishing Co. v. Tornillo*, the Supreme Court held that a Florida statute granting political candidates the right to equal newspaper space to reply to criticism violated freedom of the press under the First Amendment. The Court has allowed more stringent regulation of radio and television than of newspapers on the theory that the privilege of being awarded one of a limited number of frequencies gives the broadcaster certain obligations, including the obligations to provide equal time [*Red Lion Broadcasting Co. v. FCC*, 395 U.S. 367 (1969)]. In our case, Recent will prevail against WKRP but not *The Enquirer*, and WKRP's appeal will fail.

12. (B) Under the Abstention Doctrine, the federal courts will not decide a case based on an untested state law. The doctrine is used (1) to avoid decision of a federal question where the controversy can be based on question of state law; (2) to avoid conflict with a state's administration of its own affairs; (3) to leave to the states the resolution of unsettled questions of state law; (4) to ease congestion in the federal courts.

When taking the Multistate Exam, you must carefully note who is asserting the action, in which court, and whether it is based on a state or federal action. In the instant case, an action based on a state statute is apparently raised for the first time in a federal court.

(C) is not correct, because the case will not be based on a political question.

13. (C) The right to vote is a fundamental right. Restrictions of this right are generally subject to the strict scrutiny test. Under this test, the classification must be necessary to promote a compelling interest. A naturalized citizen has rights equal to a native citizen. See *Plyler v. Doe*, 103 S.Ct. 14 (Marshall, concurring) for an explanation of how the Equal Protection Clause protects fundamental rights.

14. (C) Arguments (1), (2), and (3) as set forth by the state of Ohio form the elements of permissible state regulation of interstate commerce. A regulation enacted to favor local consumers or industries with respect to state natural resources is generally not permissible. See *Hughes v. Oklahoma*, 441 U.S. 322 (1979).

15. (C) Plaintiff challenges the statute as allowing the unconstitutional impairment of the obligation to contract. Since South performed his work, he was owed a salary and fringe benefits. The government should argue that South violated his contract by violating the law. The Contract Clause cannot be asserted by one who has violated the contract at issue.

16. (D) Congress has the power to dispose of federal property under Article IV, Section 3, Clause 2. A taxpayer has standing to challenge a federal appropriation that has exceeded a specific limitation of the federal taxing and spending powers. In general, taxpayers have been successful only on challenges based on the Establishment Clause, a ground with little merit in the instant case.

(A), (B), and (C) are incorrect because persons have no standing as citizens to challenge the disposal of federal property.

(D) is correct because the association will be granted standing since it has a direct interest in the outcome of a decision.

17. (D) In *Jehovah's Witness v. King County Hospital*, 278 F. Supp 598 (1968) and other cases, courts have allowed the state to force medical treatment for minors despite the religious objections of their parents, on the grounds of the minors' health and safety.

(B), (C), and (D) will all be considered by the judge, but (D) is the test to be applied in this case; (B) and (C) are merely evidence toward this test.

18.   (D)   In *Dean Milk Co. v. City of Madison*, 340 U.S. 349 (1951), the court held that a Madison ordinance prohibiting the sale of milk not bottled at an approved pasteurization plant within a radius of five miles from Madison violated the Commerce Clause. In the case of *City of Philadelphia v. New Jersey*, 437 U.S. 617 (1978), the court invalidated a New Jersey waste disposal statute and ruled that the disposal of garbage was an item of interstate commerce. In our case, sections (a) and (b) of the statute place a severe burden on out-of-state firms.

19.   (B)   The statute violates the Equal Protection Clause as an invidious discrimination against the poor. The statute burdens Hilary's freedom to travel into Maricopa by denying her essential benefits. See *Memorial Hospital v. Maricopa County*, 415 U.S. 250 (1974).

20.   (B)   The Supreme Court in *Griswold v. Connecticut*, 381 U.S. 479 (1965) ruled that a statute restricting the use of contraceptives by married persons violated the right to privacy of such persons.
    (D) is incorrect because the Court ruled in *Tileston v. Ullman*, 318 U.S. 44 (1943) that a medical doctor does not have third-party standing to attack a state anti-contraceptive statute.

21.   (C)   Congress has the power to limit admission of aliens, but once aliens are admitted, discrimination is suspect and they are entitled to rights under the Equal Protection Clause.

22.   (A)   The law regards aliens as a suspect class. The burden of validating a statute that discriminates against a suspect class rests upon the state, which must prove the law accomplishes a compelling state interest.

23.   (C)   This question illustrates a Multistate trick of including two correct answers. Although (A) and (C) are both correct, (C) is the proper answer because it is narrower. When selecting among two correct choices, always select the more specific choice.

24.   (D)   The Supreme Court has ruled that not all rights assured an adult are to be guaranteed in a juvenile proceeding. The right to a trial by jury is one such example.

(A) is incorrect because habeas corpus is the correct action. The writ of habeas corpus is a judicial determination of the legality of an individual's custody. It is used to test the constitutionality of a state criminal conviction. (B) and (C) are not Adolescent's best arguments.

25. (D) The Supreme Court (387 U.S. 1, 87 S. Ct. 1428) has ruled that the Due Process Clause of the Fourteenth Amendment applies to juveniles in state court proceedings. The court ruled that sufficient advance notice must be afforded, the child and his parents must be advised of the child's right to counsel, the right to confront a witness, and the constitutional privilege against self-incrimination.

26. (C) The executive privilege will be overruled in criminal proceedings when a need for such information is demonstrated [*United States v. Nixon*, 418 U.S. 683 (1974)]. The nature in (C) refers to the fact that the indictment is a criminal proceeding. Presidential aides do share executive privilege (B), but that fact will not help them in this case. Military, diplomatic or other sensitive national security secrets (D) are given great deference, but it does not seem that a bribery investigation would fall under this exception.

27. (B) Genuth was privileged to enter the vessel for specific reasons only; he did not have the authority to consent to a search.

28. (C) One has standing to object to a search if he has a reasonable right to privacy in the premises searched.

29. (C) A grant to parochial schools to be used for teachers' salaries is a violation of the Establishment Clause, which does not allow aid to religion. Even if the teachers are involved in secular education, it is felt the aid involves a risk of excessive government entanglement with religion because the purpose of the parochial school is religious indoctrination. A similar grant to a church-related college would be permissible.

30. (B) The Taking Clause of the Fifth Amendment prohibits the taking of private property for private use, even if just compensation is made. In this case, (B) is correct because the power of eminent domain can be delegated to a private corporation or person if the taking is for public use and just compensation is given.

31. (A) State action must be involved in order for a state to protect one's constitutional rights.

(B) is not correct, because a private individual rather than a state is doing the discriminating. (C) and (D) are wrong because the discrimination is at the hands of federal officials rather than by state action.

32.   (A)   A distinction is made between religious beliefs and conduct arising from the religious beliefs. One has an absolute privilege to maintain any religious beliefs. Conduct based on these beliefs may be regulated. Hilary was prosecuted for her beliefs, not her actions; therefore, she will not be successfully prosecuted.

33.   (A)   Gender is a semi-suspect class. A constitutional challenge based on equal protection, alleging discrimination between sexes, is valid if the law is substantially related to a government interest. See *Michael M. v. Superior Court*, 450 U.S. 464 (1981).
     The stricter test in (B) is applied when the law affects a suspect class (i.e., race, alienage, citizenship).

34.   (C)   Alienage is a suspect class, and therefore the strict scrutiny test will be applied to determine if the Equal Protection Clause has been violated. Under the test, the classification must be necessary to promote a compelling state interest.

35.   (C)   The Fourteenth Amendment makes the Bill of Rights' guarantees applicable to the states. The Supreme Court has ruled that only parts of the Bill of Rights are applicable to the states. The parts applicable are the First, Fourth, Sixth, Eighth, and parts of the Fifth Amendment.

36.   (C)   *Shelley v. Kraemer*, 334 U.S. 1 (1948) states that "The Fourteenth Amendment erects no shield against merely private conduct, however discriminatory or wrongful." The Fourteenth Amendment prevents states from deprivations of equal protection of the law. In the instant case, there is no state action to trigger the Fourteenth Amendment.
     Note: The Thirteenth Amendment ("Neither slavery or involuntary servitude ... ") is the only constitutional provision that limits private individual acts on its face.
     (D) is an incorrect statement and not applicable to the fact situation.

37.   (D)   Courts will dismiss a case for lack of standing unless a challenger can demonstrate a concrete stake in the case's outcome. The injury must be real but not necessarily pecuniary. The U.S. Supreme Court has held that all tenants in a development were hurt by the exclusion of minorities.

38. (D)   Undocumented or illegal aliens are a suspect class, and therefore the strict scrutiny test should be applied to determine if the Equal Protection Clause has been violated. Under the test, the classification must be necessary to promote a compelling state interest.

39. (D)   A person has standing to raise a Fourth Amendment claim if he owned or had a right to possession of the premises searched, or if the place was, in fact, his home. Ownership of the evidence in dispute will not provide standing to challenge a search.

40. (C)   The only stage at which Harry had a right to counsel was at the preliminary hearing to determine probable cause to prosecute.

Other stages where a defendant does not have a right to counsel are taking of blood samples, pre-charge lineups, photo identifications, discretionary appeals, and parole and probation revocation proceedings.

41. (D)   Speech conveyed by physical means such as a billboard is protected by the First Amendment right to freedom of speech. Any government regulation of such speech must further an important government interest unrelated to the message being communicated, and the restriction must be as narrow as possible to further the government interest.

42. (B)   The right to privacy is considered a fundamental right. Any law that penalizes or unduly burdens a fundamental constitutional right must pass the strict equal protection test. The test requires a showing of a compelling state interest to justify the law. The right to privacy includes obscene reading material, abortion, and freedom from collection of personal data. The same test will be applied to any law affecting the right to travel, which is also a fundamental right.

43. (D)   The Supremacy Clause is the popularized title for Article VI, Section 2 of the U.S. Constitution. The clause provides that acts of the federal government operate as supreme law throughout the union. The states have no power to impede, burden, or in any manner control the operation of the laws enacted by the federal government.

44. (C)   In *Dunn v. Blumstein*, 405 U.S. 330 (1972), the Supreme Court determined that Tennessee's duration requirements for voting interfered with the fundamental right to vote and the right to travel. Fifty-day residency requirements have been upheld, however, to allow the state to maintain accurate voting records. See *Marston v. Lewis*, 410 U.S. 679 (1973).

45. (C)   Both Dutch and Swimmer have standing to challenge the statute. The statute should be found unconstitutional because it unduly infringes on Dutch's and Swimmer's rights to vote.

46. (C)   The Supremacy Clause is the popularized title for Article VI, Section 2 of the U.S. Constitution. The clause provides that acts of the federal government operate as supreme law throughout the union. The states have no power to impede, burden, or in any manner control the operation of the laws enacted by the federal government.

47. (D)   Article I, Section 6 of the U.S. Constitution provides that "for any speech or debate in either house, (members of Congress) shall not be questioned in any other place." The immunity extends to aides who engage in acts that would be immune if performed by a legislator. Offering a bribe is not in the regular course of legislative work and thus is actionable.

48. (D)   Only an action asserted by a party with standing will be judged on its merits. Cases brought by others will be dismissed on motion. The tank manufacturer has standing because, due to the president's actions, it has suffered pecuniary damages different from those of the general public.

49. (A)   Under Article I, Congress may spend to provide for the common defense and welfare.

50. (C)   A marriage taking place on the Capitol's steps would fall under the jurisdiction of the federal government because it is taking place in the District of Columbia.

51. (B)   A law affecting a suspect class must promote a compelling interest to satisfy the Equal Protection Clause. Classifications are suspect if based on race, national origin, or status of citizenship. Gender is a semi-suspect but not suspect class.

52. (A)   A court may determine the sincerity of a party who is asserting his religion as a defense. The court may also determine the exact beliefs of the religion. The court may not form a judgment as to the reasonableness of the beliefs. See *U.S. v. Ballard*, 322 U.S. 78 (1944).

53. (B)   The NALHP has not in itself suffered harm. An exception to this rule was invoked for a suit by the NAACP, because its members could not file suit without disclosing their identities.

54.   (B)   Troublemaker must have standing for his suit to be decided on its merits. A federal taxpayer has standing to challenge federal spending and spending acts if (1) the measure was enacted under Congress's taxing and spending powers, and (2) the measure exceeded some specific limitation on the taxing and spending powers.

55.   (D)   The Establishment Clause prohibits governmental assistance to religion. It does not forbid every action by the government that favors or benefits religion. A statute will not violate the Establishment Clause if it (1) has a secular purpose, (2) has a principal or primary effect that neither advances nor inhibits religion, and (3) does not produce excessive government entanglement with religion. See *Lynch v. Donnelly*, 465 U.S. 668 (1984) and *Lemon v. Kurtzman*, 403 U.S. 602 (1970).

The three-part "Lemon" test, described above, officially remains the standard in Establishment Clause cases.

56.   (D)   The three conditions are again satisfied, so the Establishment Clause is not violated.

57.   (A)   The government would not be able to determine which teachers are teaching religion and which are not without violating the element "excessive government entanglement." (See all three elements above.)

58.   (B)   Plaintiff should argue that the financial support of an institution that discriminates based on race and gender amounts to state support for this discrimination.

59.   (B)   Alleging state discrimination based on race or sex is a question for the federal court.

60.   (B)   A bill of attainder is an act of legislature that provides for punishment without trial of an individual designated by name or past conduct. Bomber is being punished under the statute, without a trial, for belonging to Freedom.

61.   (C)   The statute is inapplicable because the adult films were being shown in the privacy of motel rooms. In addition, *Stanley v. Georgia*, 394 U.S. 557 (1969) held that mere private possession of obscene matter is not a crime. Remember to read the statutes carefully.

62.   (D)   Warren was given his Miranda warning and was not interrogated. His statement was voluntary and, therefore, admissible.

63.   (C)   A state may not sue the United States without its consent. This consent may be in the form of Congressional legislation allowing a suit in a specific situation.

64.   (D)   The Establishment Clause provides that the government may not take any action that favors or benefits religion. If a regulation has a secular purpose, its primary effect does not advance religion and it does not produce excessive government entanglement, then the regulation will be valid. (A), (B), and (C) fulfill this rule. The field trips may be religious in nature, and therefore transportation for field trips has been invalidated.

65.   (C)   Congress cannot unduly burden the operation of essential state services. The work of the state senate is an essential function.

66.   (D)   Admitting the federal government has interfered with a local function, the intrusion was arguably not a great burden.

67.   (D)   Unless a specific objective is shown, the statute will be ruled discriminatory against out-of-state tailors.

68.   (C)   Federal review of state acts is a basic principle of our legal system. The specifications of the system to review these state acts is determined by Congress.

69.   (D)   Disposal of nuclear waste is an item of interstate commerce. The state statute here creates an undue burden on out-of-state nuclear firms by prohibiting them from entering New Hope to dispose of the waste. See *City of Philadelphia v. New Jersey*, 437 U.S. 617 (1978).
       (C) is not the best answer, because states can pass legislation in order to achieve a legitimate public interest even though the legislation may modify private contracts.

70.   (D)   The federal courts have jurisdiction over cases alleging a violation of the U.S. Constitution.

71.   (D)   Neither the state nor the federal government may pass an *ex post facto* law. Laws creating new crimes, an increase in punishment, or a reduction in the evidence

required are deemed *ex post facto*. A procedural change that does not affect the substantive elements is not deemed *ex post facto*.

72.   (B)   The federal judiciary's jurisdiction extends to cases to which the United States is a party. An action asserted against a federal officer qualifies as a case against the United States, if a judgment may result in federal liability. In the instant case, Grizly was an agent of the U.S. government which could be liable for his acts under *respondeat superior*.

73.   (C)   Abandoned's only chance is to argue that the Equal Protection Clause has been violated.

74.   (C)   Illegitimacy is a semi-suspect class. The state must show a rational basis for the law. Distinctions between legitimate and illegitimate children must be substantially related to a legitimate interest of the state. See *Pickett v. Brown*, 103 S.Ct. 2199 (1983).

75.   (B)   "Other evidence unknown" is a valid phrase in a search warrant. (A) will fail because it is vague. (C) contains the three elements necessary to invalidate a search based on an affidavit. They are (1) false statement; (2) recklessly or intentionally included by affiant; and (3) material. (D) will fail for lack of reason, not because the home did not belong to suspect.

76.   (A)   One's procedural due process rights have been violated only when he has been deprived of property or liberty. The court has tended to interpret these three terms broadly.

77.   (C)   The city will effectively argue that it has not breached Cleaver's contract.

78.   (D)   In *Dandridge v. Illinois* 397 U.S. 471 (1970), the Supreme Court held that wealth alone is not a suspect classification. It held that the Equal Protection Clause does not give the federal courts power to impose upon the states their views of what constitutes economic policy. If, however, the statute also deprived a citizen of a basic right, such as voting, then the Equal Protection Clause would apply.

79.   (C)   A fair procedure is required to take one's life, liberty, or property. Examples of property include rights to public education, welfare, and continued public employment. Reputation is not considered "property" under the clause.

80.   (B)   Congress may legislate but may not deprive the executive branch of its discretion in executing the laws.

81.   (B)   A witness testifying before a congressional committee may refuse to answer questions unrelated to congressional powers.

82.   (D)   Under the "affectation doctrine," Congress has the power to regulate interstate commerce. Regulation of the sale of medicine would fall under this power because courts have extended this rule to cover almost all goods.

83.   (C)   Enforcement and execution of legislation may only be performed by members of the executive branch.

84.   (C)   A commission appointed by the legislative branch may only exercise powers available to the executive branch.

85.   (C)   A different definition of obscenity may be adopted for materials sold to minors. This standard may be more restrictive than the standards applied for adults. The right of privacy encompasses the freedom to read obscene material in one's home. See *Stanley v. Georgia*, 394 U.S. 557 (1969).

86.   (A)   The weakest argument the town of Skeed could make is that the case is moot, because mootness means there is no case or controversy once the matter has been resolved. In the instant case, the question of whether or not Snowline can sell skis in the town has not been resolved.

87.   (B)   Administrative inspections are not exceptions to a warrant requirement, although the same standard of probable cause is not required. The other choices are correct. Highly regulated industries include liquor, guns, and strip mining.

88.   (B)   A defendant does not have a right to a judge who is also a lawyer in a case involving a minor misdemeanor. The other choices violate Defendant's Sixth Amendment right to a fair trial.

89.   (A)   Other stages where defendant has the right to counsel are preliminary hearings to determine probable cause to prosecute, arraignment, guilty plea and sentencing,

felony trials, misdemeanor trials where imprisonment is actually imposed, and appeals as a matter of right.

90.   (C)   The Supreme Court has not incorporated the Second Amendment right to bear arms, the Grand Jury Clause of the Fifth Amendment, and the Seventh Amendment right to a jury in civil cases into the Fourteenth Amendment. These rights may be denied by a state.

91.   (C)   Under the Commerce Clause Congress can regulate any activity, regardless of how small or local, if in the aggregate it has an appreciable effect on interstate commerce. See *Wickard v. Filburn* 317 U.S. 111 (1942) for "the aggregation doctrine."

92.   (C)   A government regulation affecting the free exercise of religion must promote a compelling government interest so as to be enforceable.

93.   (C)   Among the choices, the teacher is the only one to have standing.

94.   (A)   This answer is a description of the General Welfare Act.

95.   (D)   The statute should be held valid as an exercise of the federal spending power.

96.   (B)   The statute regulates speech, not conduct; therefore, freedom of speech guaranteed by the First Amendment is at issue. Because a guarantee is at issue, the burden is on the city to prove that the statute is constitutional.

97.   (C)   The issue in this question is standing. Only a person who seeks to demonstrate on a Sunday morning will be affected by the statute and will therefore have standing to sue.

98.   (B)   Excluding the exercise of First Amendment rights during brief periods of time and in certain places is permissible in order to achieve a compelling interest, such as access to a church.

99.   (A)   Only important and basic deprivations have been held to violate the Equal Protection Clause. (B) is clearly incorrect. (C) is incorrect because not all discrimina-

tion against the poor violates the Equal Protection Clause. (D) is wrong for the same reason that (A) is correct.

100.   (D)   Providing bus service is a state action that indirectly aids an institution discriminating on the basis of race.

101.   (C)   The bus service is secular aid and its primary effect is not to aid religion or a particular viewpoint.

102.   (B)   States cannot discriminate against aliens by denying them welfare benefits. However, Congress can deny such benefits to aliens.
         Because of Congress's plenary power over aliens, federal statutes based on alienage are usually not subject to strict scrutiny and are often held valid if they are not arbitrary and unreasonable.

103.   (A)   The arrest was not proper, because there was no cause to make a warrantless arrest. The Miranda warnings were not enough to make the evidence admissible.

104.   (C)   The First Amendment prohibits laws respecting an establishment of religion. But the U.S. Supreme Court [*Reynolds v. United States* (1879)] has ruled that polygamy is not protected under the Establishment clause. "There has never been a time in any state of the union when polygamy has not been a crime against society."

105.   (B)   Corporations are not citizens of the United States and are not protected by the Privileges and Immunities Clause.

106.   (C)   Under the Impairment of Contract Clause, a government body may interfere with a contract only if reasonable and necessary to service a public purpose.

107.   (D)   Courts will only resolve constitutional issues when a party is seeking to avoid some harm or immediate threat of harm. Dragster was too young to drive so the statute will not affect him.

108.   (A)   A citizen has a constitutional "fundamental right" to travel freely from state to state. Therefore, the federal court should apply the Equal Protection Clause. The state must overcome the burden of persuasion.

109.   (C)   Article III provides Congress with the power to determine the jurisdiction of the federal courts. Since Congress creates the courts, it must determine their jurisdiction.

110.   (B)   Congress may enforce but not limit guarantees of the Equal Protection Clause. The minimum standards are not subject to change.

111.   (C)   The Supremacy Clause provides that treaties and immigration laws take precedence over inconsistent state laws. Federal law specifies that a resident alien may not be discriminated against when seeking employment.

112.   (D)   Hersey must try to show the statute's discrimination was justified because of a compelling state interest.
        (A), (B), and (C) all advance arguments concerning the benefits of the statute to the state. Under (D), individuals within the state benefit but no compelling state interest is argued.

113.   (D)   The United States Supreme Court does not have jurisdiction to rule on the validity of a state court's invalidation of a state statute.

114.   (C)   When a state statute is declared unconstitutional, the route of appeal to the U.S. Supreme Court is by *certiorari*.

115.   (C)   A magistrate who issues search warrants must be neutral and detached. (A), (B), and (D) have all been held by courts to be biased.

116.   (B)   The statute should be found invalid because it does not put the average citizen on notice as to exactly what language is prohibited.

117.   (B)   The President, under Article II, Section 2, has the power to command and direct the military and naval forces.
        (C) is incorrect because the War Powers Act applies when the armed forces are engaged in hostilities, which is not the case here.

118.   (B)   The oath does not obligate members of the State Highway Patrol to anything that would not otherwise be required of them to do. The oath is merely a commitment to the Constitutional process.

119. (A)   Certain speech and conduct, such as vagrancy, may be prohibited by a proper statute. A statute that is overly broad or vague, or a statute that fails to give a person of ordinary intelligence fair notice that his contemplated conduct is forbidden, will be held unconstitutional.

120. (D)   The Supreme Court's interpretation of Article III's "case and controversy" requirement bars the rendition of "advisory" opinions. A moot decision is deemed advisory. When Jefferson turned eighteen, the suit became moot.

121. (C)   Mandatory retirement ages have been upheld if they pass the "rational basis standard." In order to uphold the standard, the government will have to show a rational basis for why retirement ages differ by rank.

122. (D)   Lifetime tenure is a right only enjoyed by judges appointed to Article III courts.

123. (C)   In *Kadrmas v. Dickinson Public Schools*, 108 S.Ct. 2481 (1988), a similar fact pattern applied and the court applied the rational basis test to determine that a state's decision to allow a local school board the option of charging patrons a user fee for bus service is constitutionally permissible. Encouraging local school boards to provide bus service is a legitimate state interest.
    (A) is wrong because education has never been declared a fundamental right by a majority in the Supreme Court.
    (D) is incorrect because the fact pattern does not involve interstate commerce.

124. (C)   The Commerce Clause is violated because the statute discriminates between out-of-state and in-state oil producers.

125. (C)   A police officer may search a person being lawfully arrested, without obtaining a search warrant and without probable cause of another offense.

126. (D)   A state may regulate local aspects of interstate commerce only if the local interest is substantial and reasonable, and the burden on interstate commerce is slight.

127. (B)   The constitutional basis for courts of military justice is Article I. A soldier cannot constitutionally be tried by court-martial unless his crime is service-connected. A

crime committed while on leave and far from a military base is not considered service-connected.

128. (A)   The case and controversy requirement bars the rendition of advisory or moot opinions. When an issue concerns events of a short duration and it is likely the issue will be raised again, the court will entertain the action.

129. (D)   Use immunity guarantees that neither the compelled testimony nor any fruits will be used against the witness. Shaye's confession was obtained by offering lenient treatment for a conviction obtained from Wineburger's testimony. Therefore, Shaye's testimony is fruit of Wineburger's testimony and is not admissible.

130. (B)   A search ordinarily requires a warrant. An exception to this rule would be invoked when a person exercising domain or control gives consent. Industrialist did not have such authority.

131. (D)   In *Craig v. Boren*, 429 U.S. 190 (1976), the U.S. Supreme Court held that classification by gender must serve important governmental objectives and must be substantially related to the achievement of those objectives. Therefore, classifications based on gender are "quasi-suspect."

132. (C)   A court may determine the sincerity of a party who is asserting his religion as a defense. The court may also determine the exact beliefs of the religion. The court may not form a judgment as to the reasonableness of the beliefs.

133. (D)   Certain speech and conduct, such as demonstrations and other public meetings, may be prohibited by a proper statute. A statute that is overbroad or vague will be held unconstitutional. The town of Hempstead ordinance should be ruled void.

134. (B)   The Constitution (Article IV, Section 3) expressly grants Congress the power to regulate property belonging to the United States.

135. (C)   The plaintiff's best argument would be to show that the state is so involved with the school by the accreditation process and by providing aid that the Fourteenth Amendment is applicable to the school.

136.   (D)   The statute would not inform the average citizen of the standard of speech allowable. The statute will, therefore, be held unconstitutional.

137.   (C)   Since no state action is present, the owner of a private shopping center complex may exclude persons who want to distribute pamphlets. See *Hudgens v. NLRB*, 424 U.S. 507 (1976). Pamphleteering on private property is not a constitutionally protected activity.

138.   (C)   Standing to make a federal claim requires that a decision in plaintiff's favor will eliminate plaintiff's grievance. Dorothy lacked standing to challenge the nonenforcement of the criminal laws, because criminal prosecution would not automatically cause the father to provide support.

139.   (D)   The statute will be found valid in all respects because it will not conflict with the laws of other states. No state may permit discrimination in hiring.

140.   (B)   Gender is a semi-suspect class. A constitutional challenge based on equal protection, alleging discrimination between sexes, is valid if the law is substantially related to a government interest. The stricter test in (A) applies when a law affects a suspect class, (i.e., race, alienage, citizenship).

141.   (B)   An alien is a "person" within the protection of the Due Process and Equal Protection Clauses of the Fourteenth Amendment.

142.   (D)   Jurisdiction of the federal courts is invoked because a federal question was raised (i.e., due process and equal protection).

143.   (D)   The out-of-county milk producer would have the best grounds to challenge the constitutionality of a local ordinance such as this one. Because local inspectors are not authorized to inspect out-of-county products, the other milk producers are injured in that they are prohibited from selling their product within Skim County. Such a regulation discriminates against interstate commerce [See *Dean Milk Co. v. City of Madison*, 340 U.S. 349 (1951).]

144.   (A)   The Privileges and Immunities Clause applies to "citizens," and therefore aliens are not included under the clause. Aliens are considered "persons" under the Due Process Clause of the Fourteenth Amendment.

145. (A)   Among the choices, the teacher is the only one to have standing. He has a stake in the outcome which is different from that of the general public.

146. (B)   This answer is a description of the General Welfare Act.

147. (A)   The statute should be held valid as an exercise of the federal spending power. Congress may spend to provide for the common defense and general welfare (Article I, Section 8). This spending may be for any public purpose.

148. (B)   The Supremacy Clause is the popularized title for Article VI, Section 2 of the U.S. Constitution. The clause provides that acts of the federal government are operative as supreme law throughout the union. The states have no power to impede, burden, or in any manner control the operation of the laws enacted by the government or the nation.

149. (C)   Bert's only chance is to argue that the Equal Protection Clause has been violated. In *Trimble v. Gordon*, 430 U.S. 762 (1977), the Supreme Court invalidated a portion of the Illinois intestate statute that prevented illegitimate children from inheriting from their parents.

150. (B)   Illegitimacy is a semi-suspect class. The state must show a rational basis for the law. The Supreme Court has held that a state may not attempt to influence the conduct of men and women by imposing sanctions on the illegitimate children born from their relationships.

151. (A)   The statute regulates speech, not conduct; therefore, freedom of speech guaranteed by the First Amendment is in issue. Because a guarantee is at issue, the burden is on the city to prove that the statute is constitutional.

152. (B)   The issue in this question is standing. Only a person who seeks to demonstrate during hours prohibited will be affected by the statute and will therefore have standing to sue.

153. (B)   Excluding the exercise of First Amendment rights during brief periods of time and in certain places is permissible in order to achieve a compelling interest such as access to a City Hall.

154.   (C)   Suzanne must have standing for her suit to be decided on its merits. A federal taxpayer has standing to challenge federal spending and spending acts if (1) the measure was enacted under Congress's taxing and spending powers, and (2) the measure exceeded some specific limitation on the taxing and spending powers.

155.   (C)   The Establishment Clause prohibits governmental assistance to religion. It does not forbid every action by the government that favors or benefits religion. A statute will not violate the Establishment Clause if it (1) has a secular purpose, (2) has a principal or primary effect that neither advances nor inhibits religion, and (3) does not produce excessive government entanglement with religion.

156.   (B)   The three conditions are again satisfied, so the Establishment Clause is not violated.

157.   (B)   The government would not be able to determine which teachers are teaching religion and which are not, without violating the element "excessive government entanglement." (See all three elements above.)

158.   (D)   As a general rule, one cannot assert the constitutional rights of another. A claimant must suffer a direct impairment of his own constitutional rights to have standing. Beverly Hills' zoning law did not apply to Hollywood or Westward residents. See *Warth v. Seldin,* 422 U.S. 490 (1975). There are exceptions: if third parties can show a special, indispensable relationship, they may be allowed standing.

159.   (B)   In *Maher v. Roe,* 432 U.S. 464 (1977), the Supreme Court held that a state can refuse funding for abortions that are not necessary for the mother's health (so-called non-therapeutic abortions). The state can also refuse to fund medically necessary abortions. See *Harris v. McRae,* 448 U.S. 297 (1980).

(D) is wrong because the state may prevent the use of public facilities [*Webster v. Reproductive Health Services* (1989)] and governmental abortion counseling [*Rust v. Sullivan* (1991)].

160.   (B)   The federal government has power to tax interstate commerce. Regulation of the sale of gasoline would fall under this power because courts have extended this rule to cover almost all goods.

161.   (C)   Plaintiff argues that the financial support of an institution that discriminates based on race or gender amounts to state support of this discrimination.

162. (B)   Alleging state discrimination based on race or sex is a question justiciable in a federal court.

163. (A)   Unless a specific objective is shown, the statute will be ruled discriminatory against out-of-state taxi drivers.

164. (C)   Unless a compelling state interest is shown, the clause will violate the right to travel and the Equal Protection Clause.

165. (B)   This classification discriminates based on national origin and therefore will be upheld only if it advances a compelling state interest.

166. (C)   The federal courts have jurisdiction over cases alleging a violation of the U.S. Constitution.

167. (B)   Congress may legislate but may not deprive the executive branch of its discretion in executing the laws.

168. (D)   A witness testifying before a congressional committee may refuse to answer questions unrelated to congressional powers.

169. (C)   Enforcement and execution of legislation may only be performed by members of the executive branch.

170. (A)   A commission appointed by the legislative branch may only exercise powers available to the executive branch.

171. (D)   The Speech and Debate Clause (Article I, Section 6) gives legislators immunity from criminal and grand jury investigations relating to their law-making activities. This example of "separation of powers" helps keep political vendettas from interfering with congressional work.

172. (C)   In *Metropolitan Life Insurance Co. v. Ward*, 105 S.Ct. 1676 (1985), the Supreme Court held that a similar tax would violate the Equal Protection Clause if the state could not assert any interest to support the law other than the desire to protect local businesses from out-of-state competition.

173. (C)   Congress cannot unduly burden the operation of essential state services. The work of the senate is an essential function.

174. (C)   Even though the federal government has interfered with local function, the intrusion was arguably not a great burden.

CRIMINAL LAW/PROCEDURE CONTENTS

CRIMINAL LAW/PROCEDURE QUESTIONS

1. Spoiled was given a new Ferrari sports car for her college graduation. On one occasion Spoiled had sought to impress her friends by driving the car in third gear at ninety miles per hour down a small side street. Spoiled swerved the car to avoid a squirrel running across her path. She hit the squirrel and her tires locked, causing her to lose control of the car. The car skidded onto the sidewalk, killing a poodle and its owner.

    The police arrived several moments later and questioned Spoiled. Still in a severe daze, she said, "It's all my fault. I was driving at triple the speed limit. I must have been out of my mind."

    If charged with manslaughter, should Spoiled's statement be admitted to evidence?

    (A) Yes, because Spoiled volunteered the statement.

    (B) Yes, because the questions were for an investigation in a non-custodial setting.

    (C) No, because Spoiled did not receive Miranda warnings.

    (D) No, because at the time of questioning, Spoiled was not in the proper mental state to make an admission.

2. Cynthia was arrested and charged with selling marijuana to an undercover police officer. She was given proper Miranda warnings. Cynthia chose to remain silent. At her trial, Cynthia was asked by the prosecution, "Why did you refuse to tell your frame-up story to the arresting officer?"

    Defense counsel immediately objected to the question. The trial judge twice instructed the jury, "Exercise of one's right to remain silent may not be used as an inference of guilt."

    Cynthia appealed her conviction in this trial. Is Cynthia likely to prevail?

    (A) Yes, because it would be fundamentally unfair and a deprivation of due process to allow an arrested person's silence to impeach an explanation subsequently offered at trial.

    (B) Yes, because every post-arrest silence is invariably ambiguous because of what the state is required to advise the person.

    (C) Yes, because silence in the wake of Miranda warnings may be nothing more than the exercise of one's constitutional rights.

    (D) No.

GO ON TO THE NEXT PAGE

3. Bruce, charged with murder, claims he acted in self-defense. In a common law state, which of the following choices is correct?

    (A) Self-defense is an affirmative defense that Bruce must demonstrate by a preponderance of the evidence.

    (B) Self-defense is an affirmative defense that Bruce must demonstrate beyond a reasonable doubt.

    (C) Once a self-defense claim is raised, the prosecution must disprove it by a preponderance of the evidence.

    (D) Once a self-defense claim is raised, the prosecution must demonstrate its inapplicability beyond a reasonable doubt.

4. Larry loved his wife Jane despite her infidelity. Jane had been having an affair with Elston for the past two years. Blood tests confirmed that Elston was the father of Jane's soon-to-be born baby. Larry tried everything he could think of to win back his wife's love and attention, but she continued her affair with Elston. Finally, out of desperation, and with the hope of shocking Jane, Larry filed for divorce. Jane wanted to remain married to Larry and said she would contest the divorce, but continued to see Elston. While the divorce action was pending Larry and Jane continued to share the same house. Larry took their eight-year-old twin sons to their Little League game on a beautiful Sunday afternoon. The opposing team didn't show up, and the game was canceled. Larry and the boys returned to the house to find Jane and Elston together in the brand new jacuzzi Larry had built for Jane's last birthday. Larry, usually quiet and relaxed, became enraged, grabbed one of the boy's bats, and slammed Jane in the abdomen with tremendous force. Two months later, in the middle of her seventh month of pregnancy, Jane's child was stillborn. Based on testimony by several physicians, the jury concluded that the stillbirth was due to subdural hemorrhaging and other complications arising from a skull fracture caused by the impact of Larry's bat. The testimony also revealed that the premature birth was unrelated to Larry's beating. An epidemiologist testified that a baby born in the seventh month has a 98 percent chance of surviving.

    Larry should be found guilty of

    (A) murder

    (B) first-degree murder

    (C) manslaughter

    (D) none of the above

5. Maria, a third-generation migrant worker, was tired of picking grapes for a living. She left her parents' house and went to an employment agency to find work. She told the agency that she was sixteen and available for a full-time position. The agency found her a job as a live-in domestic for a Westwood,

California, family. Steve met Maria before he hired her to cook and clean for his family. Maria admitted to Steve that she was only thirteen, but insisted that she was very mature for her age. Maria didn't mind the hard work of a domestic because they made her feel like a part of the family. One night when Steve came by Maria's room to say good-night, Maria told him that she had become pregnant with his baby.

"I am sorry, but I have to fire you" was his shocked response. "My wife can't find out you are pregnant."

Maria soon found another job to pay her bills and medical costs at an East Los Angeles McDonald's. She lived in relative poverty with Eddie, a coworker. They shared expenses and housework and took turns caring for the baby. Maria and Eddie were only friends. She longed for companionship and a father for her child. She met Todd, a young upwardly mobile professional who loved children, at a singles bar. Todd became instantly infatuated with Maria and asked her to spend a month at his ski chalet in St. Moritz, Switzerland. Maria left her infant with Eddie, who she claimed had agreed to watch the child as long as she continued to pay her share of the rent. Eddie denies the rent was ever discussed.

Both Maria and Eddie agree that Maria told Eddie, "Don't feed the kid too much. He's getting fat." Eddie ignored the baby while he was in his care. Maria and Todd returned to California two months later as husband and wife to discover that Maria's baby had died of malnutrition. Eddie is charged with involuntary manslaughter. Which of the following choices is most accurate?

(A) To be convicted, the jury must find beyond a reasonable doubt that Eddie was under a legal duty to supply food and necessities to the infant.

(B) Eddie's omission was insufficient to satisfy the requirements of involuntary manslaughter.

(C) The prosecution's best argument is that failure to act breached Eddie's legal duty in a manner sufficient to satisfy involuntary manslaughter because he stood in a special relationship to the child.

(D) The general rule that one is under no legal duty to rescue a stranger may be superseded by showing an obligation by the preponderance of the evidence.

Questions 6-7 are based upon the following fact situation.

Randolph answered his front door. It was the Avon Lady calling. Randolph, who was drunk at the time, invited the woman inside, pretending he wanted to buy some cosmetics for his wife. While they sat on the couch, Randolph first forcibly hugged the woman, then pinned her down,

GO ON TO THE NEXT PAGE

forcing her to have sexual intercourse with him while she loudly voiced her objections.

6.   Randolph, charged with rape, should be found

   (A)   not guilty, if the jury determines Randolph's intoxication was voluntary

   (B)   not guilty, regardless of how Randolph became intoxicated

   (C)   not guilty, because Randolph was physically unable to possess the requisite intent

   (D)   guilty

7.   Peeper, Randolph's neighbor, testified that he heard the Avon Lady resisting in the beginning when Randolph told her, "I am going to rape you." Peeper said he later heard the Avon Lady say, "Your caress is so nice. Let's get undressed." If the jury believes Peeper's testimony, of the following offenses, the most serious crime of which Randolph should can be found guilty is

   (A)   aggravated assault

   (B)   assault

   (C)   rape

   (D)   kidnapping

8.   Pursuant to a valid warrant, the Windsor Lodis County Police broke into Ray's house in the middle of the night. One officer stood at the foot of Ray's bed watching him sleep, while several other officers searched the premises. After the police found twelve pounds of cocaine behind a false wall, they woke Ray to ask him several questions. The police did not give Ray his Miranda warnings. Ray answered the questions and made several incriminating statements. He was then handcuffed, brought to the police station, booked, and put in a holding cell. A police officer told Ray he was being charged with possession of cocaine with the intent to sell. He did not give Ray his Miranda warnings, nor did he inform Ray he was a suspect in the murder of Robert White, a.k.a. Snow White, a cocaine importer. When asked about Snow White, Ray made several more incriminating statements.

   Ray was given his Miranda warnings during his second day in custody, but was not told about the Snow White murder investigation. Ray then made even more incriminating statements in reference to the murder. Ray's Miranda warnings were repeated to him on the third day he was incarcerated. "I will make an oral statement, but I refuse to make a written statement without my lawyer," Ray said and then made some incriminating statements about the cocaine found in his apartment as well as statements indicating that he might not be Snow White's murderer. Ray was indicted and brought to trial on cocaine and murder charges. Which of the following arguments advanced by Ray's counsel will be **LEAST** persuasive?

   (A)   Ray was under custody while he was being questioned in bed because he did not have the ability to leave, and, therefore, the Miranda rule applies to those statements.

(B)   Ray's statements regarding Snow White made at the police station during his first day in custody should be excluded because the Miranda custody requirement was fulfilled despite the fact that Ray was being held on cocaine, and not murder charges.

(C)   The incriminating statements made on the second day should not be admitted, because the failure to inform Ray about the murder investigation invalidated his Miranda warnings.

(D)   Ray's Miranda warning on the third day was insufficient because Ray demanded counsel and was not told that Miranda applies to both inculpatory statements and exculpatory statements.

9.   Steven offered Edna, a twenty-two-year-old woman, a job as a prostitute. Edna, who had never considered prostitution a viable career choice before Steven mentioned the proposition, agreed. Steven drove Edna from Yuma, Arizona, to Los Angeles, California, to put her to work on the streets.

Edna was indicted as an accomplice to Steven's violation of a criminal statute prohibiting the interstate transportation of a woman for immoral purposes.

Solomon, a twenty-four-year-old man, seduced Ethel, a fifteen-year-old girl, into having sex with him. Ethel was indicted as an accomplice to statutory rape pursuant to a criminal statute that prohibited the sexual relations of a man with a woman less than sixteen years of age.

Edith lured a seventeen-year-old into the hallway of a vacant building so Stuart could rape the woman. Edith is charged as an accomplice to rape.

Elise told Saunder she wished she had some crack. Saunder took a trip up to Washington Heights to buy ten grams of crack for Elise. He returned with the drugs and sold them to her at twice the price he had paid. Elise and Saunder were arrested. Saunder is charged with the sale of a controlled substance. Elise is charged as an accomplice to Saunder.

Which of the following persons is most likely to be convicted?

(A)   Edna

(B)   Ethel

(C)   Edith

(D)   Elise

10.   Fredrick broke into a local Chrysler dealer at midnight and took three personal computers. As he was leaving, Frederick realized that he had left his fingerprints all over the

GO ON TO THE NEXT PAGE

showroom. Fredrick took out his Bic lighter and set fire to a life-size cardboard figure of Lee Iacocca. The fire spread, consuming the entire showroom.

Frederick could be convicted of which of the following crimes under their statutory definitions but not under the common law?

(A)   burglary

(B)   arson

(C)   A and B

(D)   burglary, arson, and larceny

11.   Joe met his friend Jim while walking down the street. "Give me a boost, Joe. I want to rob that house," Jim said. Joe bent over, and Jim climbed onto Joe's shoulders to scale the wall surrounding the house. Jim entered the house through an open window and came out with a color television. "I had to kill a witness," said Jim. Jim's success convinced Joe that crime does pay. He walked over to his boss's car, which was parked in the road. Joe saw his boss sleeping in the front seat. Joe then spilled a gallon of gasoline on the car's roof and tossed a lit match onto it. His boss woke up just as the car had caught fire, and escaped unharmed.

The most serious crime Joe should be charged with is

(A)   attempted murder

(B)   murder

(C)   arson

(D)   malicious mischief

12.   Donna Dice felt betrayed by her former lover, a powerful and influential man. She waited outside his office until he appeared and then stuck a gun up his nose and demanded his diamond-studded watch. Donna took the watch, valued at several thousand dollars, to her friend, Fawn Fall. After bragging to Fawn about how she obtained the watch, Donna sold it to her for $200. Several hours later, Fawn looked out her front window to see several police officers and members of the press. "Open up, we know you possess a stolen watch," said the police. Both the police and press were unaware that there was a back door, and Fawn escaped through it. She took a taxi to the house of her friend, Jessica Jahn. "Jessica, you must help me," said Fawn. "The cops are after me because I have this stolen watch."

"Don't worry, I'll hide you," said Jessica. Jahn was arrested in her own home, along with Fawn, pursuant to a valid warrant. The trial court should rule that Jessica was a(n)

(A)   principal in the first degree

(B)   principal in the second degree

(C)   accessory after the fact

(D)   none of the above

13.   While driving on the highway Sally got a call on the car phone of her new Mercedes. After Sally said hello, the caller said, "Take that fancy ring off your finger, leave it on top of pump number nine at the Exxon

station at Exit 3, and drive away. If you don't follow directions, I will burn your Mercedes to a crisp."

Sally followed the caller's directions. The caller was later apprehended by the police. The most serious offense the caller might be found guilty of is

(A)   common law extortion

(B)   extortion

(C)   common law robbery

(D)   robbery

14.   Jan planned to hijack a plane from Dallas to Phoenix and then demand that the press print a statement advocating Eritrea's independence from Ethiopia. She filled her carry-on luggage with plastic explosives undetectable by X-rays. John was a professional luggage snatcher who searched airports for prime suitcases to snatch. He spied Jan struggling with her heavy luggage and offered to help her carry it. As soon as Jan gave John the bag loaded with explosives, John ran off and disappeared into the crowd. As he walked through another terminal, the luggage ripped open and the contents spilled out onto the floor. An undercover security officer noticed the explosives and arrested John.

John should be found guilty of

(A)   two crimes, one for taking the bag and another for carrying explosives

(B)   embezzlement

(C)   larceny

(D)   larceny by trick

15.   Dr. Knot Decent was a gynecologist in private practice. His wife, Prudence, was his nurse and assistant. Lucy Richards, Dr. Decent's last patient of the day, requested a pap smear. Prudence blindfolded Lucy while explaining to her, "This is so you can relax during the examination." Prudence knew the purpose of the blindfold was really for Knot Decent's sick and demented kicks. "I am now inserting a speculum so that I may examine you," said Knot Decent, when in fact, he inserted his penis. Decent did not release any emissions. Lucy never suspected the nature of Dr. Decent's actions. Three days later, Decent was arrested on the basis of information compiled in an investigation by the A.M.A., begun after several patients lodged similar complaints. If Dr. Decent is prosecuted under the common law for his "examination" of Lucy, should the court acquit Prudence Decent of the charge of conspiracy to commit rape?

(A)   No, because she was a principal in the second degree.

(B)   Yes, because a woman by definition may not commit a rape.

GO ON TO THE NEXT PAGE

(C) Yes, because Knot Decent's actions did not constitute rape.

(D) Yes, because a husband and wife cannot conspire to commit rape.

16. Kenneth stopped on his way to a UCLA-USC football game and purchased a new revolver. The game was very exciting and Kenneth had an excellent seat, but all he could think about was his new gun. The score was tied at the beginning of the fourth quarter. Kenneth left his seat to stand in the tunnel connecting the spectator stands with the area housing the concession stands and the exits. The tunnel seemed deserted because people were glued to their seats in this close game. Kenneth decided that this would be a nice opportunity to test his new revolver. A soda-pop concessionaire was killed by Kenneth's bullet after it ricocheted off a wall. The most serious offense of which Kenneth might be properly convicted is

(A) battery

(B) voluntary manslaughter

(C) involuntary manslaughter

(D) murder

17. Defendant will most likely be convicted of involuntary manslaughter in which of the following cases?

(A) Defendant, an attorney, worked six days a week from eight a.m. until midnight. This particular evening there was a power failure in his office, so Defendant took his work home with him at 7:00 p.m, when it began to get dark. Arriving home, Defendant opened the front door to find his wife naked and with a naked man named Johnny Holmes. The living room was lit up with bright spotlights. Three clothed men stood behind a video camera. Defendant reached over to the mantle above the fireplace where he had a ceremonial machete on display and killed Holmes with it.

(B) On his lunch hour Defendant went up to the observation deck of the Empire State Building, where he purchased a can of soda pop. Before opening the can, Defendant decided he wasn't thirsty and threw the can off the ledge of the building. The can smashed through the roof of a bus on Fifth Avenue, killing a passenger.

(C) Defendant was a passenger on a long trip from Berwick to Belefonte. Despite the beautiful scenery along Interstate 80, Defendant became extremely bored on the ride. He took out and polished his new gun to keep himself busy. Defendant had recently shoplifted the gun and did not own the statutorily required permit. "Do you think I could hit the

'P' in UPS?" Defendant asked his traveling companion as he aimed at the big brown trailer of a truck driving alongside them. Defendant did hit the "P," and he also hit a stowaway sleeping in the back of the truck. The stowaway died two days later.

(D)   Defendant had a very sensitive stomach. He was suffering from severe stomach distress during his commute to work one morning and needed to arrive at the office as quickly as he possibly could. As Defendant drove down Biscayne Boulevard, a main street leading into the downtown area, an accident ahead of him caused the traffic to come to a halt. Defendant drove onto the sidewalk to bypass the traffic, whereupon he struck and killed a pedestrian.

18.   Abe, a seller and distributor of firewood, heard a rumor that a resident of Redwood City had sold his ranch and moved away. Abe thought the ranch was to be unoccupied for two weeks so he went to the ranch for those two weeks, chopping down as many trees as he could and hauling them to his own land. About a month later, the sheriff came by with a man named Jed. "Abe, you stole these trees from Jed's ranch. We are going to have to arrest you for it," the sheriff said. Jed had the logs piled onto the back

of a trailer truck he had rented to haul them back to his ranch. On his way home, exhausted from the hectic day, Jed took a detour into town to have a drink at the Redwood City Pub. While Jed was drinking, Howie loaded all of Jed's logs on his truck and drove off with them. The sheriff thought he recognized the logs while driving behind Howie on a country road and arrested Howie.

Which of the following statements is most accurate under the common law?

(A)   Abe should be found guilty of larceny.

(B)   Howie should be found guilty of larceny.

(C)   Both Abe and Howie should be found guilty of larceny.

(D)   Neither Abe nor Howie should be found guilty of larceny.

19.   Mark, a native of Houston, Texas, decided to take his wife to New York City on the occasion of their twentieth wedding anniversary. Mark became disappointed when his order for two baseball tickets to see the New York Mets play the Houston Astros could not be filled because the game was already sold out. Mark, a professional typesetter, decided to print himself two tickets to the game.

Just before they left for New York, Mark read an article in the *Houston Post* describing a Civil War

GO ON TO THE NEXT PAGE

army poster that had recently been purchased for $5,000. Mark printed a similar poster in his shop and took it to New York with him. He sold the poster for $4,000 in New York, bragging to the collector who purchased it, "This is the finest nineteenth-century poster to be found."

Mark and his wife successfully entered Shea Stadium using the tickets he printed and sat down in two empty box seats behind the Visitor's dugout to watch the game. A man named Donald Dump sat down next to Mark. Howard Johnson hit a home run for the Mets in the third inning and Dump, like most others in the stadium, had fallen off the edge of his seat in his excitement. Mark slipped some papers out of Dump's sportcoat without Dump noticing. The papers contained the deed to Dump's Castle Casino in Atlantic City.

After the game, Mark and his wife took a taxi from Shea Stadium to Times Square, a distance of about fifteen miles. When the driver requested payment of the seventeen dollar fare, Mark screamed, "You are trying to cheat me because you can tell I am a tourist." The driver did not speak English very well and did not respond. Mark and his wife ran out of the cab without paying and got lost in the crowd.

Assume for this question only, the city of New York follows the common law.

Four statements, 1, 2, 3, and 4, are followed by four choices (A), (B), (C), and (D). Select the choice that is most accurate.

1.   Mark should be found guilty of larceny for wrongfully obtaining entrance to the baseball stadium.

2.   Mark should be found guilty of larceny for wrongfully obtaining the deed to Dump's Castle Casino.

3.   Mark should be found guilty of forgery for printing and selling the poster.

4.   Mark's failure to pay the cab fare will not result in liability for a crime unless New York has enacted a statute specifically designating theft of a service a crime.

(A)   choices 1, 2, and 3 are correct

(B)   choices 1 and 3 are correct

(C)   choices 2 and 4 are correct

(D)   choice 4 is correct

20.   Boca Towers is a complex of 350 residential units in Boca Raton. The complex, built before World War II as a rental property, was vacated in 1985 and renovated. The apartments were sold as condominiums to be occupied on December 1, 1989. On Thanksgiving Eve, 1989, James, a plumber employed by the city of Gainsville, drove to Boca Raton, broke into the complex, and took three marble bathtubs. Under the common law, the most serious offense for which James should be convicted is

(A)   larceny

(B)   robbery

(C)   burglary

(D)   common law burglary

Questions 21-22 are based upon the following fact situation.

Harry received a call at work from his mother, "Congratulations, Son, you passed the Bar exam," she said.

Harry was ecstatic. He ran through his firm's office shouting the news to everyone, pounding his hand on every desk he passed. An hour later, Harry calmed down and sat down at his desk to enjoy the view of the air shaft outside his window. Then he thought of Larry, his best friend, roommate for three years, and study partner. "Did Larry pass?" he wondered. Harry could have waited to see the Bar results in the newspaper, but that was days away, so Harry decided to call Larry that moment.

"Hi, Larry, it's Harry," he said after the receptionist transferred the call.

"Hi, Harry. What's up?" Larry answered.

"Not much. I got the results of the Bar exam today."

"What a coincidence, so did I."
"Is it good news or bad news?"
"Pretty damn good!"
"Me too!"

Larry and Harry decided to leave work that instant and meet at a nearby tavern, where they cavorted with other inebriated celebrating lawyers. Seven hours later, Larry and Harry, both extremely drunk, said good-bye to each other and walked in opposite directions toward their homes. Larry walked into a clothing store to try on the leather jacket he had admired in the window display. When the salesperson went to answer a phone call, Larry walked out

wearing the coat. Still severely intoxicated, Larry continued his walk home when he happened to see his seventh-grade teacher, Mrs. Brown, walking her dog. Larry had never forgiven Mrs. Brown for the failing grade she gave him in spelling. It had kept him out of the college of his choice, and he was ready for revenge. Before she saw him coming, Larry punched Mrs. Brown in the side of her head, and she fell to the sidewalk, suffering a serious concussion.

Harry, despite his own extreme intoxication, was still thirsty. He saw a passerby walking down the street carrying a bottle of wine and a dozen roses. It was Harry's favorite wine, a 1969 Chateau Blanc. He was in such a stupor that he thought the wine was his own.

"Give me my wine or I'll punch your lights out," Harry told the man.

The passerby knew he could defeat the drunk Harry in a brawl, but he gave Harry the wine because he was afraid he would soil his clothing. Several moments later, Harry saw his ex-wife. Threatening her with the empty wine bottle he had just drunk from, Harry led her to a dark and deserted alley and forced himself on her.

21.   Larry should be found guilty of which of the following offenses?

(A)   battery and robbery

(B)   battery and larceny

(C)   aggravated battery

(D)   only battery

22.   Harry should be found guilty of which of the following offenses?

GO ON TO THE NEXT PAGE

(A) rape and robbery

(B) rape

(C) robbery

(D) none of the above

Questions 23-24 are based upon the following fact situation.

Albert Cosby played for the Temple University Owls football team. After the Owls played their last game of the season against Rutgers, Cosby took home his football helmet, thinking it was his to keep. In reality, the helmet belonged to the school. Coach Arians had twice announced that all equipment was to be returned. Cosby skipped a practice to study for a pre-med course and did not hear the first announcement. He was present for the second announcement but was not listening when Coach Arians spoke.

On the way home, Cosby was stuck in terrible traffic due to construction on the Stuckell Expressway. Cherry White, who was driving in a car alongside Cosby's, saw the helmet and asked, "Can I try on your helmet? I always wanted to wear an Owls helmet." Cosby handed the helmet to White, who took it and quickly exited the Expressway without even signaling. Before Cosby realized what had happened, Cherry was gone.

23. If charged with embezzlement, should Cosby be found guilty?

(A) Yes, if it was unreasonable for Cosby to assume the helmet was his to keep.

(B) Yes, because Cosby took the helmet in a violation of trust.

(C) No, because embezzlement is a specific intent crime.

(D) No, only if Cosby's mistake was reasonable.

24. Cherry should be found guilty of

(A) false pretenses

(B) larceny

(C) larceny by trick

(D) none of the above

25. Corvallis attended the largest party in the history of the state of Oregon. Thousands of people celebrated in the streets for six days in honor of the Oregon State Beavers' Pac 10 Football Championship. Corvallis drank ten beers in less than an hour and became enraged when he misplaced his favorite drinking mug. He searched throughout the sorority house he had been invited into and entered a room where Davida Cragtorp and Jane Burn, Beaver cheerleaders, were practicing their leg splits. Corvallis was extremely aroused and forced himself on Davida as Jane looked on in horror. When he had finished with Davida, Corvallis began to disrobe Jane, but quarterback Wilhelm Erickson heard Jane screaming, ran into the room, and beat Corvallis severely before calling the police. In response to the charges of rape and attempted rape against him, Corvallis testified that he was so drunk that he honestly thought the cheerleaders' leg splits were meant to convey their consent to his advances. If Corvallis did

indeed honestly believe the cheerleaders had consented, he should be found

(A)   guilty, if his intoxication was voluntary

(B)   not guilty, because he lacked the required intent

(C)   guilty if a reasonable person would not have interpreted the cheerleaders' action as provocative

(D)   guilty of rape, but not guilty of attempted rape due to his lack of intent

26.   Defendant owned a hardware store on Main Street. During the energy crisis, the city council passed an ordinance requiring that all stores install a special type of glass window with better insulation than standard glass. Defendant refused to purchase the new windows, predicting that in 1986 the oil market would collapse. A young boy named Darrell rode his skateboard down Main Street. He lost control, crashed through Defendant's window, and died. The trier of fact determined that Darrell would not have been killed had a window conforming with the statutory requirements been installed. In this jurisdiction, a violation of the building code is a misdemeanor. If Defendant is charged with manslaughter, should he be found guilty?

(A)   Yes, because he violated the building code.

(B)   Yes, because his actions were the proximate cause of Darrell's death.

(C)   No, because Defendant lacked requisite intent.

(D)   No, because Defendant was not the proximate cause of Darrell's death.

27.   Sandra was fed up when the coke machine outside Joe's Exxon "ate" her money. She marched into the service station screaming in a fit of rage, spilled thousands of gallons of gasoline, and stole $100. The twenty-three-year-old attendant died of a heart attack. If Sandra is charged with felony murder, her best defense will be that

(A)   the attendant threatened her with a crowbar

(B)   Sandra didn't intend for anyone to die

(C)   Sandra was too drunk to intend to rob the gas station

(D)   Sandra was extremely angry about the coke machine and her actions were without malice aforethought.

Questions 28-30 are based upon the following fact situation.

GO ON TO THE NEXT PAGE

Donna was high on cocaine, marijuana, and alcohol. She went into a clothing store, tried on a coat, and then walked out of the store wearing the coat. She sat down on some steps in front of a house and lit another marijuana cigarette, throwing the match into a nearby garbage pail. The garbage caught fire, and the fire spread to the house next door, burning it to the ground. A statute in the jurisdiction provides that "arson is the malicious burning of a dwelling."

28.   If Donna asserts her intoxication as a defense to larceny, Donna's assertion

   (A)   will not help her case if she ingested the substances voluntarily

   (B)   will help her case only if she decided to take the coat after she was high

   (C)   may negate the element of intent and, therefore, allow Donna to defeat the charges

   (D)   will allow Donna to defeat the larceny charges, if "but for" her intoxication, she would not have taken the coat

29.   Which of the following would serve as Donna's best defense if charged with arson?

   (A)   She was so intoxicated, her acts were not voluntary.

   (B)   She was so intoxicated, she could not have formed intent.

   (C)   She was so intoxicated, her actions could not have been malicious.

   (D)   The person that provided Donna with the drugs should be held liable.

30.   The prosecution's best argument to counter the defense set forth in the previous question is that

   (A)   voluntary intoxication cannot be a defense to a general intent crime

   (B)   voluntary intoxication is a defense to a specific intent crime

   (C)   "malicious" refers to Donna's course of conduct from the time she took her first drink, knowing it would cause her to act dangerously

   (D)   "malicious" could be imputed to the seller of the drugs or the alcohol

Questions 31-37 are based upon the following fact situation.

Towhead hooked up his tow truck to a Rolls Royce car and drove away. The car's owner immediately called the police, who sent out several squad cars looking for a Rolls Royce being towed. Unbeknownst to Towhead and the police, a baby quietly slept in a car seat in the back of the Rolls Royce.

Aaron, a policeman traveling on foot, saw the tow truck speeding by. He tried to get Towhead to slow down, but Towhead kept driving. Aaron fired a shot at Towhead, but missed and killed the baby. Towhead kept driving.

Several minutes later Towhead was stopped at a roadblock. Snooper, a detective, walked over to Towhead and told him he was under arrest. When he opened the door to Towhead's truck, Snooper spotted a gun under Towhead's seat.

Towhead was taken to a nearby police station, where he was forced to fill out a form and submit to fingerprinting and a lineup. Towhead protested to all of these procedures.

Two eyewitnesses identified Towhead from the lineup. Towhead was forced to recite "The Pledge of Allegiance" to allow a third eyewitness to identify him on the basis of his voice.

Towhead was told he would get the maximum sentence, unless he confessed to his crimes. After Towhead signed a confession, he was allowed to call an attorney.

Towhead was charged with larceny and the murder of the baby. Aaron was charged with murder of the baby also.

31.   Is Aaron likely to be found guilty of murder?

   (A)   Yes, because he used deadly force.

   (B)   Yes, because he fired his gun with reckless disregard to bystanders.

   (C)   No, because Aaron was attempting to subdue a felon.

   (D)   No, because Aaron had no way of knowing that a baby was in the car.

32.   If Towhead properly objects to the introduction into evidence of the gun found in his car, the court should rule the gun

   (A)   admissible, because Towhead was in the process of being properly arrested

   (B)   admissible, because of the "fruits of the poisonous tree" rule

   (C)   inadmissible, because the officer was not privileged to look under the seat

   (D)   inadmissible, because the search was not incident to the arrest

33.   If the prosecution offers both the fingerprints taken from the Rolls Royce and Towhead's fingerprints taken shortly after his arrest, should the fingerprints be admitted over proper objection?

   (A)   Yes.

   (B)   No, because Towhead was not advised that his fingerprints could be used against him.

   (C)   No, because Towhead was not given his Miranda warnings.

   (D)   No, because Towhead had not been provided with counsel.

34.   The prosecution sought to admit the handwriting sample taken shortly after Towhead's arrest in order to compare it to a purchase order for a

GO ON TO THE NEXT PAGE

Rolls Royce. If Towhead properly objects, should the evidence be admitted?

(A)   Yes.

(B)   No, because Towhead was not advised that the handwriting could be used against him.

(C)   No, because Towhead was not given his Miranda warnings.

(D)   No, because Towhead had not been provided with counsel.

35.   Will the two witnesses be allowed to testify that they visually identified Towhead in the lineup?

(A)   Yes.

(B)   No, because Towhead was not advised that the lineup could be used against him.

(C)   No, because Towhead was not given his Miranda warnings.

(D)   No, because Towhead had not been provided with counsel.

36.   Will the third eyewitness be allowed to testify that she recognized Towhead's voice?

(A)   Yes.

(B)   No, because Towhead was not advised that his voice

sample could be used against him.

(C)   No, because Towhead was not given his Miranda warnings.

(D)   No, because Towhead had not been provided with counsel.

37.   For this question, assume that only Towhead is convicted of murder. After conviction, but before sentencing, the prosecution seeks to admit evidence of three prior felony convictions. Should these convictions be admitted as evidence?

(A)   Yes.

(B)   No, because they are highly prejudicial.

(C)   No, because they violate Towhead's right to due process.

(D)   No, because admission would violate Towhead's right to cross-examine hostile witnesses.

Questions 38-39 are based upon the following fact situation.

Jon and Don decided to rob a store. Jon volunteered to stand outside as the lookout to warn Don, who would be inside the store, if he saw a policeman coming.

Don went inside and Jon stood outside for a brief moment and then ran away. He had become too frightened to take part in the robbery.

Don told the storekeeper, "Give me your money or I'll break your neck." The storekeeper laughed, then assumed a stern expression as he pulled out a shotgun from underneath the counter and pointed it within an inch of Don's face.

38.   If Jon and Don are charged with robbery, Jon's best defense is that

    (A)   he withdrew before any crime was committed, thwarting Don's attempt

    (B)   Don performed the illegal act

    (C)   he never intended to take anything

    (D)   the storekeeper was not intimidated by Don and nothing was actually taken

39.   Plumber came to repair Al and Alice's leaky sink. Al was away on a business trip and Alice, Al's wife, was home alone. Alice let Plumber in the house, answering the door dressed in a sexy negligee. She offered Plumber a glass of champagne, which he accepted. Al arrived home unexpectedly and accused Plumber of having an affair with Alice. Al's charges enraged Plumber. Plumber smashed the bottom off the champagne bottle on the kitchen counter, and rushed toward Al with the jagged glass. Al pulled out a gun and shot Plumber in the chest, killing him instantly.

    If Al is charged with murder, should he be found guilty?

    (A)   Yes, because his accusations prompted an understandable response from Plumber.

    (B)   Yes, because his actions resulted in Plumber's death.

    (C)   No, because a broken bottle is a deadly weapon.

    (D)   No, because Plumber invited Al's reaction by allowing the circumstances.

40.   Loretta, a fourteen-year-old, lied about her age in order to join the Marines. She looked older and told everyone, including her best friends, that she was twenty-one. Loretta dated Sergeant, who also thought she was twenty-one. One night, Loretta suggested that they park the jeep alongside a lake. Loretta started kissing Sergeant, but then became frightened and cried out, "Don't touch me. I'm only fourteen." Sergeant was charged with rape and statutory rape. Sergeant is likely to be convicted of

    (A)   statutory rape if his knowledge of Loretta's true age is proved

    (B)   statutory rape if he did not stop his advances after Loretta told him her age

    (C)   both charges if Loretta resisted and Sergeant used force to accomplish intercourse

GO ON TO THE NEXT PAGE

(D)   both charges if he was inebriated while with Loretta

41.   In which of the following cases is Defendant least likely to be convicted of robbery?

(A)   By opening an unlocked door, Defendant entered an automobile that was stopped at a traffic light. "Get out of the car right now," Defendant told Driver. Driver left the car, and Defendant drove the car away.

(B)   Defendant kicked a man's hand, causing the man to drop a briefcase that he was carrying. Defendant grabbed the briefcase and ran away.

(C)   On a crowded bus, Defendant took a man's wallet out of his coat pocket. The man did not notice that his wallet was missing until after he left the bus.

(D)   Defendant grabbed a man's dog while the man was walking the dog outside the house. "Give me your money or I'll kill the dog," Defendant told the man. The man gave Defendant all of his money.

Questions 42-43 are based upon the following fact situation.

Tracie told Marc that she would love to have a new video recorder, but could not afford one. "How would you like to buy one for $100?" Marc asked Tracie. "Sure," she replied. Marc went out and stole a video recorder in order to sell it to Tracie.

Marc and Tracie were arrested and charged with several offenses, including conspiracy to commit larceny.

42.   Should Tracie be found guilty of conspiracy to commit larceny?

(A)   Yes, because Marc was solicited to take the video recorder by Tracie's offer.

(B)   Yes, because she should have known the goods were stolen.

(C)   No, because Marc acted without her knowledge or assent.

(D)   No, because Marc was the primary actor.

43.   After talking to Tracie, Marc called Dick on the phone and told him to steal a video recorder. Are Marc and Dick guilty of conspiracy?

(A)   Yes.

(B)   No, because the charge of conspiracy will be merged into a more severe offense.

(C)   No, because of the rule against double jeopardy.

(D)   No, because there was no privity between Tracie and Dick.

Questions 44-45 are based upon the following fact situation.

Nancy and four other people formed a gang. They called themselves the "McDonald's Gang." They would go into local fast food restaurants, place large and complicated orders, and when the clerk totaled their bill, they would pull out handguns and demand to be given the contents of the cash register. The gang committed twelve robberies in twelve months. As they ended a meeting finalizing the plans for another robbery, Nancy announced to all the members, "I quit this gang and I quit my life of crime!" The gang completed the thirteenth robbery, as planned.

44.   If Nancy is charged with conspiracy, in connection with the thirteenth fast food robbery, she will be found

(A)   not guilty, because she did not assist the robbery in any way

(B)   not guilty, because all the conspirators saw Nancy quit

(C)   guilty, because her withdrawal did not erase her participation in the conspiracy

(D)   guilty, because the conspiracy could not have functioned without her assistance in its planning

45.   If Nancy is charged with armed robbery of the thirteenth restaurant, she should be found

(A)   not guilty, because she did not assist the robbery in any way

(B)   not guilty, because all the conspirators saw Nancy quit

(C)   guilty, because her withdrawal did not erase her participation in the conspiracy

(D)   guilty, because the robbery was completed

46.   Bully grabbed Millie's purse and then punched her in the nose. Passerby happened to witness Bully punching Millie, who is visibly old and frail. Passerby picked up a rock and said, "Leave the old lady alone or I'll crack your skull."
       Passerby was charged with assault. The prosecution should

(A)   prevail, because Bully's fear of immediate harm was real and reasonable

(B)   prevail, because Passerby threatened Bully with deadly force

(C)   not prevail, if a reasonable person would act as Passerby did in defense of Millie.

(D)   not prevail, if Passerby was reasonable in his belief that Millie was in danger and had a right to use self-defense

Questions 47-50 are based upon the following fact situation.

Lisa wrote a letter to Marianne containing the details of her plans to rob a

GO ON TO THE NEXT PAGE

candy store. The letter stated that Marianne was to rob the store and Lisa was to wait in a getaway car. The Post Office erroneously delivered the letter to Tina instead of Marianne. Tina read the letter and at first was horrified. She considered calling the police, but then thought twice. The plan seemed flawless. Tina decided to participate in the robbery, by replacing Marianne in the scheme. Tina wrote back to Lisa saying, "Will be there, (signed) Marianne."

Lisa was involved in a car accident the morning of the planned robbery and never arrived at the scene of the crime. Tina robbed the store and escaped on foot, when she didn't see Lisa waiting outside.

47.   Lisa's best defense, if charged with conspiracy to rob, is that

(A)   the letter was merely a suggestion

(B)   her accident prevented her from participating in the robbery

(C)   there was no agreement between her and Marianne or her and Tina

(D)   the plan was too vague to be a conspiracy

48.   If Lisa argues that she withdrew from any conspiracy at the time of the accident, will the argument be persuasive?

(A)   Yes, because she had not performed an *actus reus*.

(B)   Yes, because the conspiracy was ended by impossibility of performance.

(C)   No, because a withdrawal will not negate the culpability for a past conspiracy.

(D)   No, because Tina robbed the candy store according to Lisa's plans.

49.   Is Lisa likely to be found guilty of being an accessory to Tina's robbery of the store?

(A)   Yes, because she counseled and commanded the robbery.

(B)   No, because the accident prevented her from participating in the robbery.

(C)   No, because she withdrew from the plan.

(D)   No, because she did not aid the robbery.

50.   Tina could be charged with

(A)   conspiracy only, because robbery would be merged into the conspiracy action

(B)   robbery only, because the conspiracy would be merged into a robbery action

(C)   conspiracy only, because all charges will be merged into this charge

(D)   both robbery and conspiracy

Questions 51-52 are based upon the following fact situation.

Christine and Melinda were upset because their textbooks for the fall semester cost a lot more money than they had spent the previous semester. They hadn't budgeted for this added cost. To make ends meet they decided to steal some of the books they needed from the college bookstore. According to the plan, Christine would enter the bookstore while Melinda waited outside in her new Acura. Christine entered the bookstore as planned and walked over to the anthropology section. She placed a text book under her jacket and walked down the aisle. Christine then noticed Bob, the sales clerk, staring at her, so instead of leaving the store with the book, she placed it back on the shelf.

51.   If Christine is subsequently prosecuted, she should be found guilty of

    (A)   conspiracy to commit larceny only

    (B)   attempted larceny

    (C)   conspiracy to commit larceny and attempted larceny

    (D)   conspiracy to commit larceny and actual larceny

52.   Melinda, if subsequently prosecuted, should be found guilty of

    (A)   no crime

    (B)   attempted larceny

    (C)   conspiracy to commit larceny and attempted larceny

    (D)   conspiracy to commit larceny only

Questions 53-58 are based upon the following fact situation.

Kathy met Jim at a local bar. "I drove up in my new sports car," bragged Kathy, who looked much older than her fourteen years of age. Jim assumed that Kathy was at least eighteen years old, the minimum driving age in the state. Kathy had, in fact, taken her mother's car, driven without a license, and used falsified identification to get into the bar.

Kathy invited Jim to sit in her car. She started kissing him and said, "Jim, let's go all the way." Before there was any penetration, Kathy changed her mind and demanded that Jim stop. Jim ignored Kathy's demand until she told him her age.

53.   Jim should be found guilty of attempted rape if

    (A)   the prosecution can prove that Jim knew Kathy's true age

    (B)   the defense is not allowed to submit evidence that Jim stopped before penetration

    (C)   the prosecution proves that Jim had the requisite intent

    (D)   the prosecution proves that Kathy was resisting force exerted by Jim to accomplish an act of intercourse

GO ON TO THE NEXT PAGE

54. If charged with assault with intent to rape, Jim will be found

    (A)   guilty, because Kathy told Jim to stop

    (B)   guilty, if the jury finds that Jim intended to have intercourse with Kathy, regardless of whether she consented

    (C)   not guilty, because the charges will merge into a less serious offense

    (D)   not guilty, because Jim stopped

55. Assume, for this question only, that Jim had achieved penetration before withdrawing. A jury could properly return a verdict of

    (A)   rape, but not attempted rape

    (B)   attempted rape, but not rape

    (C)   both rape and attempted rape

    (D)   neither rape nor attempted rape

56. A local ordinance recently enacted provided that "anyone adversely affecting the morals of this community will be guilty of moral degradation, an offense punishable by no more than thirty days in prison, or a fine no greater than $5,000." If prosecuted under this offense, Jim's best defense will be that

    (A)   Kathy consented to his actions

    (B)   Kathy encouraged his actions

    (C)   sex is considered acceptable in the community

    (D)   the statute should be ruled unconstitutional, as vague and overly broad

57. If prosecuted for violating the statute in the previous question, will Jim be able to assert the defense that he was under the influence of drugs and, therefore, lacked the intent to degrade the morals of the community?

    (A)   Yes, if he did not voluntarily take the drugs.

    (B)   Yes, regardless of whether he voluntarily took the drugs.

    (C)   No, because Jim's state of mind is irrelevant to the offense.

    (D)   No, because the court will not allow a defendant to benefit from an illegal act.

58. If charged with attempted statutory rape, Jim should argue that

    (A)   Kathy looked older than her age

    (B)   Kathy consented to his advances

    (C)   Kathy was the instigator of their encounter

    (D)   he stopped when he was told her age

59. Herby pretended to be a health inspector, employed by the county. He gained admission to Henry's house by showing false identification. When Henry was not looking, Herby took Henry's wallet off a table and put it in his pocket. Is Herby guilty of burglary?

   (A)   Yes, if he intended to steal the wallet.

   (B)   Yes, because he entered under false pretenses.

   (C)   No, because there was no breaking.

   (D)   No, if he truly intended to take one of Herby's pets.

60. Seth came home and found Gerald threatening Phillip, Seth's son, with a butcher knife. Seth had no idea that Gerald and Phillip were rehearsing for a school play. Seth grabbed a baseball bat and lunged toward Gerald. Gerald stabbed Seth with the very real and sharp knife he had taken from the kitchen drawer to use as a prop. Seth later died from the knife wound.

   If Gerald is charged with murder, should he be found guilty?

   (A)   Yes, because his actions prompted an understandable response from Seth.

   (B)   Yes, because his actions resulted in Seth's death.

   (C)   No, because a baseball bat is a deadly weapon.

   (D)   No, because Seth's behavior invited Gerald's reaction.

61. Lisa was placed on probation after her conviction for stock fraud. The terms of her probation provided that she was not to be permitted to purchase stock on the American or the New York Stock Exchanges. Broker, who did not know of Lisa's past, called her and, after a lengthy conversation and much cajoling, talked Lisa into opening a portfolio, which he would manage for her. Broker bought Lisa stock on both exchanges. In the jurisdiction, violating terms of probation is a felony.

   If Broker is charged with being an accessory to a violation of probation terms, he should be found

   (A)   not guilty, because he did not force Lisa to buy stock

   (B)   not guilty, because he lacked the requisite *mens rea*

   (C)   guilty, because he encouraged Lisa to buy stock

   (D)   guilty, because he was present when the crime was committed

Questions 62-66 are based upon the four cases below.

GO ON TO THE NEXT PAGE

For each question, select the case with the most applicable precedent.

(A)   Defendant was in the appliance rental business. Defendant accepted $200 and agreed to rent a refrigerator to Dorothy for three months. Dorothy sent a truck over to Defendant to pick up the refrigerator. Defendant refused to tender the appliance. Defendant was found not guilty of larceny.

(B)   Defendants saw a refrigerator outside an appliance store. They decided to take the refrigerator and use it for a party they were having that day. The Defendants could not fulfill their intention to return the refrigerator, because it was destroyed in a fire started by someone at the party who threw a match into some garbage. The defendants were held not guilty of larceny.

(C)   Using false identification and a false name, Defendant rented a refrigerator from the loading dock of an appliance store, intending to return it in exchange for a fraction of its market value. The defendants were held guilty of larceny.

(D)   Defendant was found guilty of larceny for taking an appliance he intended to return.

62.   Defendant was extremely jealous of his friend's new motorcycle, so he took the motorcycle and hid it in a local golf course. Defendant planned on returning the bike after giving his friend a "good scare."

63.   Defendant took his friend's motorcycle and rented it to others.

64.   Defendant was an elevator operator in an office building. He ran a mail order business at night. Defendant used his keys to enter the building's offices and used various companies' typewriters, computers, and desks for his own business.

65.   Defendant sold a motorcycle to Helen for $3,000. When Helen came to accept delivery, Defendant demanded $1,000 as a delivery fee.

66.   Defendant drove to a used car lot that was closed because it was Sunday. He acted as if he owned the lot. Victim looked at a flashy red car and Defendant offered him the car at a very low price. Victim gave Defendant $100 as a down payment.

67.   Charlie was walking home from work when he saw Geoffrey attempting to rape Jane. Charlie pressed the point of his umbrella against Geoffrey's neck and said, "Watch out. I am about to make a hole in your neck!"
      If the state charges Charlie with assault, Charlie most likely will

(A)   not prevail, because Geoffrey's fear of immediate harm was real and reasonable

(B)   not prevail, because Charlie threatened Geoffrey with deadly force

(C)   prevail, because Geoffrey was the aggressor

(D)   prevail, if a reasonable person would think Geoffrey was about to commit a battery

Questions 68-70 are based upon the following fact situation.

After drinking two six-packs of beer, Lush decided he wanted some pretzels. He drove to the nearest 24-hour convenience store, grabbed a carton of pretzels, and ran outside. Feeling real drunk and real good, Lush decided to burn down a neighbor's house. Lush lit a match, and the house, unoccupied at the time, burned to the ground.
The applicable statutes provide:
"Larceny is the taking of property from possession of another, without consent, with intent to steal."
"Arson is the malicious burning of a dwelling."
Lush was charged with larceny and arson.

68.   Any attempt by Lush to assert his intoxication as a defense to the larceny charge

(A)   should be dismissed because voluntary drinking is not a defense

(B)   should be dismissed only if the larceny was planned before Lush began drinking

(C)   may negate the element of intent and allow Lush to defeat the charges

(D)   will allow Lush to defeat the larceny charges if "but for" his drinking, Lush would not have committed the larceny

69.   Which of the following would serve as Lush's best defense to the arson charge?

(A)   Lush was so intoxicated, his acts were not voluntary.

(B)   Lush was so intoxicated, he could not have formed intent.

(C)   Lush was so intoxicated, his actions could not have been malicious.

(D)   The person who sold Lush the beer should be held liable.

70.   The prosecution's best argument to counter the defense set forth in the previous question is that

(A)   voluntary intoxication cannot be a defense to a general intent crime

(B)   voluntary intoxication is a defense to a specific intent crime

(C)   "malicious" refers to Lush's course of conduct from the time he took his first drink

GO ON TO THE NEXT PAGE

and knew he could become dangerous

(D)   "malicious" could be imputed to the seller of the beer

71.   The local police heard a rumor that Vicky had converted her basement into a marijuana farm. The police walked behind her house and saw empty bags of fertilizer and old fluorescent bulbs often used to provide light for indoor growth. The policemen knocked on Vicky's door and asked if they could come in. Vicky assented. One of the policemen opened Vicky's basement door, turned on a light in the stairwell leading down to the basement, and saw a sea of green plants. Vicky was arrested, and the house was searched. The police discovered several hundred marijuana plants.

Over proper objection, should evidence of the marijuana be admitted into evidence?

(A)   Yes, if the fact finder decides that Vicky voluntarily opened the door.

(B)   Yes, because the search was incident to a valid arrest.

(C)   No, if the defendant can prove that fertilizer and light bulbs are not exclusively used to grow marijuana.

(D)   No, because Vicky's reasonable expectation of privacy was violated.

72.   Mick did not like Sally, the girl that his son Harry was dating. Sally was a lawyer and Mick preferred that his son go out with physical education teachers. One night, when Mick knew that Harry and Sally were at the local movies, Mick drove up to Sally's house, poured gasoline all around the outside, and lit a match. Sally's house was engulfed in flames. Larry, a fireman who responded to the scene with the local fire department, was fatally injured when he fell through the roof into the burning inferno of the house. Mick would most likely be convicted of

(A)   endangering the life of another

(B)   criminal negligence

(C)   felony murder

(D)   voluntary manslaughter

73.   Dave punched Jay in his nose. The state prosecutor charged Dave with assault and battery. Under which of the following conditions is Dave least likely to be convicted?

(A)   Dave was severely inebriated and was, therefore, unaware of his actions.

(B)   Dave thought Jay had stolen his watch.

(C)   Dave was only joking and did not intend serious harm.

(D)   Dave had just received an electrical shock, which caused involuntary motion.

Questions 74-76 are based upon the following fact situation.

Caroll and Ann developed a scheme to rob a bank. Caroll agreed to go inside the bank and demand money, while Ann agreed to drive the getaway car. Before Caroll had demanded the money inside the bank, a policeman told Ann to move her car. Ann decided to drop the bank robbery and drove to the beach to work on her tan. Meanwhile, Caroll pulled out a watergun and demanded money from a teller.

Joe, Moe, Bo, and Crow happened to be depositing the money that they had stolen the day before from the bank next door.

"Good work lady, don't be nervous," said Joe. Moe gave her a real gun and procured an escape car after it became apparent that Ann had left. Bo watched, but did not talk or act.

74. If charged with robbery, Ann should be found

    (A) guilty, because she approved of the robbery

    (B) guilty, because she was a member of the conspiracy

    (C) not guilty, because she withdrew from the scene before a crime was committed

    (D) not guilty, because her actions did not further any crime

75. If charged with robbery, Joe should be found

    (A) guilty, because the robbery would not have been

completed without his assurances

    (B) guilty, because he shouted encouragement to Caroll

    (C) not guilty, because his words did not place the bank's employees in greater danger

    (D) not guilty, because Caroll did not manifest her acceptance of his attempt to help

76. If charged with robbery, Bo should be found

    (A) guilty, because he approved of the crime

    (B) guilty, because he did not attempt to prevent the crime

    (C) not guilty, because presence, absent overt approval, is not sufficient to charge someone with a crime

    (D) not guilty, because he did not have prior knowledge of the robbery

Questions 77-78 are based upon the following fact situation.

The local jurisdiction enacted the criminal offense of "attempted criminal battery," defined as "an attempt to perpetrate a criminal battery." "Criminal battery" was defined as "an unlawful application of force, resulting in a harmful or offensive touching."

Hugh was skiing for the very first time. He inadvertently took an expert trail marked with a black diamond. He pointed his ski tips downhill, began to gain speed, and lost all control. He closed his eyes and crouched down in order to cushion his eventual fall. He then began flying down the mountain, shooting off moguls and into the air. Janet looked up and saw Hugh coming straight toward her. She jumped out of the way, and as Hugh passed, she pushed him from the side, hoping he would fall and no longer be a menace to himself and others.

77.   If charged with attempted criminal battery, should Hugh be found guilty?

(A)   Yes, because Janet was in fear of harmful or offensive conduct.

(B)   Yes, because Hugh was obviously grossly negligent in trying to ski down a hill that was too steep for his abilities.

(C)   No, because Hugh did not intend to lose control.

(D)   No, because the collision did not in fact occur.

78.   If charged with criminal battery, should Janet be found guilty?

(A)   Yes, because she intentionally applied offensive contact.

(B)   Yes, because she touched Hugh.

(C)   No, because the touch was not offensive.

(D)   No, because Janet was privileged to touch Hugh.

79.   Anna was an eyewitness to a murder. She spent several hours at a police station, answering questions about the murder. The police gave her a book containing the photographs of several thousand people. When she came across Liz's photograph, Anna identified her as the murderer.

If Liz objects to testimony concerning the identification, the judge should rule the identification

(A)   admissible

(B)   inadmissible, if the photo is not recent

(C)   inadmissible, if the identification was done before Liz retained counsel

(D)   inadmissible, unless Anna had a perfectly clear view of the murder

80.   Mob Sterr hired Hit Manne to kill Rodney. Late one night, Manne climbed through an open window into Rodney's living room. Rodney was watching television, and Manne snuck up from behind him and shot Rodney five times in the head. Rodney lived alone, but his girlfriend, Rozy, happened to be visiting. When she heard the gunshot, Rozy screamed. Manne shot and killed Rozy. If Mob Sterr is charged with the murder of Rozy, he will be found

(A)   not guilty because Manne was only hired to kill Rodney

(B)   not guilty, if Rozy's murder was probable or foreseeable

(C)   guilty, because Rozy's murder would not have occurred but for Rodney's murder

(D)   guilty, if Rozy's murder was a probable or foreseeable result of Rodney's murder

Questions 81-83 are based upon the following fact situation.

Defendant left his keys with Neighbor before flying to his parents' home for the holidays. Neighbor had asked for permission to use the apartment on Christmas Day, when members of his own family planned to visit.

On New Year's Day, a police officer happened to pass Defendant's apartment with his drug-sniffing dog on his way to another call. The dog barked very loudly as they passed Defendant's front door.

Just then, Neighbor was in the hallway and volunteered to open the door. The police officer found cocaine and a letter from Harvey, requesting a shipment of marijuana.

81.   Neighbor's unlocking of the door was

(A)   a waiving of Defendant's rights against search and seizure, because Neighbor was consenting to the policeman's entry to the apartment

(B)   a waiving of Defendant's right against search and seizure,

because of the probable cause that existed

(C)   not a waiving of Defendant's rights against search and seizure, because the police officer lacked probable cause for a search

(D)   not a waiving of Defendant's rights against search and seizure, because Neighbor did not have a right to permit entry

82.   Does Defendant have standing to challenge the search of his apartment?

(A)   Yes, because incriminating evidence was discovered.

(B)   Yes, because the search was in an area under his dominion.

(C)   No, because Neighbor unlocked the door.

(D)   No, because he was far away at the time of the search.

83.   For this question only, assume that Defendant was never tried because he had left the country. Harvey is tried for attempt to purchase illegal drugs. If Harvey attempts to challenge the validity of the search

(A)   the evidence will be admitted because Neighbor consented to the search

GO ON TO THE NEXT PAGE

(B)   the evidence will be admitted because Harvey lacks standing to object

(C)   the evidence will not be admitted, because the search was a violation of Harvey's Fourteenth Amendment Rights.

(D)   the evidence will not be admitted, because Defendant has left the country

84.   Pam was arrested for driving without a license. Pam, who was a licensed driver but had left her wallet at home, was taken to a police station, where she was booked. Pam was searched by the police, who found two ounces of cocaine on her person. Over proper objection, will the cocaine be admitted into evidence?

(A)   Yes, because the policeman may rely upon a reasonable suspicion.

(B)   Yes, because the search was pursuant to a valid custodial arrest.

(C)   No, because the officer had no reason to be in fear or to suspect that Pam was carrying drugs.

(D)   No, because failure to carry a license is a minor offense.

85.   Ronald could not stand to watch his Grandmother Janet suffer from terminal cancer, so he decided to kill her to relieve her pain. Ronald carried Janet out of the Mercy Hospital Cancer Ward and drove her to the nearest beach, eight hours away. While Ronald and Janet were driving, a flash fire killed all the patients in the Mercy Hospital Cancer Ward. Ronald rented a sailboat, went out to sea, and threw Janet overboard. She quickly drowned.

If charged with criminal homicide, should Ronald be found guilty?

(A)   Yes.

(B)   No, because Ronald actually prolonged Janet's life.

(C)   No, because Ronald acted out of compassion and love.

(D)   No, because Janet could have survived had she known how to swim, and Ronald was not under an obligation to rescue her.

Questions 86-88 are based upon the following fact situation.

Tommy and Jan happened to sit together at a night baseball game. "I am so hungry," said Tommy. "So am I," Jan replied. Neither one of them had money to purchase food. Jan told Tommy that she had left a shopping bag full of food at her mother's house, which was nearby, but her mother was out of town. Jan also told Tommy that her mother was very absent-minded and often left the back door unlocked.

Tommy agreed to go into Jan's mother's house, but made a mistake and went into the wrong house. The owner woke up and called the police. Jan and Tommy were arrested.

86. Jan's best defense against burglary charges is that

    (A) Tommy was arrested without ever touching any groceries

    (B) Tommy entered through an unlocked door

    (C) Tommy did not intend to commit a crime

    (D) Tommy fooled her

87. Tommy's best defense against burglary charges is that

    (A) the door was not locked

    (B) he reasonably thought he had lawful permission to enter the house

    (C) only Jan should be held responsible

    (D) a mistake of law was the proximate cause of entry

88. Tommy and Jan's best defense against conspiracy charges is that

    (A) neither intended to commit a burglary

    (B) there was no meeting of the minds

    (C) the groceries were not taken

    (D) both acted under mistake of law

89. In which of the following situations will Eugene most likely be convicted of larceny?

    (A) Eugene took a stranger's car for a drive, intending to return the car before the gas ran out. Eugene was involved in a serious accident, which destroyed the car.

    (B) Eugene drove a stranger's car home, thinking that it was his own car.

    (C) Eugene walked past a convertible. The top was down, and the keys were in the ignition. Under the assumption that he was not committing larceny, Eugene drove the car away and gave it to his grandson as a graduation present.

    (D) Eugene took Eli's car, because Eli had damaged Eugene's car and had refused to pay for it. Eugene's car was much more valuable than Eli's.

90. Bobby's boiler was leaking gas, but Bobby decided to ignore the leak. He was having seventy-five people over and he could not waste time messing with the boiler. A gas explosion in the middle of the party caused the death of sixteen persons. Bobby has committed

    (A) no form of criminal homicide

GO ON TO THE NEXT PAGE

(B)   voluntary manslaughter

(C)   involuntary manslaughter

(D)   murder

91.   Elmoe was arrested and charged with armed robbery. The arresting officer gave Elmoe his Miranda warnings. Elmoe asked for counsel and was told he would receive counsel. Elmoe then proceeded to make several incriminating statements. Over proper objections, these statements should be ruled

(A)   admissible, because the period after receiving the Miranda warnings is not a critical element of the prosecution that would require counsel

(B)   admissible, because the statements were voluntary and not the result of improper questioning

(C)   not admissible, because Elmoe had requested but not received counsel

(D)   not admissible, because the right to counsel had not vested at the time the statement was made

Questions 92-97 are based upon the following fact situation.

Debra and Sandra decided to play a game. Debra, age sixteen, took a machete off the wall above her father's bed and stood Sandra, age sixteen, next to a tree. Debra threw the machete toward Sandra. The object of the game was for Debra to throw the machete as close as possible to Sandra, without striking her. Sandra knew Debra had never tried throwing a machete before.

Debra threw the machete four times. She narrowly missed Sandra the first three times. On the fourth throw, the machete struck Sandra in the throat, killing her. In the jurisdiction, one is legally accountable as an adult for committing a crime at the age of sixteen.

92.   If Debra is prosecuted, she will be found

(A)   guilty of murder

(B)   guilty of manslaughter

(C)   not guilty, because she was merely negligent

(D)   not guilty, because Sandra consented

93.   If charged with murder, Debra could be properly convicted of

(A)   involuntary manslaughter only

(B)   premeditated killing only

(C)   murder and involuntary manslaughter

(D)   murder and voluntary manslaughter

94.   Which of the following choices is the best argument to convict Debra of manslaughter?

(A)   Debra should be convicted of felony murder because throwing the machete

constituted assault with a
deadly weapon.

(B)   Debra was above the
minimum age to be convicted
of murder.

(C)   Sandra did not assent to be
killed.

(D)   Debra's actions demonstrated
carelessness in the face of an
unjustifiably high risk to
human life.

95.   Debra's father is most likely to be
charged with

(A)   assault

(B)   murder

(C)   voluntary manslaughter

(D)   contributing to the
delinquency of a minor

96.   Assume, for the next two questions
only, that the local jurisdiction
enacted a statute that states, "Murder
that is premeditated, or committed
during the perpetration of a felony, is
murder of the first degree. All other
murders are of the second degree."
    If charged with first degree
murder, Debra's best argument will
be that

(A)   she is too young to be found
guilty of such severe charges

(B)   she did not have the requisite
malice (aforethought)

(C)   the killing was not
premeditated, nor was it part
of a felony

(D)   the victim consented

97.   Assume that the prosecution
establishes a *prima facie* case of first-
degree murder. Under the above
statute, in order for the defendant to
be found innocent of first degree
murder, she

(A)   must prove both that she did
not commit a felony and that
she did not premeditate

(B)   must prove either that she did
not commit a felony or that
she did not premeditate

(C)   need not prove anything
because the prosecution has
the burden of proof

(D)   will be found guilty

98.   Defendant, a police officer, had valid
legal grounds on which to arrest
Deceased. Defendant, driving a
squad car, pursued Deceased, who
was riding a motorcycle. Realizing
that he could not keep up with the
motorcycle, Defendant forced the
motorcycle off the road. Deceased
lost control of the bike, fell down a
ravine, and died.
    Defendant will be found
guilty of murder

GO ON TO THE NEXT PAGE

(A)   unless the court determines that he was using non-deadly force, because, if he was using deadly force, he will be guilty

(B)   unless the court determines that he was using deadly force to effectuate a felony or misdemeanor arrest

(C)   unless the court determines that he was privileged to use deadly force in effectuating a felony arrest

(D)   because he was not privileged to use non-deadly or deadly force

99.   Regina always said, "I'd rather die than see any of my children in trouble." Regina's son Charlie decided to kill his mother because Regina's daughter was being investigated for running a house of prostitution. Charlie invited Regina to his house and filled her extra-strength headache relief capsules with cyanide.

Regina's house burned down, killing everyone inside, moments before Regina died of cyanide poisoning.

If charged with criminal homicide, should Charlie be found guilty?

(A)   Yes.

(B)   No, because Charlie actually prolonged Regina's life.

(C)   No, because Charlie acted out of compassion and love.

(D)   No, because Regina may have survived the fire.

100.   First-degree murder is defined by a state statute as "murder with premeditation and deliberation."

In which of the following situations is it most likely that Harris will be convicted of first-degree murder?

(A)   Harris tried to injure Russell by punching him in the nose. Russell died from the injuries he sustained.

(B)   Russell told Harris, "Your mother wears combat boots." Harris flew into a rage and killed Russell.

(C)   Severely inebriated, Harris drove ninety miles per hour in the wrong direction on a one-way street, striking and killing a pedestrian.

(D)   Russell cheated against Harris in a card game. Harris ran to a local sporting good store and bought a shotgun with which he shot and killed Russell.

Questions 101-102 are based upon the following fact situation.

Renaldo, an Olympic sprinter, was walking down the street, window-shopping. He saw a police officer chasing Hilary. Hilary was running faster than the police officer, and Renaldo joined the chase.

101. Is the police officer privileged to use force to effectuate an arrest of Hilary?

    (A) He may not use force.

    (B) He may use non-deadly force only.

    (C) He may use deadly force.

    (D) He may use deadly force only to effectuate an arrest for a felony.

102. Is Renaldo privileged to use force to effectuate an arrest of Hilary?

    (A) He may not use force.

    (B) He may use non-deadly force only.

    (C) He may use deadly force.

    (D) He may use deadly force only to effectuate an arrest for a felony if Hilary is guilty.

103. Dave knew his car's brakes were not in proper order and were about to fail. Dave continued to drive the car anyway, because he had to get to work and did not have time to take care of repairs. Dave was driving Mary home from work when the brakes ultimately failed. When they approached a red light at the bottom of a hill, Dave crashed into the car in front of him. Mary was killed in the accident. Dave has committed

    (A) no form of criminal homicide

    (B) voluntary manslaughter

    (C) involuntary manslaughter

    (D) murder

104. A local ordinance provides that one who "knowingly sells a grade of gasoline differing from the grade advertised is guilty of aggravated larceny." Chris owned a Standard Oil of New Hampshire gas station. Unbeknownst to Chris, the gas company filled Chris's 91-octane tank with 89-octane fuel. An inspector discovered the octane difference, and Chris was charged with aggravated larceny. If a jury believes Chris's testimony, will he be found guilty of aggravated larceny?

    (A) Yes, because Chris is admitting that he has not complied with the statute.

    (B) Yes, because ignorance is no excuse.

    (C) No, because Chris was not aware of the octane difference.

    (D) No, because the gas station used Standard Oil's name in relating with the public.

105. Patrick kicked Stanley, causing severe injuries. The state brought charges against Patrick for assault and battery. In which of the following

GO ON TO THE NEXT PAGE

situations is Patrick **LEAST** likely to be convicted?

(A)   Patrick was severely inebriated and was, therefore, unaware of his actions.

(B)   Patrick believed that Stanley had stolen his girlfriend.

(C)   Patrick was only joking and did not intend serious harm.

(D)   Patrick accidentally touched a live wire, and the resulting shock caused an involuntary kick.

106.   Bigamy was defined by a local statute as "having a husband or wife and marrying another person" or "marrying another person who has a husband or wife." Another statute provided that "one who has been absent for more than seven years without notice is presumed dead."

Joan and Fredrick were married in 1980, when Fredrick disappeared without notice. Joan married Kevin in 1986, without telling him that she had been married before.

If charged with bigamy

(A)   both Joan and Kevin should be held guilty

(B)   only Joan should be held guilty

(C)   only Kevin should be held guilty

(D)   neither Kevin nor Joan should be held guilty

107.   Michael, a firmly diagnosed psychotic, walked calmly into the hospital emergency room and killed seventeen nurses during a wild shooting spree. The trier of fact ruled that "the shooting spree would not have occurred but for Michael's psychosis." The conclusion of the trier of fact is closest to which of the following insanity tests?

(A)   Durham (or New Hampshire) test

(B)   irresistible impulse test

(C)   Model Penal Code provision

(D)   M'Naghten rule

108.   Acting on a "gut" feeling, a police officer knocked on Rasta's door and demanded that he be allowed to search the apartment for narcotics. Rasta refused, and the policeman told him, "If you let me use your bathroom, I won't arrest you." Rasta assented and told the officer that the bathroom was the second door on the right. The policeman turned left and found a room full of sprouting marijuana plants. Rasta was arrested. At trial for possession of drugs with intent to sell, Rasta moved to exclude the evidence. The evidence should be ruled

(A)   admissible, if the trier of fact determines that the police officer's turn to the left was an honest mistake

(B)   admissible, because the police officer entered the apartment with Rasta's permission

(C)   inadmissible, because the policeman was not privileged to do a search

(D)   inadmissible, if the police officer did not, in fact, really need to use the bathroom

109.   In which of the following fact situations is Defendant most likely to be held guilty of the crime charged?

(A)   Defendant saw $5,000 on his boss's desk. Defendant took the money, intending to return it, which he in fact did three hours later. Defendant is charged with larceny.

(B)   Defendant borrowed $5,000, using his brother's driver's license as identification. He returned the money in a timely manner. Defendant is charged with obtaining property under false pretenses.

(C)   Defendant begged his boss for a $5,000 advance against future wages. Defendant knew he was not going to return to the job or repay the money. Defendant is charged with larceny by trick.

(D)   Defendant borrowed $5,000 from his boss, intending to return the money when due. On the due date, Defendant decided not to return the money. Defendant is charged

with obtaining property under false pretenses.

110.   Defendant, an Olympic skier, wanted to neutralize Opponent. Defendant altered Opponent's ski bindings so that they would not release upon impact. Ski bindings are adjusted to release the skier's boots in a bad fall in order to mitigate any injury. Defendant hoped his alteration would cause Opponent severe leg injuries and keep Opponent from competing.

Opponent fell during a practice run and broke both his legs when his skis didn't come off. The pain was so severe that Opponent went into shock and died. Of the following offenses, which is the most serious crime that Defendant could be convicted?

(A)   involuntary manslaughter

(B)   voluntary manslaughter

(C)   murder

(D)   none of the above

111.   A police officer testified that he had ordered Jack to pull to the side of a road and produce identification because "this is a wealthy area and our orders are to pull over cars that look like they don't belong here." When asked why Jack's car looked like it did not belong, the police said, "It was old, dented, and had a Grateful Dead bumper sticker."

The officer found a packet of illegally obtained Quaaludes on the

GO ON TO THE NEXT PAGE

floor by Jack's passenger seat. If Jack makes a motion to suppress this evidence, the motion should be

(A)   sustained, because the officer was not privileged to look around the car

(B)   sustained, because the car was not lawfully stopped

(C)   denied, because the policeman was acting pursuant to an established plan

(D)   denied, because the policeman had a reasonable suspicion for which to stop the car

112.   Beverly was hit from behind by a car while riding her bicycle. She fell onto the concrete sidewalk along the road, lost consciousness, and did not waken until she reached the hospital. The driver of the car sped away from the scene of the accident. Fifteen minutes later, Phillip was cited for speeding. Phillip was also arrested on suspicion of leaving the scene of the accident.

After Phillip's arrest, a witness identified Phillip from an old photograph on file in the police station as the driver of the car that had hit Beverly.

If Phillip objects to testimony concerning the witness's identification, the judge should rule the identification

(A)   admissible

(B)   inadmissible, because the photograph was not recent

(C)   inadmissible, if the photo identification was done before Phillip retained counsel

(D)   inadmissible, if Phillip did not have a very clear view of the accident

113.   While covering a story at the local courthouse, Kent, a reporter for the local newspaper, left the courtroom in order to use the washroom. He left his notes lying on a chair. Olsen, a reporter for a rival newspaper, took Kent's notes, crumpled them up, and put them in a nearby garbage can. Olsen is not guilty of

(A)   larceny, because Kent was not present

(B)   larceny, because Olsen did not want to keep the notes

(C)   robbery, because force and/or fear were not used

(D)   robbery, because the notes did not have a monetary value

114.   Marcia was stopped by a police officer because she was not wearing a seat belt or shoulder harness while driving. Marcia was arrested, pursuant to state law, and taken to a nearby police station to be booked. In the station, Marcia was searched, and an unlicensed handgun was found on her person. Should the gun be admitted into evidence to charge her with the crime of possessing a handgun without a license?

(A) Yes, because the policeman may rely upon "reasonable suspicion" as the basis for their search.

(B) Yes, because the search was pursuant to a valid custodial arrest.

(C) No, because the officer had no reason to be in fear or to suspect that Marcia had a gun.

(D) No, because a seat-belt violation is a minor offense.

115. Cee and Dee were eating dinner in Eff's apartment. They both were dying to see the movie *Rambo*. Cee talked Dee into driving to the nearby video store to rent the movie. "Take my car," said Cee. "It's the blue car in front. The keys are in the ignition." Dee went outside and drove off in the wrong car. The owner of the car called the police, who arrested both Dee and Cee.

Cee and Dee's best defense against conspiracy charges is that

(A) neither intended to commit larceny

(B) there was no meeting of the minds

(C) the car was returned

(D) both acted under a mistake of law

116. Michael walked out of an airline terminal with a suitcase that belonged to someone else. When charged with larceny, Michael claimed he had made an honest mistake — he thought the suitcase was his own. Michael should be found

(A) guilty, for taking and carrying away property from the possession of another person

(B) guilty, because he was criminally negligent in not inspecting the suitcase

(C) not guilty, if Michael had left a suitcase in the airport with a similar appearance.

(D) not guilty, if the jury determines that Michael honestly believed that the luggage was his own

117. Aleph and Bet decided to rob a grocery store. Both agreed not to carry any weapons. When confronted by Aleph and Bet demanding the contents of the cash register and the safe, Gimmel, the grocer, pulled out a sawed-off shotgun from behind the counter. Bet whipped out a handgun and killed Gimmel. If prosecuted for murder, is Aleph likely to be convicted?

(A) Yes.

(B) No, because Bet agreed not to carry a gun.

GO ON TO THE NEXT PAGE

(C)   No, because convicting Aleph for murder would be extreme in light of the facts.

(D)   No, because the killing was justified by Gimmel's actions.

118.   Youth grew his hair long and wore an unusual hairstyle. He also changed his last name to In-Asia. Rumors circulated that Youth had joined Stay, a radical group that advocated the violent overthrow of the U.S. government.

During the predawn hours of a rainy morning, the local police sent an investigatory team to Youth's back yard. One of the police officers smelled the aroma of gunpowder emanating from an open basement window. The officers knocked on the door. Youth opened the door and was placed under arrest. The house was searched, resulting in the discovery of a large stockpile of homemade bombs.

Over proper objection, should evidence of the homemade bombs be admitted into evidence?

(A)   Yes, if the fact finder decides that Youth voluntarily opened the door.

(B)   Yes, because the search was incident to a valid arrest.

(C)   No, if Youth can prove that gunpowder smells just like several other household items.

(D)   No, because Youth's reasonable expectation of privacy was violated.

119.   Defendant killed his best friend after learning that his friend, who owed Defendant $100,000, had filed for bankruptcy. Defendant asserts that the murder charge should be reduced to manslaughter, because the killing was not premeditated, it was perpetrated in the heat of passion. The jury should be instructed that

(A)   the state must prove beyond a reasonable doubt, and by a preponderance of the evidence, that the killing was not provoked by the heat of passion

(B)   the state must prove beyond a reasonable doubt both the killing and the absence of heat of passion

(C)   the state must prove the killing beyond a reasonable doubt. Once the killing is proved, it is presumed to be murder

(D)   the state must prove the killing beyond a reasonable doubt. Once the killing is proved, Defendant has the burden of showing, by a fair preponderance of the evidence, that the killing was committed in the heat of passion

Questions 120-122 are based upon the following fact situation.

Hinkley believed he was the Messiah. He spent hours practicing long rituals, whereby he claimed to communicate with God. Hinkley, who was diagnosed by a licensed physician as a severe schizophrenic, toured the country preaching to anyone who would listen, and to some who would not listen, that they should refrain from sinning.

Hinkley decided that the government was the enemy of God. Knowing he was to be punished by the government, Hinkley shot a receptionist at the state capitol, because, he said, God ordered him to do so. The receptionist died two days later. Hinkley is charged with murder and asserts the insanity defense.

120. Hinkley's best defense, in a jurisdiction that has adopted the M'Naghten test, is that

(A) he did not know that he was killing someone

(B) he did not know that killing was wrong

(C) his mental illness was the cause of the killing

(D) he could not stop himself from killing

121. If the jurisdiction has adopted the irresistible impulse test, Hinkley will most likely be acquitted if

(A) he killed the receptionist because he was a psychotic

(B) the killing was caused by Hinkley's delusions

(C) Hinkley could not control his desire to kill

(D) Hinkley had not planned the killing in advance

122. In which of the following situations is Hinkley **LEAST** likely to be found the legal cause of the receptionist's death?

(A) The receptionist would have survived but for the fact that she was a hemophiliac and she bled to death.

(B) The receptionist was recovering from an operation and would not have died from Hinkley's shots had she not been in a weakened condition.

(C) The receptionist was killed by a fire that engulfed the hospital where she was successfully recuperating from wounds inflicted by Hinkley.

(D) Hinkley's brother Stinkly decided to shoot the receptionist too. She would not have died if just Hinkley or just Stinkly had shot her.

123. Bruce and Phil planned and committed the armed robbery of an ice cream parlor. Bruce threatened a waitress with a gun, while Phil emptied the store's cash register. Bruce fired a few shots at the store's lights and said, "Anyone that follows us gets it." Phil drove the getaway car and when it appeared that they were safe, they both relaxed. Bruce turned a corner and saw Alex walking down the street. "Boy do I hate that jerk," said Bruce. Phil took his gun

GO ON TO THE NEXT PAGE

and shot Alex, who died three weeks later.

If Bruce is charged with murder, he will most likely be found

(A)   guilty, because the killing took place during a conspiracy

(B)   guilty, because he provoked the shooting

(C)   not guilty, because Bruce and Phil did not plan on killing Alex

(D)   not guilty, because the killing was not in furtherance of the conspiracy

124.   Both Sally and Susan were less than five feet tall. They decided to become partners in the mugging business. Sally was to demand the money and Susan was to wait two blocks away. The plan was for Sally to hand all the receipts to Susan so, if Sally were caught, she would not be holding any evidence.

Sally left Susan on a street corner and started to walk two blocks away in order to mug someone. While Sally was walking away, Susan had second thoughts and decided to go back to college. She took a taxi home. Sally walked over to a man more than six feet tall and demanded his money. "You must be kidding, shrimp," said the man. He took a cigarette that he was about to light out of his mouth and threw it at Sally. Sally grabbed the man's cigarettes and ran. Sally was apprehended three blocks away, arrested, and searched.

If Susan and Sally are both charged with robbery, Susan's best defense is that

(A)   she took a taxi home before any crime was committed

(B)   Sally performed the illegal act

(C)   Sally was not successful

(D)   the man never feared Sally

125.   A local bigamy statute provided, "Any person who has a husband or wife and marries another person, or one who marries a person he or she knows has a husband or wife, is guilty of bigamy." Paul and Martha were engaged to be married. Paul never told Martha that he was married to Julie. One day Paul and Martha shared two bottles of Scotch. Paul was feeling very guilty and told Martha he was married to Julie. Martha was so drunk that his words did not register in her mind. The next morning, relieved that Martha did not remember the conversation, Paul decided never to tell her of his previous marriage. Martha and Paul married. If prosecuted for bigamy under the above listed statutes, Martha should be found

(A)   not guilty, if she was voluntarily intoxicated

(B)   not guilty, if she was involuntarily intoxicated

(C)   not guilty, regardless of how she became intoxicated

(D)   guilty

126. Beverly, a psychotic, killed her sister. The trier of fact decided that "as a result of her psychosis Beverly lacked the sustained capacity either to appreciate the wrongfulness of her conduct or to conform her conduct to the requirements of law."

    The conclusion of the trier of fact most closely resembles which of the following insanity tests?

    (A)   Durham (or New Hampshire) test

    (B)   irresistible impulse test

    (C)   the Model Penal Code's provision

    (D)   M'Naghten Rule

Questions 127-128 are based upon the following fact situation.

Kevin sold the tickets at a movie theater. On a busy weekend he often sold $5,000 worth of tickets. Kevin was heavily in debt from his recent purchase of a new house.

Late one Sunday night Kevin was the only employee on duty. He hid the day's receipts in the lining of his coat, called the police, and told them that he had been robbed at gunpoint.

127. Kevin has committed the crime of

    (A)   larceny

    (B)   embezzlement

    (C)   larceny by trick

    (D)   false pretenses

128. Assume that two months later Kevin's financial situation improves and he returns the money. If the jury determines that Kevin intended to eventually return the money at the time he put it in his coat, Kevin will be found guilty of

    (A)   larceny

    (B)   embezzlement

    (C)   larceny by trick

    (D)   false pretenses

129. A state statute provides that "any person who has a husband or wife and marries another person is guilty of bigamy." The statute further provides for exceptions: "If the prior spouse is dead or absent for more than seven years; if the prior marriage was dissolved, or the party reasonably believed it was dissolved."

    Defendant was mailed a document by his wife that certified an out-of-state divorce. Defendant mistakenly thought the decree was valid and remarried shortly thereafter. The divorce was not recognized by the state of Defendant's second marriage which follows the statutes listed above. If prosecuted for bigamy, Defendant will be held

    (A)   not guilty, if he has made a reasonable mistake of fact

GO ON TO THE NEXT PAGE

(B)   not guilty, if he has made a reasonable mistake of law

(C)   not guilty, if he has made either a reasonable mistake of fact or law

(D)   guilty, regardless of what type of mistake he had made

130.   Elizabeth and Tina together hid sixteen cases of rum in their boat when they sailed from the Virgin Islands to Miami. Elizabeth had consulted an attorney before the excursion, who advised her it would be unlawful to import rum from the Virgin Islands to Miami without paying a duty on it. Tina had also consulted an attorney, who told her of the United States Virgin Rum Exclusion Act of 1985 excluding duty collection on rum imported from the Virgin Islands.

    If charged with attempting the crime of Virgin Island Rum import-duty evasion

(A)   neither Elizabeth nor Tina should be found guilty if the Act of 1985 is valid

(B)   only Elizabeth should be found guilty if the Act of 1985 is valid

(C)   only Tina should be found guilty if the Act of 1985 is not valid

(D)   both Elizabeth and Tina should be found guilty

131.   Bookie ran an illegal gambling operation. Every day he traveled a specific route and accepted bets on games that would be played the following weekend. He confirmed the bets with printed forms that said across the top, "Bookie Wishes You Luck."

    Gregory was stopped by police because his brake lights had malfunctioned. The police searched Gregory's car and found several betting forms with Bookie's name.

    Bookie, charged with illegal gambling, seeks to prevent introduction of the forms into evidence. Should the forms be admitted?

(A)   Yes, because the search was proper.

(B)   Yes, because Bookie does not have standing to challenge the search.

(C)   No, because the search was improper.

(D)   No, because an officer may stop a car for an immediate threat, such as a broken headlight, but not for a brake light.

132.   June gift-wrapped a bomb and called April, a messenger, to deliver the bomb to May. April had no reason to be suspicious about the contents of the package. May opened the package with the bomb, triggering off an explosion. Which of the following statements is correct in respect to the crime committed?

(A)   June is a principal in the first degree.

(B)   April is a principal in the first degree.

(C)   June is a principal in the second degree.

(D)   April is an accessory before the fact.

133.   Ida was arrested and charged with murder. She was handcuffed, given her Miranda warnings, and placed in the back seat of a police car. Ida demanded to speak with a lawyer and was told she would be provided with counsel shortly. "He better be a good one because I am guilty as hell," muttered Ida. Over proper objection, Ida's confession should be ruled

(A)   admissible, because riding to the police station is not a critical element of the prosecution requiring counsel

(B)   admissible, because the statements were volunteered and not the result of improper questioning

(C)   not admissible, because Ida had requested counsel and had not received it

(D)   not admissible, because the right to counsel had not vested at the time the statement was made.

134.   In which of the following situations is Defendant most likely to be found **NOT GUILTY** as charged?

(A)   Defendant took a picnic table from his neighbor's yard. Unknown to Defendant, his neighbor had tired of the table and was planning to give it to Defendant. Defendant is charged with attempted larceny.

(B)   Believing that federal law considers it a crime to melt down U.S. coins, Defendant melted down $2,000 face value of pre-1965 silver coins. The law that prohibited the melting down of coins had been repealed years earlier, but Defendant did not know about the law's repeal. Defendant is charged with melting down coins.

(C)   Defendant hired a hit man to murder his mother-in-law. Unknown to the hit man and Defendant, Defendant's mother-in-law had died hours earlier. Defendant is charged with attempted murder.

(D)   Defendant tried to sell a car that was not his as a trade-in for a new car. The car dealer was not fooled and refused to sell a car to Defendant. Defendant is charged with attempt to obtain property under false pretenses.

GO ON TO THE NEXT PAGE

Questions 135-136 are based on the following four cases (A-D) summarized below. Decide which one of these cases best applies to each question.

(A) Defendant and Jones robbed a taxi driver. A police officer chased both assailants and caught Defendant. Jones, who was still at large, decided he should change his clothing to avoid being conspicuous. Two hours later, Jones murdered a hitchhiker and put on his clothing. Defendant's conviction for murder was upheld on appeal.

(B) Defendant rented a pornographic movie. When he realized that his wife was the movie's star, he took a gun out of his night table and shot her. On appeal, Defendant's murder conviction was reduced to manslaughter.

(C) Defendant threw a rock at his neighbor, intending only to bruise him a little, in order to "teach him a lesson." The neighbor was killed from the impact of the rock. Defendant's murder conviction was upheld on appeal.

(D) Defendant was fired from his job without cause. He went to his boss's house with a hand grenade. Defendant pulled out the grenade's pin and threatened to throw it into the house if he was not reinstated immediately.

Defendant's assault conviction was upheld on appeal.

135. Defendant, a redhead, walked past a demonstrating mob seeking to have all redheads deported from the United States. Members of the crowd grabbed Defendant and passed him over their heads in an attempt to humiliate him. When Defendant was finally released from the mob's grasp, he pulled out a gun and killed three demonstrators.

136. Defendant wanted to kidnap a famous movie star who traveled with an armed guard. Defendant tried shooting the hand in which the guard usually carried his gun, but Defendant missed the hand, hit the guard in the abdomen, and killed him.

137. A state statute provides that "members of the state legislature must not accept gifts valued at more than $500." The state was considering repealing the windfall profits tax on crude oil. For her birthday, state Senator Kay Rupt received a diamond necklace from Roller, the vice president of a large oil company. The necklace had a fair market value of $25,000.

If Roller is charged with violating the statute, his best argument is that

(A) he was not an accessory to Kay Rupt's crime

(B) the accessory may only be tried after the principal is convicted

(C) he did not intend to influence Kay Rupt with the gift

(D) the legislature did not intend to punish one who gave gifts

138. Wild Bill, a professional football player, was identified as a cocaine user from the results of a mandatory drug test he had taken. Wild Bill was granted immunity from prosecution in exchange for cooperating with authorities. He became an extremely reliable informant and was responsible for more than forty drug-related convictions.

Wild Bill told investigators that he had purchased cocaine two years earlier from Julius. A search warrant for Julius's home was issued based on Wild Bill's statements. Julius's house was subsequently raided by the narcotics squad, and 200 pounds of cocaine were found. Should Julius's motion to suppress the evidence be granted?

(A) Yes, because testimony of a drug abuser is not sufficient grounds on which to issue a search warrant.

(B) Yes, because two years had passed since Wild Bill purchased drugs from Julius.

(C) No, because Wild Bill was an extremely reliable witness.

(D) No, because testimony of a witness is sufficient to satisfy the requirements of granting a search warrant.

139. In which of the following situations is Defendant most likely to be found guilty of murder?

(A) Disturbed by the noises made when his garbage cans overturned, Defendant put some cake laced with poison in his garbage, hoping to kill the animals that frequent the area. A homeless person ate the cake and died.

(B) Defendant was threatened by a man holding a toy gun. Believing his life to be in danger, Defendant killed the man.

(C) While in the process of robbing a barber shop, Defendant threw a rock at the mirror to scare the barber out of the shop. A shard of broken glass cut the barber's jugular vein, causing his death.

(D) Defendant's boiler did not meet the efficiency standards mandated in a local ordinance. The boiler caught fire, killing three persons.

140. Mr. Chop Shop operated an automotive spare parts business. Chop Shop purchased cars or parts of cars from local felons and resold the parts to body shops and mechanics. After Chop Shop received an order for parts, he would often hire a felon to steal a same-make car.

GO ON TO THE NEXT PAGE

Jean called up Shop to ask if he needed a 1986 Cadillac. "We can always use a Cadillac" was Shop's reply.

Jean did not, in fact, have a Cadillac, but based on this reply she went out and stole one. Shop paid Jean $500 for the car.

Shop and Jean were arrested for, among other charges, conspiracy to commit larceny. Should Shop be found guilty of conspiracy to commit larceny for these dealings with Jean?

(A) Yes, because Jean took the car in reliance on Shop's offer.

(B) Yes, because Shop was aware of the theft before it occurred and had a stake in its success.

(C) No, because Shop did not help in planning, nor did he participate or assist in the theft.

(D) No, because charging Shop with conspiracy as well as other offenses would constitute double jeopardy.

141. Defendant was caught climbing the fence surrounding a new car dealer's lot. Defendant was carrying tools that are commonly used for removing radios from cars. If Defendant is charged with attempted larceny, he should be found

(A) guilty, because he was committed to completing the crime

(B) guilty, if he had the necessary mental state, because he was in close proximity to the cars

(C) not guilty, because one may not be punished for an act not yet committed

(D) not guilty, if the cars did not have radios

142. Defendant is most likely to be convicted of common law murder in which of the following situations?

(A) Defendant came home and found his wife in bed with another woman. Defendant grabbed a gun, then shot and killed both women.

(B) Defendant, driving while intoxicated, lost control of his car and killed a pedestrian on the sidewalk.

(C) Defendant shot a spitball into a classmate's eye. The eye became infected, the infection spread, and the classmate died.

(D) Defendant threw a full beer can from his seat in a baseball stadium. He intended to seriously injure a player from the visiting team. Instead, he killed a member of the home team.

143. The local police set up a roadblock to check the driver of every fifth car that passed for obvious signs of intoxication. While checking Joseph, a police officer spotted marijuana on

the back seat of his car. Joseph was ordered from the car and searched. Eight grams of cocaine were found in his pants pocket.

Joseph was charged with the illegal possession of narcotics. If Joseph makes a motion to suppress the admission of the cocaine into evidence, should he be successful?

(A)   Yes, because he was improperly searched.

(B)   Yes, because the car was stopped without cause.

(C)   No, because Joseph was stopped pursuant to a valid plan.

(D)   No, because an officer of the law may act on a "hunch."

Questions 144-145 are based on the four case summaries that follow. For each question select the case most applicable as a precedent.

(A)   Defendant rented a car for a week, using a stolen credit card and identification. Defendant never returned the car. He was convicted of larceny.

(B)   Defendant stole a bicycle and rented it to unsuspecting customers until he earned enough money to return that bicycle and buy his own. He was convicted of larceny.

(C)   Defendant, rushing to get to the post office, took an unlocked bicycle. The bicycle was then stolen from Defendant while he was in the post office. He was held not guilty of larceny.

(D)   Defendant sold a television and agreed to deliver it to the purchaser's house within three days. Defendant never delivered the television. He was held not guilty of larceny.

144.   Defendant, owner of a bar, was angry because the bar across the street installed a new large sign. Defendant took the sign down in the middle of the night, intending to return it when his new sign arrived.

145.   Defendant unscrewed the lock to a booth at the entrance of a parking lot and collected parking fees.

146.   Defendant operated a small home for retarded adults. Defendant despised Harry, one of the home's residents, because Harry was a slob. Defendant struck Harry's head as hard as he could with his fists, several times a day. On the last occasion Harry died, just moments after being hit by Defendant.

Quincy, a pathologist, performed an autopsy on Harry. "Harry died of pancreatic cancer, although, continued blows to Harry's head would have resulted in his death within two weeks," Quincy testified.

GO ON TO THE NEXT PAGE

If prosecuted for murder, Defendant should be held

(A)   not guilty, because he had the authority to discipline Harry

(B)   not guilty, because his actions did not cause Harry's death

(C)   guilty, because Harry would have died from the blows had he not died of cancer first

(D)   guilty, if Defendant did not know that Harry was ill

147.   Defendant firmly believed he was the savior of the universe. He also believed that people with freckles were polluting the world's gene pool. Defendant would stand on chairs in airports and preach his philosophy. Most people remained apathetic when Defendant made his speeches. Defendant decided it was his obligation to take definitive action. He obtained a gun through legal channels and shot three freckled people dead on a crowded street. In a jurisdiction that has adopted the M'Naghten test of insanity, Defendant's best argument is that he had a disease of the mind and

(A)   did not know the nature of the act he performed

(B)   did not know the quality of the act he performed

(C)   did not know the killings were wrong

(D)   his acts would not have occurred if not for his mental disease

148.   In which of the following situations will defendant be **LEAST** likely to be found guilty by asserting in his defense that he was intoxicated?

(A)   Defendant, charged with murder, claimed he was so drunk that he thought he was carving a turkey.

(B)   Defendant, charged with incest, claimed he was so drunk that he thought his partner was his wife.

(C)   Defendant, charged with armed robbery, claimed he was so drunk that he thought that he was carrying a watergun.

(D)   Defendant, charged with intent to commit embezzlement, claimed he was so drunk that he did not realize he was walking away with company property.

149.   William assaulted his teacher. The trier of fact determined that William, a firmly diagnosed psychotic, "lacked the ability to know the wrongfulness of his actions or understand the quality of the actions." The conclusion of the trier of fact is closest to which of the following insanity tests?

(A)   Durham (or New Hampshire) test

(B)   irresistible impulse test

(C)   Model Penal Code provision

(D)   M'Naghten Rule

150. Anthony held a wedding reception in his house for his daughter, Rebecca. Coleman pretended to be an invited guest, walked around the house, and then took Anthony's camera. Coleman was arrested and charged with common law burglary. Should Coleman be convicted?

    (A) Yes, because he took the camera with the intent of keeping it.

    (B) Yes, because he was not an invited guest.

    (C) No, because there was no breaking.

    (D) No, because he did not have the proper intent.

151. Nicholas, while visiting Leon at his apartment, noticed a bad smell. "What is that smell?" asked Nicholas. "It's a dead skunk. You know how I love to collect interesting things." Leon went to the grocery store to buy some beer, leaving Nicholas in his apartment watching television. Nicholas threw the skunk into the building's incinerator, hoping that Leon would never notice.

    If charged with larceny and burglary, Leon should be found guilty of

    (A) larceny only

    (B) burglary only

    (C) both burglary and larceny

    (D) neither burglary nor larceny

152. Fran and Janet were being investigated for a brutal murder. Fran was called before a grand jury, but she refused to testify. After being granted immunity, Fran testified that she had entered into a conspiracy with Janet to commit this murder. Both Fran and Janet were then indicted for the murder. Janet was granted immunity for agreeing to testify against Loretta, another alleged conspirator. Loretta objected to Janet's testimony at her trial.
    Should Loretta's objection be sustained?

    (A) Yes, because Janet's testimony will be biased due to her interest.

    (B) Yes, because the testimony will be a result of grand jury testimony.

    (C) No, because the investigation and indictment were proceedings without Janet's testimony.

    (D) No, because the testimony is voluntary and may be impeached.

153. Nancy and Joel were partners in the loan sharking business. While Nancy was out of town, Buffy, the company secretary, pulled out a badge and notified Joel that she was a government agent and he was under

arrest. Joel shot and wounded Buffy. Nancy was arrested two weeks later.

If Nancy and Joel are charged with assault, which of the following is most accurate?

(A)   Neither is guilty.

(B)   Both are guilty.

(C)   Only Joel is guilty, because his arrest terminated the partnership between himself and Nancy.

(D)   Only Joel is guilty, because the shooting was not approved by Nancy nor did it advance any other interests.

154.   Regina was released from prison on probation after serving ten years of a sixteen-year sentence. Regina was required to meet with her probation officer every two weeks. She was not permitted to leave the country.

Regina kept to her probation terms and got a good job. She met and fell in love with a man named Alfred, but never told him of her past life of crime. One day Alfred told Regina, "Surprise! I purchased tickets for us to fly to the Caribbean Island of Grenada for the weekend." "But I don't have a passport," Regina replied. "U.S. citizens don't need a passport to enter Grenada." Regina and Alfred flew to Grenada. A violation of the terms of probation is a felony in the jurisdiction.

If Alfred is charged with being an accessory to violating probation terms, he should be found

(A)   not guilty, because he did not force Regina to leave the country

(B)   not guilty, because he lacked the *mens rea* required for aiding and abetting a criminal

(C)   guilty, because he encouraged Regina to violate the law

(D)   guilty, because he was present when the crime was committed

155.   Defendant admitted taking Jeweler's watch in his trial for robbery. Defendant claimed that he took the watch from a display case when Jeweler was not looking and walked out of the store. Jeweler claimed that Defendant threatened to "break" his face if he did not give him the watch.

The jury may return a verdict of

(A)   robbery only

(B)   larceny only

(C)   either robbery or larceny

(D)   both robbery and larceny

156.   Lefty checked into the Holiday Den, a quiet hotel situated off an interstate highway exit. After a week, Manager, an employee of Holiday Den, became very suspicious of Lefty, who wore only white suits, black shirts, and broad-rimmed hats. Lefty also carried several violin cases back and forth from his car to his room.

Manager and the owner of Holiday Den arranged with the local rackets squad to have Lefty's room bugged. Using the tapes, a search warrant was obtained. A stockpile of automatic weapons was discovered.

At trial, Lefty objected to the admission of the guns as evidence. The trial judge should rule the evidence obtained pursuant to the search warrant

(A)   admissible, because the warrant was validly issued with probable cause shown

(B)   admissible, because Holiday Den may allow surveillance of its own premises

(C)   not admissible, because a violin case and one's taste in clothing are not inherently suspicious

(D)   not admissible, because Lefty's privacy was improperly invaded

CRIMINAL LAW/PROCEDURE ANSWERS

1. (B)   Miranda warnings are only necessary when an admission is made during custodial questioning. Whether questioning is custodial is determined by whether the person had the ability to leave. Spoiled was not in custody, hence, the admission did not need to be preceded by Miranda warnings. (A) is too vague to be the correct answer. If Spoiled had volunteered the statement in a custodial setting without a Miranda warning, it would not be admissible.

     (D) is incorrect because Spoiled was not in any way coerced into giving a statement.

2. (D)   Use of older reference materials can get you in trouble on this question. (A), (B), and (C) would have been correct under *Doyle v. Ohio*, 426 U.S. 610 (1976). This case was overturned by *Green v. Miller*, 55 U.S.L.W. 5126 (1987). The court ruled that a question concerning a defendant's post-arrest silence did not violate due process if immediately objected to, and if the court immediately issued curative instructions.

3. (A)   Under the common law, self-defense is an affirmative defense that must be demonstrated by the defendant by a preponderance of the evidence. This rule has been retained by Ohio and South Carolina. The Supreme Court recently affirmed the right of Ohio and South Carolina to follow the common law rule. In all other states, the prosecution must disprove a self-defense claim if raised by a defendant.

4. (D)   Since the baby was in Jane's womb when Larry harmed it, the baby is not legally considered a "human being"; therefore, Larry should not be found guilty of any of the listed offenses. The majority view is that a fetus becomes a human being when it is born and establishes "independent circulation." Some states (i.e., California) have enacted statutes to make the killing of a fetus murder.

5. (A)   The failure to act may constitute a breach of legal duty. A defendant will be found criminally liable if he was under a duty imposed by (1) statute, (2) a special relationship, (3) a voluntary obligation of responsibility, or (4) contract. The obligation must be proved beyond a reasonable doubt. In this case, Eddie voluntarily undertook the responsibility to care for the baby. (C) is what the prosecution must prove, it is not its best argument. Although one is not generally under a duty to rescue a stranger (Choice D), the infant was not a stranger to Eddie.

6. (D)   Intoxication may be raised to negate an element of a crime, usually intent. Rape is defined as unlawful, nonconsensual carnal knowledge of a woman by a man who is

not her husband. Intent is not an element of the crime; therefore, the defendant's intoxication will not be a defense to rape.

7.   (A)   Assault is the intentional creation of a reasonable fear in a victim that she is in danger of imminent bodily harm. While Randolph might be guilty of assault, every state also has an aggravated assault statute, which is a more serious crime. Aggravated assault includes assault with a deadly weapon and assault with the intent to rape or murder. Since the testimony that the Avon Lady manifested assent to the sexual act was accepted by the jury, Randolph cannot be convicted of rape, because rape requires penetration without consent. The elements of a kidnapping were not present. Kidnapping requires movement or concealment of the victim.

8.   (C)   Under the Miranda rule, a person must be informed of his rights to remain silent, to presence of counsel, and to the appointment of counsel at public expense, and told that his statements may be used against him. This rule applies only when the interrogation takes place in custody. (C) is the correct answer (least persuasive) because the Supreme Court has held [*Colorado v. Spring*, 1987] that the defendant need not be told the subject the authorities intend to question him about even if charges are not related. Justice Powell noted that the Miranda warnings inform a suspect that "anything" he says may be used against him. (A) is not correct, because one may be considered "in custody" although in his own home. In *Orozco v. Texas* (1969), the court held that a person questioned in his bedroom at 4:00 a.m. was deprived of his freedom of action and, therefore, was in custody for Miranda purposes. (B) is incorrect because when a person is confined to jail for any reason, regardless of its relationship to the subject matter of the questioning, that person is in custody and Miranda will apply [*Mathis v. United States* (1968)]. Although (D) is not a persuasive argument, it is more persuasive than (C) because it is true that Miranda applies to both inculpatory and exculpatory statements. An inculpatory statement is one tending to establish guilt, while an exculpatory statement tends to exonerate guilt. The Court in *Connecticut v. Barrett* (1987) ruled that police may question a suspect after he says he is willing to make an oral statement but not a written statement.

9.   (C)   One may be an accomplice to a crime although unable to be charged as a principal in the first degree. Edith could not have raped the young woman, but she can be charged as an accomplice to rape. The Model Penal Code Section 2.06 defines an accomplice as a person who with the purpose of promoting or facilitating the commission of an offense 1) solicits another person to commit it, 2) aids or agrees or attempts to aid another person in planning or committing it, or 3) having a legal duty to prevent the commission of an offense, fails to make proper effort to do so. Edith aided Stuart in the rape. (A) and (B) are incorrect because members of a limited class may not be accomplices against laws passed for their protection. Elise, (Choice D), did not solicit Saunder to commit the crime for which he was prosecuted.

He decided to buy the crack of his own volition; therefore, she was not an accomplice to that crime.

10. (C) Common law larceny consists of a taking and carrying away of personal property of another by trespass with intent to deprive. Frederick's actions constituted common law larceny; therefore, (D) is not correct. Burglary at common law was a breaking and entry into the dwelling of another at night with the intent to commit a felony. Arson at common law was the malicious burning of the dwelling of another. Frederick did not commit common law burglary or arson, because the Chrysler dealer is a business establishment and not a "dwelling." Modern statutes have extended both statutes by omitting the element "dwelling"; therefore, the answer is (C).

11. (B) Joe is guilty as an accomplice of the murder of the witness inside the house. An accomplice is liable for any probable or foreseeable result of a crime that he has assisted under the felony murder rule. (A) is correct; Joe will be liable for the attempt on his boss's life, but murder is a more serious offense than attempted murder.

12. (D) Donna is guilty of robbery, a felony, defined by the Model Penal Code Section 222.1 as: in the course of committing a theft 1) inflicting serious bodily injury upon another, or 2) threatening another with or purposely putting another in fear of immediate serious bodily injury, or 3) committing or threatening to commit any felony of the first or second degree. Fawn is guilty of receiving stolen property, a misdemeanor defined by the Model Penal Code Section 223.6 as: purposely receiving, retaining, or disposing of movable property of another knowing that it has been stolen, or believing that it probably has been stolen, unless the property is held with the intention of restoring it to the true owner.

The Multistate people like to trick you with fine-line distinctions. They want you to choose (C). There are three basic elements necessary to render a person an accessory after the fact: 1) a complete **felony** must have been committed, 2) the aider must have knowledge of the crime, and 3) the aid must be given with the purpose of impeding law enforcement. Since receiving stolen property is a **misdemeanor**, Jessica could not be an accessory after the fact for helping to hide Fawn.

13. (B) At common law, extortion was a misdemeanor defined as the unlawful collection of a fee by an officer abusing his office. Most modern statutes have expanded extortion to include the unlawful obtaining of property by means of verbal threats. Robbery requires that the threats be for (1) immediate and (2) physical harm, or (3) harm to the victim's home. Statutory extortion allows prosecution for the threat of future harm and harm to chattel.

14.   (C)   In order to be guilty of an offense, a person must have knowledge that he has committed the prohibited act. People will generally not be held strictly liable for acts they did not know they were committing. Since John was unaware that he was carrying explosives, he cannot be prosecuted for possessing them.

Larceny is defined as a trespass by the taking and carrying away of the property of another with intent to deprive the owner of that property. For larceny to have occurred the offender must have interfered with the victim's "possession" of the property as distinguished from the "custody" of it. A few examples of the distinction between legal possession and custody are: a bailor will be in constructive possession of goods in the custody of a bailee, an employer is in constructive possession of goods in the custody of the employee, and the loser of property is in constructive possession of that property if it is in the "custody" of a finder who intends to convert it. When John took the bag from Jan he obtained custody of it, and she retained possession; he then carried it away with the intent to steal it, making him guilty of larceny.

Larceny by trick has occurred where the true owner willingly surrenders **possession** of the property under false pretenses. John never obtained possession of the luggage, he only had custody; therefore he has not committed larceny by trick.

The constructive possession doctrine does not apply to property given to an employee or a bailee by a third person to be held for the employer or bailor. A taking of this property with the intent to convert it is the crime of embezzlement, not larceny, because the offender had the legal possession of the property.

15.   (D)   At common law a husband and wife could not be found guilty of conspiracy, because the law considered them to be one person. They could commit conspiracy with a third party. Although this rule has been abandoned, the question clearly asks for the common law rule, a common Multistate ploy.

Penetration is sufficient to satisfy the requirements of rape; emission is not required. If a victim is tricked into believing an act is not intercourse even though it was, rape has been committed, because the intercourse was nonconsensual.

16.   (D)   This question presents a fine-line distinction between depraved-heart murder and involuntary manslaughter. Both offenses involve (1) an unintentional killing (2) caused by a negligent act. The difference between the two is the degree of negligence. Under depraved-heart murder, the defendant should have known his actions created a very high degree of danger and risk. Involuntary manslaughter is satisfied by lesser degree of negligence than depraved-heart murder. In this question, a reasonable person would realize that another person was likely to enter the tunnel; therefore, Kenneth can be convicted of murder. Had Kenneth shot the pistol in the same place at 3:00 a.m., when the stadium was deserted, and killed a homeless person sleeping in the tunnel, he would probably be guilty of the lesser charge of involuntary manslaughter.

17. (C)   For this question, students should be able to distinguish between murder, voluntary manslaughter, and involuntary manslaughter. Murder is the unlawful killing of a human being with malice aforethought. Under the depraved-heart murder rule, extremely negligent conduct resulting in death that a reasonable person would know creates a high risk of death is murder. Defendant should be charged with murder in (B) and (D) under this rule. Voluntary manslaughter is an intentional killing prompted by an adequate provocation. Most courts have only recognized two types of provocation: (1) exposure to deadly force and (2) discovery of a spouse in bed with a stranger (Choice A). Involuntary manslaughter (Choice C) involves criminal negligence or an unlawful act causing death. Involuntary manslaughter is an appropriate charge when a reasonable person would not have assumed the action might result in death. In our case, defendant was reasonable in assuming a person would not be in a moving UPS truck's trailer. Therefore, Defendant should be charged with involuntary manslaughter. Had he fired at a passenger bus, it would have been a depraved-heart murder.

18. (B)   Larceny is a trespass in the taking and carrying away of the property of another with intent to deprive the person of that property. At common law this property needed to be personal. Realty, natural resources attached to the land, and fixtures could not be the subject of larceny unless the object was first removed from the land and later stolen, not if the removal and theft occurred together. If the landowner gains possession of the severed property, the property becomes personal and susceptible to larceny. Most states have enacted statutes to provide that larceny can be committed in respect to any property that can be moved. Abe removed and carried away fixtures from the land in a manner not culpable of common law larceny. Howie removed trees that had already become personal property and the subjects of larceny.

19. (D)   Larceny, at common law, is defined as a trespass by the taking and carrying away of the corporal personal property of another with intent to deprive the person of that property. At common law, intangibles could not give rise to larceny; therefore, entering the baseball stadium did not constitute larceny. At common law, unless documents and instruments had intrinsic value they would not be the subject of larceny. By taking the deed, Mark did not obtain title to Dump's Casino; therefore, he did not commit larceny. Forgery is the making or altering of a false writing with intent to defraud. A subject of forgery must have a legal significance, such as a deed or contract. Writings that derive their value by the fact of their existence, such as writings of historical or artistic value, cannot be the subject of forgery. Mark's poster is valued for its historic value; therefore, it could not be the subject of forgery. He may be liable if charged with misrepresentation, depending on what he said at the time of the sale. Statement 4 is correct because theft of services is not larceny under common law. Many states have made it a crime by statute.

20.   (A)   Larceny is a trespass by the taking and removing of property from the possession of another without consent and with the intent to steal that property. James's actions satisfied all the requisite elements of larceny. Larceny is the only one of the listed offenses that James could be convicted of and therefore is also the most serious offense of which he should be convicted. (B) is inapplicable because robbery is a taking of the personal property of another directly from that person by force or intimidation. (C) and (D) are not applicable, because burglary is defined, at common law, as a breaking and entry into the **dwelling** of another at night with the intent to commit a felony. A structure is a dwelling if used regularly for sleeping, even if those sleeping in the dwelling are temporarily absent. A building is not considered a dwelling if unoccupied by residents. In this question, Boca Towers would not be considered a dwelling, and James could not be found guilty of burglary.

21.   (C)   Battery is an unlawful use of force against another, resulting in bodily injury or an offensive contact. Many statutes distinguish between battery, a misdemeanor, and aggravated battery, a felony. Battery becomes aggravated if a deadly weapon is used or serious bodily injury is caused, or if the victim is a child, police officer, or woman. Intent is not an element of the criminal charge of battery; therefore, Larry should be found guilty of aggravated battery. Larceny is the taking and transporting of property from another by trespass with the **intent** to permanently deprive that person of the property. The key to this question is intent. Larry's intoxication was voluntary, and voluntary intoxication may be a defense to a crime that requires intent if the intoxication made the perpetrator incapable of forming such intent. Although Larry took the jacket, he was so intoxicated that he might not have intended to effectuate a deprivation.

22.   (B)   Robbery is the taking of personal property from another's presence by force or intimidation with intent to permanently deprive the owner. Harry's intoxication provides an excuse to the charge of robbery because he might not have had the requisite intent. Rape is the unlawful carnal knowledge of a woman by a man other than her husband, without the woman's consent. Intent is not an element of rape; therefore, voluntary intoxication will not excuse a charge of rape.

23.   (C)   Ignorance or a mistake of fact may excuse an action otherwise a crime by negating the state of mind required. For a crime requiring a general intent the mistake must be reasonable. For a specific intent crime any mistake of fact will excuse the action whether reasonable or not. Embezzlement is a specific intent crime. The elements of embezzlement are a 1) fraudulent 2) conversion of 3) the property 4) of another 5) by one who is already in lawful possession of it. Cosby had been a bailee of the helmet while he was using it, and by that fact he was already in lawful possession of it. Since Cosby believed that the helmet had been given to him (his mistake of fact) he did not act fraudulently. Therefore, he did not commit embezzlement, regardless of the reasonableness of his actions.

24. (C)   Larceny by trick is the (1) taking and transporting of (2) another's personal property (3) when possession of that property was obtained by fraud (4) with intent to steal. For the Multistate exam, students are required to make the fine-line distinctions between larceny by trick, false pretenses, and embezzlement. To satisfy the requirements of larceny by trick, defendant must only obtain possession. False pretenses applies when defendant fraudulently obtains *title*. Defendant must have been given possession under a trust for embezzlement to apply.

25. (D)   Voluntary intoxication is only a defense to a crime when it negates an element of the crime. The elements that it may negate are usually specific intent or knowledge. Rape is an offense that requires only a general intent, and not a specific one. A general intent will be present if the offender intended to perform the "bad act." Corvallis will most likely be found guilty of rape because he intended to have intercourse with her and because his mistaken belief that she consented was unreasonable. Specific intent requires that the offender intended to do even more than the "bad act" actually committed. An honest mistake of fact, no matter how unreasonable, will serve to negate a specific intent. All "attempt" crimes require the specific intent of the offender to commit the entire crime he is charged with attempting. For Corvallis to be convicted of attempted rape he must have had the specific intent to rape Jane. Such intent may be negated by his intoxication and the honest belief that she consented to acquit him of the charge.

26. (D)   The statute was not enacted for safety reasons — its purpose was for conservation. Thus, Darrell was not a member of the class designed to be protected by the statute, and his injury was not proximately caused by the statutory violation. It is for these reasons that (A) and (B) are incorrect. (C) is incorrect because intent is not an element of manslaughter.

27. (C)   In order for a death to qualify as a felony murder, it must have occurred in the process of a felony. Sandra's best course of action is to deny that a felony was committed. A completed robbery would constitute a felony. If Sandra can prove that she was inebriated and lacked the intent to forcefully deprive the gas station of its money, she will have negated a necessary element of a robbery charge. (D) is incorrect because it describes an element of manslaughter.

28. (C)   Although voluntary intoxication will not ordinarily be a valid defense, it may defeat an action by negating intent. Simply said, if a defendant was so drunk that he did not know what he was doing, he could not have formed the requisite intent to commit a crime.

29.   (C)   In this question the statute requires that the burning be done maliciously. This makes maliciousness an element of the crime. If Donna didn't act maliciously she will not be guilty of arson under this statute. She might still be guilty of another crime.

30.   (C)   This is the most logical argument. (A) and (B) cannot be correct, because intent is not an element of arson in the statute. (D) — even if true — would not relieve Donna's culpability.

31.   (C)   A police officer may use deadly force to apprehend a person accused of a felony. Although (D) is correct, it is not the reason why Aaron isn't guilty.

32.   (A)   The police may conduct a search incident to a lawful arrest without a warrant.

33.   (A)   The accused does not have a right to counsel when physical evidence, such as fingerprints, is taken. His right to due process was not violated.

34.   (A)   Handwriting is another type of physical evidence that may be taken before counsel is appointed.

35.   (D)   One has a right to have counsel at a lineup to observe any suggestive aspects of the procedure.

36.   (A)   The voice sample would qualify as physical identification that does not invoke the right to counsel.

37.   (A)   Evidence of prior felonies is admissible in the sentencing following a conviction. The other choices are appropriate if this evidence was admitted prior to conviction.

38.   (D)   The elements of robbery are 1) a taking 2) of personal property of another 3) from the other's person or presence 4) by force or intimidation 5) with intent of permanent deprivation. Don was not successful in using fear or in effectuating a deprivation; thus, the elements of robbery have not been fulfilled, and neither Jon nor Don have committed robbery.

39.   (C)   A person may use deadly force in self-defense if she is without fault in creating the situation, confronted with unlawful force, and threatened with imminent death or

great bodily harm. (A) and (D) are ridiculous; Plumber's response was irrational. (B) is incorrect since the elements required for Al to be guilty of murder are missing.

40.   (C)   Statutory rape is the carnal knowledge of a female under the age of consent. The age of consent generally varies from sixteen to eighteen years old. This is usually a strict liability crime. A mistake as to the woman's age, no matter how reasonable, is not a defense. Rape is the unlawful carnal knowledge of a woman by a man who is not her husband.

41.   (C)   The elements of robbery are 1) a taking 2) of personal property of another 3) from another's presence 4) by force or intimidation 5) with intent to permanently deprive him of it. The element of "force or intimidation" is missing in (C). The prosecution should charge Defendant with larceny in such a fact pattern.

42.   (C)   Conspiracy is an agreement between two or more persons formed with the objective to commit an unlawful act. Tracie and Marc never entered into an agreement to steal a video recorder.

43.   (A)   Dick and Marc fulfilled all the elements of conspiracy as defined in the previous question. (D) is incorrect since the question doesn't involve Tracie. Double jeopardy is the doctrine preventing a defendant from being tried more than once for a single offense.

44.   (C)   Under the common law, withdrawal cannot be a defense to a charge of conspiracy after actually participating in the plan to commit a crime.

45.   (B)   A person may limit her liability for subsequent acts of the other members of a conspiracy if she withdraws. In order to withdraw, she must perform an affirmative act that notifies all members of the conspiracy and gives them an opportunity to abandon their plans. It is not necessary that she thwart the objective of the conspiracy.

46.   (D)   Passerby was trying to rescue Millie and, therefore, assumes her privilege of self-defense. He must have been reasonable in his belief that she was in danger. If Millie had not been in danger and Passerby was unreasonable to believe she needed rescue, he would be liable for battery. Whether a reasonable person would intervene on Millie's behalf is unrelated to the issue of self-defense (Choice C).

47.   (C)   Since conspiracy, by definition, is an agreement, an absence of an agreement will preclude a conspiracy conviction.

48.   (C)   Withdrawal is never a defense to the charge of conspiracy. A conspiracy is an agreement formed between people with the objective of committing an unlawful act. In this question the conspiracy has already taken place and the conspirators may be prosecuted. The liability for subsequent acts of conspirators may be limited by withdrawal, but not the liability for conspiracy. An *actus reus* is a "bad act" that is prohibited by law. The act of conspiring will constitute an *actus reus*.

49.   (A)   An accessory before the fact is one who has aided, abetted, procured, or commanded the commission of a crime, but was not present at the scene.

50.   (D)   Robbery and conspiracy are crimes separate and complete in and of themselves and will not merge.

51.   (C)   Christine would be found guilty of conspiracy to commit larceny because she entered into an agreement with Melinda to carry out their criminal objective. Christine would also be guilty of attempted larceny because she formulated the intent to steal before entering the bookstore. If she had formed the intent to steal after removing the book from the shelf, then the removal of the book from the shelf would have been a non-trespassory taking.

52.   (C)   Melinda should be found guilty of conspiracy to commit larceny because she entered into an agreement with Christine. She should also be found guilty of attempted larceny since she was Christine's accomplice. The crime of attempted larceny was committed when Christine, with intent to steal, took the book from the shelf. She cannot be charged with larceny, because the crime was never completed.

53.   (D)   Rape is the unlawful carnal knowledge of a woman without her consent. If Kathy was resisting, she obviously did not consent. Jim would be guilty of attempt if his act fell short of a crime that he meant to commit.

54.   (B)   Intent is the key here. Assault with intent to rape is a specific intent crime. Jim must have had the state of mind required, because he attempted to have intercourse without regard for Kathy's consent.

55.   (A)   The crime of rape has been committed once there has been a nonconsensual penetration. Jim could be found guilty of rape. He could no longer be charged with attempted rape because the attempted rape merged into the more serious rape charge.

56.   (D)   The statute is vague and overly broad on its face. Under the U.S. Constitution, a criminal statute must provide notice of what constitutes the crime. This statute gives no warning or indication as to what constitutes moral degradation. It will be void for vagueness because the reasonable citizen would have no idea when he or she is violating the law.

57.   (C)   Intent is not an element of the offense. Remember to read all statutes very carefully.

58.   (D)   Statutory rape is the crime of carnal knowledge of a woman under the age of consent. Kathy was under the age of consent. This is a strict liability crime; an honest mistake as to a woman's age is not a defense. However, attempt crimes require specific intent. Therefore, Jim could be acquitted of **attempted** statutory rape if he shows that he did not intend to have sex with a woman under the age of consent.

59.   (A)   The elements of burglary are 1) a breaking and entry 2) into the dwelling of another 3) with the intent to commit a crime inside. Entry obtained by fraud will satisfy the "breaking" requirement of burglary. Henry must have also intended to commit a crime inside; that crime is the theft of Herby's wallet.

60.   (C)   A person may justifiably use deadly force in self-defense if he has a reasonable belief that it is necessary to prevent his own unlawful death or serious bodily harm. However, an initial aggressor, who instigated the attack, is not entitled to self-defense. The amount of force allowed in self-defense must also be in proportion to the threat. The right to use deadly force will generally not be justified against an unarmed aggressor. Gerald reasonably believed that his life was threatened when Seth lunged toward him with a bat.

61.   (B)   Since Broker did not know of Lisa's criminal history, he lacked the mental state (*mens rea*) to assist in a crime.

62.   (B)   The element of "intent to steal" required to satisfy a larceny charge is missing from both of these cases.

63.   (D)   The elements of larceny have been satisfied. The property was taken from the possession of another, without consent and with intent to steal. The key to the similarity between both of these cases is that stealing includes the use of an item.

64.   (D)   Here, again, we have Defendant guilty of larceny for using the property of others.

65.   (A)   The element of the "taking and carrying away of the property of another" is missing, so the defendants should not be found guilty of larceny. They should be prosecuted for embezzlement.

66.   (A)   This is another embezzlement action. Victim voluntarily tendered the $100.

67.   (D)   Charlie was trying to rescue Jane and, therefore, assumes her privilege of self-defense.

68.   (C)   Although voluntary intoxication will not ordinarily be a valid defense, it may defeat an action by negating intent. If Lush was so drunk that he did not know what he was doing, he could not have intended to steal the pretzels.

69.   (C)   Again, voluntary intoxication cannot negate a crime but can negate an element of that crime. In this question the element is "maliciousness." Read the statute in the fact pattern carefully. A quick reading could lead to selecting (B), but "intent" is not mentioned in the statute.

70.   (C)   This is the prosecution's most logical argument.

71.   (D)   The warrantless search behind Vicky's house was illegal, as was turning the basement light on. Both acts were violations of the defendant's expectation of privacy. The evidence would be inadmissible under the exclusionary rule, as "fruits of the poisonous tree."

72.   (C)   Mick would be found guilty of felony murder since the fireman's death resulted as a natural consequence of his felonious conduct. Mick would be held accountable since it was foreseeable that firefighters would come to the house and could be endangered.

(D) is incorrect. Voluntary manslaughter consists of an intentional homicide committed under extenuating circumstances (the rule in most jurisdictions).

73. (D)   An act must be voluntary, or the result of extremely gross behavior, to be considered criminal. Dave's punch was beyond his control.

74. (B)   Since Ann was a member of the conspiracy to commit that crime, she is guilty as an accessory to the crime, even after she withdraws. In order for Ann to have successfully withdrawn from the conspiracy, she must repudiate her encouragement of the crime or she must notify authorities to take some action to prevent the commission of the offense. Her repudiation would be sufficient if it is determined that Ann merely discouraged the commission of the crime. If it is determined that Ann assisted in providing some material (e.g., a car) to Caroll, then Ann would have had to neutralize this assistance in order to have successfully withdrawn (e.g., by notifying authorities before the chain of events leading to the crime became unstoppable).

75. (B)   Joe's shouts were intended to encourage Caroll. Therefore, he is guilty of any crime Caroll commits because he aided and abetted her crime. Actual assistance is not necessary (Choice A), only the attempt to help.

76. (C)   Bo would have had to have taken some positive action or spoken some words of approval in order to be considered part of the conspiracy.

77. (C)   The statute and its definition include the word "attempt." Specific intent is an element of attempt crimes. Since Hugh accidentally lost control, the element of intent was not satisfied.

78. (D)   Justification is a valid defense for battery. Janet was justified in touching Hugh, to prevent more serious injury.

79. (A)   The accused does not have a right to counsel during photo identifications.

80. (D)   An accessory before the fact is responsible for the crimes he did or counseled and for any crimes committed in the course of committing the crime contemplated, so long as the other crimes were probable or foreseeable.

81. (D)   Neighbor did not have authority to use the apartment on New Year's Day, nor did he have the authority to permit a search.

82.   (B)   One has standing to object to a search of his own apartment, regardless of his whereabouts at the time of the search.

83.   (B)   One may not object to an illegal search of the premises of another, even if evidence obtained by the search incriminates him.

84.   (B)   Police may conduct a full search of a person as incident to a lawful arrest, with or without probable cause.

85.   (A)   Ronald is guilty of murder because his actions were the proximate cause of Janet's death. The reasons for his actions and what could have happened are irrelevant.

86.   (C)   The elements of burglary are 1) breaking 2) and entry 3) into the dwelling, 4) of another 5) at night 6) with intent to commit a crime. Jan should assert the defense that she did not intend to commit a felony.
                  (B) is incorrect because opening an unlocked door will constitute "breaking."

87.   (B)   The same reasoning as in the preceding question applies here.

88.   (A)   The parties will not be held guilty of conspiracy, because there was no agreement formed to commit a crime.

89.   (C)   Larceny is the taking and asportation (carrying away) of property from the possession of another person without consent and with intent to steal. The "intent to steal" element was satisfied in this choice. Eugene took a car that he knew belonged to another. A mistake of law, a person's honest belief that his actions do not constitute a crime, is generally not a defense.

90.   (C)   Death caused by criminal negligence is involuntary manslaughter. The negligence must be further from "the reasonable man" standard than required for civil liability. The element of "intent" is missing to invoke voluntary manslaughter. Bobby did not intend to kill anyone.

91.   (B)   Statements are not admissible if made under custodial interrogation without Miranda warnings. Elmoe's statements were voluntary and subsequent to a valid Miranda warning. By volunteering his statements, Elmoe waived his right to counsel for that period of time.

92. (A)   Murder is the unlawful killing of a human being with malice aforethought. Awareness of an unjustifiably high risk to human life will satisfy the malice aforethought element.

93. (C)   The charge may be properly reduced from murder to involuntary manslaughter, based on the degree of recklessness in Debra's actions. Conviction for voluntary manslaughter would not be proper, because the killing was unintentional.

94. (D)   This would satisfy "malice aforethought." The others are obviously false answers.

95. (D)   This question is best answered by eliminating obviously false answers.

96. (C)   Common sense will help for this one. Look at the elements of first-degree murder. Debra should argue that she has not satisfied these elements.

97. (A)   Proving a *prima facie* case shifts the burden to the defendant. The defendant must show that she has not fulfilled the elements brought forth by the prosecution.

98. (C)   Deadly force may be used if the officer reasonably believes it is necessary to effectuate the arrest of a person that he reasonably believes has committed a felony. (A) and (D) are incorrect because a police officer is privileged to use deadly force under certain circumstances. (B) is incorrect because deadly force is not allowed in misdemeanor cases.

99. (A)   Charlie is guilty of murder because his actions were the proximate cause of Regina's death. His motives and what could have happened are irrelevant.

100. (D)   This is the only choice where premeditation and intent are shown. In (A), Harris had intent to injure but not murder. (B) involved the heat of passion and not premeditation. (C) was a case of involuntary murder.

101. (D)   Deadly force may be used if it appears reasonably necessary in order for the officer to effectuate an arrest of a person he reasonably believes committed a felony.

102.   (D)   A private person has the same right to use force to make an arrest as a police officer except that the private person has a valid defense *only* if the person being harmed is actually guilty of the offense for which the arrest is being made.

103.   (C)   Death caused by criminal negligence is involuntary manslaughter. The negligence must be more grievous than the "reasonable man" standard required for civil liability. Since Dave did not intend to kill Mary, the element of "intent" is missing; therefore, he cannot be charged with voluntary manslaughter. For the same reason, Dave could not be convicted of murder.

104.   (C)   The statute specifically provides that the offense must be perpetrated "knowingly." Therefore, knowledge must be an element of the crime. Since the jury believed Chris' story, they must acquit him of the crime.

105.   (D)   An act must be voluntary, or the result of extremely gross behavior, to be criminal. Patrick's kick was beyond his control.

106.   (B)   Bigamy is not a strict liability offense. Only Joan could have had the requisite intent to commit bigamy since she knew she was already legally betrothed. Kevin has a valid defense of mistake of fact because he had no idea that Joan was legally married. He will not be held guilty.

107.   (A)   The Durham test, also called the "but for" test, provides that a defendant is entitled to acquittal if proof establishes that the crime was a product of his mental disease. Under the irresistible impulse test (Choice B), a defendant will be acquitted if, because of his mental illness, he is unable to control his actions. The Model Penal Code provision (Choice C) provides acquittal for one who lacks the capacity to appreciate the criminality of his conduct or to conform his conduct to the law's requirements. Under the M'Naghten Rule (Choice D), a defendant will be acquitted if mental disease left him without the ability to know the wrongfulness of his actions or understand the quality of the actions.

108.   (C)   The evidence was the fruit of an unlawful search because a warrant was not obtained. This question simply tests your knowledge of the obvious.

109.   (C)   Larceny by trick is the taking of property from possession of another, with consent obtained by fraud and with intent to steal. (C) is the only choice satisfying all the elements of the crime charged. (A) is incorrect because larceny requires an intent to steal, and Defendant did not intend to steal the money. The elements of false

pretenses (Choices B and D) are 1) a lie concerning a material fact, 2) intending to defraud the true owner, and 3) causing the owner to transfer title. In (B), the victim did not transfer title, and the loan was repaid. In (D), Defendant originally intended to return the money; therefore, Defendant did not make a misrepresentation.

110. (C)   Since Defendant intended to seriously injure Opponent, he is liable for his act's resulting in death.

111. (B)   A car may not be stopped merely because it is old and has a bumper sticker the police dislike. The search was not valid.

112. (A)   The accused does not have a right to counsel at photo identifications. (D) is irrelevant to the quality of the photo identification. The witness's view of the accident would be important, but not Phillip's.

113. (C)   The elements of robbery are 1) a taking 2) of personal property of another 3) from another's person 4) by force or intimidation 5) with the intent to permanently deprive him of it. The element of "by force or intimidation" was missing. The elements of larceny were all present. They are 1) a taking 2) and carrying away 3) of corporal personal property 4) of another 5) by trespass 6) with intent of permanent deprivation. The value of the notes is irrelevant (Choice D). The law prohibits the theft of worthless property as well as valuable property.

114. (B)   Police may conduct a full search of a person as incident to a lawful arrest with or without probable cause. (D) is incorrect because the question states that the law provides for an arrest for this offense.

115. (A)   Intent to commit a crime is an element of conspiracy. Conspiracy requires an agreement, the object of which is to commit a crime, or requires that a crime be committed. Dee's taking of the wrong car was a mistake of fact. A mistake of law (Choice D) occurs when an offender has misinterpreted the law or was ignorant of the law. Mistake of law will usually not be a valid defense.

116. (D)   Larceny is the taking and asportation (carrying away) of property from the possession of another person without consent, or with consent obtained by fraud, with intent to steal. If Michael honestly believed that the suitcase was his, the element of "intent to steal" would be absent and he would not be guilty of larceny. The fact that the two pieces of luggage resembled each other and that Michael left one behind (Choice C) may help in proving the honest mistake theory, but a person might

mistakenly take luggage not resembling his own or intentionally take luggage resembling his own.

117. (A)   A conspirator is liable for the crimes of a co-conspirator, if the crime was committed in furtherance of the conspiracy, and the crime was a "natural and probable" consequence of the conspiracy. Although Aleph and Bet agreed not to carry weapons, (B) is incorrect because it is probable that a death might result during the course of such a crime. Aleph and Bet cannot use self-defense to justify the death (Choice D), because they were at fault as the initial aggressors.

118. (D)   The warrantless entry into the back yard was illegal as a violation of the defendant's expectation of privacy. The evidence is inadmissible under the exclusionary rule, as "fruits of the poisonous tree."

119. (B)   The prosecution has the burden of proving all elements of a crime beyond a reasonable doubt to obtain a conviction. A killing is not presumed to be murder (Choice C).

120. (B)   Under the M'Naghten rule, a defendant is entitled to acquittal if he proved that he possessed a disease of the mind that caused a defect of reason, causing the defendant to either 1) not know the wrongfulness of his actions or 2) not understand the nature and quality of his actions.

121. (C)   A defendant is entitled to acquittal under the irresistible impulse test if he is able to establish that, because of mental illness, he was unable to control his actions to conform to the law.

122. (C)   Hinkley will be guilty of murder in any of the other situations. In regard to (A), (B), and (D), a wrongdoer is responsible for any unusual conditions that make the victim susceptible to suffer worse consequences. In (C) the death was independently caused by the fire. Hinkley would still have been guilty of murder if the receptionist was at death's door at the time of the fire.

123. (D)   One is liable for the crimes of other conspirators provided the crimes were committed in furtherance of the conspiracy's objectives and the crimes were a natural and probable outcome of the conspiracy. Alex's killing was not related to the conspiracy, even though it occurred while the conspiracy was still viable (Choice A). (B) is false. (C) is incorrect because if the killing had been related to the conspiracy Bruce would be liable despite the fact that the killing was unplanned.

124.   (D)   The elements of robbery are 1) a taking 2) of personal property of another 3) from the other's person or presence 4) by force or intimidation 5) with intent to permanently deprive the person. The man's lack of fear made Sally unsuccessful in using force or intimidation. Therefore, she did not commit a robbery. If Sally did not commit a robbery, Susan cannot be liable for the same. (A) and (B) are incorrect because a co-conspirator is liable for the actions of other conspirators acting in furtherance of the conspiracy.

125.   (C)   The statute demands "knowledge." Martha did not obtain that knowledge. The reasons for her intoxication are not relevant.

126.   (C)   The fact pattern used a duplicate of the Model Penal Code Section 4.01 provision stating, "A person is not responsible for criminal conduct if at the time of such conduct as a result of a mental disease of defect he lacks substantial capacity either to appreciate the criminality [wrongfulness] of his conduct or to conform his conduct to the requirements of law." The Model Penal Code standard includes the M'Naghten Rule (Choice D), which provides for acquittal if mental disease left the defendant without the ability to know the wrongfulness of his actions or to understand the quality of the actions, and the irresistible impulse test (Choice B), which provides that a defendant will be acquitted if because of his mental illness he is unable to control his actions. However, (C) is the correct answer since the standard used by the trier of fact is most closely in accordance with the Model Penal Code. The Durham test (Choice A) provides that a defendant is entitled to acquittal if it is established that his crime was a product of mental disease or defect.

127.   (B)   Embezzlement is the conversion of property held pursuant to a trust agreement, using the property in a way inconsistent with the terms of that trust, and with intent to defraud. Larceny is defined as the taking and carrying away of corporal personal property of another by trespass with intent to deprive that person of the property. False pretenses involves the taking of property fraudulently.

128.   (B)   The elements of embezzlement have still been satisfied.

129.   (C)   This law has an exception for people with a "reasonable belief" that they have been divorced. Both a mistake of fact or a mistake of law qualify as a reasonable belief. Normally only a mistake of fact will qualify as a valid defense.

130.   (A)   If the Act of 1985 was valid there was no law requiring an import duty be paid on Virgin Island Rum. Individuals cannot be charged with the attempt to violate a law

that does not exist. This is the doctrine of legal impossibility. Although Elizabeth believed she was committing a crime, people may not be prosecuted for "bad" thoughts alone. There must be an accompanying "bad act."

131. (B)   Bookie does not have standing to challenge the search, despite the fact that the evidence is being used against him. The search, not the stopping of the car, was improper because the officer had no reason to suspect that Gregory had violated the law. Only Gregory may prevent the evidence from being used.

132. (A)   A "principal in the first degree" is one with the requisite mental state who actually engages in an act or omission that causes a criminal result. Anyone who acts through an innocent agent (in the manner that June acted through April) will be classified as principal in the first degree. To be an accessory before the fact (Choice D), April would have had to participate in June's plans. Since April was free of any knowledge-able involvement she cannot be an accessory to the crime.

133. (B)   Statements are admissible if made under custodial interrogation after Miranda warnings. Ida's statements were voluntary and subsequent to a valid Miranda warning. By speaking without counsel present she waived her objection.

134. (B)   Repeal of an offense negates any action for attempt of the repealed offense regardless of Defendant's intent. This is called legal impossibility. You cannot be convicted of a law that does not exist. Each of the other choices are bungled attempts at violating a law that is in effect.

135. (B)   These are both classic manslaughter cases. The killings will be ruled manslaughter because they were committed in the heat of passion.

136. (C)   In both cases the defendant will be held guilty of murder. Harm was planned and intended, and a killing resulted.

137. (D)   There was no conspiracy between Rupt and Roller to violate the statute. The language of the statute clearly places all obligations on Rupt. The legislature would need to have intended to hold criminally liable the givers of the gifts for Roller to be prosecuted.

138. (B)   The remoteness in time of the Wild Bill-Julius drug deal would make Wild Bill's testimony insufficient grounds upon which to issue a search warrant. Since the

warrant was not valid, the evidence is not admissible. Under average circumstances, (D) will be correct. How else would prosecutors prove their cases? (C) is incorrect because the jury (or other trier of fact) determines a witness's reliability.

139. (C)   Defendant is liable for the unforeseen consequences of his illegal act. Intent is lacking under (A). Defendant may assert self-defense to (B). In (D), the statute was not enacted to prevent death and no "bad" intent or gross negligence was shown.

140. (C)   Conspiracy is an agreement between two or more persons with intent to enter into an agreement and intent to achieve the unlawful objective of the agreement. Shop and Jean never entered into any agreement to steal a car.

141. (B)   Defendant began performing the crime when he started climbing the fence into the dealership. He also had the intent necessary to be guilty of attempt. (D) is irrelevant. (A) merely proves that Defendant had the necessary mental state.

142. (D)   Common law murder is the unlawful killing of a human being with malice aforethought. Malice aforethought is an intent to kill or inflict great bodily injury, awareness of an unjustifiably high risk to human life, or an intent to commit a felony. The level below murder is voluntary manslaughter, an intentional killing caused by adequate provocation. (A) involves voluntary manslaughter. (B) and (C) involve either involuntary manslaughter or extremely negligent conduct.

143. (C)   A search conducted in accordance with a plan, whereby some cars are systematically stopped, is valid. Since the marijuana was seen pursuant to a valid search, the police were then empowered to arrest Joseph and further search him.

144. (C)   Larceny is the taking and carrying away of property from the possession of another, without consent or with consent obtained by fraud, with intent to steal that property. There was no intent to steal in these two cases.

145. (B)   All the elements of larceny are satisfied here.

146. (B)   Defendant's actions were nasty, but not the cause of Harry's death. The fact that Harry would have died from more blows but for the cancer will not impose liability for murder on Defendant. Defendant had not delivered those additional blows that would have killed Harry.

147. (C)   The M'Naghten Insanity Test provides that a defendant is entitled to assert the defense of insanity if the proof establishes that the defendant had a disease of the mind causing a defect of reason such that the defendant lacked the ability, at the time of his actions, to either know the wrongfulness of his actions (Choice C) or understand the nature (Choice A) and the quality (Choice B) of his actions. (A) and (B) are both partially correct, but a failure to understand the nature of the action will not satisfy the test without a failure to understand the quality of the action and vice versa.

148. (D)   Intoxication is not a valid defense; however, if a defendant is not capable of forming the "intent" necessary for a crime his intoxication will prevent liability.

149. (D)   The fact pattern is a duplicate of the M'Naghten rule. Under the Durham Test (Choice A), a defendant is entitled to acquittal if proof establishes that his crime was a product of mental disease or defect. A crime is a "product" of the disease if it would not have occurred "but for" the disease. Under the irresistible impulse test (Choice B), a defendant will be acquitted if, because of his mental illness, he is unable to control his actions. The Model Penal Code provision (Choice C), provides acquittal for one who lacks the capacity to appreciate the criminality of his conduct or conform this conduct to the law's requirements.

150. (C)   The elements of burglary are 1) a breaking and 2) entry 3) into the dwelling 4) of another 5) at night 6) with the intent of committing a felony. Coleman did not commit a breaking. The mere fact that he was uninvited does not automatically mean that a breaking occurred (Choice B).

151. (A)   Since Leon took the property of another, he has committed larceny. Neither force nor fear were employed to obtain possession; therefore, Leon has not committed a burglary. Even though the item taken was a dead, smelly skunk, it was property nonetheless and capable of being stolen.

152. (B)   Janet's testimony was an indirect result of Fran's grand jury testimony.

153. (B)   Since the shooting was the result of the conspiracy, both parties should be held liable.

154. (B)   Since Alfred did not know of Regina's history, he lacked the mental state (*mens rea*) to assist in a crime.

155. (C)   The difference between larceny and robbery is that robbery is accomplished by the use of force. The jury could return a verdict of either larceny or robbery, depending on who they believe. (D) is not correct, because a conviction for both crimes is impossible. Larceny would be merged into the more serious crime of robbery.

156. (D)   Electronic surveillance is a "search and seizure" requiring a warrant. Holiday Den did not possess any rights capable of defeating Lefty's expectations of privacy.

CONTRACTS CONTENTS

CONTRACTS QUESTIONS

Questions 1-2 are based upon the following fact situation.

International Nose Cones (INC) contracted with Total Destruction Bombers (TDB) to design a nose cone for the B-2 bomber. TDB had just received a two-trillion-dollar contract from the Pentagon to produce a B-2 prototype. The INC-TDB contract provided that INC would receive a twenty-nine-million-dollar payment within ninety days after a wind tunnel test and other procedures confirmed that the finished nose cone complied with all of the specific technical requirements.

On June 1, INC cabled TDB: "Final test completed on nose cone, will expect payment within ninety days."

On July 1, the federal government notified TDB that all weapons systems development was suspended for two years, due to budgetary restrictions, and that payment would not be made for systems under development but not yet completed.

TDB's legal department advised management that they had grounds for a successful action against the federal government based on breach of contract. Management decided not to sue, fearing it would affect the likelihood of receiving a contract to supply Sri Lanka's Sinhalese Tamil rebels with arms. TDB notified INC that due to the government's new policy, it intended to cancel the nose cone contract because it could not afford to pay for the nose cone.

1. In an action brought by INC against TDB, which of the following statements is the best answer?

    (A) INC will not recover.

    (B) INC will recover costs incurred thus far.

    (C) INC will recover market value.

    (D) INC will recover the full contract price.

2. INC consults its counsel about asserting an action against the federal government for breaching its agreement with TDB. Should counsel advise INC to file suit?

    (A) Yes, because there was privity of contract between INC as a creditor beneficiary and the federal government.

    (B) Yes, because INC was a third-party beneficiary to the TDB-federal government agreement.

    (C) No, because the federal government-TDB agreement did not create an obligation to INC.

    (D) No, because a non-party to a contract may not enforce such agreement against a party who ultimately did not benefit from the agreement.

3. Todd owned a yacht, but he had become dissatisfied with it. Todd was infatuated with the magnificent yacht owned by Ron, who rented an

adjacent slip at the dock. Todd let Ron know that if and when Ron decides to sell his yacht, Todd will be interested in purchasing it. Several months later, Ron called Todd and told him, "Good news, I'm buying a real boat. You can have my scrap heap for $650,000."

"You have a deal," said an excited Todd. Ron immediately sent a letter confirming transfer of ownership of his yacht in three weeks for a price of $650,000 and signed it "Sincerely, Ron."

Ron's yacht was only one year old. Conforming models were still in limited distribution by its manufacturer, Uniform Yachts.

Several days later, Ron's wife Ronnie confessed that she had been having an affair with Todd. Ron immediately called Todd and said, "Our deal is off. You can have my wife, but never my boat. Not at any price." An identical boat was listed for sale at one million dollars. Todd asserted an action demanding specific performance. Is Todd likely to prevail?

(A) No, because the agreement did not satisfy the relevant Statute of Frauds.

(B) Yes, because there was an offer and acceptance.

(C) No, because there is an adequate remedy at law.

(D) Yes, because Ron's letter satisfied the requirement of a writing.

4. On October 19, 1987, a day that became known as "Black Monday," stock markets across the world plunged. The Dow Jones Industrial Average, which gauges the value of thirty New York Stock Exchange "Blue Chip" issues, declined more than 500 points. This represents 20 percent of its value.

Investor enjoyed the view of Riverside Park as he listened to the business reports on the radio. It was autumn, the leaves on the trees had changed their colors, the day was sunny with a refreshing breeze, but as Investor looked past the park to the Hudson River and the New Jersey high-rise buildings, he wondered if people would be jumping out of their windows, as they did in 1929.

At 2 p.m., Investor decided to sell his entire portfolio. He dialed his broker but the line was busy. For the next half-hour, Investor kept redialing his broker's number but could not get through. At 2:30 p.m., Investor heard a report that many people could not reach their swamped brokers. Those who did reach their brokers still could not sell their stocks because buyers were nowhere to be found.

"My God, my stocks are worthless! I better pull my money out of the bank before the banks go, too," Investor thought.

Investor ran to his bank, withdrew $100,000, stuffed the cash in his attaché case, and ran home. When he arrived home, he heard a report that the dollar had fallen to postwar lows against the Japanese yen, Swiss franc, and German mark. On that basis, Investor decided to trade in his cash for gold.

"I'd better buy some gold before this green is worthless," Investor thought. He was too exhausted to run around any more so he made Larry, his building's doorman, a proposition.

"Larry, I need your help. I have to invest in gold. I'll pay you $5,000 if you take this money downtown to Goldco and buy as many one-ounce Canadian gold coins as they'll give you. Don't worry about the door, I'll open it for whoever comes by," Investor said.

Larry agreed to the deal, hailed a cab, and went to Goldco to find that their supply of Canadian coins had already been depleted. He could not contact Investor because the apartment house's lobby did not have a phone. Larry decided to buy one-ounce South African Krugerands instead. The Krugerands were composed of the same percentage of gold as the Canadian coins. When Larry returned with the coins, Investor told him, "I can't believe you did this. I refuse to lend my support to apartheid. Forget about the money I promised you."

In an action asserted by Larry against Investor, the trial judge should rule that Larry's purchase of Krugerands

(A) failed to satisfy a condition precedent

(B) effected a rescission

(C) was a justifiable modification

(D) was conditional on satisfaction

5. Jeremy signed a contract with Grand Prix Motors, a local Ronzoni car dealer, on January 1. The price of the car was $42,000, including options, license fees, taxes, and dealer preparation. Jeremy gave a certified check for $4,000 to Grand Prix as a deposit and was told by a salesman, "Delivery time varies, but it should take no longer than three months." Later that day, as was its custom, Grand Prix contracted to pay Ronzoni Motors, a Balogna company, $32,000 to procure the car it had promised to Jeremy. Ronzoni promised delivery on February 28.

On January 15, Enzo Ronzoni, the president of Ronzoni Motors, who was afraid to fly, died in a train crash en route to a race in Monaco. A public concern that the Ronzoni cars in production might decrease in quality due to Enzo's death caused the demand for the cars to plummet. Jeremy notified Grand Prix that he wanted to cancel his order. Grand Prix notified Ronzoni that it could not accept delivery of the car Jeremy had ordered because of Jeremy's actions. Ronzoni Motors asserted an action against Jeremy based on Jeremy's failure to honor his contract with Grand Prix. Which of the following assertions would most aid Jeremy's defense?

(A) The order was subject to Jeremy's satisfaction.

(B) Ronzoni was not an intended beneficiary of the contract.

(C)   Jeremy contracted for a car built under Enzo's supervision, and his death rendered the contract's performance impossible.

(D)   The proper suit is between Ronzoni and Grand Prix because Grand Prix has a deeper pocket.

6.   Drillco manufactured parts for offshore oil rigs. Some of the parts were custom-made for specific rigs, while other standard parts were also made by the company.

        On August 1, Hopefourstrike, a company that specializes in offshore drilling, signed an agreement to purchase "all of the filters Drillco produces, for twelve months at a price of $300 per filter. Drillco guarantees to produce 500 filters per month at a minimum. Any modification to this agreement must be in writing." Moments after signing the agreement, the parties orally agreed that in September the production minimum would be 1,000 filters. On August 18, Iraqi bombers destroyed Fahesti Filter Works, Iran's major producer of oil drilling filters. Iran responded by attacking Assadfilco, Iraq's oil filter state monopoly. Worldwide prices of the filters quadrupled. On August 21, Hopefourstrike cabled Drillco to confirm September delivery of 1,000 filters at $300 per unit. Drillco did not respond to the cable.

        Hopefourstrike then called Drillco. In this conversation, Hopefourstrike agreed to accept 1,000 filters in September at $600 per filter. On September 15,

Hopefourstrike received 1,000 filters and immediately sent a check in the amount of $300,000 to Drillco. Drillco asserted an action for $300,000 against Hopefourstrike. Which of the following arguments will be most helpful to Hopefourstrike?

(D)   The Parol Evidence Rule will not allow admission of the modifications.

(B)   The modifications were void because the Statute of Frauds applies to contracts for the sale of goods valued above $500.

(C)   The UCC requires that these modifications be in writing and signed by Drillco.

(D)   The price modification will fail because it was not supported by consideration.

7.   A symbiotic relationship existed between several small stores located in the Smallsville Mall and the two large department stores at either end of the mall. Persons walking from one large department store to the other often patronized the smaller stores. The small stores attracted customers to the large stores and provided an atmosphere that made shopping more pleasant.

        O'Reilly's, one of the large stores, was experiencing terrible financial difficulties and was thinking of closing. Fearful that the closing of O'Reilly's would be a fatal blow to the entire mall, the owners of eight small stores and O'Reilly's entered into an agreement that provided, "In consideration of O'Reilly's agreement not to close their Smallsville Mall Store for at least five years, the owners of the other stores in the mall agree that O'Reilly's will no longer have to pay for maintenance of the mall's common areas."

At the time the contract was signed, the small store owners assumed "common areas" included only the interior of the mall. O'Reilly's owners assumed the agreement covered the mall's interior, exterior, and parking areas, a significant expense in the winter. Industry custom includes parking areas when contracting to maintain common areas. Which of the following statements is correct?

(A) The parties will be obligated to perform in a manner conforming with the small store owners' understanding.

(B) The parties will be obligated to perform in a manner conforming with O'Reilly's understanding.

(C) The parties will be obligated to perform, and the court will decide the industry definition of "common areas."

(D) The agreement is null and void.

8. On January 1, 1985, Forest City, a developer of shopping centers, signed a contract with Social Insurance to insure the San Andreas Shopping Center, a two-year-old complex located near Los Angeles. The agreement provided for a maximum of $75,000,000 in coverage in exchange for a monthly premium of $5,000 to be paid by Forest City by the fifteenth day of every month. The agreement provided that "This contract may not be assigned."

On January 1, 1986, Forest City decided to raise $17,000,000 in cash for a new project. The money, raised by issuing debentures and additional common stock, was underwritten by Tuna Brothers, a Wall Street brokerage firm. Tuna received $1,700,000 in cash, warrants, and assignment of all proceeds from Forest City's earthquake insurance in exchange for its services. The earthquake that struck Southern California in October of 1987 caused $7,000,000 in damages to the San Andreas Shopping Center. At the time of the accident, Forest City had not paid Social any of its insurance premiums. Will Tuna Brothers recover $7,000,000 from Social Insurance?

(A) Yes, because Social's obligation to pay was independent of Forest City's obligation to pay.

(B) Yes, because the agreements contained adequate consideration.

(C) No, because of the anti-assignment clause.

(D) No, because Forest City was behind in its payments.

GO ON TO THE NEXT PAGE

9.   Glaser was hired by Eastwood to install the windows in the new mayor's mansion that was under construction on a cliff overlooking Carmel Beach. The agreement between Glaser and Eastwood incorporated the architects' plans and specified, "Glaser agrees to purchase and install all windows, as illustrated in the attached plans, within sixty days of construction of the house's frame for the sum of $78,000 to be paid within ten days of completion of installation."

An earthquake struck Carmel Beach forty-eight days after the frame was constructed. Glaser had completed 90 percent of his work and incurred substantial expenses. The cliff on which the house rested collapsed and fell into the sea.

Glaser's best chance to recover compensation for his work will be to base his action on

(A)   equitable restitution

(B)   impossibility

(C)   quasi-contract

(D)   commercial impracticability

10.   After several weeks of negotiations, Ellen and Hellen agreed over the phone that Ellen would buy Hellen's art collection. "Let me review our agreement," Ellen said to Hellen, "I will purchase all seventy-four of the oils listed in your letter of last week, including their frames, for $874,000 to be paid in twenty-four monthly installments, after a down payment of $374,000."

"Exactly," said Hellen, "Just apprise your lawyer of the terms and let him prepare a contract."

Ellen's lawyer prepared the contract, which provided, "Ellen agrees to purchase from Hellen, and Hellen agrees to sell to Ellen, the seventy-four oil paintings named below. Ellen agrees to compensate Hellen $374,000 at this signing, followed by twenty-four monthly payments of $20,833.33 to be paid on the thirteenth of each month."

Ellen made the down payment, and Hellen delivered the paintings without their frames. Ellen asserted an action against Hellen to recover the frames. Which of the following statements is most accurate?

(A)   If the contract between Ellen and Hellen is ruled a total integration, evidence of their phone call agreement will be accepted.

(B)   If the contract between Ellen and Hellen is ruled a total integration, evidence of their phone call agreement will be accepted only if it does not contradict the writing.

(C)   The question of whether a written agreement is an integration is a question of fact to be decided by the judge.

(D)   The question of whether a written agreement is an integration is a question of fact to be decided by the jury.

Questions 11-12 are based upon the following fact situation.

Jason, a dedicated Coors beer drinker, was inspired to participate when he saw advertised a bicycle race sponsored by his favorite beer. Jason decided to buy a $500 Fuji touring bike to help him compete.

"Why don't you buy one for your wife?" the salesman said. "I can give you two bikes for $1,000."

"But I only have $550 with me," Jason replied.

"That's okay," said the salesman as he took Jason's $550. "I'll ship both bikes when you pay the rest."

Jason walked past another bicycle store on his way home and saw the same Fuji bike on sale for $400. He immediately called the salesman and told him to cancel the order and refund his deposit.

"Forget it. We made a deal," the salesman responded.

Gary had always wanted a video camera. When he saw the sign "Big Videocams Sale" in a store window, he walked inside and ordered a video camera for $750. After a little coaxing, Gary agreed to order a stereo sound Super VHS player for $500.

"I don't have my wallet with me," said Gary.

"Don't worry," the salesman responded. "You are a lawyer, which tells me that you are both trustworthy and wealthy. Send us a check when you get the goods."

Several days later, Gary received the camera. He was about to mail a check but his wife came in screaming, "You stupid fool. That camera sells everywhere for only $500, and *Consumer Reports* rated that VCR the 'worst buy'!"

Gary called to cancel his order.

"Sorry," said the salesman, "I told you all orders were final during the sale."

11. Is Jason's contract wholly enforceable?

   (A)   Yes, under the common law Statute of Frauds.

   (B)   No, under the common law Statute of Frauds.

   (C)   Yes, under UCC provisions.

   (D)   No, under UCC provisions.

12. Is Gary's contract wholly enforceable?

   (A)   Yes, under common law.

   (B)   No, under common law.

   (C)   Yes, under modern law.

   (D)   No, under modern law.

Questions 13-14 are based upon the following fact situation.

Walden, owner of a chain of bookstores, occupied a store in Lewis and Clark Mall in Portland. Walden's lease for this store, from Northwestern Associates, the owners of the Mall, provided him with 5,000 square feet of space. When the lease was about to expire, Walden devoted significant time and effort to find a suitable new site for his Portland store. After months of negotiation, Walden was about to sign a lease on the new location he had found, when he received a phone call from

GO ON TO THE NEXT PAGE

Northwestern. Northwestern's representative convinced Walden to stay on by stating, "We'll give you a two-month option to renew your five-year lease." Walden subsequently paid an architect $9,000 to redesign the store and included the mall's address when preparing a $24,000 direct-mail campaign. With more than a week remaining on the option, Walden was notified by Northwestern that they were revoking the option because the mall was to be demolished. Walden brought an action to compel Northwestern to honor its option and the lease.

13. Of the following arguments, which will be most persuasive in Northwestern's favor?

   (A) A business context will not negate a donative intent.

   (B) Consideration must be given to render an option irrevocable.

   (C) Plans to do remodeling in the future do not constitute a detriment.

   (D) An offeror may revoke an offer at any time before acceptance.

14. Walden's best argument is

   (A) promissory estoppel

   (B) an option may not be revoked if supported by consideration

   (C) the option was part of a bargained-for agreement

   (D) Walden's expenses before and after the agreement constitute consideration

15. After many months of intense bargaining, Distritoy sent the following letter to Stear's on January 1, 1987.

   "Distritoy hereby offers Stear's 10,000 Rice Paddy Dolls at $120 per dozen, shipped freight collect UPS. Terms are 50 percent down payment with acceptance, balance 2/10, net/30. This offer is not revocable and will be held open until April 30, 1987." On April 12, Distritoy cabled Stear's, "Rice Paddy offer withdrawn."

   On April 15, Stear's responded to Distritoy with the following letter: "Accept your January 1 offer, but want dolls shipped parcel post. Will prepay."

   Distritoy called Stear's upon receipt of the acceptance letter and said, "We are sorry. Hong Kong has doubled prices of Rice Paddy Dolls, and we cannot deliver. Don't worry about this one; we'll give you a good deal on Speed Racers instead."

   In an action brought by Stear's, the court should rule in favor of

   (A) Distritoy, because Stear's counteroffer was a rejection of Distritoy's offer

   (B) Distritoy, because an offeree can demand performance only if it had extended consideration for the offer

   (C) Distritoy, because it could revoke the offer

(D) Stear's, because a merchant may not withdraw an offer to sell goods when he has stated that the offer will be irrevocable

16. Swarmer Brothers, a movie studio, mailed the following letter to the Biz, a large video retailer, on January 15: "Due to an oversupply, we can offer you 29,000 videos of our $50,000,000 movie Wishtar for $27.50 per unit. We will also sell any quantity of Fatal Construction at $59.00 per unit. Delivery for both movies in March. This offer will expire on February 15." Swarmer Brothers sent a cable to the Biz on February 10 that stated, "Offer regarding Wishtar and Fatal Contraction is hereby revoked."
On February 15, the Biz nonetheless cabled Swarmer Brothers: "We accept your offer, send 20,000 Wishtars in March, balance by April 15; 50,000 copies Fatal Contraction in March." What is the legal relationship between the parties on February 16?

(A) Swarmer Brothers' February 10 cable was an effective revocation because consideration was not given for the offer.

(B) The Biz's modification constituted a counteroffer that invalidated the original offer.

(C) Swarmer Brothers is obligated to ship Fatal Construction, but not Wishtar.

(D) The Biz's February 15 cable constituted a valid acceptance.

17. On March 1, Southrealty sent a letter to Northrealty via U.S. Postal Service Express Overnight mail stating: "We hereby offer Southacre and all of its fixtures for $2,000,000 cash." The offer did not reach Northrealty until March 3, and Southrealty received a $10.75 refund from the Postal Service. On March 5, Northrealty sent a letter via Express Mail to Southrealty responding: "Thank you for your offer; it sounds agreeable, but would you be willing to accept $500,000 cash, monthly installments of $100,000 plus interest of 8 percent on unpaid principal?" Southrealty sent a letter back the same day it received Northrealty's missive: "Forget about it. Money talks; everything else walks." On March 10, Northrealty mailed a certified check for $2,000,000 and a letter advising that Southrealty's original offer had been accepted. Northrealty had not yet received Southrealty's response to it's March 5 letter. Was there a valid contract between Northrealty and Southrealty?

(A) Yes, as soon as Northrealty mailed the acceptance.

(B) Yes, as soon as Southrealty received the acceptance.

(C) No, because Northrealty's March 5 counteroffer terminated the offer.

GO ON TO THE NEXT PAGE

(D)   No, because there is no
        evidence that a "meeting of
        the minds" occurred.

18.   Razorback's Kosher Clam Bar was
        the only restaurant of its kind in all
        of Fayetteville, Arkansas. Toby, who
        had tired after forty years of Kosher
        clam baking, decided to sell the
        restaurant. She contacted a broker
        who brought the restaurant to his
        client Ginny's attention. When Toby
        met Ginny and saw that Ginny was
        serious about buying the restaurant,
        Toby made the following offer on
        October 25: "I hereby offer
        Razorback's Kosher Clam Bar to
        Ginny for $1,000,000 to be received
        on December 15." On November 15,
        Ginny wired $1,000,000 to Toby's
        account and mailed a certified letter
        stating her acceptance of Toby's
        offer. On December 13, Toby told
        Ginny, "Forget our deal. There's no
        way I can give up the restaurant."
        Toby's statement

(A)   was an anticipatory
        repudiation

(B)   will void any agreement

(C)   must be written to be
        effective

(D)   is not effective

19.   Slumlord owned residential property
        in Philadelphia, Center City, Camden,
        and Atlantic City. The maintenance
        for some of his properties became
        economically burdensome during the
        oil crisis. In 1974, Slumlord decided
        to abandon an ocean-front apartment
        building when he could not find a
        buyer. The building rapidly
        deteriorated and was vandalized
        considerably. When the state of New
        Jersey legalized gambling, the value
        of Slumlord's building skyrocketed.
        Slumlord turned down several
        multimillion dollar offers for his
        abandoned building. He assumed
        the value would continue to rise. He
        had good information that the new
        Resorts International Taj Mahal
        Casino was to be built to the east of
        his property and that the Showboat
        Casino was to be built to the west.
        However, Resorts International and
        Showboat were concerned that
        Slumlord's building would be an
        eyesore, and offered to pay for the
        building's demolition. Finally, in
        1987, Slumlord signed a contract to
        sell the land to Heritage U.S.A.,
        Inc., represented by Jim and Tammy
        Faker, who planned to build a
        Heritage U.S.A. Theme Park and
        "God's Faker Casino" on Slumlord's
        property. "The Lord should receive
        money from blackjack and craps, not
        only from bingo," said Jim at a press
        conference. Slumlord was to receive
        3 percent of God's Casino's profits in
        exchange for his land.
              Jim and Tammy were forced
        to resign from Heritage U.S.A., Inc.,
        several months later, when Heritage
        experienced severe financial
        difficulties. As part of their
        economic retrenchment, Heritage
        U.S.A. announced that they would
        not begin any new projects.
        Slumlord's building was in worse
        condition than ever before. Now, it
        was filled with nasty graffiti criticizing
        Tammy's makeup. If Resorts
        International asserts an action against
        Heritage U.S.A. to compel

performance of the contract with Slumlord, should the action succeed?

(A) Yes, because Resorts suffered actual pecuniary damage and was a third-party beneficiary.

(B) No, because privity of contract is absent between a party to a contract and one who is not a party but receives a benefit from the contract.

(C) No, because Resorts was an incidental beneficiary to the contract.

(D) No, because the damages to Resorts were abstract and difficult to substantiate.

20. Crystal, a first-year student at Oklahoma City University School of Law, worked nights as a stripper to support herself. When her grandfather in Wheatland found out how Crystal supported herself, he became furious and called her up. "Why didn't you tell me you needed money? Quit your job and I'll send you signed notes guaranteeing you support for the next three years. You can even use these notes for collateral if you need a loan," he said.

Crystal received C's in all her first-year courses. She was elated and celebrated by buying herself a brand new Hyundai. OK Hyundai extended her a loan to finance the car with her grandfather's notes as security. Crystal's grandfather died before the Hyundai had been driven

1,000 miles. The executor of the estate refused to honor the notes. OK Hyundai brought an action against the estate after Crystal defaulted on her loan and they couldn't find any other assets to seize. Is the estate likely to prevail?

(A) Yes, because there was no bargained-for exchange between Crystal and her grandfather.

(B) Yes, because the validity of the notes is in issue between the estate and Crystal, not OK Hyundai.

(C) No, because Crystal's grandfather authorized her to use the notes as collateral.

(D) No, because Crystal relied on the notes, which were intended to benefit Crystal's creditors.

21. Bahrain Shipping, incorporated in the State of Delaware, owned six super-tankers and was engaged in shipping crude and refined oil between the Persian Gulf and Europe, and Asia and North America. Bahrain signed a ten-year contract with Texaco, agreeing to ship 100,000,000 barrels of oil per year from Kuwait to New Orleans at a price of $2.05 per barrel. Cost accountants at Bahrain estimated a gross profit of nine cents per barrel on the transaction. In 1985, Persian Gulf hostilities between Iran and Iraq caused Bahrain's insurance premiums to quintuple.

GO ON TO THE NEXT PAGE

Bahrain continued to ship Texaco's oil despite the reality that it could not earn a profit at the $2.05 per barrel price. Texaco earned a substantial windfall when crude prices rose $6.00 per barrel in response to the Gulf hostilities.

In 1987, the Gulf became closed to shipping. Texaco notified Bahrain that it expected Bahrain to honor its shipping agreements. The most economical means to ship the oil was to truck it 1,200 miles over land to the Saudi Arabian Ru-Ba-Khali pipeline and then on to Oman, where tankers could be filled in the safe waters of the Arabian Sea. The total shipping cost to Bahrain was approximately $8.00 a barrel. Bahrain's best chance to suspend its agreement with Texaco is by pleading the doctrine of

(A)   mutual mistake

(B)   unilateral mistake

(C)   impossibility

(D)   impracticability

22.   Robbie was embarrassed that his friend Dave dressed like a slob and a pauper. Robbie, a fashion designer, constantly nagged Dave about his appearance. "What can I do?" Dave replied. "I am a law student. I can't afford nice clothing."

"Come on, Dave. Your father is loaded, and he gives you plenty of cash," Robbie replied.

"Yeah, but my girlfriend Cherry won't eat in a restaurant that charges less than $100 for dinner. I also buy lots of lottery tickets in the

hope that I might be able to drop out of law school," answered Dave.

Robbie went to Regent's, a local clothing store, and ordered $400 worth of clothing for Dave. Regent's delivered the clothing on the basis of Robbie's statement that "Davie's honest, he'll pay. If he doesn't, I will."

Dave wore the clothing but could not and did not pay the bill. Regent's brought an action against Robbie for $400. Is Regent's likely to prevail?

(A)   No, because a promise to pay the debt of another must be in writing to be enforceable.

(B)   No, because a suretyship agreement is within the Statute of Frauds.

(C)   Yes, because Robbie's promise to pay for the clothing is enforceable.

(D)   Yes, but only if Regent's has exhausted its recourse against Dave.

23.   Tommy, a rookie fullback for the Cleveland Browns football team, was excited that, after years of hard work at Barberton High School and Kent State University, he finally achieved his lifetime dream of playing for a professional team. Tommy purchased a condominium and a new car shortly after he signed a three-year $240,000 contract. On October 1, 1987, the National Football League Players Association decided to call a strike. Tommy was called into the management office of the Browns.

"We need you for our next game, Tommy. This is your chance to get off the bench and become a star," the general manager said.

Tommy replied, "I know. But I can't be a scab."

Management: "You don't want to lose your new car and condo because you can't pay your bills?"

Tommy: "That's true, but I'm afraid those guys are going kill me. After the strike is resolved, every time I get tackled I'll be afraid for my life."

Tommy watched the next three Browns games on TV, knowing he could have been the hero of those games.

On October 18, Tommy received an envelope from the Browns that said, "Inside, an offer you can't refuse." Inside the envelope a letter stated, "In exchange for five dollars which we have received from you, we hereby guarantee to give you a three-day option to accept a contract for the balance of the season at $20,000 per game."

The strike was settled on October 19. Hours after the settlement, Tommy conveyed his acceptance of the October 18 offer. "The offer has been revoked. You are going to collect splinters on the bench at your regular salary," the Browns told Tommy. Tommy then brought an action to recover $20,000 per game. Which of the following statements is the best answer?

(A)   Tommy's action will succeed if he can prove he gave five dollars for the three-day option.

(B)   Tommy's action will succeed regardless of whether he tendered five dollars because a signed, written offer may not be revoked if it has a clause that guarantees it will stay open.

(C)   Tommy will not succeed because the end of the strike reinstated his previous contract and made the option impossible to perform.

(D)   Tommy will succeed because he made a proper acceptance of a valid offer.

24.   Carlos, an attorney, invested his life savings in a new company that manufactured tests for AIDS. The contract stipulated that Carlos was to receive 49 percent of the company's profit and provided, "This contract may not be assigned." After producing the capital for the new company, Carlos had completed his performance, and he assigned all of his rights in the company to his grandmother, Sadie.

Hector, a mechanic and car designer, formed a partnership with Mario Spagehti. The contract provided that Hector would receive 49 percent of all winnings in exchange for providing Spagehti with a customized racing car. The contract between Hector and Spagehti provided, "Rights under this contract may not be assigned." Two

GO ON TO THE NEXT PAGE

weeks after delivering the car and one day before its first race, Hector assigned all his rights in the car's profits to his grandmother, Bella.

Jose ran ten miles every morning before he went to school. One day, he wrote the following:

"I, Jose, am going to be an Olympic marathon champion. I hereby assign to my grandmother, Therese, all proceeds from any running shoe endorsement I might receive." Jose gave this writing to Therese. Which of the following grandmothers will be able to successfully enforce their assignment?

(A)   Sadie

(B)   Bella

(C)   Therese

(D)   none of the above

25.   Henry, Steve, and Joe were medical school classmates and were also housemates who became lifetime friends. The three men, though very different, complemented each other perfectly. Steve, a very tense and efficient person, was always in bed by midnight. Henry and Joe resented Steve, because they both needed to stay up until 3 a.m. every night to finish their studying. Henry had a master's degree in biochemistry, and he helped Steve and Joe with courses in that subject. Joe, an extremely mellow person, whose mere presence had a relaxing effect on his high-strung housemates, loved to cook, and made sure his housemates ate well, even while cramming for exams. Henry loved to wash dishes and pots;

the dirtier the pots, the more fun Henry had. The reason was that the harder Henry scrubbed, the more nervous energy he expended.

Four fact patterns are summarized below. In which one should the trial judge's ruling be affirmed?

(A)   Steve convinced Henry to purchase Cranston's biochemistry notes from Ardis. The notes were for Steve's benefit because Henry, a biochemist, was breezing through the course, but Ardis delivered the notes to Henry, who then turned them over to Steve. Henry orally promised Ardis that he would pay for the notes, and Steve guaranteed Henry's promise to Ardis, who did not know that Henry was a surety. When Henry decided not to pay Ardis, Ardis asserted an action against Steve. The trial judge ruled that Steve's promise was within the Statute of Frauds and, therefore, unenforceable because it was not written.

(B)   Joe negotiated an agreement with his landlord to pay $10 per month for the right to pick all the fruit growing in their yard. The agreement provided that the three students could eat but not sell any fruit. After a severe storm damaged many trees and the price of breadfruit quintupled, the landlord sought to have the agreement declared null and void. The trial judge ruled that the contract was within the Statute of Frauds under the Land Contract Provision and was, therefore, void because it was not written.

(C)   Henry decided to insure his microscope, valued at $2,000. Hensly Insurance agreed to insure it for ten dollars per month. After six months, Henry decided to sell the microscope to Bernard, a pharmacologist. Henry brought an action to cancel the insurance agreement on the ground that it was void. Henry alleged that the agreement was oral and within the Statute of Frauds because performance would not be completed within a one-year period. The trial judge ruled against Henry.

(D)   Joe and Steve entered into an oral contract with Food Fair to purchase $750 worth of food and drink so they could throw a wild party for their classmates. Steve wrote a letter carefully and accurately stating the terms of the contract and finished the letter by saying, "Our agreement was oral and, therefore, not binding. I regret to tell you to forget the entire matter. My roommates think we don't have time to party three weeks before a histology exam." Steven signed his name at the bottom. Food Fair asserted an action against Joe and Steve based on breach of contract. The trial judge ruled that the agreement for the sale of goods valued at more than $500 was within the Statute of Frauds and, therefore, was void because it was oral.

Questions 26-27 are based upon the following fact situation.

Professor Alzheimer hired Digger Doug to search an ancient Aztec Indian burial site for artifacts. Professor told Digger, "I will pay you twenty dollars for every day you spend digging, regardless of how many artifacts you find, so long as you spend ten hours a day digging."

26.   Which of the following provides the best description of Professor and Digger's relationship?

(A)   A unilateral offer of employment, revocable after giving reasonable notice.

(B)   A series of bilateral contracts.

(C)   A series of unilateral contracts.

(D)   Employment subject to the condition that Digger discovers artifacts.

27.   Professor can terminate his offer

GO ON TO THE NEXT PAGE

(A)   only after lapse of a
reasonable amount of time

(B)   only by effective revocation

(C)   by either effective revocation
or by lapse of a reasonable
amount of time

(D)   only after giving Digger
sufficient notice

28.   The University of Ganja contracted
with Splifco, a general contractor, to
build an academic building. The
contract stated that all work should
be completed by August 1, and
contained a clause stating that "both
parties are aware that classes begin
the Wednesday after Labor Day."
The building was not completed until
the middle of October and the
university withheld all payment. The
court's decision on whether the
University will be liable for the
contractual price of the construction
will most likely be determined by
whether

(A)   the clause stating the date the
school began classes is
construed to make time of
the essence

(B)   each party acted in good faith

(C)   the university can prove
undue hardship

(D)   Splifco acted in good faith

29.   Stripper spent two hours inside Paul's
house checking all of the windows in
expectation of doing repair work on

them. On April 1, Paul wrote
Stripper a letter that said, "If you
strip and seal all of my windows, I
will pay you $750. I promise to keep
this offer open for thirty days."
Stripper wrote back on April
5, "I cannot do the work for one
penny less than $1,000." On April 10
Stripper wrote again, "I'll do it for
$750; your silence will constitute an
acceptance." Paul received Stripper's
second letter on April 13 and chose
not to respond. Stripper performed
the work on April 30. Paul was out
of town at the time.
A contract between Stripper
and Paul was formed on

(A)   April 10, the date Stripper
mailed his letter

(B)   April 13, the date Paul
received Stripper's offer

(C)   April 30, the date Stripper
performed the work

(D)   Paul and Stripper did not
form a contract

30.   Producer signed a written agreement
to purchase 100 cases of film from
Filmco. The parties had orally
agreed that the contract would be
voided if Producer could not obtain
financing for the movie for which he
needed the film. Will Producer's
failure to obtain financing act as a
defense to a breach of contract
action brought by Filmco when
Producer refuses to purchase the
film?

(A)   Yes, because the financing
clause need not be a written

modification of a contract not within the Statute of Frauds.

(B)   Yes, because obtaining the financing was a condition precedent to the formation of the contract.

(C)   No, because of the Parol Evidence Rule.

(D)   No, because Producer will be estopped from denying his agreement with Filmco.

31.   Harold and George agreed to trade title to their cars. Harold drove his Lamboerghini to George's house, where George had his Rolls Royce parked. Which of the following statements is **LEAST** accurate?

(A)   Harold's conveying his car to George is a concurrent condition to George's duty to convey his car to Harold.

(B)   Harold's conveying his car to George is a condition precedent to George's duty to convey his car to Harold.

(C)   George's conveying his car to Harold is a condition precedent to Harold's duty to convey his car to George.

(D)   Harold's conveying his car to George is a condition subsequent to George's duty to convey his car to Harold.

Questions 32-36 are based upon the following fact situation.

Lisa, an interior designer, claimed that she could increase the sales volume of any store by remodeling it in a scientific manner. Lisa orally agreed with Creased to remodel Creased's Designer Sportswear Store within ninety days.

Both parties later signed an agreement whereby Creased was to pay a $75,000 remodeling fee in ten equal payments of $7,500. Payment in full was due within ten days of the completion of construction, provided that Creased's retail sales increased by 25 percent. The agreement further provided that it could be modified only by a writing signed by both parties.

Two weeks after construction began, Lisa demanded payment of $7,500, which was the amount of the first installment. She showed Creased bills for materials she used totaling $8,200. Creased denied any obligation to pay until the job was completed, but, reluctantly, he orally agreed to pay half of Lisa's out-of-pocket expenses while the job progressed to show his goodwill.

When the renovation was complete, Creased's sales increased by $200,000, 24 percent above the previous year. Lisa said Creased could further increase his sales (at least another 1 percent) if he changed his advertisements. Creased refused to pay the remaining balance on the remodeling expenses and demanded that Lisa return the money he had advanced.

32.   If Lisa claims that Creased orally agreed to change his advertisements as part of the plan to increase sales by 25 percent, Creased will most

GO ON TO THE NEXT PAGE

likely be able to exclude the agreement by arguing

(A)   that the original written agreement was completely integrated

(B)   that under the Parol Evidence Rule, a contract may not be interpreted by subsequent evidence

(C)   that the original written agreement was partially integrated

(D)   promissory estoppel

33.   Assume for this question only that Lisa completed construction on January 10, and sales had already increased 27 percent before New Year's Day. Could Lisa have demanded full payment on January 10?

(A)   Yes, because the contract provided for payment within ten days of completion of work.

(B)   No, because a debt that matures on a national holiday is not due until the following work day.

(C)   No, because a reasonable person would interpret the contract to mean ten days after completion.

(D)   Yes, because the sales had increased before January 1.

34.   Was the agreement to pay half the expenses as construction proceeded a valid modification?

(A)   Yes, because the contract was a partially integrated agreement.

(B)   Yes, if the agreement was a compromise by both parties reached after an honest dispute.

(C)   No, because it was not in writing.

(D)   No, because of an absence of valid consideration.

35.   Assume for this question only, the renovation was completed three weeks behind schedule and sales increased 32 percent. Would Creased be able to rescind the contract because of Lisa's delay?

(A)   Yes, because timely completion was an express condition of the contract.

(B)   Yes, because the contract did not mention any other means of redress for a violation of the contractual deadline.

(C)   No, if the contract was substantially performed within the specified time.

(D)   No, because time was not of the essence.

36.   Assume for this question only, Creased is ruled to have breached

the contract by demanding that Lisa install purple carpeting on January 15, while the contract gives Lisa carte blanche to choose the color scheme of the store. What will Lisa be able to recover in an action for breach of contract?

(A) $75,000

(B)   her expenses

(C)   a pro rata recovery

(D)   nothing

37.   Potamkin Roller Bearing agreed in writing to supply Sisler Motors with 1,000,000 roller bearings for $7,000,000 on March 1. On March 1, Potamkin had in its inventory only 970,000 roller bearings, and they delivered that number to Sisler. Sisler refused delivery and payment and asserted an action against Potamkin for breach of contract. Should Sisler prevail?

(A)   Yes, because Potamkin has not fulfilled its contractual obligations.

(B)   Yes, if Potamkin does not deliver 30,000 additional roller bearings in a reasonable amount of time.

(C)   No, because Potamkin has substantially performed the contract.

(D)   No, Potamkin will be excused under the doctrine of impossibility.

Questions 38-41 are based upon the following fact situation.

Disney was a graphic designer who had created many wonderfully entertaining cartoon characters. He decided that he could no longer put as much energy into his business as he had because he was growing older and felt it was time to semi-retire. He decided to sell the license for Pluto, one of his cartoon characters, to Mickey. The written contract between Disney and Mickey provided that Mickey would receive all rights to Pluto. Mickey agreed to provide Disney with 50 percent of Pluto's earnings for a ten-year period, measured from the time that the contract was signed in 1976. The contract further provided that Mickey agreed to pay $100,000 to Disney in 1986. After the 1986 payment, Mickey would own Pluto outright. Disney named his son, Walter, as the beneficiary of the $100,000 in 1986. Disney reserved the right to change the beneficiary at any time prior to payment.

In 1977, Pluto became much more popular as a result of Mickey's aggressive marketing campaign. Pluto was on everything from bed sheets to yo-yos. Mickey brought in more capital by selling his future rights in Pluto, from 1986 on, to Minnie for $500,000.

In 1977, Disney learned that his son Walter had a drug abuse problem. Disney checked Walter into the Betty Ford Clinic where he supposedly sobered up, but Disney wasn't sure that he could ever trust Walter again. Since he was afraid that Walter would waste the proceeds from Pluto, Disney changed the beneficiary to his other son, Woodpecker.

Woodpecker was ecstatic over the assignment. He thanked his father, made a "Pluto party" for Mickey and Minnie, and, in reliance on the money Woodpecker expected to receive from the assignment, quit his partnership in a prestigious law firm.

In 1979, Disney's finances and his health were in terrible condition. A retired professional football player named Refrigerator contacted Disney. Refrigerator was currently the sales representative for an innovative scientist who had developed a process where people could be frozen for the low price of $10,000 and then thawed when a cure was found for their illnesses. Refrigerator agreed to accept Disney's 1986 rights to Pluto as security for the $10,000 payment.

In 1980 Pluto's value plummeted because video games had begun marketing their own characters with names like "Dr. Destructor." Pluto just couldn't compete. Mickey bought back the rights he had sold to Minnie for $25,000.

38.   In 1986, Walter sued Mickey for $100,000. Should the court rule in favor of Walter?

(A)   Yes, because Walter was a donee beneficiary and, therefore, his rights vested in 1976.

(B)   Yes, because Walter was a creditor beneficiary and, therefore, his rights vested in 1976.

(C)   No, because Disney exercised the power that he had reserved for himself to change the beneficiary.

(D)   No, because Walter was an incidental beneficiary and, therefore, was left without rights.

39.   If Mickey does not make the $100,000 payment in 1986 and Woodpecker brings an action against Mickey, is Woodpecker likely to prevail?

(A)   Yes, because the value of Pluto is still substantial.

(B)   Yes, because Woodpecker has a valid claim to payment pursuant to the Disney-Mickey contract.

(C)   No, because Woodpecker must sue Minnie first.

(D)   No, because Woodpecker should have sued Minnie and Mickey.

40.   Assume for this question only that Woodpecker is unable to recover from Mickey. If Woodpecker asserts a claim against Minnie to recover the $100,000 payment, should Woodpecker recover?

(A)   Yes, because Woodpecker is a beneficiary who changed his position in reliance on the contract.

(B)   Yes, because Woodpecker is a donee beneficiary of whom Minnie had knowledge.

(C)   No, because Woodpecker is an incidental beneficiary.

(D)   No, because under the contract Minnie was no longer liable.

41.   Refrigerator, who was never paid, asserted an action against Mickey for $10,000. Woodpecker objected to Refrigerator's claim, arguing that Refrigerator had no legitimate interest in the Pluto payments. Should the court rule in favor of Refrigerator?

(A)   Yes, because Disney had the right to change the beneficiary to the Pluto contract.

(B)   Yes, because Refrigerator provided consideration.

(C)   No, because Woodpecker was named as beneficiary before Refrigerator and, therefore, prevails in time.

(D)   No, because as a donee beneficiary, Woodpecker's right had already vested.

Questions 42-44 are based upon the following fact situation.

Mechanic rebuilt the engine in Hot Rod's car, pursuant to a written contract, at an agreed price of $1,400. Hot Rod called Mechanic and told him in good faith that the car was still not operating properly and he refused to tender payment.
Mechanic sent Hot Rod a letter reminding him that payment was overdue. On January 1, Hot Rod responded with a letter agreeing to pay $1,200 if Mechanic agreed to rebuild the car again within ten days. Mechanic did not answer the letter. Hot Rod mailed a check for $1,200 and wrote, "Payment in full in accordance with terms of letter sent January 1." Mechanic cashed the check but did not rebuild the car within ten days. Hot Rod sent letters and called to demand performance, but Mechanic has not responded.

42.   When Mechanic first rebuilt the car, Hot Rod refused to tender payment. Hot Rod's actions did not constitute a breach because

(A)   Mechanic had substantially or properly rebuilt the engine

(B)   Mechanic acted in bad faith

(C)   the engine was improperly repaired

(D)   Mechanic refused to re-check the engine

43.   If Mechanic asserts an action against Hot Rod for $200 (i.e., the difference between the price agreed upon in the original contract and the amount actually tendered), Mechanic will most likely

(A)   prevail, because he never assented to the new terms

(B)   prevail, if he can prove he properly rebuilt the car

(C)   not prevail, if the original price was excessive

GO ON TO THE NEXT PAGE

(D)   not prevail, because the check was cashed without objection

44.   If Hot Rod asserts an action against Mechanic for damages sustained because the car was not repaired again after the check was cashed, Hot Rod will most likely

(A)   prevail, because Mechanic agreed to fix the car within ten days by cashing the check

(B)   prevail, because Mechanic was obligated to fix the car again to satisfy the original contractual terms

(C)   not prevail, because the January 1 letter was a counteroffer

(D)   not prevail, because the agreement is unenforceable due to a lack of consideration

Questions 45-47 are based upon the following fact situation.

Waldman, owner of a chain of supermarkets, and Pimple, owner of a department store chain, agreed on a cooperative advertising program whereby both parties would share the costs of the campaign based on their respective average retail sales. They appointed an independent auditor to monitor their sales and bill them for their respective shares. Waldman paid several bills without complaint, but then he said he had discovered an accounting error made by the auditor that had led him to pay a disproportionate amount. Waldman asked Pimple to refund the amount the auditor had caused him to overpay. Pimple refused to give Waldman a refund. Pimple found it hard to believe that the auditor had erred.

Waldman proposed a settlement to their dispute. Waldman offered not to pursue his claim for the refund in exchange for Pimple's promise to pay Waldman's maintenance costs for the common areas of their shopping center for a two-year period. Pimple said, "Okay, I'll agree because you're stubborn, but I still think that you're wrong."

Six months after the advertising agreement was signed, Pimple's department store in the mall experienced a sharp decline in sales. Pimple closed the store to cut her losses. She managed to sublease the store to Fazio, who agreed in the sublease to maintain the common areas as per the Pimple-Waldman agreement. Shortly after Fazio subleased Pimple's store, he realized his sales were very low and moved the store to another shopping center. Waldman was forced to pay for maintaining the common areas.

45.   Was Pimple's promise to maintain the common areas supported by consideration if the accountant did not in fact err?

(A)   Yes.

(B)   No, if Pimple never believed Waldman had a valid claim.

(C)   No, because Waldman would have lost any claim asserted against Pimple.

(D)   No, because Pimple's settlement was vague.

46.   If the court rules that Pimple and Waldman's maintenance agreement was an enforceable contract, will

Waldman be successful in an action against Fazio?

(A)   Yes, because Waldman is a third-party creditor beneficiary to the Pimple-Fazio agreement.

(B)   Yes, because Waldman is a donee third-party beneficiary to the Pimple-Fazio agreement.

(C)   No, because Waldman cannot claim privity with Fazio.

(D)   No, because Waldman is an incidental beneficiary to the Pimple-Fazio agreement.

47.   If the court rules that the Pimple-Waldman maintenance agreement was an enforceable contract, will Waldman be able to bring an action against Pimple for Fazio's refusal to maintain the common areas?

(A)   Yes, because Waldman is a third-party beneficiary.

(B)   Yes, because Pimple remains liable to fulfill the maintenance agreement.

(C)   No, because Waldman may assert an action against Fazio.

(D)   No, because the Pimple-Fazio contract ended the obligation between Waldman and Pimple.

Questions 48-50 are based upon the following fact situation.

Mayor Ted Scotch placed full-page advertisements in Metropolis's three daily newspapers offering a $100,000 reward to anyone who supplied information leading to the arrest and conviction of the murderer of Scotch's predecessor, Mayor Stream.

48.   Mayor Scotch's offer could be accepted by

(A)   arresting and convicting the murderer

(B)   apprehending the murderer

(C)   agreeing to make every possible effort to bring about the arrest and conviction of the murderer

(D)   supplying the information necessary to identify the murderer and have him arrested and convicted

49.   Scotch's offer terminated

(A)   only after lapse of a reasonable time

(B)   only by effective revocation

(C)   either by effective revocation or by lapse of a reasonable time

(D)   at the end of Mayor Scotch's term

GO ON TO THE NEXT PAGE

50. Mayor Scotch can effectively revoke the offer

    (A) only by placing full-page ads in Metropolis's three dailies

    (B) by placing small advertisements in the newspapers

    (C) by notifying any person actively pursuing the murderer

    (D) by placing a full-page advertisement in the Metropolis dailies, or by a comparable medium and frequency of publicity

Questions 51-55 are based upon the following fact situation.

Supportco agreed with Realco to build the steel support frame for an office tower to be constructed on Marshacre. Realco assumed that the frame would be completed in six weeks. During protracted negotiations, Supportco and Realco orally agreed that an additional charge of twenty-seven dollars per man hour would be charged if the project required more than 2,000 man hours. The parties signed a written contract, with Supportco agreeing to build the steel frame and Realco agreeing to make six equal weekly installments of $6,000. The agreement to pay twenty-seven dollars per man hour, after 2,000 man hours had been completed, was omitted from the written agreement. A clause in the contract provided, "All prior agreements between Supportco and Realco are specified in this document. Any amendments or changes to this contract must be in writing."

The work proceeded for three weeks, and Realco made three payments. Marshacre was unable to support the structure, and the project was partially suspended while the foundation was being reinforced with pilings driven into the ground. Such a delay had not been anticipated by either party.

Supportco served Realco with notice that the delays would cause their work time to exceed 2,000 man hours, and they planned to invoke the overtime clause. Realco orally agreed, for a second time, to make the twenty-seven-dollars-per-hour payments.

Supportco submitted invoices for ten weeks of work; the final four weeks were billed at twenty-seven dollars per man hour.

Realco refused payment, saying, "Have some compassion. I am almost bankrupt. I can't pay now." Realco later asserted that the oral agreements were unenforceable due to lack of consideration and under the Parol Evidence Rule. Supportco brought an action against Realco for the additional seven dollars per hour.

51. Should the court rule in favor of Realco on the parol evidence issue?

    (A) Yes, because the contract contained a clause prohibiting oral modifications.

    (B) Yes, because the oral agreement contradicts the terms of the written agreement.

    (C) No, because the oral agreement addresses issues not mentioned in the written agreement.

(D) No, because an oral agreement was formed after the written agreement.

52. Which of the following arguments should Supportco set forth to have the first overtime agreement admitted?

(A) Testimony concerning negotiations is admissible to aid in the interpretation of an agreement.

(B) Testimony of oral conditions precedent to a contract is admissible.

(C) Testimony of a collateral agreement is admissible.

(D) The Parol Evidence Rule does not apply to contracts involving unforeseen results.

53. Supportco is likely to defeat Realco's absence of consideration argument by advancing which of the following arguments?

(A) Neither party could or should have foreseen the construction delays.

(B) Both Realco and Supportco acted in good faith to resolve a legitimate dispute.

(C) Both of the above arguments.

(D) Neither of the above arguments.

54. Which of the following arguments will **LEAST** support Supportco's attempt to enforce the overtime agreement?

(A) The parties were attempting to resolve an honest dispute.

(B) The overtime agreement rescinded the written contract.

(C) The oral agreement added new duties for Supportco.

(D) The oral agreement was a collateral agreement.

55. Supportco should argue that Realco's statement "I am almost bankrupt. I can't pay now"

(A) was an admission of obligation and an implied promise to pay at a later date

(B) should have been expected to induce Supportco's reliance

(C) was a fraudulent misrepresentation

(D) should confer criminal as well as civil liability on Realco

Questions 56-60 are based upon the following fact situation.

Hustler, a taxi driver, dreamed of becoming a real estate tycoon. Hustler's parents had taught him that dreams can come true if you work hard enough. He

GO ON TO THE NEXT PAGE

commissioned Architect to draw plans for a forty-two-story office tower. Although Hustler had no means to pay Architect for his work, Architect agreed to produce the plans on the condition that Hustler engage reputable subcontractors, obtain land, and give Architect a 10 percent share in the ownership of the building. After receiving a commitment from Architect, Hustler approached Landseller to enlist his assistance. Landseller was trying to sell a downtown parking lot he owned for $500,000. Landseller agreed to give Hustler the parking lot in exchange for the promise that Hustler engage reputable subcontractors and compensate Landseller with a 10 percent share in the ownership of the building.

Architect wrote to University, "In consideration of the fine education I received at this institution, I pledge 10 percent of future payments from my new building."

Hustler was able to retain the necessary subcontractors to supply the materials and construct the building by offering each one a small percentage of ownership in the building. The total number of shares promised to subcontractors amounted to 70 percent of the ownership of the building.

Architect contracted to sell his interest to Loafer, a twenty-four-year-old high school dropout, for $750,000 in cash. Loafer had just inherited four million dollars from his father. Loafer did not notify any of the parties in ownership of the building of Architect's assignment to him.

Architect took a vacation with the money he had collected from Loafer. On this vacation, Architect met Surfer, a twenty-four-year-old high school dropout who spent his days on the beach. Surfer had just inherited eight million dollars. Architect sold his contract with Hustler to Surfer for $850,000 cash. Surfer promptly notified all the parties involved.

Hustler was enamored of his new status as a real estate tycoon, but became impatient with the project. The construction was scheduled to take three years. Hustler decided to sell his interest to Fatcat for $850,000. Hustler immediately began work on another scheme. Fatcat notified all parties of the assignment. Surfer protested the assignment on the grounds that Fatcat was too staid to effectively perform Hustler's duties. Surfer believed that Hustler would do a better job of keeping the subcontractors motivated. Fatcat did, in fact, complete the project in a sloppy manner.

When the first profits were earned through the rental of office space, Fatcat credited $10,000 to the account of Architect. Loanshark, a creditor of Architect, asserted a lien on Architect's $10,000. University, Loafer, and Surfer each claimed to Fatcat that they were assignees. Fatcat refused to make any further payments on Architect's account.

56. If University asserts a claim against Fatcat, is University likely to prevail?

    (A) Yes, if University provided notice of Architect's assignment.

    (B) Yes, because Architect's assignment to University was earlier in time than his other assignments.

    (C) No, because Architect did not manifest an intent of present transfer.

    (D) No, only if University did not provide notice of the assignment.

57. Loafer and Surfer both asserted actions against Fatcat to recover

Architect's share of the profits. Should the court rule in favor of Loafer?

(A) Yes, because even though Surfer provided notice first, Loafer was a prior assignee.

(B) No, because even though Surfer provided notice first, Loafer was a prior assignee.

(C) No, because Hustler did not have the legal right to assign his interest to Fatcat.

(D) No, because Surfer gave notice before Loafer.

58. In an action by Loanshark versus Loafer, which of the following choices is the most accurate?

(A) Loanshark will prevail over Loafer because the debt owed Loanshark is a defense against Architect's assignment.

(B) Loanshark will prevail over Loafer because a creditor has priority over an assignee for value.

(C) Loafer will prevail over Loanshark because a creditor has no standing to sue an assignee.

(D) Loafer will prevail over Loanshark because the assignment left Architect

without any rights to the building's profits.

59. Loafer asserted an action against Hustler in recourse for Hustler's assignment of his contract to Fatcat. Loafer alleges the building was not properly built because Fatcat was an inept supervisor. As a result, the rents are lower than they should have been and the expenses are higher. The trial court should rule that Hustler is

(A) not liable, because public policy allows the unimpeded transfer of assets

(B) not liable, because construction supervision is not performance of a personal nature

(C) liable, because supervising a construction contract requires personal skill and discretion

(D) liable, because Hustler was given consideration for a job

60. Which of the following choices is **LEAST** accurate?

(A) Hustler's obtaining land was a condition precedent to Architect's obligation to draw plans.

(B) Landseller's conveyance of land to Hustler partially fulfilled Hustler's condition

GO ON TO THE NEXT PAGE

precedent to Architect's duty to draw plans.

(C)   An ineffective conveyance by Architect to Surfer would be a condition precedent to Loafer's receiving a share of the profits.

(D)   Hustler had more than one condition precedent to Landseller's obligations.

Questions 61-64 are based upon the following fact situation.

Paul and Saul orally agreed that Paul sell to Saul his office building for two million dollars. Saul agreed to send a check for one million dollars to Carol to satisfy a debt owed her by Paul. Paul and Saul agreed that the title would pass immediately even though the agreement was not yet in writing.

Saul had the agreement typed a week later. He failed to include a clause in reference to the debt he had agreed to pay Carol.

There was a typographical error in the printing of the contract that erroneously stated the sale price to be $1,500,000. Neither party noticed the error, nor questioned the omission of the payment to Carol. Both Paul and Saul signed the contract.

61.   If Carol asserts a claim against Saul for one million dollars

(A)   Saul could raise the Statute of Frauds as a defense because the oral agreement was for the purchase of real property

(B)   Saul could raise the Statute of Frauds as a defense because the oral agreement contained a promise to answer for the debt of another

(C)   Saul could raise the Statute of Frauds as a defense because the oral agreement was for the sale of real property and contained a promise to answer for the debt of another

(D)   the Statute of Frauds will not be at issue.

62.   Carol's action against Saul will be most significantly affected by whether

(A)   Saul was negligent by not exercising care in reading the agreement

(B)   Paul was negligent by not exercising care in reading the agreement

(C)   Paul's agreement with Saul was fully integrated

(D)   the Statute of Frauds will be at issue

63.   Which of the following will be Saul's best argument in his defense?

(A)   Paul and Saul agreed not to pay any part of the purchase price to Carol before she found out about the original agreement.

(B)   Saul's original agreement to pay one million dollars of the purchase price to Carol will fail due to lack of consideration.

(C)   Carol was obligated to notify both parties in writing of the acceptance of the contract.

(D)   The action will fail due to the Statute of Limitations.

64.   If Saul refused to pay more than $1,500,000 for the building and Paul brought an action for the remaining $500,000, Paul should argue that

(A)   he never agreed on a price with Saul

(B)   there was a mistake in the integration

(C)   there was no intent to regard the writing as a contract since an oral agreement had already been reached

(D)   the written contract was a partial integration

Questions 65-69 are based upon the following fact situation.

Driver operated a tractor for Constructor. Without informing Constructor, Driver drove the tractor home after work to use in the landscaping of his neighbor's yard. The neighbor was so thankful that he gave Driver a six-pack of beer that Driver drank

while driving the tractor back to the construction site.

Driver negligently lost control of the tractor, ramming into a crowd of pedestrians and a puppy on the sidewalk. Walker, one of the pedestrians, was seriously injured, requiring six months of physical therapy for a fractured hip. Constructor mistakenly believed that he was liable for the damages in the accident. He visited Walker in the hospital and told the very distraught man, "Don't worry about anything. I am going to pay for everything." Constructor then told Walker's physical therapist, "Take care of Walker, and I'll take care of you."

Feefee, owner of the puppy who died a slow painful death from wounds received in the accident, threatened to sue Driver, who had no assets. Constructor contacted Feefee and told her, "If you agree not to sue Driver, I will compensate you for all of your damages."

65.   If Walker brings an action against Constructor for pain and suffering, Constructor should assert in his defense

(A)   mistake of fact

(B)   the Statute of Frauds

(C)   lack of consideration

(D)   indefiniteness

66.   Evidence of which of the following will **NOT** affect an action by the physical therapist against Constructor?

(A)   Constructor's promise to pay for all of Walker's injury-related expenses created an enforceable contract.

(B) the therapist began treatment of Walker only after Constructor told the therapist he would take care of it.

(C) Both of the above.

(D) None of the above.

67. If the therapist decided not to treat Walker anymore and Walker asserted a claim based on breach of contract, is the therapist likely to prevail?

(A) Yes, because the therapist contracted with Constructor, not Walker.

(B) Yes, because the therapist's obligations to Walker were discharged upon the therapist's agreement with Constructor.

(C) Yes, because Walker did not provide any consideration.

(D) No, because Walker was a third-party beneficiary.

(E) Yes, because the therapist never promised to treat Walker.

68. Feefee did not sue Driver pursuant to her agreement with Constructor. If Feefee brings an action against Constructor for the value of her dog, should she prevail?

(A) Yes, because Feefee's promise to Constructor was a bargained-for exchange.

(B) Yes, because a dog is considered personal property.

(C) No, because Feefee would not have been able to recover from Driver.

(D) No, because Constructor was not liable for the accident.

69. Assume for this question only that Constructor changed his mind about compensating Feefee for the loss of her dog and honestly and in good faith believed that Feefee would not succeed in a suit against him. He agreed with Feefee to settle all claims between them for one thousand dollars, half the value of the dog. If Feefee later asserts a claim against Constructor for one thousand dollars, representing the balance of the dog's value, and for her own emotional damages, Feefee will most likely

(A) recover the balance of the dog's value only

(B) recover her emotional damages only

(C) recover the balance of the dog's value and her emotional changes

(D) not recover any damages

Questions 70-73 are based upon the following fact situation.

John signed a written agreement to purchase 100 gross plush toys at $288 per gross from Fred. The contract provided that John would not be bound if the stuffed animals were not delivered by June 1 or if they did not meet certain specifications. If John accepted the delivery, he then had ninety days in which to pay Fred. Fred delivered ninety-two gross on June 1 and promised that the remaining stuffed animals would be delivered on June 4. "Don't bother," said John, "keep all of them." The stuffed animals that were delivered had met John's specifications.

70. If Fred asserts an action against John for breach of contract, which of the following will be John's best defense?

   (A)   The market value had steadily increased from the date the parties contracted until delivery date.

   (B)   The market value had steadily decreased from the date the parties contracted until delivery date.

   (C)   Fred had not substantially performed by the agreed date.

   (D)   A stuffing shortage caused the delay.

71. The obligation of Fred to deliver 100 gross of stuffed animals on June 1 was

   (A)   an implied condition precedent to payment

   (B)   an express condition precedent to payment

   (C)   a condition subsequent

   (D)   a concurrent condition

72. The contract between John and Fred was

   (A)   divisible

   (B)   indivisible

   (C)   partially divisible

   (D)   none of the above

73. Which of the following choices, if true, would best support Fred's position?

   (A)   The stuffed animals were custom-made.

   (B)   John had cash-flow problems.

   (C)   The stuffing factory had burned down.

   (D)   On April 15, John had told Fred, "Don't worry about the delivery date, just do a good job."

Questions 74-78 are based upon the following fact situation.

Ellen, a computer manufacturer, contracted to buy 300 cathode ray screens at $100 each, F.O.B. buyer, from Cathodco.

GO ON TO THE NEXT PAGE

The contract provided that thirty screens would be delivered on the first of each month; payment was to be due ten days thereafter.

Ellen purchased the cathode ray screens with the expectation that her computers would become 10 percent faster once the new screens were installed.

The contract specified that the screens were purchased to increase efficiency.

Ellen mailed Cathodco a check for payment of the first installment within ten days after the first delivery. She performed tests on the screens to measure their speed, taking sixteen days and costing $2,000. These tests showed that the new screens were actually slower than the ones she was replacing.

Ellen installed five of the new screens in her computers and, as expected, the computers slowed down. Ellen notified Cathodco that she was returning the screens that had been delivered and repudiating the rest of the contract because the screens did not meet contractual specifications.

74.   Which of the following statements is the most accurate?

(A)   Ellen had a right to inspect the cathode ray screens only before she paid for them.

(B)   Ellen had a right to inspect the screens.

(C)   Ellen's rights to inspect the screens terminated when she signed the contract.

(D)   Ellen had rights to inspect the screens only if the rights were expressly set forth in the contract.

75.   If the court determines the fair market value of a slow cathode ray screen to be sixty-five dollars, what will be Ellen's liability be for the installed screens?

(A) $175.

(B) $500.

(C) $325.

(D)   Nothing, because they are returnable.

76.   How much will Ellen recover for the twenty-five screens delivered but not installed?

(A) $2,500, and she may keep them.

(B) $2,500, if she returns them.

(C) $875 after she sells them at fair market value.

(D)   Nothing.

77.   Besides the price paid for the screens, Ellen may recover

(A)   punitive damages

(B)   lost profits

(C)   damages for the aggravation caused by Cathodco

(D)   inspection and handling costs for the screens

78.   Assume for this question that Ellen has the opportunity to "cover."

Which of the following choices is the best?

(A) Ellen will be reimbursed for expenses incurred in rewrapping the screens.

(B) Ellen may purchase more efficient cathode ray screens elsewhere.

(C) Ellen may sell the screens delivered and recover the difference between the contractual price and the sales price.

(D) Ellen may repair the screens and recover the price.

Questions 79-84 are based upon the following fact situation.

Kool, a twenty-one-year-old college senior, loved cars. He worked long hours after school to make the payments on his Standard Motors Firefly. Bank had extended him a two-year loan with no pre-payment penalty. Kool fell behind in his payments, prompting Bank to write him a letter stating, "If payments are not resumed by January 15, we will be forced to repossess your Firefly." Kool dropped out of school to work longer hours at McDavids, the local fast food restaurant, so that he would be able to resume his payments.

On January 6, Kool's Uncle Henry, a fifty-five-year-old real estate tycoon and bachelor, discovered Kool's plans to pay his debt. He called Kool on the telephone and said, "I can't let my favorite nephew mess up his life. If you stay in school and quit your part-time job I will assume all payments on your car and provide you with $200 spending money every month until next May."

Kool agreed to quit his job and stay in school.

Henry called Bank and left a message with the receptionist stating, "I will pay you all the money Kool owes and assume all his future payments if you guarantee not to repossess his car. If Bank does not return my call, I will assume he has accepted the offer."

Bank did not respond to Henry's call, did not repossess the car, and cashed Henry's checks over the next six months.

Kool drove off the side of a winding mountain road four months before his graduation from college. Kool died in the crash and the car was reduced to ashes. Bank sued Henry for the remaining payments due on the car. Kool's estate brought suit against Henry for six remaining monthly payments of $200 spending money promised to Kool.

79. If Henry argues that the Bank's original agreement to give Kool a two-year loan to buy the car was void because it was oral, will the court rule in Henry's favor on this issue?

(A) Yes, because the contract could not have been performed in less than a year.

(B) Yes, because the contract was for the sale of goods in excess of $500.

(C) No, because the contract could have been satisfied in less than a year.

(D) Yes, because in some jurisdictions Kool would have

GO ON TO THE NEXT PAGE

been considered a minor at the time of the contract.

80. Did Henry and Kool enter into an enforceable contract on January 6?

    (A) Yes, because Henry sought to induce Kool to refrain from working and to stay in school.

    (B) Yes, because Henry received pecuniary benefit from the agreement.

    (C) No, because Henry did not receive any consideration.

    (D) No, because the promise of a gift is not enforceable.

81. If Henry seeks to assert that he never formed a contract with Bank to assume the car payments, which of the following arguments will help Henry's case?

    I. The contract was never formed because it violated the Statute of Frauds.

    II. The contract was revocable at will.

    (A) I only

    (B) II only

    (C) both I and II

    (D) neither I nor II

82. If Bank seeks to assert that he did form a contract with Henry, which of

the following arguments will help Bank's case?

    I. Bank made an objective manifestation of assent by not calling Henry back

    II. Bank made an objective manifestation of assent by not repossessing the car

    (A) I only

    (B) II only

    (C) both I and II

    (D) neither I nor II

83. Assume for this question only that Henry is unemployed and indigent. Also assume Kool legally delegated the duty to pay the loan to Henry. Will Bank be able to assert an action against Kool's estate to recover the balance of the loan?

    (A) Yes, because Bank has a cause of action against Kool if the loan is not repaid.

    (B) Yes, because Bank has a cause of action against Kool for nonpayment of the loan, regardless of whether remedies against Henry are exhausted.

    (C) No, because only Henry is liable to Bank in case of breach.

    (D) No, because there was a novation.

84. If Kool's estate asserts an action against Henry for the balance of spending money due in the contract, the estate most likely will

    (A) prevail

    (B) not prevail, because Kool's death terminated the agreement

    (C) not prevail, because the agreement was not in writing

    (D) not prevail because Kool's death frustrated the purpose of the agreement

85. Stephanie and Grace, brokers at the Metropolis Mercantile Exchange, signed a written agreement on January 1 stating that Stephanie would sell Grace ten contracts for crude oil at a specified price on May 1. In February, the price of oil fell from thirty dollars to fifteen dollars. When May 1 came Stephanie refused to perform. If Grace asserts an action against Stephanie for breach of their contract, and Stephanie asserts in her defense that the contract was void because the term "contract" was vague, is Grace likely to prevail?

    (A) Yes, because parol evidence can be admitted as to how the parties defined the term "contract" in their negotiations.

    (B) Yes, because "contract" is a standard term whose definition is easily ascertainable.

    (C) No, because of the Parol Evidence Rule.

    (D) No, because the price fluctuation amounted to a mutual mistake.

Questions 86-87 are based upon the following fact situation.

The University of Rasta hired Paul Tosh under a one-year contract as an adjunct professor of music. Tosh taught two classes every Monday and Wednesday. Tosh missed the second week of classes because of injuries he had sustained in a car accident. When he returned to class on the third week, Tosh discovered he had been replaced by Bunny Wailer, who was teaching his classes. The University of Rasta refused to reinstate Tosh or allow him to teach. Tosh brought a claim for breach of contract against the University.

86. Which of the following arguments will help Tosh's case most?

    (A) Tosh's one-week absence was not a material breach.

    (B) Tosh had relied on the contract with Rasta when he refused other offers.

    (C) The contract may be divided into a series of agreements, one for each week of teaching.

GO ON TO THE NEXT PAGE

(D)   Tosh was excused from his obligation due to physical impossibility.

87.   If the University of Rasta can prove any of the following, which one will help their case most?

(A)   Bunny is a better teacher than Tosh.

(B)   Bunny was the only substitute available, and she demanded a full-semester contract.

(C)   Tosh was offered a substitute's job at half his salary as an adjunct professor.

(D)   Tosh was offered an office job at the same salary as an adjunct professor.

Questions 88-90 are based upon the following fact situation.

Trouthead owned a fishing-supply store. In the course of business, he purchased 10,000 yards of 12-pound test fishing line from Fishycorp. The contract provided that Trouthead would remit payment immediately upon receiving the merchandise. Trouthead received delivery, mailed a check for payment in full, and then inspected the fishing line. It was only 10-pound test. Trouthead tried to return the line, but Fishycorp refused to take it back, claiming that 10-pound line was as good as 12-pound line.

88.   In general, a contract clause providing for payment before inspection of goods

(A)   is void as against public policy

(B)   does not preclude a buyer from inspecting the goods and pursuing remedies for non-conformance

(C)   will preclude the buyer from seeking redress for non-conformance

(D)   will preclude the buyer from recovering the incidental damages associated with the inspection of non-conforming goods.

89.   Trouthead should try to

(A)   return the goods and demand Fishycorp supply him with 10,000 yards of 12-pound test fishing line

(B)   return the goods and recover damages based on the difference in the value of 10,000 yards of 12-pound and 10-pound test lines

(C)   return the goods and recover the contract price and damages based on the difference between the contract price and the cost of procuring substitute goods

(D)   keep the goods and not recover damages because he waived his remedies by agreeing to the payment before inspection clause

90. Will Trouthead be justified in reselling the 10-pound test line?

  (A) No.

  (B) Only at a public sale.

  (C) In a private sale.

  (D) In a private sale, but only after providing Fishycorp with notice.

91. Lincoln orally agreed to sell his mercantile shop to Nebraska. Nebraska remodeled the store for $15,000 and spent $3,000 in moving expenses and supplies. Lincoln repudiated the contract, relying on the Statute of Frauds. Which of the following facts will the judge rely on in reaching a decision that the contract is enforceable?

  (A) The contractual price of the store.

  (B) Whether Lincoln was aware of the repairs.

  (C) The doctrine of part performance.

  (D) The local real estate market.

Questions 92-95 are based upon the following fact situation.

Guess Oil had the following contract with Spell Refineries:

"Guess agrees to purchase all of its refined heating oil for the next six months from Spell. The price will be determined by the heating oil price on the New York Mercantile Exchange on the day of delivery. Guess reserves the right to purchase all or part of Spell's output. Spell agrees to produce a minimum of 10,000 barrels of heating oil per day." The contract was written and properly authenticated.

After three months, Spell asked Guess if they would agree to lower the minimum to 5,000 barrels per day. Guess agreed, but only if Spell agreed to accept payment after twenty days rather than after ten days as they had previously agreed. Spell and Guess shook hands on this new arrangement.

Four months into the contract, a tremendous explosion destroyed Spell's primary refinery. Spell stopped delivering oil to Guess.

92. Was the original agreement between Guess and Spell enforceable?

  (A) Yes.

  (B) No, because of lack of consideration.

  (C) No, because the contract was replaced.

  (D) No, because the price, an essential term, was missing.

93. Assume for this question only that the original agreement was fully valid. Was the second agreement, providing for a reduction in the minimum oil output enforceable?

GO ON TO THE NEXT PAGE

(A)   Yes.

(B)   No, because of a lack of consideration.

(C)   No, because the contract was too vague.

(D)   No, because an essential element was missing.

94.   Assume for this question only that the contract and modification were valid. For what reason would Guess not be able to win an action for breach after the explosion?

(A)   Because Guess assumed the risk of explosion as per the contract.

(B)   Because the explosion excused Spell from fulfilling the contract.

(C)   Because Spell had not violated the contract by not supplying the daily quota.

(D)   Because the explosion was due to Spell's negligence.

95.   If Spell sold the refinery and assigned its contracts to Cramco before the accident and Cramco refused to supply its output to Guess without reason, which of the following choices would be most accurate?

(A)   Spell's agreement with Guess would be void.

(B)   Spell would have breached its agreement with Guess.

(C)   Spell would be liable to Guess for Cramco's breach.

(D)   Only Cramco would be liable for the minimum output.

Questions 96-98 are based upon the following fact situation.

Solomon wanted to purchase the Morne View apartment complex from Nadia, but he was unsure whether he could raise the necessary capital. Solomon and Nadia signed a written agreement whereby Nadia granted Solomon a sixty-day option to purchase Morne View. The contract provided that the option was revocable by Nadia at any time prior to acceptance. At the time of the contract Solomon had orally agreed to pay $1,000 for the option. Two days later Nadia revoked the option.

96.   If Nadia sues Solomon for the $1,000 option price, is Nadia likely to prevail?

(A)   No, because there was no consideration for the option.

(B)   No, because evidence of the agreement for Solomon to pay Nadia could not be admitted.

(C)   Yes, because the offer was actually irrevocable.

(D)   Yes, because the option was exactly what Solomon bargained for.

97.   Which of the following arguments will most definitely **NOT** support Solomon's position?

(A)   Nadia induced his promise through fraud.

(B)   The agreement was unconscionable.

(C)   An offer for the sale of real property may be revoked only in writing.

(D)   Nadia acted in bad faith.

98.   The arrangement between Nadia and Solomon could be described as a

(A)   unilateral contract

(B)   firm option

(C)   quasi-contract

(D)   pre-contract by estoppel

99.   Jones contracted to sell Farmacre to Smith. The written signed contract contained the exact boundaries and description of the land selling price, terms of payment, and effective date of contract.
      The contract contained all essential information except for the quality of title to be conveyed. Which of the following statements is most accurate?

(A)   The contract is voidable by either party.

(B)   Jones is obligated to convey whatever interest he owned in Farmacre on the contractual date.

(C)   Jones will be required to convey a marketable title.

(D)   Jones will be required to convey the title he owned on the date of contractual closing.

Questions 100-104 are based upon the following fact situation.

Sailbrow sold a sixty-foot boat to Marcos pursuant to a signed contract. The contract provided that Marcos make sixty monthly payments of $20,000 starting January 1. On January 15 of the following year, reasonably fearing Marcos would lose his job and leave the country, Sailbrow conveyed his rights under the contract to Aquino for a lump sum. Neither party notified Marcos, who made six payments to Sailbrow before learning that Aquino had obtained the right to payment.

100.   If Aquino asserts an action against Marcos for $120,000 to recover the six payments Marcos erroneously paid to Sailbrow, should Aquino prevail?

(A)   Yes, because Aquino was legally entitled to the payments.

(B)   Yes, if the conveyance was properly reported to the appropriate government officials.

(C)   No, because Marcos did not receive notice of the conveyance.

GO ON TO THE NEXT PAGE

(D)   No, only if Marcos can prove the parties intended to deceive him.

101.   Marcos subsequently sold the boat to Ver, who assumed Marcos's payments on his contract but failed to keep up with them. Aquino asserted an action against Ver for payments of $20,000 per month. Aquino will most likely be successful

(A)   because there is privity of contract between Aquino and Ver

(B)   because justice demands payment for services

(C)   if Marcos defaulted on his obligations

(D)   until Ver gives notice of default

102.   Was Marcos's assignment to Ver valid?

(A)   Yes, if the Marcos-Sailbrow contract did not contain a clause prohibiting a Marcos assignment.

(B)   Yes, even if the assignment was oral.

(C)   No, unless the Marcos-Sailbrow contract contained a clause specifically allowing Marcos to assign.

(D)   No, unless Marcos gave prompt notice to Sailbrow.

103.   If Ver dies or declares bankruptcy

(A)   his rights in the boat are extinguished

(B)   his rights in the boat are extinguished unless the jurisdiction has community property laws

(C)   his rights in the boat survive and are treated as assets or liabilities

(D)   his rights in the boat revert to Marcos

104.   If Ver had leased the boat from Marcos rather than received an assignment, which of the following statements would be most accurate?

(A)   Ver would be unable to enforce his sublease unless it was specifically allowed under the Marcos-Sailbrow agreement.

(B)   Ver would be in the same legal position as if he were an assignee.

(C)   Ver would be liable to Marcos, as well as Aquino.

(D)   Ver could enforce his sublease unless it was specifically prohibited by the Marcos-Sailbrow agreement.

Questions 105-107 are based upon the following fact situation.

Roundmouth, a dealer in rare coins, cabled Investor on April 1, "We will sell you up to fifty 1885 gold U.S. twenty-dollar pieces at $500 each. Specifics have been sent by U.S. Mail." The letter, containing the legal details including postage, insurance, grantees, and a clause stating, "the offer will be held open for one hundred days," was received by Investor on April 4. On April 3, Investor sent a cable to Roundmouth that said, "I accept your offer for five gold coins." Three hours after Investor sent the cable, a riot in South Africa set off a panic that caused the price of gold to immediately double.

105. Assume, for this question only, Investor's cable formed a valid contract. On April 4, Roundmouth called Investor and said, "I regret that due to the riots I must charge $1,000 per coin." Investor replied, "Send me all fifty of them at $1,000 per coin." If the trial judge rules that two separate contracts were formed, Investor will owe Roundmouth

    (A) $1,000 for each of 50 coins

    (B) $500 for each of 50 coins

    (C) $500 for each of 5 coins and $1,000 for each of 45 coins

    (D) $1,000 for each of 5 coins and $500 for each of 45 coins

106. Assume for this question only that on April 4 Roundmouth sent a cable to Investor, "Confirm your order of five coins, must retract offer for other coins." Investor responded, "Pursuant to the offer you promised to keep open, I purchase the remaining 45 coins at $500 each." Roundmouth refused to send the coins. If Investor asserts an action based on breach of contract against Roundmouth, should Investor succeed?

    (A)   Yes, because Roundmouth expressly promised to keep the offer open for one hundred days.

    (B)   Yes, because the attempted revocation was ineffective.

    (C)   No, because the contract's material terms were changed by the South African riots.

    (D)   No, because the revocation was effective.

107. Assume for this question only that before Roundmouth was able to revoke his offer, Investor sent a second cable requesting delivery of all fifty coins. Shortly after receiving the second cable, Roundmouth discovered that the coins had been stolen. Roundmouth's best defense to an action brought by Investor for breach of contract is

    (A)   unilateral mistake

    (B)   impossibility of performance

    (C)   the offer had been terminated by Investor's prior actions

    (D)   an absence of condition precedent

GO ON TO THE NEXT PAGE

Questions 108-109 are based upon the following fact situation.

On May 1, Scott told Muney, "If you paint my house, I will give you $5,000. This offer will not be revoked or altered until September 1."

108. What is the legal effect of the clause "This offer will not be revoked or changed until September 1?"

    (A) It provides Muney with a binding non-negotiable option.

    (B) It provides Muney with a binding negotiable option.

    (C) It does not affect Scott's power of revocation.

    (D) It prevents Scott from revoking the offer any time before September 1.

109. On May 15, Muney started painting Scott's house. On June 1, Scott told Muney, "I retract my offer of May 1." Scott had painted one-third of the house. Which of the following choices is most accurate?

    (A) Muney may complete painting the house and recover in full because Scott could not revoke the offer before September 1.

    (B) Muney could complete the painting and recover in full because he started painting before Scott revoked the offer.

    (C) Muney must stop painting on June 1, but will recover for his work between May 15 and June 1.

    (D) Muney must stop painting. He will not recover for his work.

Questions 110-112 are based upon the following fact situation.

Planter contracted with Homeowner to plant grass, trees, and bushes on the plot where Homeowner was constructing a new house. Homeowner was afraid that the job would not be completed before the first frost, so the parties agreed that "all work will be completed by November 1." Planter also agreed to extend a warranty of "Homeowner's 100 percent satisfaction." The contract provided that Homeowner would be obligated to pay in full within fifteen days of the work's completion.

Planter's work was delayed because Homeowner was delinquent in paying the general contractor building the house. The general contractor suspended work for two months. Planter could not begin the landscaping until the house was completed and all building-related refuse was carted away. Planter completed landscaping on November 7. Homeowner was dissatisfied with the results. When Planter asked what he specifically did not care for, Homeowner shrugged his shoulders and said, "I don't know, I just don't like it."

110. If Planter asserts an action to recover the value of the landscaping, Homeowner could assert which of the following defenses?

    (A) The job was not completed by November 1.

(B)   The bushes were unsatisfactory by objective standards.

(C)   The bushes were unsatisfactory by subjective standards.

(D)   The general contractor is responsible for landscaping.

111.   Which of the following statements is most accurate?

(A)   Homeowner's duty to pay was a condition precedent to Planter's duty to landscape.

(B)   Planter's duty to landscape was a condition precedent to Homeowner's duty to pay.

(C)   Homeowner's duty to pay was a condition subsequent to Planter's duty to landscape.

(D)   Planter's duty to landscape was a condition subsequent to Homeowner's duty to pay.

112.   Which of the following choices is **LEAST** accurate?

(A)   Homeowner's dispute with the general contractor excused Planter from the November 1 deadline.

(B)   Homeowner was obligated to give prompt notice to Planter when the house was ready to be landscaped.

(C)   By allowing Planter to proceed with the job, Homeowner waived the November 1 deadline.

(D)   The November 1 deadline was not affected by developments subsequent to the signing of the contract.

113.   Far Rock Away, a company engaged in hauling boulders, contracted to provide its services, charging $2.00 per pound hauled, to Wood Mere, a construction company engaged in clearing timber. The agreement provided that Far Rock Away would remove boulders from all Wood Mere construction sites for the next four years. The agreement further provided that payments would be made to Cedar Hurst, a creditor of Away. Mere shut down its operations. Hurst asserted an action against Mere for breach of contract. Mere should assert which of the following defenses?

(A)   Far Rock Away's rights were not assignable.

(B)   Wood Mere's contract with Far Rock Away was not enforceable, due to a lack of consideration.

(C)   Wood Mere, in good faith, did not have any need for Far Rock Away's services.

(D)   Wood Mere's rights were personal.

GO ON TO THE NEXT PAGE

114. Centre, the owner of the Centre Center shopping mall, entered into a contract with Undecided to sell a store located in Centre Center. Undecided tendered a $1,000 down payment, as required by the contract, to buy "the Center's northernmost store and a small amount of land surrounding the store." The purchase price was set at $200,000, and both parties signed a written agreement. Undecided seeks to repudiate the contract. Should the trial court allow it?

    (A) Yes, because contracts for the sale of real property are not final until "closed."

    (B) Yes, because the agreement is too vague to be enforced.

    (C) No, because the agreement satisfies the Statute of Frauds.

    (D) No, because $1,000 is more than sufficient consideration.

Questions 115-118 are based upon the following fact situation.

   Sheldon signed a thirty-year lease with Norman for a wire-hanger factory. The lease provided that Norman pay $100,000 rent per year plus all taxes due on the factory. Norman had an option in the lease to purchase the premises at any time for $1,000,000 in cash.
   Sheldon conveyed the factory to Debra soon thereafter. Norman assigned the lease to Barbara without mentioning the clause specifying payment of taxes.

115. Must Barbara pay taxes?

    (A) Yes.

    (B) No, because the agreement to pay taxes does not touch or concern the land.

    (C) No, because the agreement to pay taxes is collateral and does not run with the land.

    (D) No, because Barbara never agreed to pay the taxes.

116. Barbara stopped making payments two years after she assumed the lease, prompting Debra to bring a breach of contract action against Norman. Is Debra likely to prevail?

    (A) Yes, if Norman occupied the premises.

    (B) Yes, regardless of whether Norman occupied the premises.

    (C) No, because his obligations terminated with the assignment.

    (D) Norman will be liable for the taxes only.

117. Assume for this question only that Barbara fulfilled all of her contractual obligations. She notified Debra that she had decided to exercise her option to purchase the factory. Debra refused to sell it. Barbara brought an action for specific performance. Is Barbara likely to prevail?

    (A) Yes.

(B)   No, because the option did not run with the land.

(C)   No, because the option did not touch or concern the land.

(D)   No, because Barbara merely had priority over other purchasers.

118.   Assume for this question only that Barbara fulfilled all her obligations over a two-year period. Barbara then assigned her interest in the factory to Heidi. Heidi was well known in the community as a dead beat. Heidi did not pay her rent, and Debra asserted an action against Barbara. Is Debra likely to prevail?

(A)   Yes, because as the assignor Barbara remained liable.

(B)   Yes, because of Heidi's reputation.

(C)   No, because Barbara had the right to repudiate her own contract.

(D)   No, because Barbara's assignments ended her privity of estate.

Questions 119-122 are based upon the following fact situation.

Davinci and Lisa entered into a written contract providing, "Davinci is to paint a portrait of Lisa at Lisa's house. The painter guarantees the subject's satisfaction.

If satisfied, she must pay Davinci $1,000 within thirty days of completion of the painting."

Although Lisa's husband was thrilled with the painting, Lisa did not like it and refused to make payment. Davinci asserted an action based on breach of contract.

119.   Of the following arguments, which is **LEAST** helpful to Davinci?

(A)   Lisa's dissatisfaction with the portrait was not genuine.

(B)   Lisa never looked at the portrait.

(C)   Lisa refused to accept the portrait because a personality conflict arose between artist and subject during the long hours Lisa spend modeling for Davinci.

(D)   Davinci's portrait was an accurate reproduction of Lisa's appearance.

120.   Assume for this question only that Lisa refused to make herself available to model for Davinci. Which of the following statements would be **LEAST** accurate?

(A)   Lisa's cooperation with Davinci was an implied condition of the contract.

(B)   Davinci assumed the risk of Lisa not cooperating.

GO ON TO THE NEXT PAGE

(C)   Davinci was under an implied obligation to cooperate with Lisa's schedule.

(D)   If Lisa refused to cooperate, Davinci would be excused from performance and could maintain an action for breach of contract.

Questions 121-127 are based upon the following fact situation.

Joe and Bill had known each other for twenty years. Bill heard through Steve that Joe was thinking of selling his lawn mower. The warranty on Bill's mower had recently expired, and the mower had expired as well. Since Bill was in need of a mower he wrote a signed letter to Joe, dated March 1, that said: "If you deliver your lawn mower in working condition to my house by 6:00 p.m. on March 15, I will pay you $400. This offer is not subject to change or revocation."

Joe wrote to Bill on March 3 and told him, "I accept your offer, and will deliver the lawn mower before March 15." The letter was properly addressed and posted on March 3, but did not arrive until March 14, two days after Bill purchased a mower from Mocco for $450.

Mocco was also Joe's friend. Mocco bragged to Joe on March 13 that he had sold his used mower to Bill at a very high price.

Joe brought the mower to Bill's house at 5:30 p.m. on March 15. Bill was out, but Joe waited until Bill arrived at 7:00 p.m. Bill refused to pay for the mower.

121.   Bill's letter to Joe on March 1 was, in effect,

(A)   a firm option

(B)   a unilateral contract

(C)   a bilateral contract

(D)   a void contract

122.   What is the legal effect of the clause "this offer is not subject to change or revocation" in Bill's letter of March 1?

(A)   It prevented Bill from revoking the offer any time before March 15.

(B)   It created a binding non-negotiable option for Joe.

(C)   It created a binding negotiable option for Joe.

(D)   It did not affect Bill's power of revocation.

123.   If Joe asserts an action based on breach of contract against Bill, the court should rule that Joe's March 3 letter

(A)   did not affect Bill's rights to revoke his offer

(B)   bound both parties to a unilateral contract

(C)   bound both parties to a bilateral contract

(D)   is an effective acceptance

124.   Joe and Mocco's March 13 conversation affected Joe and Bill's relationship in what manner?

(A)   It had no legal effect

(B) It had no legal effect because Joe's offer was irrevocable until March 15.

(C) It terminated Joe's power to accept Bill's offer.

(D) It made Mocco a third-party beneficiary.

125. Assume for this question only that Bill extended a valid offer to Joe. Assume further that Joe's conversation with Mocco did not affect the offer. Joe's act of bringing the mower to Bill's house will have which of the following effects?

(A) It will not have any legal effect because Bill was not home.

(B) It will not have effect until Bill agrees to form a contract.

(C) A valid contract will be formed because delivery at 7:00 p.m. is considered substantial performance.

(D) A valid contract will be formed at 5:30 p.m.

126. Joe had the legal power to form a contract to sell his lawn mower to Bill

(A) from March 1 to March 15

(B) from March 1 to March 13

(C) during a time period other than the two above

(D) never

127. Lockspeed personally owns a large company that manufactures commercial airplanes. Don, a neighbor, told Lockspeed, "I convinced a friend of mine to buy three of your airplanes for his company." The planes were indeed sold by Lockspeed to the friend. Don demanded a 1 percent commission, as is customarily given to airplane salesmen. Which of the following arguments would support Lockspeed's refusal to pay the commission?

(A) Lockspeed never promised to pay a commission.

(B) Even if Lockspeed had promised to pay a commission, the promise would not have been supported by consideration.

(C) The contractual elements of offer and acceptance were absent.

(D) A and C

Questions 128-130 are based upon the following fact situation.

General Helicopters purchased its steel from Mahoning Steel Corp. The companies signed a two-year agreement that contained a clause prohibiting either party from assigning its rights under the contract. The contract further provided that General Helicopters tender its payment directly to Narduzzi, a creditor of Mahoning.

GO ON TO THE NEXT PAGE

Mahoning subsequently assigned its rights to Penguin Bank, as collateral for a loan. Mahoning billed General Helicopters upon completion of the contract. General Helicopters tendered payment of the full contract price to Mahoning ten days later.

128.   The clause in the original agreement prohibiting either party from assigning its rights will

(A)   be enforceable only against General Helicopters

(B)   not be enforceable by any party

(C)   invalidate any rights Penguin may have had

(D)   make Mahoning's assignment to Penguin a breach of contract although the assignment will be enforceable

129.   If the court rules that Mahoning's assignment to Penguin was valid, and General, unaware of the assignment, paid his debt to Mahoning,

(A)   Penguin will not be able to recover from either Mahoning or General Helicopters

(B)   Penguin will recover from Mahoning only

(C)   Penguin will recover from both Mahoning and General Helicopters

(D)   Penguin will recover from General Helicopters only

130.   Assume the court ruled that the assignment from Mahoning to Penguin was valid. If Narduzzi was unaware of the assignment, and he brings suit for his payment,

(A)   Narduzzi will recover from Penguin

(B)   Narduzzi will recover from Mahoning

(C)   Narduzzi will recover from General Helicopters

(D)   Narduzzi will not recover if he had not relied on or manifested assent to the contract

Questions 131-132 are based upon the following fact situation.

Sam told his paternal grandfather, Joe, that he was thinking of trying to quit smoking. Joe decided to encourage Sam, so he signed a written agreement promising to give Sam $10,000 if Sam completely refrained from smoking for the next year. Sam's maternal grandfather, Rob, found out about Joe's promise and told Sam, "I will also give you $10,000." Sam did not smoke for a year, and he asked Joe for the money. Joe replied, "I was just kidding. I never intended to give you ten grand, but I really did you a favor, since you quit smoking." Sam then contacted Rob who also refused to pay.

131.   Sam asserted an action against Joe, who raised the argument of lack of consideration as his only defense. Is Sam likely to prevail?

(A)   Yes, if he asserts the theory of promissory estoppel.

(B)   Yes, if he asserts there was a bargained-for exchange.

(C)   No, because Sam was thinking about quitting.

(D)   No, because Sam received the benefit of no longer being a smoker.

132.   Assume for this question only that Sam is unable to recover against Joe. If Sam asserts a claim against Rob, which of the following arguments will best support Rob's position?

(A)   Sam was going to stop smoking anyway.

(B)   Sam has not provided any consideration.

(C)   The agreement between Rob and Sam was oral.

(D)   There was no intent by Rob to form a contract.

133.   On March 1, Daisey looked at Rose's boat. Rose said, "You can have the boat for $20,000. I promise to keep this offer open for thirty days." On March 15, Rose called Daisey and told her, "the boat was destroyed in a fire." On March 22, Daisey found out Rose had lied, the boat was actually in good condition, and she told Rose that she wanted to buy the boat. Rose refused. If Daisey brings an action against Rose for breach of contract, Daisey will most likely

(A)   prevail, because Rose promised to keep the offer open

(B)   prevail, because the boat had not been destroyed

(C)   not succeed, because of the March 15 phone call

(D)   not succeed, because the offer of March 1 was not valid

134.   Byron wanted to purchase a car, but he didn't have any free time to go to the dealers. He authorized Lee to buy him a new Dragon car from Dragon Motors. Lee signed the contract, "Byron by Lee, his agent." When the car arrived at the showroom three weeks later, Byron refused to accept or pay for it. Dragon Motors asserted an action against Byron based on breach of contract. Which of the following choices is **LEAST** accurate?

(A)   Dragon will prevail if Lee's authority was in writing.

(B)   Dragon will prevail if the car was custom-made and is not suitable for use by others.

(C)   Byron will prevail despite written authority for Lee.

(D)   Byron will prevail because a contract for the sale of goods valued at more than $500 must satisfy the Statute of Frauds.

GO ON TO THE NEXT PAGE

135. Leroy hired Roofer to build the roof on his new house. Leroy agreed to pay $14,000 to Roofer upon completion of the work. After Roofer had completed approximately half the roof, he sent a signed writing to Leroy asking him to send the $14,000 that would be coming due to him to his creditor, Bank Two. Roofer completed the work. Bank Two brought an action against Leroy for refusing to pay the $14,000. Leroy's best defense will be

    (A) Bank Two could not have completed the roofing project

    (B) Roofer had previously agreed not to assign the contract

    (C) The roof leaks

    (D) Bank Two was not an intended beneficiary of the original contract.

Questions 136-137 are based on the following fact situation.

Prodigey, a fifteen-year-old computer wizard, owned a computer software company that he had started at the age of ten. In 1985, the company had sales of $41,000,000. Sleezex, one of Prodigey's clients, gave Prodigey a 6-month note for $10,000 to settle an insurance claim between them. Prodigey sold the note to Banco Uno for $9,000, and then told Sleezex that the note had been ruined when he left it in the pocket of a pair of jeans that his mother washed.

Sleezex gave Prodigey a note identical to the first. Prodigey sold the second note to Banco Quatro for $9,500.

Sleezex had still not paid the note thirty days after it was due.

136. Will Prodigey be able to assert an action against Sleezex for failure to pay on the note?

    (A) Yes, because Prodigey still owned the right to collect $10,000 from Sleezex.

    (B) No, because a minor cannot collect the value of a note.

    (C) No, because Prodigey assigned the note to a third party.

    (D) No, because the note is no longer physically possessed by Prodigey

137. Assume Banco Uno and Banco Quatro bring actions against Sleezex for payment on the notes. Assume further that Sleezex argues, *inter alia*, Prodigey was a minor. The trial court will rule

    (A) one of the banks may recover, based on priority

    (B) neither may recover, because Prodigey's minor status voided the note

    (C) neither may recover if Sleezex knew that Prodigey was a minor

(D)   neither may recover, because a holder in due course can never receive more than his predecessor

CONTRACTS ANSWERS

1. (D) A contractor's duty to a subcontractor is independent of any other agreement. TDB's problems with the government do not have legal bearing on its agreement with INC. In awarding damages, courts generally seek to place the non-breaching party in the same position that he would have been in had the contract been performed as expected. These are called expectation damages. Since INC completed its end of the bargain, it can only be made whole if it receives the entire contract price. If INC had not completed the nose cone, it most likely would recover for costs incurred plus lost profit.

2. (C) A third party to a contract may enforce the contract against the contracting parties only if she is an intended beneficiary of that contract. The third party must either be a creditor beneficiary (the contract called for the fulfillment of a pre-existing debt or obligation to the third party) or a donee beneficiary (the contracting parties intended to bestow a gift upon the third party). INC is not a creditor beneficiary, because its contract with TDB was subsequent to TDB's contract with the government. INC is also not a donee beneficiary, because the government contract was not entered into with the intent to bestow a gift upon INC. Therefore, INC has no right to enforce TDB's contract with the government. (A) is incorrect because there was no privity of contract. (B) is incorrect because INC does not satisfy the elements required to be considered a third-party beneficiary. (D) is false.

3. (C) In a contract for the sale of goods, a buyer may demand specific performance when the goods are unique (UCC 2-716). This contract was valid because there was an offer and acceptance, and the letter satisfied the Statute of Frauds' requirement of a writing. However, the existence of a valid contract will not automatically justify the remedy of specific performance. A mass-produced boat will not be considered a unique good. Todd should sue at law for the difference between his contract price with Ron and the cost of a comparable boat. These are his expectation damages and "an adequate remedy." If this had been a custom-made yacht, Todd would have had a good probability of obtaining specific performance.

4. (A) The oral agreement between Larry and Investor was a unilateral contract. There was no obligation on Investor's part until Larry bought Canadian coins. When Larry bought Krugerands, he did not fulfill the contract's condition for payment. Investor specifically stated that he would pay Larry if Larry bought Canadian coins for him. Larry's performance was a condition precedent to Investor's obligation to compensate him. (D) is incorrect because personal satisfaction must be contracted for. Larry's purchase was neither a rescission nor a modification (Choices B and C), because no contract existed until Larry bought the proper coins.

5.   (B)   Only an intended beneficiary may sue, i.e., Grand Prix, and Jeremy must have, by the contract, intended to confer a benefit on Ronzoni. According to these facts, Ronzoni is not a creditor beneficiary or a donee beneficiary. Ronzoni merely "happens to gain" by virtue of the agreement. This makes Ronzoni an incidental beneficiary who will not be entitled to sue on the contract. See Rest 2d § 302 illus. 17. (A) is incorrect because a condition of personal satisfaction must be expressly provided for in the contract. (C) assumes too many facts not in the question. (D) is true, but will not aid Jeremy in his defense.

6.   (D)   A modification to a bilateral contract must be supported by additional consideration to be binding upon the parties. This was an output contract. Hopefourstrike got nothing more than it was already entitled to in exchange for the promise to pay $300 more per filter. Drillco had already agreed to supply 1,000 filters in September. Therefore, this promise will not be binding upon Hopefourstrike. The UCC does not allow the oral addition of inconsistent terms to a contract. (UCC 2-202, 2-209). These terms are in direct conflict with the original contract and will be binding only if in writing. (C) seems to be the best answer, but it is an incorrect statement of law. To satisfy the UCC's Statute of Frauds, the writing must be signed by the party to be charged, that is Hopefourstrike and not Drillco. (A) is incorrect because the Parol Evidence Rule only bars *prior* oral agreements. (B) is not very persuasive, because the original contract was in writing.

7.   (D)   A contract was never formed because there was no meeting of the minds. The formal name given to such a fact pattern is "misunderstanding." Where there has been a misunderstanding as to the meaning of a material term in a contract and neither party knows, nor has reason to know, that the other party's interpretation differs from their own, the contract will be voided. Parties will not be charged with knowledge of industry custom. If one party knows or should know of the misunderstanding, then the innocent party's interpretation will prevail and the contract will be binding.

8.   (A)   The agreement between Social and Forest City was an aleatory contract, a mutual agreement the effects of which depend on an uncertain event. The duties of the parties to an aleatory contract are independent, and each may sue the other for breach even though she is also in default. Social was obligated to pay the damages despite the fact that the premiums were not paid. (But Social may also sue Forest City for breach on the unpaid premium). Social would only be relieved from liability if it had already cancelled the insurance contract for failure to pay premiums. (C) and (D) are incorrect, as explained above. (B) is not of any concern here. According to Restatement of Contracts 2d, an anti-assignment clause will be interpreted to bar delegation of duties but not rights; hence, Forest City was free to delegate its coverage despite the anti-assignment clause. The results would have been different

had the clause prohibited assignment of "rights," instead of assignment of the contract, or if it had provided that any assignment shall be void.

9. (C)   Glaser cannot recover "on the contract," because the contract's conditions have not been fulfilled. However, a court will attempt to rectify the inequity of forcing Glaser to bear all of his expenses by allowing him an action in quasi-contract. Quasi-contract is a legal fiction used to prevent unjust enrichment of one party to the detriment of another when there was no contract or the contract is unenforceable. The party who suffered a detriment is awarded restitution for expenses and labor or damages to the extent of his reasonable reliance. In this fact pattern, Glaser should recover for the work he completed despite his inability to contractually bind Eastwood for the entire $78,000. (D) is not applicable. It arises when the terms of a contract have become economically onerous and neither party assumed such a risk. Impossibility (Choice B), though applicable, only serves to discharge all of the parties' duties.

10. (C)   If parties to a written agreement intend the written agreement to be an expression of their oral understandings, the written agreement is said to be an *integration*. An integration is either (1) partial: i.e., not containing all details of the agreement or (2) total: i.e., containing *all* relevant details of the agreement. Evidence of prior oral understandings that contradict an integration may not be admitted in court under the Parol Evidence Rule. Such evidence supplementing but not contradicting an integration may be admitted in the case of a partial integration but not a total integration. In our case, it must be decided whether the written agreement between Hellen and Ellen was a partial or total integration, because the integration (written contract) was silent concerning the frames. If the contract is ruled to be a partial integration, evidence of the frames will be admissible because it supplements but does not contradict the written agreement. If the contract is ruled a total integration, no evidence of prior or contemporaneous agreements may be admitted. Under the majority view, the question whether a written agreement is an integration, partial or total, is a question of law that is decided by a judge, not a jury.

11. (D)   An agreement for the sale of goods valued at $500 or more is within the Statute of Frauds and, therefore, not enforceable unless it is supported by a writing. At common law, the agreement was taken out of the statute and enforced if payment was made or the goods had been received. This rule was changed by the UCC [2 -211-(3)(a)], which states that oral contracts for amounts greater than $500 are enforceable only "with respect to goods for which payment has been made and accepted or for which goods have been received and accepted." In our cases, the UCC would make only part of the agreement enforceable.

12. (A)   For the same reason as above, the contract is enforceable only under common law.

13.   (B)   The promise of a gift is as unenforceable in a business context as it is in a personal matter (Choice A), but the promise to extend Walden's time period in which he could enter a new lease was represented as an option. Therefore, the principal issue is whether this "option" will be enforceable. To be binding, an option must be supported by consideration. Since there was no consideration given by Walden, Northwestern's statement amounted to an offer that may be revoked at any point prior to acceptance, unless there is partial performance by the offeree (Choice D). Walden suffered a detriment by expending money in reliance on the offer, but this reliance was not reasonable since he did not have a binding agreement, and Northwestern did not receive a benefit, rendering (C) incorrect.

14.   (A)   Since Walden did act in reliance on the promise, this will be his best argument. The main issue will be whether this reliance was reasonable. Since no consideration was given, and Northwestern did not bargain for Walden's reliance, (B) and (C) are incorrect. (D) will not qualify as consideration; it is evidence of reliance.

15.   (C)   Under UCC 2-205, "An offer by a merchant to buy or sell goods in a signed writing which by its terms gives assurance that it will be held open is not revocable, for lack of consideration during the time stated or if no time is stated for a reasonable time, but in no event may such period of irrevocability exceed three months." The offer exceeded three months, and therefore, it will not be enforceable under this UCC provision. Under the common law, consideration must be exchanged for the offeror's promise to keep the offer open to be enforceable. Under the common law (but not under the UCC), Stear's attempt at acceptance would have been considered a counteroffer (Choice A), since it changed the terms of the original offer. A counteroffer rejects an original offer and ends Stear's power of acceptance. However, the counteroffer is irrelevant because Distritoy had already revoked its offer on April 12, before it was sent the counteroffer. (D) is incorrect because of the three-month time limit.

16.   (D)   Since the correspondence between the Biz and Swarmer Brothers is between merchants, it is within the scope of UCC Article 2. UCC 2-205 provides that "an offer by a merchant to buy or sell goods in a signed writing by its terms that gives assurance that it will be held open is not revocable, for lack of consideration during this time stated." Swarmer Brothers was prevented by this section from revoking its offer (that makes (A) incorrect). According to UCC 2-207, "A definite and seasonable acceptance or a written confirmation which is sent within a reasonable time operates as an acceptance even though it states terms additional to or different from those offered or agreed upon, unless acceptance is expressly made conditional on assent to the addition of different terms." (B) simply describes the common law method of interpreting acceptances, and (C) is incorrect because Biz's additional terms do not invalidate the Wishtar deal.

17.   (A)   The common law "mailbox rule" provides that an acceptance is valid upon its mailing, not upon its receipt (Choice B). A revocation or a rejection, on the other hand, is effective upon receipt. Since Northrealty's acceptance was mailed before it received Southrealty's revocation, a valid contract was formed. (C) is incorrect because Northrealty's March 5 response was not a counteroffer. It was merely an inquiry as to whether Southrealty was willing to change the terms. An inquiry will not terminate an original offer. The Multistate examiners like to test the fine-line distinction between a counteroffer and an inquiry. (D) is false — the facts of the question provide sufficient evidence that there was a meeting of the minds on the original offer.

18.   (D)   The statement is not effective, because the contract was already formed and could not be revoked by either party. (A) does not apply because there cannot be an anticipatory breach when one party to a unilateral or bilateral contract has already fully performed (in our case, Ginny).

19.   (C)   One who is not a party to a contract but stands to receive a benefit is called a *third-party beneficiary*. The Restatement (Second) § 302 distinguishes between an intended third-party beneficiary, who has standing to sue a party for a breach of the contract, and an incidental beneficiary, who may not sue. (See Answer #5.) Resorts was not a creditor or a donee beneficiary, but merely "happened to gain" from the agreement. This makes Resorts an incidental beneficiary without standing to sue on the contract.

20.   (D)   This question addresses two issues: consideration and third-party beneficiaries. The promise to Crystal was not a bargained-for exchange, since Crystal did not supply any formal consideration. However, it was still a valid contract after the application of the theory of promissory estoppel. Restatement (Second) § 90(1) provides, "a promise which the promisor should reasonably expect to induce action or forbearance and does induce such on the part of the promisee or a third person, will be enforceable against the promisor to the extent justice requires." Estoppel, in essence, allows reasonable detrimental reliance to hold a contract valid where there is a lack of consideration. Since Crystal quit her job, she relied to her detriment on the promise and the promise was binding.

Crystal's quitting of her job might also be viewed as consideration for the grandfather's notes. Her grandfather received the benefit he bargained for — his granddaughter stopped stripping.

One who is a beneficiary but not a party to an agreement is called a third-party beneficiary. The Restatement (Second) § 302 has done away with the distinction between creditor and donee beneficiaries and instead divides beneficiaries into intended, who may enforce a contract, and incidental, who may not. Since Crystal's grandfather clearly expected the notes to be used as collateral, he can be considered to have intended to be her surety, and creditors such as OK Hyundai may enforce the agreement between Crystal and her grandfather (Illus. 12) Although (C) is true, (D) is the better answer because it addresses both issues.

21. (D)   Under the traditional view, performance would not be excused unless it was utterly impossible to perform. Many modern courts [Restatement (Second) ch. 11] and the UCC [2-615(a)] allow a promisor's performance to be excused if changed circumstances make performance commercially infeasible. But if the party assumed the risk of such an occurrence, the party may not be excused. This view equates extreme impracticability with impossibility. The elements necessary for impossibility (Choice C) are much more strict. Impossibility requires that it be objectively impossible to perform the contract through no fault of either party. The contract will then be discharged. Mistake, (A) and (B), is irrelevant to this fact pattern.

22. (C)   A promise to pay the debts of another falls within the Statute of Frauds and must be in writing to be enforceable. Such an agreement is called a suretyship. (A) and (B) are correct statements of law, but do not answer the question. In our case, Robbie was not a surety for Dave, because Robbie incurred the debt; Dave did not. Dave never ordered the clothing and, therefore, was never liable to pay for it. Robbie owed Regent's the money. Whether Regent's has exhausted its recourse against Dave is irrelevant (Choice D). Robbie might be able to recover the $400 from Dave since Dave kept the clothing and wore it.

23. (D)   A promise to keep an offer open is valid only if supported by consideration. The five dollars given in exchange for the option is that consideration. A court will generally not inquire into the adequacy of the consideration (Choice A). Since the offer recites consideration, the court will most likely take it at face value. Because the offer had not been revoked before he accepted it, Tommy's acceptance will be valid whether he had an option for three days or not. If not supported by consideration, an offer will be open for a reasonable time or until it is expressly revoked. (B) is the law [UCC 2-205] regarding the sale of goods; it is not applicable to an employment contract. (C) is incorrect because the offer did not mention that it was conditional upon the status of the strike.

24. (A)   An anti-assignment clause barring assignment of a contract will be interpreted to allow assignment of rights only and not duties. An example of a right is to collect payment, while a duty would be to render a performance. Thus, Sadie's assignment was valid and enforceable. Bella will not be able to enforce her assignment, because Hector's contract stipulated, "Rights under the contract may not be assigned." Compare the clauses in the agreements.

An assignment of the future rights to a future contract is not enforceable. Jose's assignment to Therese will not be enforceable, because Jose assigned rights to a contract that was not yet in existence.

To make a contract completely unassignable the clause should provide that any assignment shall be void.

25.   (C)   The Statute of Frauds requires that an agreement that cannot be performed within one year must be in writing. Since Henry could have collected on his insurance policy within the one year period, for example if the microscope had been stolen, the oral agreement is valid. Note that whether this particular agreement is fulfilled within one year is not the issue; the issue is whether the agreement is capable of being fulfilled within one year. (A) is not correct because the surety provision of the Statute of Frauds requiring that a promise to pay the debt of another be in writing only applies when the promisee knows, or has reason to know, of the surety relationship.

(B) is incorrect. The Statute of Frauds requires that an agreement for an interest in land be in writing. The right to pick the fruit from trees will not qualify as an interest in the land the trees are on.

(D) is incorrect. Joe's memorandum may satisfy the writing requirement of the Statute of Frauds. In this writing he memorialized the agreement with Food Fair. A writing may suffice despite the fact that it was executed for a different purpose.

26.   (C)   A unilateral contract is one in which the offeror bargains for the actual performance only, rather than a promise to perform. Digger was not bound to do the work for the Professor, but once he performed, the Professor was obligated to pay him. The Professor's offer created a series of contracts. Digger's daily work constituted a separate acceptance of each offer. (A) describes the Professor's offer, but not the relationship of the Professor and Digger. (D) contradicts the facts of the question. (B) is incorrect. A bilateral contract is one in which the offeree, either expressly or impliedly, accepts the offer by promising to perform. That is not the case here. Digger can accept only through performance.

27.   (C)   A unilateral contract offer is automatically revoked by the passage of a reasonable amount of time. The offeror may also revoke the offer prior to acceptance where there has not been partial performance.

28.   (A)   The court must consider the intent of both parties. In real estate contracts, courts are reluctant to impose a completion date as a condition precedent to payment on the contract, but there are exceptions, as when the contract stipulates, as it does here, that time is of the essence. The University will be bound to pay some compensation for the building because it has kept it and will be enjoying the benefit of it, but may be able to subtract damages for the time it expected to have use of the building, but did not. In situations such as these, the best device is to insert a liquidated damages clause in the contract which sets specific money damages for late performance. (B) and (D) are incorrect because the state of mind of the breaching party is generally

not considered. Undue hardship (Choice C) is also not generally considered grounds for discharge.

29.   (D)   Paul's letter of April 1 was an offer. The promise to keep the offer open was unenforceable because no consideration was given for it and it was not for the sale of goods (i.e., not under the UCC). Stripper's letter of April 5 was a counteroffer and a rejection of Paul's offer. Therefore, Stripper had relinquished his power of acceptance. Stripper's letter of April 13 was not an acceptance, it was a new offer extended to Paul. Under the common law, silence will never be considered an acceptance. The Rest 2d § 69(1) has attempted to change this rule. It states, "Where the offeror has given the offeree reason to understand that silence or inaction of the offeree will constitute acceptance, the silence or inaction of the offeree will operate as an acceptance if he subjectively intends to be bound." The facts of the question do not show that Paul intended to be bound by Stripper's offer. Other exceptions exist to the "silence is not acceptance" rule. Where the offeree silently accepts the benefit of the offeror's services or past dealings of the parties indicate that silence might be an acceptance, the offeree may be held to a contract. Since Paul was unaware of Stripper's work and they had no past dealings, Stripper cannot claim that a contract had been formed.

30.   (B)   A written contract can be attacked by oral evidence without violating the Parol Evidence Rule if the evidence points to the agreement's validity. Here, Producer is arguing that the agreement never came into being. If the oral modification was subsequent to the written agreement, the Parol Evidence Rule would not come into play at all. Where a party asserts that the contract could not become effective until a condition occurred, all evidence (written or oral) is admissible. Remember, the parties are not altering a written agreement (Choice A), but challenging it.

31.   (D)   A condition precedent is one that must occur before an absolute duty of immediate performance arises in the other party. A concurrent condition is when two conditions are supposed to occur simultaneously. A condition subsequent differs significantly from the previous two types. The occurrence of a condition subsequent cuts off an already existing duty. Each party in this question was obligated to convey his car upon the other's performance (condition precedent) or to convey simultaneously (concurrent condition).

32.   (A)   A final and complete written integration of a contract may not be contradicted or supplemented by extrinsic evidence. A partially integrated agreement cannot be contradicted, but may be supplemented with proof of consistent additional terms (Choice C). The statements regarding advertising would be consistent additional terms that are admissible if the writing were a partial integration, but not a complete integration. If Creased successfully proves that the original agreement was completely

integrated, the court may not allow any evidence of supplemental agreements. (B) is false; subsequent statements are never barred by the Parol Evidence Rule. Promissory estoppel (Choice D) is inapplicable since it is a theory that Lisa would rely upon.

33.   (C)   The plain meaning of the contract is that payment is due ten days after completion of the work and increased sales. Lisa cannot demand payment in full on January 10 because the contract gives Creased another ten days in which to make his payment. The completion and increase in sales are a condition precedent to the obligation of Creased to pay.

34.   (B)   A compromise settling an honest dispute may always be a valid contract unless the Statute of Frauds has been violated. Both parties' concessions will serve as consideration for each other. This compromise did not violate the Statute of Frauds, because the agreement could be performed within one year.

35.   (D)   A "time is of the essence" provision must be stipulated in the contract for the contract to be voided due to tardy performance. There was no such provision in Creased's contract with Lisa. "Time is of the essence" provisions will generally not void a construction contract, because the owner of the premises cannot return the benefit despite the fact that it was not completed on schedule. The law abhors a forfeiture; therefore, Creased must still compensate Lisa for the work she performed.

36.   (C)   Creased's breach of the contract will give Lisa the right to restitution for her time and labor. The condition that Creased's sales increase by 25 percent will be excused because Creased's actions made fulfillment of the condition impossible. She will not necessarily receive the full $75,000, unless she completed performance and sales rose 25 percent.

37.   (A)   This question deals with the perfect tender rule. If a party tenders an imperfect performance, that party is in breach of contract. This rule is codified in UCC 2-601, which provides, "unless otherwise agreed. . . , if the goods or tender of delivery fail in any respect to conform to the contract, the buyer may (a) reject the whole; or (b) accept the whole; or (c) accept any commercial unit or units and reject the rest." The perfect tender rule will not apply to installment contracts; those are covered in UCC 2-612. Courts will also make exceptions if they find the breach insubstantial.

38.   (C)   Disney had a right to revoke Walter's interest at any time because the promise was gratuitous. While Walter was named to receive payment from Mickey, he was an intended beneficiary of the contract, but once Disney removed Walter's name, his

rights were extinguished. Disney's reservation of right to change the beneficiary prevented Walter's rights from vesting.

39.   (B)   Woodpecker was named as the beneficiary of the contract between Disney and Mickey. He is a bona fide intended beneficiary of this contract who may assert his rights. Refrigerator has a claim on only $10,000 out of the $100,000. Mickey will not be released from his contractual obligation, because Pluto decreased in value (Choice A). Mickey assumed the risk that Pluto's value might fluctuate. Woodpecker has no cause of action against Minnie because she had sold her rights to the contract with Disney back to Mickey (Choices C and D).

40.   (D)   Mickey had purchased all rights back from Minnie; therefore, Minnie could not be held liable for the payment since she was no longer a party to the Mickey-Disney contract.

41.   (A)   Disney could have assigned these rights to anyone he chose.

42.   (C)   Hot Rod and Mechanic had a contract for repairs. In such an instance, the performance of the repair (rebuilding of the engine) is a condition precedent to the obligation to pay. Hot Rod had no obligations and could not be in breach until Mechanic had completely repaired the car. Bad faith (Choice B) is of no concern; neither, for the purposes of this question, is (D). (A) is incorrect because if Mechanic had substantially performed, then Hot Rod might be in breach.

43.   (D)   When terms are written on the back of a check above the place of endorsement, cashing the check constitutes a valid accord and satisfaction of those terms, unless words such as "under protest" or the like are written under the signature. Since Mechanic accepted Hot Rod's check, he also accepted Hot Rod's terms of payment. The words "payment in full" release Mechanic's claim to another $200 regardless of whether he had properly fixed the car.

44.   (A)   Mechanic is liable to fix the car because, by cashing the check, he agreed to the terms of Hot Rod's letter, which required him to repair the car within ten days. (B) is incorrect because the original contract did not provide for subsequent repairs. (C) is incorrect because the original offer had already been accepted. A counteroffer is meaningless once a contract has already been formed. (D) is incorrect. Since there was a valid dispute as to whether the car had been repaired, the terms of the agreement formed when the check was cashed represented a compromise supported

by concessions by both parties. Hot Rod would get his car fixed and Mechanic would get paid.

45. (A)   A promise to forego an action brought in good faith is sufficient consideration to complete a contract even if the action would have failed (Choice C). (B) is incorrect because Pimple's subjective belief is irrelevant. There is no evidence in the question that the settlement was vague (Choice D).

46. (A)   Since the court ruled the Pimple-Waldman agreement was enforceable, Pimple owes a duty to Waldman. Waldman is Pimple's creditor. The Fazio-Pimple sublease calls for Fazio to satisfy the pre-existing duty owed to Waldman by Pimple. Waldman is a classic example of a creditor beneficiary to this sublease and may sue Fazio on the basis of his contractual obligation. A donee beneficiary (Choice B) is one upon whom the contracting parties intended to confer a gift. An incidental beneficiary (Choice D) is someone who "happens to gain," but is not directly intended to gain by the contract and has no third-party rights to sue.

47. (B)   Despite the fact that Pimple had obtained an agreement from Fazio to pay Waldman's maintenance costs, Pimple will still be liable on her contract with Waldman. Pimple did not delegate her duties in the maintenance agreement to Fazio, but entered another agreement with Fazio that called for satisfaction of the maintenance agreement. As a third-party creditor beneficiary to the Pimple-Fazio contract, Waldman has the choice to sue either Pimple (on the basis of their agreement) or Fazio (on the basis of the sublease). (A) is the reason that Waldman may sue Fazio, but not the reason that Pimple remains liable to Waldman. (C) assumes that Waldman may have standing to sue only one person for breach of contract, and that is incorrect.

48. (D)   Rewards are usually unilateral contracts that may be accepted only by performance. The answer to this question is contained within the facts. The offer was not for an arrest of the murderer (Choice A) or apprehending the murderer (Choice B), but for information leading to the arrest and conviction.

49. (C)   Any offer can be terminated by revocation or upon passage of a reasonable amount of time.

50. (D)   An offer may be revoked through reasonable attempts at substantially similar publicity informing of its revocation. Since the original offer was extended through a full-page ad in the daily newspapers, the revocation must be through a substantially similar medium.

51.   (D)   Parol evidence (oral evidence) can be offered to show that subsequent modifications were made to a written contract. The Parol Evidence Rule, forbidding the admission of oral evidence when there has been a complete and final written integration of a contract, applies only to contemporaneous or prior negotiations. This written contract was a complete and final integration because it contained a "merger clause" stating that it was a full embodiment of all prior agreements. Although the oral agreement prior to the written contract will be inadmissible, the oral agreement subsequent to the written contract will be admissible. The parol evidence issue will only control whether evidence of the oral agreement is admissible in court, it will not have bearing on the enforceability of that oral agreement.

52.   (C)   Extrinsic evidence is admissible to show agreements between the parties that are collateral to the integrated writing. A collateral agreement must be supported by separate consideration. For (A) to be relevant to the admissibility of the overtime agreement, that agreement would need to have been mentioned in the writing. (B) and (D) are false.

53.   (C)   The circumstances delaying the work were not contemplated by either party when Supportco and Realco formed their contract. Unforeseen circumstances not anticipated within the terms of the contract will give the parties the potential right to avoid the contract. Supportco's forbearance of this right by agreeing to continue the work despite these unforeseen circumstances will constitute sufficient consideration for the promise to pay the overtime rate. Supportco and Realco also had a bona fide dispute over Realco's obligations to Supportco. The subsequent oral agreement was their settlement. In an honest dispute, a modifying agreement will ordinarily be given effect.

54.   (B)   This is the least supportive answer because it is contrary to the evidence of the question. There was no attempt to rescind the written agreement. (C) and (D) make the same argument, that the oral agreement was collateral to the written agreement and, therefore, is admissible. (A) will show that there was consideration for the oral agreement.

55.   (A)   This is the most reasonable interpretation of Realco's statement listed in the answer choices. Realco's statement did not look to induce reliance, and it could not have induced reliance because Supportco had already completed performance (Choice B). There is no evidence in the question to support (C), and Realco did nothing to incur criminal liability (Choice D).

56. (C) Architect bestowed a gift upon University. Although the letter purports to recite Architect's fine education as consideration, "past consideration is no consideration." The education that Architect has already received was not given in exchange for ownership in this building; therefore, Architect's promise will not be binding unless he intended to transfer the rights at the time of the promise. Architect has impliedly reserved the right to revoke a promise of a future assignment since it was not supported by consideration. However, promises to charities will often be enforced under the doctrine of promissory estoppel without any proof of detrimental reliance. Whether this standard would apply to University depends upon whether it qualifies as a charitable institution.

57. (A) Hustler's assignment to Loafer was irrevocable because it was given for consideration. When an assignor makes two assignments of the same right and the first assignment is irrevocable, the first assignee will prevail. Providing notice of the assignment will not give a subsequent assignee priority.

58. (D) Loanshark had notice of the assignment and did not act to prevent it. He may not claim an interest in something that does not belong to Architect anymore. Although (C) may be correct in this instance, it is not a general rule.

59. (C) An assignment involving contractual duties is called a delegation. All duties may generally be delegated; however, duties involving personal judgment and skill may not be delegated without the consent of the other party to the contract. Hustler's duties clearly fit into this category. Loafer will most likely be able to collect those damages that he can prove were a result of Fatcat's sloppy management.

60. (C) A condition precedent is an occurrence that must take place before the other party has an obligation to perform. The lack of validity of one agreement (Architect with Surfer) will not be a "condition precedent" in contract law to the validity of another contract (Architect with Loafer) unless it is so provided within that contract.

61. (D) The Statute of Frauds would not be at issue. A promise to pay the debt of another must be made to the creditor, not solely the debtor, to fall within the Statute of Frauds protection of suretyship. When the promise is made to the debtor, the creditor is a third-party beneficiary and may enforce the promise without considering the Statute of Frauds. This agreement was in writing despite the fact that it omitted the portion requiring that partial payment be made directly to Carol. A correction to a writing is never barred by the Statute of Frauds.

62.   (C)   This is a parol evidence issue. If the court decides that the written contract was a complete and final integration, Carol will not be allowed to submit evidence that payment was to be made to her. Therefore, she will not be able to show that she was a third-party beneficiary to the agreement with standing to sue.

63.   (A)   Carol's rights would have vested if she were aware of the agreement, preventing Paul and Saul from revoking the benefits conferred upon Carol in the contract. Paul and Saul were free to rescind their agreement until it vested. (C) is incorrect; such formal notice is not required to vest third-party rights.

64.   (B)   A typographical error usually provides the ground for a reformation of the contract to reflect the true intentions of the parties.

65.   (C)   Constructor's promise to pay for Walker's damages is not enforceable because Constructor did not receive consideration in exchange for the promise. Construction has no legal obligation to Walker; therefore, Walker did not give up any valid legal claims against him. This is the most important issue in the question since gratuitous promises are not enforceable. The contract would not fall within the Statute of Frauds since the elements of a surety relationship are missing. Although the contract was vague, it could have been enforceable if supported by consideration, because the court might reasonably interpret what Constructor meant by "everything." This is not a situation that would fall under the doctrine of mistake (Choice A). Restatement (Second) § 152 defines a mutual mistake as where both parties have been in error concerning a basic factual assumption that materially affects the exchange, and the party seeking relief has not born the risk. Restatement (Second) § 153 addresses a unilateral mistake. It occurs when only one of the parties was in error, and requires that all of the elements of mutual mistake exist plus either the non-mistaking party knew of the error or enforcement of the contract would be unconscionable.

66.   (D)   (D) is the correct answer because both (A) and (B) will affect an action by the therapist. (B) indicates reliance by Therapist that may invoke the doctrine of promissory estoppel. (A) might render the therapist an intended third-party beneficiary of a valid contract between Constructor and Walker.

67.   (E)   The arrangement between Constructor and the therapist was a unilateral contract. No enforceable contract was formed until the act requested was performed. Each time the therapist treated Walker, Constructor was bound to pay for it. However, the therapist was never bound to treat Walker. The therapist may stop treating Walker at any time without being in breach. Walker is clearly the intended (donee) beneficiary of the Constructor-Therapist contract (Choice D), but this will not prevent the therapist from winning the suit. The therapist cannot raise any claims that Walker

and Constructor may have against each other, and Walker cannot sue Constructor. The proper suit is against the therapist (making (A) and (C) incorrect). (B) is simply false.

68.   (A)   Feefee gave up her valid rights to sue Driver as consideration for Constructor's promise. Driver's inability to pay is irrelevant. (B) is not a reason upon which Feefee might prevail, but merely the reason why she would choose to sue. (D) might apply in a tort setting, but in this situation Constructor agreed with Feefee that he would assume Driver's liability.

69.   (D)   The settlement was in good faith. Therefore, it acts as an accord and satisfaction in discharge of the remaining debt. Agreeing not to file a suit is valid consideration for a binding agreement as long as a party honestly believes that she had a valid claim. Even if Feefee could recover, she would not be able to collect for her emotional loss in a contract action. The law of contract seeks to redress economic losses only.

70.   (C)   This question deals with the perfect tender rule. If a party tenders an imperfect performance, that party is in breach of contract. This rule is codified in UCC 2-601 which provides, "unless otherwise agreed. . . , if the goods or tender of delivery fail in any respect to conform to the contract, the buyer may (a) reject the whole; or (b) accept the whole; or (c) accept any commercial unit or units and reject the rest." The perfect tender rule will not apply to installment contracts; those are covered in UCC 2-612. Courts will also make exceptions if they find the breach very insubstantial. This defense will help prove that Fred's failure to deliver the entire contractual amount on time was a material breach.

71.   (B)   A condition is an event other than the passage of time that creates, limits, or extinguishes the duty to perform. An express condition is stated within the contract. Some conditions that are not expressly stated will be implied by operation of law. A condition is "precedent" if its occurrence creates a duty in one party. Here, delivery of the proper amount and quality of animals was required within the contract before John had a duty to pay, so it was an express condition precedent. A concurrent condition requires that both parties exchange performances simultaneously. This question did not deal with a concurrent condition, because John had 90 days in which to pay after he had received delivery.

72.   (B)   This contract called for one transaction that could not be partitioned; therefore it is indivisible. If a contract is divisible, the UCC will consider it an installment contract. Under UCC 2-612, "An 'installment contract' is one which requires or authorizes delivery of goods in separate lots to be separately accepted." Neither

party to this contract could choose to fulfill part of the contract without another part, so the contract was complete.

73.   (D)   The perfect tender rule makes "time of the essence" an implied condition precedent in contracts for the sale of goods. This means that a late tender will constitute a material breach of contract, giving the buyer a right to reject the goods. This contract made "time of the essence" an express condition by relieving John's liability if there was a late delivery. (A) and (C) would not be the best answers. The fact that the animals were custom-made does not relieve the "time of the essence" provision, although it may aid in proving liability for the delivered animals. At first glance, (C) sounds like an impossibility or impracticability defense; however, Fred could have searched for additional stuffing sources. (D) is the best answer since it provides evidence of a subsequent modification (that does not fall within the Parol Evidence Rule) waiving the timeliness provision.

74.   (B)   Ellen had a right at any time to inspect the goods to determine if contractual specifications were met. (A) is incorrect; under many contracts, goods are paid for prior to their receipt. Ellen still has a reasonable time to inspect the screens after she receives them. (C) and (D) were fabricated. The opposite of (D) is true; a right to inspection must be expressly waived.

75.   (B)   Cathodco can recover the full contractual price of $100 for each screen Ellen keeps regardless of the market value. (D) is incorrect since the screens once inspected, tested, and installed were accepted and nonreturnable barring contractual provisions stating otherwise. If you chose (A), you should consider taking a remedial math course after the bar. If the court subsequently finds that Cathodco breached a warranty with Ellen that the screens would be faster than the ones she was replacing, Ellen will recover the difference between the value of the screens and the value they would have had if they had been as warranted under UCC 2-714.

76.   (B)   Ellen may recover the full price paid for the nonconforming screens provided that she returns them. (C) is incorrect since Ellen is not obligated to sell the screens.

77.   (D)   Under UCC 2-715(1) Ellen will be allowed to recover her incidental costs. This section provides, "Incidental damages resulting from the seller's breach include expenses reasonably incurred in inspection, receipt, transportation and care and custody of goods rightfully rejected, any commercially reasonable charges, expenses or commissions in connection with effecting cover and any other reasonable expense incident to the delay or other breach."

78. (B)   UCC 2-712 provides that if a seller is in breach, a buyer has the right to purchase substitute goods at a reasonable price. This is called "cover." Under the UCC "the buyer may 'cover' by making in good faith and without unreasonable delay any reasonable purchase of or contract to purchase" substitute goods. "The buyer may recover from the seller as damages the difference between the cost of cover and the contract price together with any incidental or consequential damages . . . less expenses saved. . . ." If the purchaser decides not to "cover," he will be limited to recovery of the difference between contract price and market value at the time of the breach (Choice C).

79. (C)   The pre-payment clause made the agreement performable within one year. (B) is deceptive. Although the UCC requires a writing with a contract for the sale of goods over $500, an oral contract will be enforceable when the goods have already been accepted by the buyer. (D) is incorrect; contracts made by minors are not automatically void, but voidable at the minor's discretion if not for the purchase of a necessity.

80. (A)   When one party acts to his detriment in exchange for a benefit conferred in the contract, there will be sufficient consideration to support the contract. A legal detriment will result if the promisee performs an act he is not otherwise legally obliged to perform or refrains from an action permissible to him. Since Kool gave up his legal right to have a part-time job or quit school, there was consideration for Henry's promise to pay for the car and provide spending money. A contract is formed despite the absence of a monetary loss to the promisee (Choice B) or monetary gain to the promisor. A promise to confer a gift without the intent to induce reliance is not enforceable. In this question, the promise reasonably induced acts by the promisees. (C) is incorrect because peace of mind may be sufficient consideration in some instances (see *Hamer v. Sidway*).

81. (A)   The Statute of Frauds provides that an agreement to answer for the debt of another must be in writing. There is no evidence in the question that the contract might be revocable at will.

82. (C)   Acceptance is a manifestation of assent to an offer in a manner understood or specified by the offerer. Since Henry indicated that silence would be an acceptance and he wanted a guarantee that the car would not be repossessed, both arguments I and II would help Bank's case.

83. (A)   Although contractual duties may be delegated, the delegator (Kool) still remains liable should there be a default by the delegatee (Henry). Henry is primarily liable for the debt, but Kool remains secondarily liable as the surety for the debt. (B) is

incorrect because Bank must first attempt to recoup the amount due from Henry. A novation (Choice D) occurs when a new contract is substituted for the original one. A novation will extinguish all prior obligations. The contract in this case was delegated, it was not replaced.

84.   (D)   Kool and Henry satisfied the elements required to form a valid contract. There was an offer, acceptance, and consideration. The contract did not contain a provision to terminate upon the death of the party. Contracts will ordinarily be discharged upon death only if they require personal services, which this did not. However, Kool's death destroyed Henry's purpose in entering into the contract. The Restatement 2d § 265 provides that a contract may be rescinded if an event frustrates the purpose of the contract depending upon the unforeseeability of the intervening event and the extent that the event deprived the promisor of benefit from the contract. It is relatively unforeseeable that Kool should die at such a young age. Since Henry sought to keep Kool in school without a part-time job, Kool's death completely prevents Henry from benefitting from the contract. (C) is incorrect; the Statute of Frauds does not require a contract with a six-month duration to be in writing.

85.   (B)   The January 1 agreement was an option contract. An option contract occurs when a party pays for the right to contract at a later date. Parties enter such an agreement specifically to protect themselves from price fluctuations. (D) is incorrect because Stephanie and Grace both bore the risk that the price would change. "Contract" is a standard term that is easily defined by the custom and usage of the trade. It will not allow a rescission of the contract for vagueness.

86.   (A)   Tosh must argue that perfect attendance was not an implied condition of the job. If he can prove that a short absence for legitimate reasons does not impair the quality of his teaching services, it would follow that the absence will not amount to a breach. In fact, the University of Rasta would be in breach for replacing Tosh. The estoppel argument (Choice B), only gives Tosh relief to the extent that justice requires and will be harder to prove than the immateriality of Tosh's absence.

          (C) is an inappropriate argument because it would permit the University to fire Tosh for a material breach of any one segment of the contract.

          (D) is also inappropriate because impossibility discharges all parties from performance.

          Tosh is not in a strong position because most contracts for employment are "at will," meaning that the employer may fire the employee at will.

87.   (B)   This answer is the best justification for a legal breach. The difficulty in obtaining a substitute would tend to demonstrate that Tosh's absence was a material breach and had the effect of ending the contract.

88.   (B)   Trouthead still has a right to inspect the goods and has maintained his remedies (UCC 2-513). Public policy will not prevent a seller from demanding payment before this point.

89.   (C)   A buyer of goods is entitled to "cover" in the event of a breach by the seller. This is the best course of action and will make Trouthead "whole" because he will have obtained the goods he wanted at the price he bargained for. "Cover" allows one to buy substitute goods and recover the difference between the price of the substitute goods and the contractual price (UCC 2-712, 2-725). If the substitute goods are bought below the original contract price, there is no additional recovery. In no event will the breaching party be permitted to benefit from the breach.

90.   (D)   A remedy for the buyer when the breaching seller refuses to accept a return of the goods is to resell the goods and then recover the difference between the sales price and the contract price from the seller. The original seller must be notified of the sale.

91.   (C)   This contract would ordinarily be void under the Statute of Frauds as an oral contract for the sale of land; however, Nebraska may be able to enforce the contract under the quasi-contract theory because of the substantial improvements he made to the store in expectation of ownership. The other choices would not be considered.

92.   (A)   The original agreement was fully enforceable. Both parties supplied consideration. Spell was guaranteed a buyer for its oil, and Guess was guaranteed a seller at the market price in exchange for their concessions. Although there was not a consistent price each month, the method of determining the price was definite. All essential elements were present for a contract. The subsequent agreement entered into by the parties modified, but did not replace or invalidate, the original contract.

93.   (A)   Again, all elements needed for a contract were fulfilled. Guess lowered the output requirement in exchange for Spell's extending the time for payment.

94.   (B)   Spell will be excused from performance under the doctrine of impossibility. This doctrine states that a contract is discharged when, through no fault of the parties, the subject matter essential to the performance of the contract is destroyed. (D) would help Guess win an action for breach. Neither party assumed the risk of explosion (Choice A). If Spell had assumed the risk, it would still be held liable to perform the contract. (C) may be true, but impossibility excuses it.

95.   (C)   The sale and assignment to Cramco would delegate Spell's duties in the contract with Guess to Cramco. One may delegate duties, but she remains liable if the duties are not properly satisfied. A delegation of duties does not void the original agreement (Choice A). (B) is incorrect since Cramco is the party in breach of contract, although Spell is secondarily liable for that breach. Spell would only be in breach if the contract had forbidden the delegation of duties.

96.   (D)   One is free to negotiate a revocable option. Solomon received consideration because the offer was held open beyond the time of an ordinary offer despite the fact that Nadia had the power to revoke it. An acceptance by Solomon would also extinguish Nadia's power of revocation. (B) depends upon whether the option contract was fully or partially integrated. An option contract that does not recite consideration will most likely not be regarded as a full integration. Payment of $1,000 to Nadia by Solomon does not contradict the written agreement.

97.   (C)   There is no general requirement that the revocation of an offer must be in writing. However, parties may always create such a requirement within their contracts.

98.   (A)   Nadia has extended an offer that can be accepted by performance (acceptance of the offer) and revoked any time before such performance. It resembles a unilateral contract. (B) is incorrect; a firm option is not revocable.

99.   (C)   A contract for the sale of land will not be defeated due to a failure to specify the kind of title to be conveyed. The seller will be required to supply a marketable title. The contract is not voidable for indefiniteness, since the court has the power to supply the omitted term (Choice A).

100.   (C)   If an obligor renders performance before he has notice of an assignment, the assignee takes title subject to the obligor's defense of ignorance. Sailbrow is the proper party for Aquino to sue since he was unjustly enriched by accepting payment.

101.   (A)   Aquino may enforce the contract against Ver because an assignment puts assignees in privity of contract.

102.   (A)   All contractual rights may generally be assigned unless the contract expressly forbids it. Assignments relating to the sale of goods over $500 must be in writing.

103.   (C)   Ver's rights as an assignee are treated as any other asset or liability he may have had at death or bankruptcy.

104.   (D)   A sublease is permitted unless the original lease specifically prohibits it. (This is really a property question so relax!) A sublessee will not be liable to anyone other than the sublessor.

105.   (C)   Since the court found that two separate contracts had been formed, Investor's first cable formed a contract for the sale of five coins at $500. Investor's cable was received prior to revocation. Despite the clause to the contrary, Roundmouth had the power to revoke the offer at any time prior to acceptance because there was no consideration given for an option and the offer was to be held open for longer than the three months the UCC allows an option contract to be irrevocable without consideration. Roundmouth could only revoke the offer in regard to the remaining coins, which he did. Investor's subsequent acceptance was for the remaining 45 coins at $1000 apiece.

106.   (D)   A written offer for the sale of goods is revocable, despite a clause stating the offer would be kept open, (1) if no consideration is paid for the option and (2) if the time period is more than three months. Since the time period stated here was 100 days, Roundmouth was free to revoke the offer at any time prior to acceptance. (C) is incorrect because Roundmouth assumed the risk that the price of gold would rise when he extended the offer.

107.   (C)   Once Investor accepted the offer by ordering five coins, a contract had been formed and Investor terminated any future power of acceptance on that offer. Although Roundmouth might also have a good argument for impossibility, that defense is much more difficult to prove. Roundmouth's performance would not be objectively impossible unless there were no other source of these coins. He most likely would be held responsible for insuring against theft and replacing the coins, even at a loss.

108.   (C)   Offers not supported by consideration or reasonably relied upon may be revoked at will by the offeror, despite promises not to modify or revoke the contract. See explanation for Question 106. This question does not fall under the UCC exception allowing a firm offer spanning less than three months to remain irrevocable without consideration, because the contract is for personal services and not the sale of goods.

109.   (B)   Scott's offer was for a unilateral contract because Scott was bargaining for performance, not a promise to perform. Under the Restatement, an offer to form a

unilateral contract becomes irrevocable once performance has begun. The unilateral contract will not be formed until the act requested has been completed, but once the offeree begins to perform, he will be given a reasonable time to complete performance, during which the offer is irrevocable. This rule was established to prevent capricious acts of offeror's from damaging the offeree in a unilateral contract.

110. (C)   Payment to Planter was conditioned upon satisfaction of a party to the contract. The agreement clearly specified that Homeowner could reject the goods if not 100 percent satisfied. This allows Homeowner's subjective tastes to be the standard and not the objective standard of a reasonable person in Homeowner's position. Homeowner's dissatisfaction must be in good faith, and she must give Planter an opportunity to cure performance to conform to her taste. This is not a contract for the sale of goods. Therefore, completion of performance by the date specified in the contract will not be "of the essence" or a material breach unless expressly specified in the contract (Choice A). Additionally, the reason for the delay is partially attributable to the actions of Homeowner.

111. (B)   Since Homeowner was not obligated to pay until Planter had fulfilled his obligations, Planter's duty to perform was a condition precedent to Homeowner's duty. (C) and (D) are incorrect because a condition subsequent is an event discharging a previous duty to perform. Such conditions are rarely used in contracts and are not involved here.

112. (D)   Since the delay was caused by Homeowner, Planter will be excused from the deadline. A court will estop Homeowner from enforcing the deadline. All of the other choices are relevant.

113. (C)   Cedar Hurst was a third-party beneficiary to an output contract between Far Rock Away and Wood Mere. UCC 2-306 provides that parties must make good faith efforts under such contracts, which they did. The contracts will not fail due to lack of consideration (Choice B), because both parties had obligated themselves. Wood Mere agreed to use Far Rock Away as its services were needed, and Far Rock Away agreed on a set price. (A) is irrelevant because there was no assignment of a contract. (D) is also irrelevant.

114. (B)   A court will not enforce this contract, because it lacks the specifics of the transfer. A contract for the sale of land needs to detail the amount of land. This agreement is in writing and satisfies the Statute of Frauds (Choice C). (A) is simply false.

115. (A)   As an assignee of the lease, Barbara assumed all terms and liabilities in the lease, regardless of her actual awareness. (B) and (C) deal with property law issues and are not relevant to this question.

116. (B)   Norman's contractual obligation survived the lease. One who assigns obligations remains liable as a surety if those obligations are not properly performed.

117. (A)   Both the burdens and benefits of the Sheldon-Norman agreement were conveyed to Barbara and Debra. Debra will be bound to allow Barbara to exercise the option.

118. (A)   An assignor remains secondarily liable on a contract as a surety for the assignee. Debra may assert an action against Heidi, Norman, or Barbara.

119. (D)   Lisa was required to act in good faith. If (A), (B), or (C) are correct, she did not. (D) will not help Davinci's case, because Lisa may, in good faith, dislike an accurate portrait of herself.

120. (B)   Both parties were obligated to cooperate. Failure of either party to do so would constitute a breach, and the usual remedies for breach would be available.

121. (B)   A unilateral contract is formed when the offerer requests performance (delivery of the mowers) rather than a promise to perform. Here Bill clearly and unambiguously requested performance, not a promise to perform. (A) is incorrect despite the fact that this offer related to the sale of goods because the UCC will only apply to merchants. Joe is a casual seller, and Bill is a casual buyer; they are not merchants. The UCC will render an option irrevocable without consideration if its duration is less than three months.

122. (D)   Offers not supported by consideration or detrimental reliance can be revoked at will by the offeror, even if he has promised not to do so for a certain period of time. The UCC carves out an exception for a firm offer between merchants to last for less than three months.

123. (A)   Bill was not asking for a promise of performance, but only the performance itself. He had the right to revoke his offer until Joe began performance. The offer was automatically revoked when the time for performance passed. The "Mailbox Rule" provides that acceptance by mail of a bilateral contract creates a contract at the moment of posting, so long as the acceptance is properly addressed and stamped.

This rule will not apply to a unilateral contract. (B) is incorrect since Bill is not effectively bound until Joe commences performance.

124. (C)   The conversation gave Joe reliable information inconsistent with Bill's offer. Joe's new knowledge will constitute a revocation of Bill's offer.

125. (D)   Under a unilateral contract, acceptance is generally accomplished by performance of the requested act. Bill asked that Joe deliver the mower to his home by 6:00 p.m., which Joe did. Notice to the offeror will not be a condition unless expressly provided for.

126. (B)   Joe had the power to form a contract by delivering the mower from March 1, the date Bill sent the letter, until March 13, the day his conversation with Mocco terminated his power of acceptance.

127. (D)   A contract is formed only after a "meeting of the minds," offer, acceptance, and consideration. Offer and acceptance were absent. The name of the individual who wanted to buy the airplanes would have constituted sufficient consideration to make a promise to pay a commission enforceable.

128. (D)   An agreement not to assign is not a condition of the obligor's promise to pay; therefore, breach of the promise does not excuse the obligor, but does provide an action for damages. (A) is incorrect since Mahoning may also be liable. Assignment of rights may be prohibited by an express clause (Choice B). The most effective way to prevent assignment of a contract is to write that "any assignment will be void."

129. (B)   Since General Helicopters did not know of the assignment, it will not be liable to Penguin. Mahoning is liable to Penguin because it was the assignor of the rights.

130. (D)   Narduzzi was a third-party beneficiary to the contract. Until a third-party beneficiary's rights vest, the original parties may modify the contract. The Restatement (Second) § 311 provides that a third-party beneficiary's rights will vest if 1) the beneficiary materially changes his position in justifiable reliance on the contract, 2) brings suit on the promise, or 3) manifests assent to it at the request of the promisor or the promisee.

131. (B)   Abstaining from smoking is sufficient consideration in a bargained for exchange. Although promissory estoppel may help Sam to prevail, proving bargained-for

exchange is a safer avenue to pursue. Under the Restatement (Second) § 90, reasonable reliance will be compensated only to the extent necessary to prevent injustice.

132. (B)   Rob should argue that since Sam had already promised Joe to quit smoking, Rob received no binding consideration for his promise. (C) implies that this case presents a Statute of Frauds problem, but the contract was to be performed within one year, and (D) is incorrect since subjective intent is not an element of contract formation. A valid offer and acceptance depends upon the objective manifestation of the exchange, not upon whether an offer or an acceptance was intended.

133. (C)   An offer may be revoked despite a promise not to do so, unless the promise to hold the offer open was made in exchange for valid consideration. Between merchants, a firm offer will be held open for up to three months without consideration. Rose and Daisey are a casual buyer and seller; they will not qualify as merchants. The March 15 phone call was an effective revocation because it gave Daisey information inconsistent with the offer. (D) is incorrect — the March 1 offer was valid at the time.

134. (C)   Under the Statute of Frauds, a contract for the sale of goods over $500 must be in writing [UCC 2-201(1)] and signed by the party to be charged. This contract was signed by Lee and not Byron. Contracts for goods specifically manufactured and not suitable for use by others need not be in writing. If an agent seeks to enter into a contract that ordinarily must be in writing, the agent's authority must be in writing. (C) is the least accurate choice because if Lee's authority was written, Dragon will most likely prevail.

135. (C)   An assignee takes his rights subject to the defenses of the obligor. Leroy could only owe Bank Two what he owed Roofer. If Leroy did not owe Roofer money on the contract because the work was not satisfactorily completed then he would not be liable to pay Bank Two. (B) is incorrect because contractual rights may be assigned despite a clause to the contrary. Violation of the clause may be a breach of the contract, but will not be a breach material enough to excuse payment.

136. (C)   When one sells a note, he assigns all benefits and loses standing to bring an action on the note. The fact that Prodigey is a minor is irrelevant.

137. (A)   The bank with priority will have an action for the money due on the note. One of the notes will be fully enforceable. An infant may choose to avoid a contract he

has entered into with certain exceptions. Sleezex may not choose to avoid Prodigey's contract for him. These exceptions include necessities, military service, student loans, and insurance contracts. Courts sometimes refuse to void a contract when the minor involved is in an ongoing business.

EVIDENCE CONTENTS

EVIDENCE QUESTIONS

1. Wiz was in need of an extremely sophisticated computer chip for a computer mainframe he was designing. Wiz contacted Finder, a broker who bought and sold computer components, to see if Finder could obtain the chip. "I may be able to find the chip," Finder told Wiz, "but it won't be cheap. It will cost $20,000 plus my fee." Finder successfully delivered the chip and demanded $22,000. Wiz offered $21,000 for both the chip and commission. In a suit brought by Finder to recover $22,000, Finder seeks to introduce copies of prior receipts of transactions with Wiz and others that show Finder charges a 10 percent commission for finding similar computer components. Wiz seeks to admit the testimony of six other brokers who specialize in the sale of computer components. They plan to testify that they charge 5 percent commission on rare computer components. Which of the following statements is most accurate?

(A) Finder's copies should be admitted as a past recollection recorded.

(B) Finder's copies should not be admitted because of the Best Evidence Rule.

(C) The testimony of the six brokers should be admitted to determine the customary business practice in the community.

(D) The testimony of the six brokers should not be admitted because it is not relevant.

2. Fox was severely injured when the flux capacitor of his DeLorean sports car exploded as he was driving through the Twin Pines Shopping Center. Fox asserted an action against Doc, manufacturer of the automobile, Goody Wilson, owner of the mall, and Futureback, Inc., owners of a truck unlawfully parked near the scene of the accident. Fox is seeking damages for his pain and suffering due to the flux capacitor burning his hand. Over proper objection, should the court permit Spielberg to testify that Fox jumped out of his car while screaming, "My hand hurts like it was struck by lightning"?

(A) Yes, as a declaration of a past bodily condition.

(B) Yes, as a declaration of a then existing bodily condition.

(C) Yes, as a declaration of a then existing bodily condition, but only if Spielberg was a licensed physician.

GO ON TO THE NEXT PAGE

(D)   Yes, as an exception to the Hearsay Rule, but only if Spielberg was a licensed physician and the statements were made pertinent to diagnosis and treatment.

Questions 3-4 are based on the following fact situation.

Six residents of the State of Valley brought suit against the State to rescind a new regulation permitting the operation of tandem trucks on the state's freeway system. Plaintiffs, a group of farmers with land adjacent to the Ventura Freeway in the County of Encino, allege that their crops were damaged by increased vibrations, noise, and exhaust from the passing tandems. Reseda, plaintiff's counsel, called Sepulveda, a state highway engineer who had supervised a report concerning the vehicular traffic on the disputed highway. Reseda asked Sepulveda, "Could you please tell us, according to the report you supervised, what percentage of the state's freeway traffic the tandems represent?" The state objected to the question despite their admission that Sepulveda was a bona fide expert. Reseda then called Balboa, one of the plaintiffs, to the stand. While being questioned, Balboa coughed in a seemingly uncontrollable manner and said, "I am sorry. Ever since the tandems have been allowed to pass, I can hardly breathe." On cross-examination, Balboa was asked, "Is it not true that you told your neighbor, Van Nuys, that you did not even notice a difference in your breathing when the law changed?" Reseda objected to the question.

3.   The trial judge should rule Reseda's question of Sepulveda

(A)   admissible under the business records exception to the Hearsay Rule

(B)   admissible, since the witness had personal knowledge of the matter

(C)   inadmissible, despite its probative value toward the main issue in the case, because it violates the Best Evidence Rule

(D)   inadmissible as extrinsic evidence of a collateral matter

4.   Which of the following statements is most accurate?

(A)   Balboa's statement about her breathing problem should be ruled inadmissible as a self-serving declaration.

(B)   Balboa's statement about her breathing problem should be ruled unfairly prejudicial.

(C)   The question asked of Balboa on cross-examination should be ruled improper regardless of whether it was set forth for impeachment purposes.

(D)   The admissibility of the question asked of Balboa will be determined by the professional status of the person to whom Balboa originally directed her comments.

5. Skunk delivered the keynote speech at the annual international convention of Racoons held at Grossinger's Country Club resort. Five thousand Racoons heard the speech live, and hundreds of thousands of others heard the speech over short-wave radios and by official tape recordings. Skunk said, "It is indeed an honor to be allowed to address such a distinguished audience. Please allow me to comment on the previous administration of President Chipmunk. Although sincere in its actions, much more could have been accomplished during his administration's tenure. We have an obligation to our society, and we must address this obligation in the best way possible. This organization can and will accomplish more in the future than it has in the past." Chipmunk asserted an action against Skunk for slander. Counsel for Chipmunk called Mongoose to relate to the court the contents of the speech. Skunk objected to Mongoose's testimony. The court should

(A) sustain the objection because Mongoose's recollection amounted to hearsay

(B) sustain the objection because a more perfect means of achieving the objective of Mongoose's testimony was available

(C) overrule the objection if Skunk's speech was identical to the script from which he read

(D) overrule the objection because a defamatory statement is not hearsay

6. Mr. and Mrs. Idiot left Junior, their six-year-old child, at home alone while they went to the movies. Junior cooked himself dinner, made some popcorn, and was about to watch a foreign movie when he heard some glass break. He saw Grizzly, a tall bearded man, climbing through the broken window. Junior was able to identify Grizzly in a proper lineup. If Junior is asked to testify against Grizzly, his testimony should be ruled

(A) admissible in a civil but not a criminal action

(B) admissible in either a criminal or a civil action after a court-approved preliminary inquiry

(C) admissible if the court determines Junior has the intellectual capacity of observation, recollection, and the ability to communicate his experience

(D) admissible in a civil action unless Grizzly can prove Junior is not competent to testify

7. Boss closed his office door and told his secretary, "I am going out to

GO ON TO THE NEXT PAGE

lunch. Please record all my phone calls in the company log." Company policy provided a standard log book to record messages when an employee was not present to receive the call. Boss was gone from his office less than five minutes when Rosemary called. Secretary recorded the following entry in her log book: "Rosemary called and said that her husband Bill landed safely at O'Hare Airport and he was going to take a cab to Hoffman Estates." A taxi driver was found murdered in his cab. The taxi was parked in Shaumberg, a town between O'Hare Airport and Hoffman Estates. Bill was charged with first-degree murder. The prosecution moved to admit both Secretary's phone log entry, made when Rosemary called, as well as the driver's own fare log stating his destination as Shaumberg. Which of the following statements is most accurate?

(A)   Both entries will be admitted under the business record exception to the Hearsay Rule.

(B)   Secretary's entry will be admitted as a record of regularly conducted activity.

(C)   Secretary's entry will be admitted because hearsay within hearsay is not excluded if each part of the combined statements conforms with an exception to the Hearsay Rule.

(D)   Secretary's entry will not be admitted because hearsay within hearsay is excluded under the Hearsay Rule if a component of the statement fails to qualify as an exception to the Hearsay Rule.

8.   Hasenfaus and Abrams owned a small incorporated charter airline called Aircontra. Aircontra operated charter flights between the United States and Central America. Poindexter and North were pilot and copilot, respectively, of an Aircontra plane flying from El Salvador to Washington. The plane landed in Miami for refueling. Shortly after take-off from Miami, en route to Washington, the plane exploded, and both Poindexter and North were killed. Poindexter's estate asserted an action against Aircontra. At trial, Aircontra called Buchanan, a surviving member of the ill-fated plane's crew, to testify. Buchanan invoked the protection of the Fifth Amendment and refused to testify. Aircontra then offered properly authenticated transcripts of testimony given by Buchanan in his criminal trial for freebasing cocaine on board the Aircontra flight and testimony in a suit asserted by North's estate against Aircontra. The transcripts contained testimony that Buchanan, Poindexter, and North were freebasing cocaine on board the plane. The fire used in the freebasing process caused the plane to explode. Aircontra offered the court stenographer to attest to the transcripts' accuracy. Poindexter's estate objected to the admission of the transcripts. The court should rule

(A)   the transcript of the criminal trial admissible, but the transcript of the civil trial inadmissible

(B)   the transcripts inadmissable because of the constitutional right to cross-examine a witness

(C)   the transcripts inadmissible because they are hearsay and not within any exception

(D)   the transcripts of both trials admissible

9.   Ivan Blowsky was the star witness in a trial of eleven codefendants accused of trading Colt Industries stock with information not available to the general public. Blowsky was granted immunity in exchange for his testimony. Blowsky owns 100 percent of the stock and is chief executive officer of Blowsky, Ltd. He was indicted and charged with tax evasion for failing to report income received from the eleven codefendants named in the Colt Industries suit. The prosecutor argued that Blowsky, Ltd., was paid for providing information about Colt that was unavailable to the general public. Blowsky, Ltd.'s business records were subpoenaed, but Blowsky refused to present the records. Will Blowsky be compelled to produce the records?

(A)   No, if he was granted transactional or use immunity in the first proceeding.

(B)   No, if he exercises his Fifth Amendment privilege.

(C)   Yes, even if he exercises his Fifth Amendment privilege.

(D)   Yes, because he must show that the prosecutor lacks an independent source for his evidence.

10.   Hawke was stabbed sixteen times in the pre-frontal lobe of his brain and three times in his left eyeball. The assailant left Hawke, a champion hand-wrestler, in a deserted alley where Hawke bled to death. Cobra is charged with the murder of Hawke. The prosecution called Dr. John Rambo, a forensic pathologist, who testified that Hawke's wounds were inflicted by a thin tool much like a unique tool used by jewelers. Cobra was employed by Clubber Lang Jewelers as a repairman. Rambo was about to show a photograph of Hawke's face but Ivan Drago, Cobra's counsel, objected. The prosecution called Balboa to the stand, who testified, "I heard a guy scream, 'You should have seen the jeweler's tool go right into the dude's brain.'" Drago objected to Balboa's testimony.
        Which of the following choices is most accurate?

GO ON TO THE NEXT PAGE

(A)   The photograph will be ruled admissible because it is relevant to the prosecution's case. Balboa's testimony will be ruled admissible if it was made immediately after the stabbing.

(B)   The photograph will be ruled inadmissible even though it is relevant, and Balboa's testimony will be ruled admissible even if the declarant is available, despite being hearsay.

(C)   The photograph will be ruled admissible, but only for the limited purpose of showing the tool was used to inflict the stab wounds. Balboa's testimony will be ruled inadmissible because Balboa was not a participant in the stabbing.

(D)   The photograph will be ruled admissible and Balboa's statement will be ruled admissible, under the "excited utterance" exception to the Hearsay Rule, but only if the declarant is shown to be unavailable.

11.   Lisa Dollar testified that she saw Defendant Bill Bogus holding a gun and demanding cash from a woman near an automatic cash machine. On cross-examination, Dollar admitted she had once told her husband, "It was snowing so heavily that night, I really can't be sure who tried to rob the woman." Dollar's testimony

about what she had told her husband is

(A)   inadmissible, because it is hearsay not within any exception

(B)   admissible to impeach her credibility but not as substantive evidence

(C)   admissible as substantive evidence alone

(D)   admissible as past recollection recorded

12.   Killer and Murderer were veterans of the United States Marine Corps. They wanted nothing more in life than to see those regimes they believed to be dominated by communists fall. Frustrated at what they perceived as the failure of the United States government to take concrete action against the Nicaraguan Sandinistas, Killer and Murderer decided to form an army of their own to obliterate the Sandinistas. Killer and Murderer formed a corporation with the intent of arranging an army.
Killer was named president and Murderer was named vice-president for purchasing. Killer and Murderer were arrested after a lawful search of Murderer's apartment yielded 200 M-16 rifles. The prosecution seeks to admit a statement made by Killer to Fat Louie, an arms merchant, in which Killer said, "There ain't no way I'm gonna need any guns from you; my man Murderer is vice-president

for purchasing." Killer's counsel objects to admission of the statement. The court will not rule against Killer on this issue if

(A)   the statement was made during the course and in furtherance of the conspiracy

(B)   the statement was not made during the course and in furtherance of the conspiracy

(C)   Louie was not a party opponent

(D)   Killer had been legally obligated to perform separate duties under the corporate charter

13.   Ginsburg was the subject of a Senate Judiciary Committee investigation of marijuana abuse among federal judges. Biden, a committee member, asked Ginsburg, "Did you ever smoke pot?" "No, and I never plagiarized my law school papers either," Ginsburg replied.

      Three months later, Ginsburg was prosecuted for perjury in relation to the statements he made before the committee. Bork testified that he was asked by Ginsburg to consult on a case before Ginsburg's District of Columbia Federal Court of Appeals.

      "I went into Ginsburg's chambers," Bork testified, "and he was sitting on the floor with three clerks. Their shoes and ties were off and they were passing around a joint the size of a cigar. Ginsburg said

something about smoking dope to help him find a creative solution to a difficult equal protection problem, and that a congressman had brought the pot back from a Nicaraguan fact-finding mission, along with some cocaine that they had already snorted." Which of the following statements is most accurate?

(A)   Bork's testimony concerning the cocaine is inadmissible as hearsay not within any exception.

(B)   Bork's testimony concerning the cocaine is certainly admissible.

(C)   Introduction of a transcript of Ginsburg's alleged perjurious statements will be prevented by the Best Evidence Rule.

(D)   The Best Evidence Rule is inapplicable to the transcripts of Ginsburg's testimony.

14.   Tim was killed in an airplane crash. His estate asserted a wrongful death action based on *res ipsa loquitur*. Lilian, his mother, testified, "Tim called from the airport and told me he was wearing a yellow shirt." The testimony is objectionable primarily because it is

(A)   hearsay

(B)   not relevant

(C)   admissible as *res gestae*

GO ON TO THE NEXT PAGE

(D)   leading

15.   Sandy was a passenger in her sister Jane's car when the car was hit by Ron's truck, which had just jackknifed after hitting a patch of ice. Sandy was not injured, but Jane suffered a fractured tibia. Jane asserted an action against Ron. Sandy was called by Jane's counsel to testify and was asked, "Do you think Ron was driving recklessly and/or at a speed far over the speed limit?" Is the question proper?

(A)   Yes, if counsel establishes Sandy had driving experience and could estimate speeds.

(B)   Yes, if Sandy was alert and observing Ron's driving.

(C)   No, because Sandy is testifying on Jane's behalf.

(D)   No, unless counsel establishes Sandy is an expert witness.

16.   Isaac went to City High School with Jacob and Sara. On homecoming night, Sara was murdered in a biology classroom. Isaac plans to testify that Jacob told Isaac and two other people that he killed Sara. Isaac's testimony will be admitted if

(A)   Jacob is exempt from testifying about Sarah's death on the ground of privilege

(B)   Jacob is held in contempt of court for refusing to testify about Sarah's death

(C)   Jacob cannot be forced to testify about Sarah's death because he shares a house with Robert Vesco in the Bahamas, outside the court's jurisdiction

(D)   all of the above

17.   Wally owned a small company in the business of building, installing, and maintaining a machine used in the purification of steel. The company did not sell the machine invented and designed by Wally. It would only lease it accompanied with a service contract.

On May 15, Wally inspected a machine leased to the Daisy Steel Company, as required by the service contract. Two days later, an explosion on Daisy's premises caused severe damage and injured Pete, a United Parcel Service employee in the process of making a delivery.

Wally inspected the premises after the accident and told his friend Wendy, "The explosion was caused by my machine. I should have opened it up when I had last inspected it, but I was running late."

Pete asserted an action against Daisy. Wally was not available to testify at the trial because he had subsequently died from injuries he sustained when another one of his boilers exploded. Should Wendy be allowed to recount

Wally's statements about the cause of the Daisy Steel accident?

(A)   Yes, under the "admission" hearsay exception.

(B)   Yes, under the "declaration against interest" hearsay exception.

(C)   No, Wally's statement to Wendy was hearsay since he did not witness the accident.

(D)   No, because Wendy's testimony is hearsay not within any exception.

18.   Executive, an attorney, was arrested for possession of marijuana after a drug-sniffing dog alerted airport officials that Executive's briefcase was stuffed with the drug.

Executive took the stand in his own defense and testified, "As soon as the officials grabbed me, I realized the briefcase was not mine. I must have taken it instead of my own when I left the men's room. I never smoked those funny cigarettes in my life." The prosecution concluded its cross-examination by asking Executive to smile, so that Dr. Dentine, a forensic dentist, could get a good look at his teeth. Dentine claimed he could examine the stains on a person's teeth and determine if the person had recently abused any form of delta-9-tetrahydrocannabinol, marijuana's active ingredient.

May the prosecution force Executive to smile if the defense makes a timely objection?

(A)   Yes, because the evidence is relevant.

(B)   Yes, because defendant elected to testify.

(C)   No, because the defendant may assert his privilege against self-incrimination.

(D)   No, unless Dr. Dentine's observations are not arbitrary and are scientifically sound.

19.   In which of the following situations should the defense's objection be sustained?

(A)   Witness testified at the trial of Francis, "Fred knew he was as good as dead. He had been given his last rites and could barely talk, but said, 'I saw Francis cut my throat.' He died within moments." The defense sought to exclude the testimony on the grounds it was hearsay.

(B)   Mary Beth asserted an action to recover custody of Baby Jane, her natural child. The case became complicated when an adoption referee fled the country with his mistress and all the relevant case files. Witness testified that Bobbie Beth, Mary's sister, had told

GO ON TO THE NEXT PAGE

the referee that Baby's natural father was William Booth, a notorious alcoholic. This statement was used to impeach Bobbie because she had subsequently stated under oath that the father was Richard Nixon, the former President. Bobbie, who fled the country in the middle of the trial, had given key testimony because she was present when Mary Beth and the adoptive parents signed their agreement that was now lost. Counsel for the adopting parents, defendants in the action, objected to Witness's testimony as hearsay.

(C)   In a breach of contract action, Plaintiff sought to introduce the testimony of a witness from a previous action between the same parties. This witness had stated that he was present at the making of an oral agreement between the parties. The witness had since been diagnosed as having Kuru, a disease endemic to Africa that is spread by eating infected human brains. As a result the witness was not asked to testify in this action. Defendant objected to the admissibility of the previous testimony.

(D)   Plaintiff sought to establish that Denise died on October 13, 1987, by showing that the date was inscribed on her tombstone. Defendant objected to the evidence, claiming it was hearsay and Plaintiff had not subpoenaed the person who carved the inscription, even though he lived less than two miles from the courthouse.

20.   Black, the author of a best-selling dictionary, died intestate. Several persons claimed entitlement to his estate. White asserted a claim based on her allegation that she was Black's biological daughter. White called upon Green, a postal worker who had delivered mail to her home for twenty years, to testify. Green testified, "Black often spent weeks at a time at the White's. White's mother's mail was often received addressed to 'Mrs. Black.' Black once picked White up into his arms and asked me if I thought his 'daughter' was cute." Should all of Green's testimony be admitted?

(A)   No, because of the Best Evidence Rule.

(B)   No, because of the Hearsay Rule.

(C)   Both of the above.

(D)   None of the above.

21.   In which of the following fact situations must David be unavailable for the testimony to be ruled admissible?

I. Defendant seeks to admit testimony given by David, a witness to a deposition for a civil proceeding between two persons not involved in Defendant's case.

II. Defendant seeks to admit testimony given by David, who heard Declarant say, while laughing, "Did you see that idiot go through the light and crack up his new Ferrari?"

III. Defendant seeks to introduce the testimony of David, a nurse, who heard Declarant's statements after he was told he had three minutes to live.

IV. Defendant seeks to admit a family Bible containing his family history and genealogy as compiled by David.

(A) I and III

(B) II and IV

(C) I, II, and III

(D) IV only

22. In a suit asserted by Reagan against Gorbachev, Reagan seeks to admit before the court transcripts of Gorbachev's testimony from a prior suit between the parties. The transcripts will be admitted if

(A) Gorbachev cannot remember the subject of the testimony

(B) Gorbachev is ill and refuses to testify

(C) Gorbachev is dead

(D) all of the above

23. Ellen, a computer wizard at Barney Smith, was accused by her employer of embezzlement. Ellen had, by her own admission, taken 200 computer software programs home and resold them to Columbus Avenue software, a discount retailer. Ellen used the proceeds from this sale to refurnish her apartment in a tony neighborhood near Central Park. The prosecution presented Ellen's employment contract as evidence. The contract contained a standard clause providing, "Employee understands that all supplies and equipment used by employee, including but not limited to, writing instruments, paper, stationery, reference books, computer hardware and software, and duplicating equipment, remains the property of employer, and may not be removed by employee from employer's premises without express written permission." On direct examination, Ellen testified, "During my contractual negotiations, I complained about the low salary I had been offered. Mr. Upham, the vice-president said, 'You can make lots of extra money by taking the obsolete software programs we no

GO ON TO THE NEXT PAGE

longer use. They aren't worth enough for the company to bother with, but you can substantially increase your income.'"

A timely objection to Ellen's testimony should be

(A)   sustained, because of the Best Evidence Rule

(B)   sustained, as hearsay not within any exception

(C)   sustained, because of the Parol Evidence Rule

(D)   overruled, because the testimony may be used to show the absence of criminal intent

24.   Which of the following persons would be ruled competent to testify under common law?

(A)   When asked under oath why he did not attend church, Eldred said, "I believe that the existence of any Supreme Being such as God is unknown and probably unknowable."

(B)   Benedict, an investment banker working on Wall Street, was convicted of treason after it was revealed that he had orchestrated a hostile takeover of McDonnell Douglas with Ivan "the Terrible" Boesky and a KGB agent on behalf of a corporation registered in the Netherlands Antilles and

controlled by the Soviet government.

(C)   Henry, a forensic toxicologist, was called to testify that an ingredient in Acme toothpaste could have decomposed and caused plaintiff's internal bleeding. Henry owned shares of Red Top Toothpaste which he had received in exchange for testing its safety.

(D)   none of the above

Questions 25-29 are based upon the following fact situation.

Speeder, who frequently drives quickly in residential neighborhoods, ran into and injured Timmy. Timmy filed suit, alleging that Speeder was driving drunk and struck him while he was lawfully in the crosswalk.

25.   Timmy called Freeloader, a passenger in Speeder's car, to testify that moments before the accident, Hitcher, another passenger, had exclaimed, "You're going too fast! We'll never be able to stop in time for a pedestrian." The trial judge should rule this testimony

(A)   inadmissible, as hearsay not within any exception

(B)   inadmissible, unless Hitcher corroborates Freeloader's testimony

(C)　admissible, as a spontaneous utterance reflecting Hitcher's impression at the time the statement was made

(D)　admissible, as a declaration against interest

26.　Timmy asked Freeloader if Speeder had been drunk with the expectation that he would say yes. Instead, Freeloader testified, "Speeder was without a doubt sober." Timmy then called Crosser, a witness from the scene of the accident, who testified, "Speeder was very drunk!" The trial judge should rule Crosser's testimony

(A)　admissible, as relevant to material issues

(B)　admissible, because Timmy was surprised by Freeloader's testimony

(C)　inadmissible, because a party may not impeach his own witness

(D)　inadmissible, because Crosser is not an expert in determining intoxication

27.　Timmy asked Crosser to testify that she had heard Timmy say to Speeder, "The accident was all your fault," and that Speeder had not answered. The trial judge should rule this testimony

(A)　inadmissible, as hearsay not within any exception

(B)　inadmissible, since all the witnesses are available to testify

(C)　admissible, since it is double hearsay

(D)　inadmissible, because Speeder's silence could be interpreted as an admission

28.　Speeder's counsel, on cross-examination of Crosser, asked her if she had been drunk when she witnessed the accident. Crosser responded, "I have been on the wagon for some time. I haven't had a drink in six months." Speeder then called Lusch to the stand, who testified, "Crosser and I got drunk together Saturday night." The trial judge should rule Lusch's testimony

(A)　admissible, to show Crosser's ability to recollect the accident

(B)　admissible, to show Crosser's character

(C)　inadmissible, because probative value is outweighed by prejudicial effect

(D)　inadmissible, because it is a collateral matter

29.　Speeder seeks to testify that an hour after the accident he said to Freeloader, "I can't move my arm, it

GO ON TO THE NEXT PAGE

must be broken." The trial judge
should rule Speeder's testimony

(A)   admissible, as a present sense
impression

(B)   admissible, to prove Speeder's
physical suffering

(C)   inadmissible, as self-serving

(D)   inadmissible, as hearsay not
within any exception

Questions 30-33 are based upon the
following fact situation.

One morning, Farmer Frank looked
out his window and to his horror saw that
the white picket fence surrounding his house
had been overturned. The yard was covered
with unusual tire tracks. Frank decided that
the tracks could only have been made by
Tommy's truck. Tommy was an alcoholic,
and Frank assumed that Tommy had driven
onto his lawn, destroying the fence in the
process. Frank brought suit against Tommy.

30.   Frank testified that he had called
Tommy's home and that a woman
had answered the phone. The
woman said she was Tommy's wife
and a partner in Tommy's Trucking
Company, Inc. Frank told her, "I
want to talk to Tommy about his
ruining my fence with his truck."
Mrs. Tommy replied, "Calm down; we
know our truck hit your fence.
Tommy will call you back." It was
the first time Frank had ever spoken
with Mrs. Tommy. The trial judge
should rule Frank's testimony of his
conversation with Mrs. Tommy

(A)   admissible, because the
accuracy of the phone system
and Mrs. Tommy's
identification of herself is
sufficient authentication

(B)   admissible, because the
accuracy of the phone system
is sufficient authentication

(C)   inadmissible, because Frank
could not have recognized
Mrs. Tommy's voice

(D)   inadmissible, as hearsay not
within any exception

31.   Frank further testified that a man
had called him. The man never
identified himself, but Frank and
Tommy knew each other well and
Frank was sure that the man who
called him was Tommy. Frank said
that Tommy told him, "I'm sorry
about the fence; send me a bill and
I'll take care of it." This testimony
should be ruled

(A)   admissible, because Frank
recognized Tommy's voice

(B)   admissible, because of the
accuracy of the phone system

(C)   inadmissible, as hearsay not
within any exception

(D)   inadmissible, because Tommy
did not identify himself

32.   Later that day, Frank called Tommy's
Trucking. A man answered,
"Tommy's Trucking, Nick here."

After Frank identified himself the man said, "I was driving the truck that drove onto your lawn this morning. I hope you'll forgive me." Frank knew Nick, but could not recognize his voice during the phone call. "I guess it was a bad connection," Frank explained on cross-examination. Frank's testimony of his phone conversation with Nick should be ruled

(A)   admissible, because of the accuracy of the phone system

(B)   admissible, because of the accuracy of the phone system, and because the speaker identified the company and acted as if he worked there

(C)   inadmissible, as hearsay not within any exception

(D)   inadmissible, because Frank did not recognize the voice as Nick's

33.   To illustrate the damages, Frank offered a photograph of the damaged lawn and fence. The trial judge should rule the photograph

(A)   admissible, if Frank testifies that the photograph accurately illustrates the damage caused by the truck

(B)   admissible, only if Frank testifies that the photograph was taken on the day the damage was discovered

(C)   inadmissible, because it violates the Best Evidence Rule

(D)   inadmissible, unless the photographer testifies that the photo is accurate

34.   Trucker agreed to transport oranges for Citrus, Inc., at his cost plus ten cents per mile. In a breach of contract suit, Seatcover, Trucker's assistant, recounted under oath the expenses she could remember that Trucker incurred. Citrus objected to Seatcover's testimony, because Trucker had kept a written record of all his expenses. Citrus's objection should be

(A)   sustained, because of the Best Evidence Rule

(B)   sustained, because the records were not so voluminous that they required a summary

(C)   overruled, since it is a record of regularly conducted activity

(D)   overruled, since it is a testimony of firsthand knowledge

35.   Bob and Ray were arrested and brought to police headquarters. The officer interrogating them said, "I am going to ask you one more time, what do you know about the computer scheme?" Ray said, "I admit it. My family needed the money, so I

GO ON TO THE NEXT PAGE

figured out a way to tap into the bank's code. I needed a connection in the bank, so I approached Bob and offered him $10,000." Bob remained silent during the confession. The fact that Bob remained silent while being implicated by Ray should be ruled

(A)   admissible, as an implied admission

(B)   admissible, because Ray's confession was an admission against interest for the co-defendants

(C)   inadmissible, because Ray's statements were not relevant to Bob's guilt

(D)   inadmissible, if a reasonable man in Bob's situation would not have felt obligated to answer

36.   Lori testified that she saw Bruce hit Joel, who then shot Bruce in self-defense. On cross-examination, Lori was asked, "Isn't it true that during the pre-trial hearing you said that Joel had shot Bruce without provocation?" The trial judge should rule the question

(A)   proper, as substantive evidence only

(B)   proper, for impeachment purposes only

(C)   proper, for substantive evidence and impeachment purposes

(D)   improper, since it is hearsay not within any exception

37.   Deena broke Richie's nose in a bar-room brawl and was arrested for assault and battery. Deena protested that the prosecutor failed to call Wendy, a witness to the fight, to testify. Wendy would have testified in Deena's favor. The prosecutor answered, "If Wendy's testimony was in favor of Deena, Deena should have called Wendy to testify." This statement by the prosecutor should be ruled

(A)   admissible, as within an exception to the Hearsay Rule

(B)   admissible, as a rebuttal to an inference that the evidence would be unfavorable to Deena

(C)   inadmissible, since it draws attention to the criminal defendant's right to refuse to testify

(D)   inadmissible, as an argument not based on evidence set forth

38.   A judge would least likely permit a leading question over an objection in which of the following choices?

(A)   direct examination of an adverse party

(B)   direct examination of a hostile witness

(C) direct examination of a disinterested witness

(D) issues related to preliminary matter, such as age or address of witness

39. Doris Night, a macrobiotic who works in a nut shop in Los Angeles, was arrested for auto theft on New Year's Eve. Joe Hudson, a new assistant district attorney who had only recently been admitted to practice in California, was assigned to prosecute the case. At trial, Hudson asked ten-year-old Molly Day, who claimed she saw Doris driving a car that night on Elm Street, "Molly, was the car that you saw on Elm Street red?" An objection to Hudson's question would be

(A) overruled, because the question is relevant to the State's case

(B) sustained, because the question is leading

(C) overruled, even though the question is leading

(D) sustained, because it is extrinsic evidence offered to prove a collateral matter

Questions 40-43 are based upon the following fact situation.

Givens is being tried for his kidnapping of Altamonte after forcing

Altamonte to rob a bank in Wyoming. Givens denies all charges.

40. Givens calls Douglas to testify that Altamonte is paranoid and schizophrenic. The trial judge should rule this testimony inadmissible

(A) because Altamonte is not the defendant

(B) because the issue must be raised by the defendant

(C) if Douglas is not an expert

(D) because a victim's psychosis cannot justify the crime

41. Charles testified for Givens. The prosecution chose not to cross-examine Charles. The defense then called Jay, who testified that Charles had a reputation as a very honest and truthful man. Over proper objection, Jay's testimony should be ruled

(A) admissible, assuming Jay knew Charles well enough

(B) admissible, as relevant to Charles's veracity

(C) inadmissible, as hearsay not within any exception

(D) inadmissible, because Charles's veracity was not brought into issue

GO ON TO THE NEXT PAGE

42. Givens testified on his own behalf. On cross-examination, the prosecution may ask Givens if

    (A) it is true that he received a three-month suspended sentence for perjury

    (B) it is true that he was convicted three years earlier for kidnapping

    (C) he was ever previously arrested

    (D) it is true that he was released from prison fourteen years earlier, after serving two years for manslaughter

43. Elaine testified that she had heard Altamonte scream as she was entering Givens's car. On cross-examination, Elaine was asked, "Is it true that you have been indicted and are awaiting trial for a misdemeanor?" The trial judge should rule this question

    (A) not proper, because leading

    (B) not proper, because irrelevant

    (C) not proper, because its probative value is outweighed by possible prejudice

    (D) proper, because relevant to witness's possible bias to the prosecutor

Questions 44-48 are based upon the following fact situation.

Jeff Stone, who formed his own rock band when he was eight, is on trial for murdering his mother, Debby. Jeff claims he was in Atlantic City on the night in question. He says his mother committed suicide.

44. Helen, a guitarist who was fired by Jeff many years ago, testifies that Debby had been very depressed because of Jeff's gambling habits and had told Helen she was going to kill herself. The trial judge should rule Helen's testimony

    (A) inadmissible, because it is hearsay

    (B) inadmissible, because it is irrelevant

    (C) admissible, as a dying declaration

    (D) admissible, as an exception to the Hearsay Rule

45. The prosecutor, on cross-examination, asks Helen, "Are you not Jeff's aunt?" The trial judge should rule the question

    (A) improper, because the issue was not raised by the defense

    (B) improper, because the answer sought is irrelevant

    (C) proper, since a relative is incompetent as a witness

    (D) proper, to show bias

46. Jeff called Bruce, a neighbor, who testified that Jeff had a reputation in the community as a law-abiding and nonviolent citizen. The trial judge should rule this testimony

    (A) inadmissible, because only the prosecution may raise the issue of reputation

    (B) inadmissible, because actions in a particular instance may not be proved by reputation

    (C) admissible, only to prove the defendant's veracity

    (D) admissible, because a criminal defendant may introduce evidence of his character as substantive evidence of his innocence

47. Jeff's defense attorney offered into evidence a letter that Jeff claimed he had written to his mother three days before she was found dead. The note said: "Thank you for helping me with my career. I will take care of you even when you are old and gray." At trial, Jeff's business manager, Zack Harris, was called to testify that the handwriting was actually Jeff's. The prosecution objected. This objection should be

    (A) sustained, because Zack's testimony would be inadmissible opinion evidence

    (B) overruled, because Zack can qualify as an authenticating witness

    (C) overruled, under the "past recollection recorded" exception to the Hearsay Rule

    (D) sustained, because an expert must identify the handwriting in a criminal case

48. Jeff testified that he was in Atlantic City at the time of his mother's death and, therefore, could not have committed the murder. The prosecutor asked Jeff, on cross-examination, "Were you convicted of perjury last year?" Jeff answered, "I have never been convicted of perjury." The prosecutor seeks to submit evidence of Jeff's conviction. The trial judge should rule this evidence

    (A) inadmissible, because the prosecutor may not impeach Jeff

    (B) inadmissible, because specific instances of conduct are not relevant to the issue of whether Jeff murdered Debby

    (C) admissible, because of the nature of the crime of perjury

    (D) admissible, because the crime of perjury is relevant to the issue of whether Jeff murdered Debby

GO ON TO THE NEXT PAGE

Questions 49-51 are based upon the following fact situation.

Dan and Stan signed a contract in which Dan agreed to lease Hotel Shlock to Stan, who agreed to maintain the premises. Stan brought an action for loss of profits.

49.   Dan called Janitor, who often cleaned Stan's office. Janitor testified that he heard Stan say, while talking on the phone, "The value of Shlock has tripled. I have to figure out a way to break the lease." The trial judge should rule Janitor's testimony

    (A)   admissible, on the issue of Stan's state of mind

    (B)   admissible, to prove the value of the hotel

    (C)   admissible, for both Stan's state of mind and the value of the hotel

    (D)   inadmissible, because it is hearsay not within any exception

50.   Esquire, who proofread the contract just before it was signed, was called to testify about the terms of the contract. This testimony should be ruled

    (A)   admissible

    (B)   inadmissible, because of the Best Evidence Rule

    (C)   inadmissible, because of the Parole Evidence Rule

    (D)   inadmissible, because it is hearsay not within any exception

51.   Dan denied that the signature on the contract was his. Stan called Miss Parker, who had taught Dan in high school. Parker testified that she remembered Dan's signature and that the signature on the contract was his. Dan is thirty-two years old. The court should rule Miss Parker's testimony

    (A)   admissible

    (B)   inadmissible, because she is not an expert

    (C)   inadmissible, because genuineness is a question for the jury and not for a witness

    (D)   inadmissible, because Dan has not been a high school student for many years

Questions 52-54 are based on the following fact situation.

Sleepy sued Lazy for damages arising out of a car accident.

52.   Sleepy produced a photocopy of Lazy's car registration to prove Lazy's ownership. Lazy objected to the photocopy, but did not deny that he owned the car. The trial judge should rule that the copy is

    (A)   admissible, only if the original is shown to be unavailable

(B)   admissible, regardless of the availability of the original

(C)   inadmissible, because of the Best Evidence Rule

(D)   inadmissible, unless the car is owned by a business and the photocopy was a business record

53.   Nervous happened to be returning from the grocery store with his wife Mary when he witnessed the accident between Lazy and Sleepy. Mary testified, "Just before the accident Nervous screamed that Lazy was driving on the wrong side of the street." The trial judge should rule Mary's testimony

(A)   admissible, only if Nervous is shown to be unavailable

(B)   admissible, regardless of Nervous's availability

(C)   inadmissible, as hearsay not within any exception

(D)   inadmissible, because of the Best Evidence Rule

54.   Sleepy called Dr. Casey to testify that Lazy came to his office minutes after the accident. When Dr. Casey saw the bruises and asked, "What happened?" Lazy answered, "I cracked up my car because I was driving on the wrong side of the

street." Dr. Casey's testimony should be ruled

(A)   admissible, as an admission against interest

(B)   inadmissible, if Lazy objects

(C)   inadmissible, as hearsay not within any exception

(D)   inadmissible, because of the physician-patient privilege

Questions 55-58 are based on the following fact situation.

Alison sued David for injuries suffered in an automobile accident caused by Steve, who had rented David's car. Alison claims David knew that Steve was under the legal driving age.

55.   Hertz, present at the accident, sought to testify that he had remarked to another witness, "Steve is so young, he can't drive!" Hertz's remark to his companion is

(A)   inadmissible, unless evidence was put forth showing Hertz was an expert in determining age

(B)   admissible, as an excited utterance

(C)   admissible, as a prior statement

GO ON TO THE NEXT PAGE

(D)   admissible, as a statement by Hertz regarding a condition he had observed, made while he was observing it

56.   David called Steve to testify. David expected Steve to say that he was eighteen years old. However, on direct examination, Steve testified that he was fifteen. David then tried to confront Steve with a statement he had made in his deposition claiming that he was eighteen. Which of the following is true in regard to Steve's statement at trial?

(A)   It is inadmissible, because David cannot impeach his own witness.

(B)   It is inadmissible, because it is hearsay not within any exception.

(C)   It may be used to refresh Steve's memory.

(D)   It is admissible for impeachment and as substantive evidence that Steve is above the legal age.

57.   Alison offered evidence that after the accident David's employees required proof of age from anyone who sought to rent a car from David, regardless of how old the person appeared. This evidence is

(A)   inadmissible, on the grounds of irrelevancy

(B)   admissible, to show that David was aware of the need to take remedial measures

(C)   inadmissible, on the grounds of public policy

(D)   admissible, to show that David's prior conduct was negligent

58.   Alison offered evidence that after the accident David visited her in the hospital and offered a $10,000 settlement, saying, "I am sorry I rented my car to a fifteen-year-old kid." The statement "fifteen-year-old kid" is

(A)   inadmissible, as hearsay not within any exception

(B)   admissible, as a factual admission made in connection with an offer of compromise

(C)   inadmissible, as a statement made in connection with an offer to pay medical expenses

(D)   admissible, as an admission by David that Steve was below the legal driving age

Questions 59-63 are based upon the following fact situation.

Sean was charged with the crime of assaulting Shaheid. Sean admitted to slamming a coconut into Shaheid's face, thereby causing him to lose seven teeth, but he claimed that he was acting in self-defense because Shaheid, while heavily intoxicated, had blocked the road with his Volkswagon and threatened to harm Sean.

59. The prosecutor, in her case in chief, introduced testimony that Sean has a reputation in his community as one who likes to settle arguments in a violent manner. The court should rule this testimony

   (A) admissible, to show the possibility of conformity in this instance

   (B) admissible, because the probative value of the evidence outweighs its possible prejudice

   (C) inadmissible, because the defendant's character has not been placed at issue

   (D) inadmissible, as irrelevant

60. Dr. Kilpatrick, president of North Side Hospital, where Sean was employed as a physician, testified, "I have known Sean since he was a young boy and he is a hard-working, law-abiding, and peace-loving man." Kilpatrick's testimony should be ruled

   (A) admissible, because relevant to the issue of whether Sean was the aggressor

   (B) admissible, because relevant to decide an appropriate punishment if convicted

   (C) inadmissible, because conduct in specific instances may not be proved by character references

   (D) inadmissible, as hearsay not within any exception

61. Kilpatrick was asked, on cross-examination, if he was aware that Sean had a reputation in the community of having a "hot temper." The trial judge should rule this question

   (A) proper, because previous acts may be used to prove conformity on a specific occasion

   (B) proper, to determine Kilpatrick's knowledge of Sean's reputation

   (C) not proper, because specific acts may not be proved by reputation

   (D) not proper, because overly vague

62. Sean called Chris, who testified that Shaheid was known in the community to be a violent man, a molester of women, and an alcoholic, who had spent many years in a unique Caribbean camp for alcoholics. The court should rule the testimony

GO ON TO THE NEXT PAGE

(A)   admissible, only if Chris testifies of specific acts that could have been felonies

(B)   admissible, as relevant to the issue of self-defense claimed by Sean

(C)   inadmissible, because the witness did not lay a proper foundation

(D)   inadmissible, unless Shaheid was actually convicted of the crimes mentioned

63.   The prosecution called Nellie, an admitted prostitute, who testified she had seen Sean drive through a stop sign less than a mile from the altercation, without even slowing down. The trial judge should rule this testimony

(A)   admissible, because it shows Sean has a propensity to ignore the law

(B)   admissible, even if Sean was not convicted of passing a stop sign

(C)   inadmissible, because testimony of such an act is not allowed on the issue of Sean's guilt or innocence

(D)   inadmissible, because of Nellie's character

64.   Clyde sued Lee for damages arising out of an auto accident in which Lee had plowed into Clyde's 1969 Mustang. The accident took place on the corner of Willson Avenue and 3rd Street on October 3, 1987. Clyde filed his lawsuit on September 2, 1990. After the parties could not reach a settlement agreement, the matter was scheduled for trial on December 1, 1991. One day prior to trial, Clyde went to the corner where the accident took place and took four photos with his expensive Nikon. At trial, the photographs are

(A)   admissible, as a then existing physical condition

(B)   admissible, but only if Clyde testifies that he took the photos

(C)   inadmissible upon objection by Lee, because the photos were taken more than four years after the accident

(D)   admissible, if the photos accurately and correctly portray the scene of the accident

Questions 65-69 are based upon the following fact situation.

Elmo, while crossing the street, was hit by a car driven by Ernie. Larry and Harry were passengers in Ernie's car. Vincent, another pedestrian, witnessed the accident and called the police, who sent Croker to investigate.

65.   The plaintiff called Larry as a witness, who testified that just before the accident Harry had screamed, "You're going too fast. You'll never

be able to stop for that pedestrian."
Larry's testimony should be ruled

(A)   admissible, as a spontaneous utterance

(B)   admissible, as a declaration against interest

(C)   inadmissible, because speed must be determined by an expert

(D)   inadmissible, because it violates the Best Evidence Rule

66.   Vincent testified, "Ernie offered me $5,000 to testify it was all Elmo's fault." The trial judge should rule this testimony

(A)   admissible, as a declaration against interest

(B)   admissible, as an admission by a party opponent

(C)   inadmissible, because not relevant to the issue of negligence

(D)   inadmissible, as hearsay not within any exception

67.   Elmo's counsel introduced evidence that Ernie offered Elmo $5,000 to release him from all liability arising from the accident. This evidence should be ruled

(A)   admissible, only on the issue of liability

(B)   admissible, only on the issue of damages

(C)   inadmissible, because of public policy

(D)   inadmissible, because not relevant

68.   Suzy testified that Ernie had a reputation in the community as a safe and careful driver. Suzy and Ernie lived on the same block for more than thirty years. The trial judge should rule Suzy's testimony

(A)   admissible, as tending to prove that Ernie was driving safely prior to the accident

(B)   admissible, only if the plaintiff asks for punitive damages

(C)   inadmissible, unless the plaintiff has raised the character issue

(D)   inadmissible, because general reputation cannot be used to prove lack of negligence on a particular occasion

69.   Croker testified that three days after the accident he ran into Ernie in a barber shop where Ernie told him, "My lawyer said I may get away with it, but it was actually my fault." Croker's testimony should be ruled

GO ON TO THE NEXT PAGE

(A) admissible, because Croker is a police officer

(B) admissible, as a party admission

(C) inadmissible, because the statement was made three days after the accident

(D) inadmissible, as hearsay not within any exception

Questions 70-71 are based upon the following fact situation.

Mary Slope and her best friend, Dana Dover, were driving to a ski resort in late December when Mary's car was hit head-on by a pick-up truck driven by Barry Burros. No one was injured, but Mary's car was badly wrecked and Dana began to have nightmares that she was an auto mechanic for Chrysler. Mary alleges that Burros was driving without windshield wipers and that that was the cause of the accident.

70. A passenger in Burros's car said to Tim, who happened to be walking his dog at the scene of the accident, "We couldn't see a thing; the wipers weren't working." Tim's testimony concerning the passenger's statement should be ruled

(A) admissible, as a declaration against interest

(B) admissible, as an admission of party opponent

(C) inadmissible, because of possible bias

(D) inadmissible, because it is hearsay not within any exception

71. Tim also seeks to testify that, just before the cars crashed, a man next to him screamed, "That driver can't possibly see where he's going without windshield wipers!" The testimony should be ruled

(A) admissible, only if the man who screamed is not available to testify

(B) admissible, even if the man who screamed is available to testify

(C) inadmissible, as hearsay not within any exception

(D) inadmissible, because no recording was made

72. The defense called Eli to testify on behalf of the defendant in a burglary trial. On cross-examination, the prosecutor may properly ask Eli, as a witness,

(A) about his past felony convictions, but the prosecutor is bound by Eli's answer

(B) about his past misdemeanor convictions, but the prosecutor is bound by Eli's answer

(C)   about Eli's arrest record

(D)   about Eli's thirty-day
       suspended sentence for
       embezzlement

Questions 73-76 are based on the following fact situation.

Robert was returning home after seeing a Broadway show in New York City. Robert had a fascination with tunnels. As he was driving through the Holland Tunnel, he was involved in an accident with Billy Smith, who happened to be in the cast of the Broadway show Robert had just seen. Joe Johnson, a carpenter, saw the whole accident in his rear-view mirror and was present at the trial.

73.   Joe Johnson testified that Robert
       exceeded the speed limit by "at least
       twenty miles per hour." On cross-
       examination, Robert asked Joe,
       "What color is my car?" Joe replied,
       "Green." Robert seeks to introduce
       evidence that his car is red. The trial
       judge should rule this evidence

       (A)   admissible, as bearing on
              Joe's recollection of the facts

       (B)   admissible, as bearing on
              Joe's veracity

       (C)   inadmissible, because
              remembering the color of the
              car is not relevant to the issue
              of remembering the accident

(D)   inadmissible, because the
       issue of the color of the car is
       a collateral matter

74.   Joe further testified that Patti, a
       passenger in Robert's car, told him a
       half an hour after the accident, "I
       knew we would crack up. He was
       driving like a wild man. Don't tell
       Robert I told you this." The trial
       judge should rule Patti's testimony

       (A)   admissible, as a declaration
              against interest

       (B)   admissible, as an admission of
              a party

       (C)   inadmissible, unless Robert
              refuses to testify

       (D)   inadmissible, as hearsay not
              within any exception

75.   Patti testified that Robert was
       speeding and was looking all around
       him instead of keeping his eyes on
       the road because he was so
       fascinated with the engineering of the
       tunnel. In support of this testimony,
       Billy Smith called Judy, who has car-
       pooled to work with Robert for the
       past twenty years. Judy testified that
       every time Robert drives through a
       tunnel, he speeds uncontrollably and
       looks all around him in fascination.
       Judy's testimony will most likely be

       (A)   excluded, because prior acts
              on a particular occasion are

GO ON TO THE NEXT PAGE

inadmissible to prove conformity therewith

(B)   admitted, because it is reputation as to character

(C)   excluded, because Judy was not present at the time of the occurrence

(D)   admitted, as proof of Robert's habit of speeding in tunnels.

76.   Approximately four hours after the accident, Robert, who is an artist, went home and painted a watercolor of the accident. At trial, Robert claimed he could not remember details of the accident. Billy seeks to show him the watercolor to assist his testimony. The trial judge should rule presentation of the artwork

(A)   permissible, as a past recollection recorded

(B)   permissible, as a present recollection refreshed

(C)   not permissible, because Robert had time to reflect before he started painting

(D)   not permissible, because the painting is of no evidentiary value

77.   Dorothy was assaulted, robbed, and raped. Her injuries required four weeks of hospitalization. As she was leaving the hospital she screamed, "That's the man who did it." Her husband, Mark, grabbed the man she

was pointing at. Mark's testimony of Dorothy's statement should be ruled

(A)   admissible, only if Dorothy is shown to be unavailable

(B)   admissible, regardless of Dorothy's availability

(C)   inadmissible, as hearsay not within any exception

(D)   inadmissible, because of the husband-wife privilege

Questions 78-79 are based upon the following fact situation.

Sal stopped by an all-night store to pick up some cat food. As he left the store, he saw his good friend Mike pull up in his old Rambler. Mike and Sal started talking. A few minutes later, Duran pulled up in his new Honda and ran into the store. Shots were fired inside and Duran came running out, but he collapsed as he tried to get into his car. Betty, the cashier, came running out of the store screaming, "No one robs my store and gets away with it." Suddenly, Duran took out a gun and shot Sal in the chest, killing him instantly. Duran then aimed at Mike and took a shot at him. When the police arrived, Sergeant Cox ran over to Mike, who was bleeding profusely and said, "I don't think you're gonna make it, kid." Mike then said, "That man shot and killed my good friend Sal." Within moments, Mike died.

78.   At Duran's trial for double murder and robbery, the prosecutor sought to admit Sergeant Cox's testimony as to Mike's statement about the man who

killed Sal. The defense objected.
This testimony should most likely be

(A) admissible, under the "dying declaration" exception

(B) admissible, as a then-existing mental condition

(C) inadmissible, because Cox is a police sergeant

(D) inadmissible, because the declaration was made by Mike

79. Evan testified that he was watching television with Duran at the time of the incident. When asked on cross-examination, Evan denied that he had loaned Duran money to pay for the television they had been watching. The prosecution called Spider, the salesman who sold the television to Duran, to testify that he saw Evan loan Duran the money for a television. The trial judge should rule Spider's testimony

(A) admissible, to impeach Evan

(B) admissible, to show Duran was in debt and had a motive to rob the store

(C) inadmissible, because not relevant

(D) inadmissible, because prejudicial

Questions 80-82 are based upon the following fact situation.

Jon walked into a house that he thought belonged to his girlfriend Mary, but it was really the house next door to Mary's. Ron, the owner of the house, had just finished exercising in his basement and was walking upstairs, wearing a black sweatsuit, just as Jon walked in through the front door, which had been left open. Jon attacked Ron, causing grave injuries. Jon was charged with assault, battery, and attempted burglary. He claimed that he had thought the house was Mary's, that Ron was a burglar, and that he had used force in self-defense.

80. Jon's long-time neighbor, Lam, testified that Jon had a reputation in the community as a hard-working and peaceful man. The trial judge should rule this testimony

(A) admissible, to assess damages in a possible civil suit

(B) admissible, to show the unlikeliness that Jon had criminal intent

(C) inadmissible, because reputation cannot be used to prove behavior in a specific instance

(D) inadmissible, as hearsay not within any exception

81. Lam was asked, on cross-examination, whether he knew that Jon had been prosecuted for assault and attempted

burglary on two prior occasions. The trial judge should rule this question

(A)   proper, to determine Lam's familiarity with Jon

(B)   proper, because relevant to prove Jon acted in a criminal manner in this instance

(C)   not proper, because the probative value is outweighed by possible prejudice

(D)   not proper, because the incidents are not related

82.   Henry testified that Jon is a karate expert and has a reputation in the community as "the kind of guy who likes action — he loves to pick fights." The trial judge should rule Henry's testimony

(A)   admissible, only if Henry has personal knowledge

(B)   admissible, to prove Jon acted in self-defense

(C)   inadmissible, unless Jon is not available to testify

(D)   inadmissible, because of lack of proper foundation

83.   Abe hired Judy to defend him against charges arising out of an armed robbery. Dave, Judy's secretary, was present during the questioning and took notes. The charges were dropped when Abe agreed to testify against Harry. Judy was called by the prosecution during Harry's trial to testify about what Abe had told her regarding the robbery. Judy refused to testify. The judge should rule that Judy

(A)   must testify, because an attorney-client privilege may only be claimed by the client

(B)   must testify, because Abe has turned State's witness

(C)   cannot testify, because of the Hearsay Rule

(D)   cannot be forced to testify, because of the attorney-client privilege

84.   Harry Munster was involved in a collision with Lilly Adams on Mockingbird Lane. While they were exchanging phone numbers, Harry said to Lilly: "Oh my gosh! My insurance company is reliable. They'll pay for your broken nose!" Lilly sued Harry for personal injuries and plans to testify as to what Harry said to her. Lilly's testimony will be

(A)   admissible, as an excited utterance

(B)   admissible, but only to prove ownership or control of the vehicle

(C)   admissible, to prove negligence

(D)   inadmissible, as hearsay not within any exception.

Questions 85-87 are based upon the following fact situation.

Flyer owned a private plane, which he used for recreational purposes. One clear afternoon, Flyer experienced mechanical difficulties and was forced to eject himself from the plane. Flyer parachuted safely to the ground, but the plane crashed into Smiley's barn, causing substantial damage to the structure. Flyer was rescued by two policemen, who noticed that Flyer was acting strangely. Flyer was brought to a hospital, where he was diagnosed as heavily intoxicated. Criminal charges were brought against Flyer for operating an airplane while under the influence of alcohol.

85. When brought to the hospital, a videotape of Flyer was made to aid the diagnosis. The tape showed that Flyer's speech was slurred and his walk unsteady. The prosecution seeks to admit the tape into evidence. Should the court allow the prosecution to show the tape to the jury?

(A) Yes, because the probative value is not outweighed by unfair prejudice.

(B) Yes, because it is an admission against interest.

(C) No, because the defendant's privilege against self-incrimination was violated.

(D) No, because it would be impossible to lay a proper foundation.

86. Smiley filed suit against Flyer, alleging that the damages to his barn were a direct result of Flyer's intoxication. Smiley offers the properly authenticated records of Flyer's criminal conviction for flying while intoxicated. The conviction should be ruled

(A) admissible, only to prove intoxication

(B) admissible, only to prove character

(C) inadmissible, because Flyer pleaded guilty only for criminal purposes

(D) inadmissible, because it is hearsay not within any exception

87. Smiley joined Pee Wee Airport in his suit, alleging that the airport was negligent for allowing Flyer to fly while obviously inebriated. Smiley seeks to introduce evidence that shortly after Flyer's accident, the airport instituted a new screening procedure in which an airport employee monitors pilots to be sure that they are fit to fly. The trial judge should rule this evidence

(A) admissible, to show Pee Wee could have prevented the accident

(B) admissible, to show Flyer was intoxicated

GO ON TO THE NEXT PAGE

(C)   inadmissible, because not relevant to Pee Wee's negligence

(D)   inadmissible, because the policy of the court is to encourage remedial measures

88.   Jagger suffered ankle injuries when a heel fell off his shoe while he was dancing. The shoe company called Dr. Dimento to testify about statements made to him by Jagger. In which of the following situations would the judge be most likely to admit the testimony over Jagger's objections?

(A)   The trial judge ruled that the discussion between Jagger and Dimento occurred during preliminary discussions, and Jagger eventually received treatment.

(B)   The trial judge ruled that the discussion between Jagger and Dimento occurred during preliminary discussions, and Jagger left the office without being treated.

(C)   The trial judge ruled that Jagger had been Dimento's patient for two years, and the statements were made when the two happened to meet at a cocktail party.

(D)   The trial judge ruled that Jagger and Dimento discussed the matter at a cocktail party, where they met for the first

time and were trying to "make conversation."

89.   Three days after having been shot point-blank in the face, Ryan knew he was about to die. He said to Nurse, "I only have a couple hours to live. I want you to know Sammy shot me." Ryan died less than an hour later. Sammy's counsel called Susan to testify. Susan said that she had visited Ryan three days before he died and "Ryan said he could not tell who shot him." Susan's testimony should be ruled

(A)   admissible, to impeach Ryan

(B)   admissible, as a statement under belief at impending death

(C)   inadmissible, because not relevant

(D)   inadmissible, because the last implication is deemed controlling

Questions 90-92 are based upon the following fact situation.

Gary was caught trying to burglarize a jewelry store. The police obtained a search warrant for Gary's apartment and found a handwritten map of the jewelry store, marked with possible escape routes.

90.   Rob testified that he had shared a cell with Gary in the state penitentiary seven years earlier and had seen Gary write letters. Rob further testified that the map was

written by Gary. The trial judge should rule Rob's testimony

(A) admissible, because Rob is qualified to form an opinion on the handwriting

(B) admissible, only if corroborated by collateral evidence such as fingerprints

(C) inadmissible, because Rob is not an expert

(D) inadmissible, because Rob's character is inherently flawed due to his imprisonment

91. Rob offered to testify that five days after the robbery, Rob, Gary, and Joyce, Gary's girlfriend, were drinking at a local bar. When the check came, Gary slipped out a roll of hundreds from his pocket and winked at Joyce. Then Joyce said, "That's nothing. You should see all the money in his apartment." Rob's testimony should be ruled

(A) admissible, for attacking the credibility of the defendant

(B) admissible, as an admission

(C) inadmissible, as hearsay not within any exception

(D) inadmissible, unless the conversation can be corroborated by another witness

92. Gary was found guilty of all charges. At the sentencing hearing, the prosecution introduced evidence of eleven previous felony convictions. The trial judge should rule the prior convictions

(A) admissible

(B) inadmissible, because prior convictions not admitted at trial are not admissible at sentencing hearings

(C) inadmissible, because highly prejudicial

(D) inadmissible, if the previous convictions were for crimes unrelated to burglary

Questions 93-94 are based upon the following fact situation.

Abby was familiar with Crabby's voice. Abby testified, during Crabby's suit for negligence, "I received a call and recognized Crabby's voice. After I asked her what was new, she told me she had 'just been driving drunk and hit an old lady.'"

93. Crabby's counsel objected to Abby's identification of Crabby's voice. The trial judge should rule that the phone call was

(A) properly authenticated, only if a recording was made and examined by an expert

GO ON TO THE NEXT PAGE

(B)   properly authenticated, because Abby was familiar with Crabby's voice

(C)   not properly authenticated, because Crabby never identified herself

(D)   not properly authenticated, because Abby was the one who received the call

94.   Even if the phone call was ruled authenticated, Crabby's counsel will still object to the contents of the conversation. The trial judge should rule the contents

(A)   admissible, as a then-existing mental condition

(B)   admissible, as an admission against interest

(C)   inadmissible, as hearsay not within any exception

(D)   inadmissible, because no blood alcohol level was taken

Questions 95-96 are based upon the following fact situation.

Smith brought suit against Goldberg for injuries Smith said he had suffered when Goldberg stepped on his toe in Charlie's Clam Bar. Goldberg claimed he had never been to Charlie's Clam Bar, nor had he stepped on Smith's toe.

95.   Ayatollah testified that Goldberg was a very religious Jew and therefore always told the truth. Over proper objection, Ayatollah's testimony should be ruled

(A)   admissible, as proper character evidence

(B)   admissible, as relevant to Goldberg's veracity

(C)   inadmissible, as hearsay not within any exception

(D)   inadmissible, because credibility may not be proved by a person's religious beliefs

96.   Ayatollah testified further that since Goldberg was so religious, his diet was restricted and he did not eat shellfish under any circumstances. The trial judge should rule this testimony

(A)   admissible, to prove Goldberg would never lie

(B)   admissible, as tending to prove Goldberg would not be found in a clam bar

(C)   inadmissible, because not relevant

(D)   inadmissible, because religious beliefs may not be used as evidence

97.   Greta sued Lebow Health Spas, alleging that while jogging on the spa's track she slipped on a wet spot left negligently by Salezar, an employee who had just cleaned and dried the track. She alleges that she

suffered a broken hip due to the health spa's negligence.

Rogers, another employee at the spa, testified that he saw Greta trip over her own shoelace as she left the locker room. After assisting her and calling an ambulance, he immediately filled out an accident report, pursuant to spa policy. Lebow Health Spas seeks to admit this report into evidence.

The trial judge should rule the report

(A) inadmissible, because both Rogers and Salezar are available to testify

(B) inadmissible, because it is hearsay not within any exception

(C) admissible, as a recorded recollection

(D) admissible, as a business record

98. Shadey pleaded guilty to armed robbery and told the judge, "I did it because my girlfriend is pregnant and I needed the money." Shadey was later allowed to withdraw his guilty plea. During his trial, the prosecutor seeks to introduce evidence of Shadey's plea of guilty and accompanying admission. The trial judge should rule

(A) the guilty plea admissible, the admission inadmissible

(B) the admission admissible, the guilty plea inadmissible

(C) both the admission and the guilty plea admissible

(D) neither the admission nor the guilty plea admissible

Questions 99-103 are based upon the following fact situation.

Dreamer sued Trucker for injuries he claimed to have suffered as a result of Trucker's hitting him with his pickup truck while he crossed the street. Mac and Peter were riding with Trucker. Joseph was taking his dog on a midnight walk.

99. Joseph testified that Trucker offered him $10,000 to falsely testify that the accident was due to Dreamer's negligence. The trial judge should rule this evidence

(A) inadmissible, as hearsay not within any exception

(B) inadmissible, because probative value is outweighed by possible prejudice

(C) admissible, as an admission by conduct

(D) admissible, as a declaration against interest

100. Dreamer testified, "Mac and Peter told me that Trucker was driving

GO ON TO THE NEXT PAGE

thirty miles an hour above the speed limit." The trial judge should rule this statement

(A)   inadmissible, as hearsay not within any exception

(B)   inadmissible, because Trucker's interest in the outcome counteracts the hearsay exception

(C)   admissible, as a party declaration

(D)   admissible, as a declaration against interest

101.   Trucker was asked, "Is it true you offered Dreamer a $50,000 settlement?" The trial judge should rule the question

(A)   not proper, because it is not relevant to either liability or damages

(B)   not proper, though relevant, because public policy is to encourage settlements

(C)   proper, as probative of claim value

(D)   proper, as an admission by a party

102.   On the evening of the accident, Joseph wrote about it in his diary. At the trial, he cannot remember details of the accident, and Dreamer requests to allow Joseph to look at

his diary. The trial judge should rule this request

(A)   not proper, because of the amount of time that elapsed since the notes were taken

(B)   not proper, because the notes are hearsay not within any exception

(C)   proper, as a past recollection recorded

(D)   proper, as a present recollection refreshed

103.   Dreamer called Greasy, who testified that he had installed a new speedometer on the day after the accident. The trial judge should rule Greasy's testimony

(A)   inadmissible, because public policy overrides relevancy

(B)   inadmissible, because not probative as to negligence

(C)   admissible, because relevant as negligence

(D)   admissible, because it was a declaration against interest

Questions 104-108 are based upon the following fact situation.

On a clear day in May, the Wallingford National Bank was robbed of $400,050.00. As the robber ran out of the bank with the money bags, he shot and killed a depositor. Betty Buick, a new teller at the bank, pushed the alarm button under the counter as soon as the robber ran out to the street. The next day, Betty identified Tony in a lineup as the robber.

104. At Tony's trial, the prosecutor called a car salesman to testify that when Tony offered to pay for a car in cash, he told Tony, "The only way to get that much cash is to rob a bank." Tony made no reply. This statement should be ruled

   (A) admissible, as a statement not denied by the defendant

   (B) admissible, only for the purpose of proving that the salesman believed Tony to be guilty of the felony murder

   (C) inadmissible, because the Fifth Amendment provides Tony with a privilege against self-incrimination

   (D) inadmissible, because Tony had no reason to respond to the salesman

105. The prosecution called Mouth, an attorney, to testify that Tony consulted him about accepting his case and that during their initial discussion Tony admitted that he had robbed the bank and murdered a depositor. Mouth and Tony could not agree on the fee, so Tony hired Roy as his counsel instead. Mouth's testimony should be ruled

   (A) inadmissible, because Tony was not warned by Mouth that the statements could be used against him

   (B) inadmissible, because the discussion was privileged

   (C) admissible, because the discussion occurred before the attorney agreed to represent the client

   (D) admissible, because the attorney has the right to waive the privilege

106. The defense called Dorothy, owner of Oz Donut Shop, who testified that Tony is an "honest and peace-loving man." Dorothy's testimony is

   (A) inadmissible, because Tony has not testified

   (B) inadmissible, because character may not be proved by reputation

   (C) admissible, to prove Tony's innocence

   (D) admissible, to prove Tony is believable

107. Tony's counsel called Moses, who claimed he was at a baseball game with Tony on the day of the crimes. On cross-examination, the prosecutor asked, "Is it true that you testified at the trial at which Tony was recently

acquitted of the charge of murdering a bus driver?" The most persuasive argument to sustain an objection to this question is that

(A)   it is a leading question

(B)   the tendency to mislead outweighs its probative value

(C)   the question raises issues not raised on direct examination

(D)   the question is relevant

108.   At Tony's trial the prosecutor asked Tony, on cross-examination, whether he had been convicted of burglary five years earlier. The court should rule, over an objection by defense counsel, that this question is most likely

(A)   improper, because burglary does not involve dishonesty or false statement

(B)   improper, because of the Best Evidence Rule

(C)   proper, if the court finds that the probative value for impeachment will outweigh any prejudice to Tony

(D)   proper, because the prosecutor can lead a defendant on cross-examination

109.   Sophie, a caterer, sued Craig for failure to pay for a bar mitzvah she had catered for Craig's son. At trial,

Sophie plans to testify that she personally supervises every affair, and plans to explain the amount of money expended on the bar mitzvah by testifying as to how much food was served, the rental cost of the ballroom, and the cost of hired help. Craig objects on the ground that Sophie regularly records all this information in the plan book in her office. Sophie's testimony is

(A)   inadmissible because it violates the Best Evidence Rule

(B)   inadmissible, as hearsay

(C)   admissible, because based on firsthand knowledge

(D)   admissible, as a business record

Questions 110-114 are based upon the following fact situation.

Speeder injured Jogger with his automobile at an intersection. Reebock, Jogger's wife, was with him and witnessed the accident, as did Senile, who happened to be walking by. Senile called the police, who sent Kojack to investigate.

110.   Reebock testified that her husband entered the intersection after the light turned green. As a witness, Reebock is

(A)   incompetent, because a wife cannot testify for her husband

(B) incompetent, because a relative is biased and cannot testify as a witness

(C) competent, even if she had an interest in the outcome

(D) competent, only if she is not suing for consortium and loss of services

111. Kojack testified, "I brought Senile to the police station about an hour after the accident, and as soon as I questioned him, he started screaming about Speeder running the light. I included his statements in my notes." The trial judge should rule Kojack's testimony

(A) admissible, as a present sense impression

(B) admissible, as an excited utterance

(C) admissible, as a public report

(D) inadmissible, as an excited utterance, because it could have been a product of reflection

112. Kojack testified that he had heard Speeder offer Jogger $3,000 to settle the claim. The trial judge should rule this testimony

(A) admissible, because Speeder's statement was a party admission

(B) admissible, only to the issue of liability, but not to the issue of damages

(C) inadmissible, because it is an offer to compromise a disputed claim

(D) inadmissible, because it is hearsay

113. Jogger seeks to allow Kojack's testimony that Speeder told him, "I was driving about eighty-five miles an hour." The trial judge should rule this testimony

(A) admissible, as a party admission

(B) inadmissible, because it is hearsay

(C) inadmissible, because Speeder does not qualify as an expert in determining automobile speeds

(D) inadmissible, as an opinion

114. Andretti testified that Speeder had a reputation in their hometown, Daytona, of being a safe and cautious driver. The trial judge should rule the testimony

(A) admissible, as tending to prove that Speeder was driving safely at the time of the accident

GO ON TO THE NEXT PAGE

(B)   admissible, only if the judge determines that Andretti had personal knowledge of Speeder's driving habits

(C)   inadmissible, because in a civil case character evidence may be used only after the plaintiff has attacked the defendant's character

(D)   inadmissible, because evidence of reputation cannot be used to prove that a defendant acted in conformity with that reputation in a specific instance

115.   Fred sues Rasta Restaurant for injuries he says he suffered after eating an allegedly contaminated bowl of calaloo soup. Rasta testified that more than forty other customers ate the same calaloo soup and none of them got sick. Fred called Dr. Breadnut, who testified, "I treated six patients for stomach ailments. All of them had eaten calaloo soup at Rasta's on the same day that Fred did." The trial judge should rule Dr. Breadnut's testimony

(A)   admissible, as long as other testimony linked the stomach ailments to contaminated calaloo

(B)   admissible, as long as the doctor is accepted as an expert

(C)   inadmissible, because the patients' statements to the doctor are hearsay

(D)   inadmissible, because it is not relevant

Questions 116-117 are based on the following fact situation.

Walker sued Owner for injuries sustained when Walker slipped on Owner's negligently maintained sidewalk. Owner denies that Walker suffered any injuries.

116.   Dr. Paul offers to testify for Walker that the day after the accident, Walker came to see him in his office and said, "I fell on a sidewalk that was all cracked and uneven." Dr. Paul's testimony would be

(A)   inadmissible, because it states a fact not in issue

(B)   inadmissible, except the portion of the statement that the sidewalk was cracked and uneven

(C)   admissible, in full

(D)   admissible, but only as to the cause of the injury

117.   Owner called Listener, who testified that Walker told him he fell down some steps, seriously injuring himself, the day before he slipped on Owner's sidewalk. Listener's testimony should be ruled

(A)   inadmissible, because it is hearsay not within any exception

(B)   inadmissible, because it is irrelevant

(C)   admissible, as an admission of a party opponent

(D)   admissible, as a spontaneous declaration

118.   Ortega sued Duarte in a dispute over the ownership of a pond located between their ranches. Ortega seeks to introduce photocopies of deeds authenticated by the county recorder that were made from microfilm kept in the county recorder's office pursuant to statute. The trial judge should rule the photocopies

(A)   admissible as a recorded recollection

(B)   admissible as a record of a document affecting an interest in property

(C)   inadmissible, due to the Best Evidence Rule

(D)   inadmissible unless the deeds are more than twenty years old

119.   Larry, the fourteen-year-old mentally retarded brother of the defendant, is called to testify. The trial judge should rule Larry's testimony

(A)   admissible

(B)   inadmissible because of Larry's age

(C)   inadmissible because Larry is mentally retarded

(D)   inadmissible because Larry is the defendant's brother

Questions 120-122 are based upon the following fact situation.

Clumsy's auto collided with a truck owned by Patton Trucking. Clumsy's car slid beneath the truck's trailer, crushing the roof of the sedan and causing Clumsy severe head injuries. Clumsy sued Cheepo, the truck's manufacturer, alleging that his injuries were caused by their negligent design, since the truck did not have a protective device to prevent cars from driving under the trailer. Cheepo answered that it would be impossible to design a trailer with equipment to prevent a car from driving under it.

120.   Clumsy seeks to introduce evidence that two days after his accident, Cheepo's engineers began to work on a bumper that would wrap all around the truck's trailer, at the same height as a car bumper. The bumpers became standard equipment on all of Cheepo trucks within two years later. The trial court should rule this evidence

(A)   inadmissible, because public policy is to avoid discouraging remedial measures

(B)   admissible, to show the prior design was negligent

GO ON TO THE NEXT PAGE

(C)   admissible, to show Cheepo was aware of the need to take precautionary measures

(D)   admissible, to refute Cheepo's argument that the protection was impossible to design

121.   Clumsy offered as evidence a pamphlet put out by the United States Highway Safety Board, a government regulatory agency. Cheepo objected. The trial judge should

(A)   sustain the objection, because the document was not properly authenticated

(B)   sustain the objection, because of the Best Evidence Rule

(C)   overrule the objection, because the document is a statement against interest

(D)   overrule the objection, because the pamphlet is an official publication

122.   Witness, a disinterested bystander, was called to testify. She refused to declare by oath or affirmation that she would testify truthfully, saying "such a statement would be an insult to my integrity." The trial judge should rule Witness's testimony

(A)   admissible, only if investigation shows she is without motive to lie

(B)   admissible, if Witness's veracity is established by community reputation

(C)   inadmissible, unless corroborated by other witnesses

(D)   inadmissible, regardless of corroboration by other witnesses

Questions 123-126 are based on Loser's trial for robbing 47th St. Diamond Corp.

123.   The prosecution seeks to offer evidence, obtained in a valid search of Loser's apartment, showing he was heavily in debt from an illegal gambling habit. This evidence should be

(A)   inadmissible, because the defendant did not put his character at issue

(B)   inadmissible, because the prejudicial effect will outweigh its probative value

(C)   admissible, to prove Loser's motive to rob the Diamond Corp.

(D)   admissible, to prove Loser's motive to commit crimes

124.   The prosecution offers a description, given to police by an employee of the Diamond Corp., implicating Loser. The employee died of a heart attack before Loser was arrested. The description is

(A)   inadmissible, because it is not very precise

(B)   admissible, as a recorded past recollection

(C)   inadmissible, as hearsay not within any exception

(D)   admissible, as a valid identification

125.   On direct examination, Loser testified that he does not know how to drive cars with manual transmissions. The car used to escape the scene of the crime was recovered by the police, and it had a manual transmission. Loser's counsel asked him, "What did you tell the police on the day of the crime?" Loser's answer was, "I do not drive a manual transmission." Loser's answer is

(A)   inadmissible, as hearsay not within any exception

(B)   inadmissible, because Loser's answer helps his case, giving him a motive to lie

(C)   admissible, only as a prior consistent statement

(D)   admissible, only to prove that Loser does not know how to drive a manual transmission

126.   The prosecution seeks to impeach Loser on cross-examination by showing that he was recently

convicted for possession of narcotics. This strategy is

(A)   a proper way to question Loser's veracity

(B)   improper, because robbery and drug possession are not sufficiently similar

(C)   proper, to show Loser is inclined to commit crimes

(D)   improper, because the prejudicial value outweighs the probative value

127.   Tinker Motor Company was sued in a product liability action when the axle of one of its cars broke. The company asked Conant, an assembly line worker, to tell Eddie, Tinker's counsel, exactly how the axle is assembled. Conant said to the lawyer, "Quite frankly, I was drunk a lot last year and luckily nobody noticed." Plaintiff asks Eddie to testify about his conversation with Conant. The trial judge should rule that

(A)   Eddie may be forced to testify because the conversation is relevant

(B)   Eddie may be forced to testify because Conant is only a factory worker

(C)   Eddie cannot be forced to testify because of the attorney-client privilege

GO ON TO THE NEXT PAGE

(D) Eddie cannot be forced to testify because Conant is not an expert

Questions 128-130 are based upon the following fact situation.

Marty sued Wilbur after Wilbur's horse, Mr. Ed, kicked Marty.

128. Wilbur's counsel objected when he was asked, "Has Mr. Ed ever kicked a person before?" The question should be ruled

(A) proper

(B) improper, because not relevant to the facts

(C) improper, because past actions cannot be used to prove propensity to act in a certain matter

(D) improper, because the probative value is outweighed by possible prejudice

129. Wilbur's counsel asked him, "Couldn't Marty have mistaken your neighbor's horse for Mr. Ed?" The trial judge should rule this question

(A) proper, only if the neighbor is unavailable to testify

(B) proper, because the Best Evidence Rule is inapplicable

(C) not proper, because the question calls for an opinion of the witness

(D) not proper, because not relevant

130. Wilbur's counsel called Ted to testify that he heard Ralph say, "Wilbur's and his neighbor's horse must be twins, they look and act so alike." The trial judge should rule this testimony inadmissible, because

(A) neither the witness nor the declarant were experts

(B) the declarant gave an improper conclusion

(C) the testimony is hearsay not within any exception

(D) the Best Evidence Rule has not been satisfied

Questions 131-132 are based upon the following fact situation.

Hershy went to Dr. Nestle to treat his cold. Nestle erroneously prescribed a drug known to have severe side effects and generally used only by terminally ill patients. Hershy had a high fever for the next three days, then suffered a heart attack and died. Nestle's records were admitted into evidence.

131. Dr. Maimon carefully examined Nestle's records. He was asked, "In your opinion, could the medication have caused Hershy's heart attack?" Dr. Maimon's opinion should be ruled

(A) inadmissible, because an expert may not be asked a

hypothetical question based on prior testimony

(B) inadmissible, because an expert may not be asked a hypothetical question based on a party's records

(C) admissible, as a response to a hypothetical question

(D) admissible, since Maimon is an expert and is in a position to weigh the evidence

132. Dr. Cutter, the pathologist who performed the autopsy on Hershy, seeks to state his opinion as to the cause of Hershy's death. His opinion is based upon his examination of microscopic tissues that were prepared by an assistant in his office and not admitted into evidence. The trial judge should rule Cutter's testimony

(A) proper, if such tissues are reasonably relied upon by physicians

(B) proper, as a record of regularly conducted activity

(C) not proper, unless the slides were admitted into evidence

(D) not proper, because Cutter did not prepare the slides himself

133. Charles was present with his counsel at a preliminary examination where James was being questioned under the suspicion that he had been an accessory after the fact in a bank robbery case. James testified, "Charles jumped into my back seat with a bag full of cash." Charles was charged with armed robbery. The prosecution was unable to locate James to testify at Charles's trial, so they moved to admit James's pretrial testimony. The trial judge should rule this testimony

(A) admissible, as a past recollection recorded

(B) admissible, as former testimony

(C) inadmissible, as hearsay not within any exception

(D) inadmissible, because James is a codefendant and has a right against self-incrimination

Questions 134-135 are based upon the following fact situation.

Mike sued for injuries sustained in a shopping mall when he tripped over a broken step and fell. The defendant, Elvira Malls, Inc., maintained that the lease for Reads Restaurant provided it with complete responsibility for the condition of those steps.

134. Mike brought a witness who testified that he was hired by Elvira on the

GO ON TO THE NEXT PAGE

day after the accident to fix the steps. The court should rule this testimony

(A)   inadmissible, because the law seeks to encourage repairs and prevent injuries

(B)   inadmissible, because of the confidential relationship

(C)   admissible, because the repairs are relevant to prove that the prior condition constituted negligence

(D)   admissible, as relevant to the issue of who maintained control over the steps

135.   Elvira offered the testimony of its employee, James, who said, "Hundreds of people use those steps every day, and I have no knowledge of any accidents." This evidence should be

(A)   inadmissible, because James's testimony is not relevant

(B)   inadmissible, because the testimony is not relevant to the issue of due care

(C)   admissible, because it tends to prove proper maintenance of the steps

(D)   admissible, because it has no bearing on the issue of due care

Questions 136-137 are based upon the following fact situation.

Dealer and his employee Mechanic were both sued by Purchaser for damages incurred when his brakes failed. Sleezy, an attorney, was retained to defend Dealer and Mechanic. The three had a conference; the only other person present was Debra, Sleezy's secretary, who took notes.

136.   Purchaser seeks to have Mechanic testify to what was said at the conference. The trial judge should rule the testimony

(A)   admissible, because the conference was attended by persons other than the attorney and client

(B)   admissible, as an admission against interest

(C)   inadmissible, as violating the Best Evidence Rule

(D)   inadmissible, because of the attorney-client privilege

137.   Mechanic files a cross-claim against Dealer. He calls Debra to testify to Dealer's statements during their conference. The trial judge should rule Debra's testimony

(A)   inadmissible, if Dealer asserts the attorney-client privilege

(B)   admissible, because the conference was not privileged as to suits between Dealer and Mechanic

(C)   admissible, because the privilege could only be

asserted by Dealer since he paid the attorney's fees

(D) admissible, because Dealer's statements were not meant to be concealed from Mechanic

Questions 138-141 are based upon the following fact situation.

Nifty was driving his car and listening to Roberta Flack's "Killing Me Softly" on the radio when he suddenly crashed into Swifty. Sheriff Erp arrived approximately one hour later.

138. A witness, who has since moved overseas, ran over to Erp and exclaimed, "I was right there and saw it perfectly. Swifty jumped the light, it was all his fault." Erp made notes of the witness's statement. The trial judge should rule Erp's testimony regarding his notes

(A) inadmissible, as hearsay not within any exception

(B) inadmissible, because the passerby is unavailable

(C) admissible, as a spontaneous utterance

(D) admissible, as a past recollection recorded

139. Nifty called Spify, who testified that she saw Swifty run the light. Swifty called Squeeky and asked him about Spify's reputation for veracity in the community. The trial judge should rule this question

(A) proper, because Spify and Squeeky lived together in a very close community

(B) proper, because Swifty is laying a foundation to impeach Spify

(C) improper, because Swifty is trying to impeach the witness whom he is cross-examining on a collateral matter

(D) not proper, because reputation for veracity may not be used to prove truthfulness on a specific occasion

140. Swifty sat in Erp's car and answered questions for a police report. At one point, Swifty said, "I most likely did jump the light." Nifty seeks to admit Erp's testimony of Swifty's statement. The trial judge should rule the testimony

(A) inadmissible, as hearsay not within any exception

(B) inadmissible, unless Swifty confirms the statement

(C) admissible, as a written recollection

(D) admissible, as an admission against interest

GO ON TO THE NEXT PAGE

141. Nifty seeks to testify that Swifty had offered him a new car if he would agree to drop the suit. The trial judge should rule this evidence

   (A) admissible, as a party admission

   (B) admissible, on the issue of liability, but not on the issue of damages

   (C) inadmissible, because a settlement offer is not relevant to liability or damages

   (D) inadmissible, even though relevant, due to legal policy

142. In 1986 Suzie brought a suit to challenge the validity of a conveyance made by Eddie in 1973. Suzie, alleging Eddie's incompetence, offers valid affidavits by two of Eddie's neighbors, stating that they have observed Eddie hanging from a tree branch by his legs for hours at a time. The affidavits further allege that Eddie had walked around the neighborhood during a snowstorm clad only in his underwear. These affidavits should be

   (A) admissible, as a record of documents affecting an interest in property

   (B) admissible, as ancient documents

   (C) admissible, as official documents

   (D) inadmissible, since they are hearsay not within any exception

143. Samuel, charged with murder, has testified on his own behalf. The prosecutor seeks to impeach Samuel by admitting Samuel's thirteen-year-old conviction for voluntary manslaughter and his two-year-old conviction for perjury. The trial judge should rule

   (A) both the manslaughter and perjury convictions admissible

   (B) only the perjury conviction admissible

   (C) only the manslaughter conviction admissible

   (D) neither the perjury conviction nor the manslaughter charge admissible

Questions 144-146 are based upon the following fact situation.

Cautious sued Sandy for injuries suffered in an automobile accident.

144. On direct examination Cautious was asked, "Is it true that you were driving below the speed limit?" The trial judge should rule this question

   (A) proper

   (B) proper, only if Cautious testifies that he looked at his speedometer just before the accident, and an expert witness certifies the accuracy of the speedometer

(C)   not proper, because Cautious is not an expert

(D)   not proper in form

145.   On cross-examination, Cautious was asked about a tape of a conversation he'd had with Denny the Snake, a convicted child molester who was planning a drug deal. Cautious objected on the grounds that the content of his conversation with Denny the Snake was obtained by an improper wiretap and had been excluded in a prior criminal trial. The question about the taped conversation is

(A)   proper

(B)   proper, to impeach Cautious's veracity, but not to prove that Cautious was a drug dealer

(C)   proper, to prove that Cautious was a drug dealer, but not proper to impeach him

(D)   not proper

146.   Sandy asked Bystander, a witness at the scene of the accident, if she thought Cautious had been speeding. Cautious's counsel jumped up and shouted, "I object," then sat down. The trial judge should

(A)   sustain the objection, because Bystander may not provide an ultimate conclusion

(B)   sustain the objection, because a proper foundation has not been laid

(C)   overrule the objection, because it is not proper

(D)   overrule the objection, because a lay witness is qualified to judge if a car is speeding

147.   Reverend Ike is called as a witness in a civil case between Winky and Dinky. Ike is questioned about a conversation he'd had when Stinky, a witness of the fight between Winky and Dinky, came to the Reverend for counseling. Stinky's attorney was present at trial and was allowed to speak. Which of the following will most likely result in exclusion of Ike's testimony, based upon the clergyman-penitent privilege?

(A)   Winky objects, invoking the clergyman-penitent privilege.

(B)   Reverend Ike objects, invoking the clergyman-penitent privilege.

(C)   Stinky's attorney objects.

(D)   Stinky admits that he never saw Ike before or after their conversation.

GO ON TO THE NEXT PAGE

148. Victim testified at the trial of Mugger for criminal battery. Mugger had allegedly struck Victim with a metal pipe, just outside the Howard Street Post Office. The prosecutor asked Victim to recount the entire event. "I got this form from school to fill out. I typed it and walked to the post office." Mugger objects to the testimony concerning the school form. The trial judge should

   (A)   sustain Mugger's objection, because of the Best Evidence Rule

   (B)   sustain Mugger's objection, because the prosecution did not lay a proper foundation

   (C)   overrule Mugger's objection, because Victim can refer to the document without producing it

   (D)   overrule Mugger's objection, only if Victim is deemed believable

149. Gilbert sued Hatfield for injuries sustained in an automobile accident. Gilbert's lawyer, Ratelle, sought to call Gilbert to the stand for a redirect examination. This should be permitted in which of the following circumstances?

   (A)   Ratelle seeks to review the facts of the case.

   (B)   Ratelle seeks to introduce new evidence that he feels will make his case "airtight."

   (C)   Ratelle seeks to reply to several minor matters raised by Hatfield's counsel on cross-examination of Gilbert.

   (D)   Ratelle seeks to reply to a significant issue raised by Hatfield's counsel on cross-examination of Gilbert.

Questions 150-153 are based upon the following fact situation.

A bus driven by Denise collided with a car owned by Johnson. Denise claimed Johnson's left headlight had not been on, causing her to think the car was a motorcycle.

150. Johnson's attorney Bill Boal wants the sheriff, who was at the scene, to testify that Lou Weed, a passenger in the bus, said to him, outside the presence of Denise, "Denise was going fifty-five miles per hour in a thirty-mile-per-hour zone!" This statement is

   (A)   inadmissible, as hearsay not within any exception

   (B)   inadmissible, because it states a conclusion

   (C)   admissible, as a spontaneous utterance

   (D)   admissible, as an admission of a party

151. Denise asked Johnson, "How much does a new headlight cost?" The trial

judge should rule this question improper because

(A)   it is a question for an expert

(B)   Denise has not laid a proper foundation

(C)   it is not the best evidence of cost

(D)   it is not relevant

152.   Denise seeks to introduce the testimony of Bystander, a disinterested witness who had heard Mechanic, a repairman who worked for Johnson, say, "I told you yesterday that broken headlight would be trouble." The trial judge should rule the testimony admissible only if

(A)   Denise proves that Mechanic is an agent of Johnson, his statement was within the scope of his employment, and he is unavailable to testify

(B)   Denise proves that Mechanic is an agent of Johnson and is unavailable to testify

(C)   Denise proves that Mechanic is an agent of Johnson, is unavailable to testify, and produces evidence that the bulb was out for at least one day

(D)   Denise proves that Mechanic is not available to testify

153.   Bystander testified that she heard Johnson reply to Mechanic, "It's your fault, you were supposed to fix it." Johnson objects to Bystander's testimony. The trial judge should

(A)   sustain the objection because it is hearsay not within any exception

(B)   sustain the objection because Johnson was the principal, not the agent

(C)   overrule the objection only if Mechanic is unavailable

(D)   overrule the objection, as an admission of a party

Questions 154-155 are based upon the following fact situation.

Cane sued Abel for breach of contract. Both the contents and authenticity of the contract are in dispute.

154.   Cane's secretary testified that she had mailed to Abel what Cane had told her was the contract. The trial judge should rule this testimony

(A)   admissible, only if the actual contract is produced

(B)   admissible, regardless of the authenticity of the contract

GO ON TO THE NEXT PAGE

(C) inadmissible, unless the actual contract is shown to be unavailable

(D) inadmissible, because of the Best Evidence Rule

155. Cane's secretary testified further, "The contract stated, 'Abel agreed to ship ten gross of widgets within ten days.'" The trial judge should rule this testimony admissible only if

   (A) he is convinced that the letter is precisely quoted

   (B) he finds the original letter unavailable

   (C) the jury is convinced that the letter is precisely quoted

   (D) the jury finds that the original letter is unavailable

Questions 156-157 are based upon the following fact situation.

Lorraine filed suit against the White Church for breach of contract.

156. Harvey testified that Lorraine had a reputation in the community as a very religious person. This testimony should be ruled

   (A) admissible, as relevant to prove that Lorraine would not lie

   (B) inadmissible, as hearsay not within any exception

(C) inadmissible, because religious beliefs may not be used to prove veracity

(D) inadmissible, because of the Best Evidence Rule

157. Debby testified in favor of the church. On cross-examination, Lorraine asked Debby, "Is it not true that you are a member of White Church?" The trial judge should rule this question

   (A) proper, to show bias

   (B) proper, despite the Best Evidence Rule

   (C) not proper, because leading

   (D) not proper, because religious beliefs may not be introduced to prove veracity

158. Harvey was shopping at Value Town Department Store and happened to see Abe pickpocket Sherry. The prosecution called Harvey to testify. Harvey refused to testify, claiming the privilege against self-incrimination. Harvey should be allowed to remain silent only if the judge believes

   (A) there is some reasonable possibility that Harvey will incriminate himself

   (B) there is a preponderance of evidence that Harvey will incriminate himself

(C) there is clear and convincing evidence that Harvey will incriminate himself

(D) Harvey will definitely incriminate himself

159. Elroy brought an action against both Acme Bus Company and Stinker, a driver for Acme, to recover for damages he allegedly suffered when hit by the bus Stinker was driving for Acme. Elroy found a witness who testified that Acme is known in the community to hire reckless drivers. The witness also testified that Stinker has a reputation in the community as a flagrant violator of traffic laws. The trial judge should rule the testimony

(A) admissible, as tending to prove the accident was caused by the negligence of Acme and of Stinker

(B) admissible, because the issue of character was raised by one of the defendants

(C) inadmissible, because the issue of character was raised by a defendant

(D) inadmissible, to prove negligence

160. Mark was hit by a distinctly painted Corvette and died from the injuries. The side of the car said "Soap Box Derby" in pink and red paint. Nick is charged with both leaving the scene of an accident and vehicular homicide.

The prosecution called Dave, who testified, "I was once hit by a speeding Corvette driven by Nick. The car was pink and red and said 'Soap Box Derby' on the sides. Nick then drove away." Dave's testimony is

(A) admissible, to show Dave exhibited a propensity to drive recklessly

(B) admissible, only to establish an identifying circumstance

(C) inadmissible, because Dave's character is not in issue

(D) inadmissible, because its probative value is outweighed by the danger of unfair prejudice

161. Linda sued S.H. Kress Company for injuries she claims she suffered from an accident in Kress's department store. Franz, an employee, completed a standard form provided by the company's attorney in order to assist him in defending Kress. Linda requests that the report be submitted into evidence. The trial judge should rule the report

(A) admissible, as a statement against interest

(B) admissible, as recorded recollection

GO ON TO THE NEXT PAGE

(C)   inadmissible, as hearsay not within any exception

(D)   inadmissible, because the report is a privileged communication between client and attorney.

Questions 162-163 are based upon the following fact situation.

Samuel suffered from food poisoning after eating dinner at Pirate's Seafood Restaurant. In a suit against Pirate's, Samuel alleges that its negligence and breach of warranty caused him severe illness and lost wages.

162.   Samuel planned to testify that he was asked to sign a sheet of paper with his name and address before he ate his shrimp dinner, because the owners of Pirate's wanted to send thank-you cards to all its customers who ordered seafood. This testimony is

(A)   admissible, if Samuel has a witness to verify the signature

(B)   admissible, if the original paper is in the possession of Pirate's

(C)   inadmissible, if the original is in the possession of Pirate's

(D)   inadmissible, if the court determines it is a collateral matter

163.   After Pirate's tried to prove that Samuel was allergic to shrimp,

Samuel testified that he had been eating shrimp twice per week for several years, often at Pirate's. He also testified about a fact of minor importance in the case, citing his business travel and entertainment records, but not admitting these records to evidence. This evidence should be ruled

(A)   admissible, because the records relate to a collateral matter

(B)   admissible, regardless of the importance of the matter to be proved

(C)   inadmissible, regardless of the importance of the issue, because it is hearsay

(D)   inadmissible, because the records relate to a collateral matter

164.   Marty Tall was a plaintiff in a medical malpractice suit against Dr. Good. Dr. Dunce was called as an expert and asked on direct examination, "In your opinion, could a mistake like the one made by Dr. Good cause the symptoms exhibited by the plaintiff?" The defendant objected. The trial judge should rule the question

(A)   proper

(B)   not proper, because leading

(C)   not proper, if the opinion is based on facts not submitted in evidence

(D)   not proper, because the ultimate opinion should be left for the trier of fact

165.   Lowlife is on trial for putting razor blades inside candy bars and giving the candy to children on Halloween. Teddy, a six-year-old boy, answered "yes" when asked, "Did a man in a yellow convertible call you over and give you candy that made your mouth hurt?" Over proper objection, Teddy's answer should be ruled

(A)   admissible, as an answer to a proper question

(B)   admissible, only if corroborated by an adult

(C)   inadmissible, because the question was leading

(D)   inadmissible, because Teddy's age prevents him from being a competent witness

166.   Farmer had watched as Deliverer drove his heavy truck onto an old bridge. Farmer testified, "Deliverer should have stopped the truck and estimated the bridge's ability to bear the truck's weight." Farmer's testimony should be

(A)   inadmissible, because the issue of negligence should be decided by a trier of fact

(B)   inadmissible, because Farmer is not an engineering expert

(C)   admissible, only on the issue of Deliverer's character

(D)   admissible, because the opinion would be helpful to the trier of fact

167.   Sandusky sues Ashtabula for breach of contract. Cuyahoga is called to testify on behalf of Sandusky. Ashtabula cross-examines Cuyahoga. Which of the following questions should the trial judge rule improper?

(A)   "Isn't it true you are Sandusky's cousin?"

(B)   "Weren't you convicted of larceny three years ago?"

(C)   "You just testified that the two parties sealed the contract with a handshake. Didn't you testify during the pre-trial deposition that the parties did not shake hands?"

(D)   "Isn't true everyone in Twinsburg, your hometown, knows you are an alcoholic?"

168.   Faust sued Bo in tort, and Bo called Woody as a witness. Faust discredited Woody, and Bo seeks to offer evidence of Woody's reputation as a truthful man. The trial judge will be most likely to permit rehabilitation evidence if the content of the discrediting evidence was that

(A)   Bo and Woody played on the same football team

(B)   Woody was not present at the scene of the accident

(C)   Woody was a frequent blackjack player in Atlantic City

GO ON TO THE NEXT PAGE

(D)   Woody had an extremely low I.Q.

169.   Ralph is on trial for drunk driving. When Ralph was booked at police headquarters on New Year's Eve, a police officer made a videotape of Ralph showing him to be dizzy, rude, and garbling his words. Assuming proper authentication, is the judge likely to admit this evidence?

(A)   No, because specific instances of conduct cannot be proved by extrinsic evidence.

(B)   No, because it is hearsay not within any exception.

(C)   Yes, because it is an admission.

(D)   Yes, because its value is not substantially outweighed by unfair prejudice.

170.   Talker is on trial for conspiracy. Nosey testified that she heard Talker's conversation through a wall separating their hotel rooms. The defense denies that the voice she heard was Talker's. Which of the following would be the **LEAST** sufficient basis for admitting the testimony?

(A)   Nosey also listened to Talker speak through a wall in the courtroom and identified it as the same voice.

(B)   Nosey was familiar with Talker's voice, but had never

heard the voice through a wall.

(C)   Nosey knew Talker was staying in the room next to hers before she heard the voice.

(D)   Nosey shared a room with Talker's mother, who had identified Talker's voice.

171.   Rick sued Dick for injuries suffered when he slipped in a hallway outside Dick's office. Dick sought to admit evidence that he did not carry liability insurance for accidents occurring in the hallway. This evidence should be ruled

(A)   admissible, to determine damages

(B)   admissible, to prove ownership of the hallway

(C)   inadmissible, because irrelevant

(D)   inadmissible, because of the Best Evidence Rule

172.   Mary and John were involved in an automobile accident. Olson, a bystander, happened to be carrying a camera and took several photographs. Before the photographs may be admitted into evidence, a proper foundation must include, as a minimum, testimony of which of the following?

(A) Possession of the photographs must be traced from the time they were developed until the time they reached the courtroom.

(B) Someone present at the scene of the accident must attest to the photos' accuracy.

(C) Olson must testify.

(D) An expert must testify that the photos were not retouched.

173. Anne sued Dan for damages to her automobile occurring when it was struck by an empty trash can on a windy day. Dan denies ownership of the trash can and seeks to offer testimony that he puts his empty trash cans inside his garage when he returns from work in the evening. Both parties agree that the accident took place late at night. The trial judge should rule the evidence

(A) admissible, as evidence of habit

(B) inadmissible, as a conclusion

(C) inadmissible, as a self-serving declaration

(D) inadmissible, because propensity may not be proved by specific instances

174. Mantle hit Maris over his head with a bat. Whitey and Elston testified as witnesses to the event. A leading question will be permitted over objection in all of the following situations except

(A) Mantle's direct examination of Maris

(B) Mantle's cross-examination of Whitey

(C) Mantle's direct examination of Elston

(D) Mantle's cross-examination of a physician who testified as an expert witness

175. In the felony murder trial of Jason Jr. arising out of an armed robbery, Jason Sr. was called to testify. The prosecution objected to Jason Sr.'s testimony on the grounds that Jason Sr. just completed a five-year prison sentence for manslaughter and is Jason Jr.'s father. The trial judge should rule the testimony

(A) admissible

(B) inadmissible, because of Jason Sr.'s relationship to the defendant

(C) inadmissible, because of Jason Sr.'s manslaughter conviction

(D) inadmissible, because of Jason Sr.'s manslaughter conviction

GO ON TO THE NEXT PAGE

and his relationship to the
defendant

176.   Greedy refused to testify during his
trial for drug smuggling, claiming his
right against self-incrimination. The
prosecution called Esquire, who
testified that he had incorporated
Columbia Express, Inc., for Greedy.
Columbia Express's boats were later
found to be carrying cocaine. Greedy
moved to strike Esquire's testimony.

(A)   admissible, under the
"business record" exception to
the Hearsay Rule

(B)   admissible, because Esquire is
merely stating the general
nature of the legal services
rendered

(C)   inadmissible, because it is
hearsay not within any
exceptions

(D)   inadmissible, because of the
attorney-client privilege

EVIDENCE ANSWERS

1.   (C)   The Multistate Exam often contains questions that draw from different subjects. This question requires knowledge of the law of both evidence and contracts. In a court action based on a contract between a buyer and a seller, if the seller is a merchant, the UCC will apply. Finder is a merchant, thus the UCC rule controls the outcome in this question. "The express terms of an agreement and an applicable course of dealing or usage of trade shall be construed whenever reasonable as consistent with each other; but when such construction is unreasonable, express terms control both course of dealing and usage of trade and course of dealings controls usage of trade" [UCC 1-205(4)]. In accordance with this provision, the court should admit evidence of customary business practices to aid in interpreting the contract between Finder and Wiz.

(A) is not correct, because Finder's copies are not a past recollection recorded. A past recollection recorded is a written record made by a witness unable to remember the facts.

(B) is not correct, because FRE (Federal Rule of Evidence) 1003 provides, "A duplicate is admissible to the same extent as an original unless (1) a genuine question is raised as to the authenticity of the original or (2) in the circumstances it would be unfair to admit the duplicate in lieu of the original."

(D) is not correct because the custom and usage of the trade is relevant to the contract and therefore admissible under FRE 402.

Note: Finder's copies should be admitted under the business records exception of the FRE.

2.   (B)   Although Fox's statement is hearsay as an out-of-court statement, it is admissible under FRE 803(3) as a then existing physical condition. Fox's declaration will be admitted to prove his symptoms, including pain and suffering, but not to prove the actual injury itself.

(A) is incorrect because statements of past symptoms are admissible under FRE 803(4) if made to a doctor to assist in his diagnosis.

(C) and (D) are not correct, because declarations of a then existing physical condition are admissible even if they are made to a non-physician.

3.   (C)   Under the Best Evidence Rule, the law requires that the most persuasive evidence available be used to prove the terms of a writing. For material terms, the original writing must be produced unless it is shown to be unavailable for a reason not attributable to the fault of the party seeking to admit the evidence. Reseda's question violated this rule because the original report was available.

(A) is not correct, because the Business Exception Rule [FRE 803(6)] is an exception to the Hearsay Rule to allow a business record into evidence. No attempt was made by Reseda to enter any record into evidence.

(B) is not correct, because Reseda's question calls for information in the report, not for the witness's personal knowledge.

4.   (B)   Balboa's statements will not be admissible because their probative value is outweighed by the danger of unfair prejudice they create.

(A) is also correct, but it is not as good an answer as (B). "Self-serving declaration" is a frequently used Multistate Exam choice. It is rarely correct.

(C) is not correct, because such a question is proper for impeachment purposes only. One may introduce evidence of a prior statement that is inconsistent with present testimony. The question would not be proper if set forth for another purpose.

(D) is not correct, because the status of the person who heard the comments is not at issue.

5.   (B)   The Best Evidence Rule requires that the most persuasive form of evidence be used to prove the content of a disputed matter. In this question, the most persuasive form of evidence available would be the tape recording, not Mongoose's recollections.

(A) is incorrect because recounting defamatory statements is not hearsay. The words are not set forth to prove the content of the statements, but merely to establish that the defamatory statements were made.

(C) is relevant only to determine if a suit should be brought for libel or for slander.

(D) would have been correct under the reasoning set forth in (A), but the Best Evidence issue makes the objection sustainable.

6.   (B)   The court determines whether a person is competent to be a witness. The court decides, as a matter of law, if a child is competent by conducting a preliminary inquiry. The elements of a child's competency are (1) comprehension of the obligation to tell the truth, (2) intellectual capacity of observation, (3) recollection, and (4) communication of his observations.

Even though the standard of competency of a witness is more strict in a criminal case than in a civil case, due to the constitutional right to confront and cross-examine witnesses, (A) is not correct because the choice omits reference to a preliminary hearing.

(C) lacks the competency element of comprehension of the obligation to tell the truth.

(D) is an incorrect statement of a defendant's burden in a competency issue.

7.   (D)   Both the taxi driver's log and the Secretary's writing are hearsay. Rosemary's statement regarding Bill is hearsay within hearsay. FRE 805 provides, "Hearsay included within hearsay is not excluded under the Hearsay Rule if each part of the combined statements conforms with an exception to the Hearsay Rule. ..." In other words, each component of the hearsay must meet an exception to the Hearsay Rule. Secretary's phone log entry will be considered a business record and is admissible on its own as a "business record" exception to the Hearsay Rule. However, Rosemary's statement about Bill that was written in the log was hearsay and inadmissible because Rosemary did not have personal knowledge of Bill's plans after he arrived at O'Hare. As a result, Secretary's notation in the log book would be inadmissible. The driver's log is admissible under the "business record" exception to the Hearsay Rule.

The rule of law stated in (C) is correct; however, the choice is incorrect because the entry is not admissible in this question.

8.   (D)   Although Buchanan's testimony is constituted of out-of-court statements, FRE 804(b)(1) gives a hearsay exception for former testimony if the declarant is unavailable (Buchanan's refusal to testify makes him "unavailable" under FRE 804(a)(1)), the testimony was given by the declarant as a witness in another proceeding, and the criminal defendant (or a "predecessor in interest" in a civil case) had an opportunity to develop cross-examination. All the above listed conditions have been met and both transcripts are admissible.

9.   (C)   The Supreme Court has ruled that the Fifth Amendment right against self-incrimination does not extend to a taxpayer seeking to exclude his business and tax records. "Use immunity" prohibits direct or indirect use of evidence given in a subsequent criminal prosecution. "Transactional immunity" is absolute immunity from prosecution for any offense.

10.   (B)   FRE 403 provides that despite its relevance "evidence may be excluded if its probative value is substantially outweighed by the danger of unfair prejudice, confusion of the issues, or misleading the jury." The photograph should be ruled inadmissible as highly prejudicial. Balboa's statement will be ruled admissible under the "excited utterance" exception to the Hearsay Rule.

(C) is incorrect because the "excited utterance" exception to the Hearsay Rule does not require participation by the declarant. A nonparticipant may be moved to describe what he perceives, and one may be startled by an event in which he is not an actor.

(D) is incorrect because an excited utterance is not excluded by the Hearsay Rule even though the declarant is available as a witness. Balboa certainly heard a statement made under the stress of a situation.

11. (B)   Although Dollar's statement to her husband constitutes hearsay not within any exception, it will be ruled admissible for the limited purpose of impeaching the witness. It will not be admissible for substantive purposes.

     (D) is not correct because there is no written document whose contents are being offered for their truth, as is required for a past recollection recorded.

12. (B)   A statement made by the co-conspirator of a party during the course and in furtherance of the conspiracy is admissible under the "admission by a party opponent" exception to the Hearsay Rule [FRE 801(D)(2)]. If this statement was not made in furtherance of the conspiracy it will be inadmissible as hearsay. Read the question carefully. It asks under what circumstances the court will rule for Killer to disallow the testimony by using the double negative "will not rule against."

     (A) is incorrect because if the statement was made during the course and in furtherance of the conspiracy, then the court would rule against Killer.

     (C) is incorrect because the statement does not have to be made directly to a party opponent.

13. (D)   The Best Evidence Rule applies only where the contents of a writing are to be proved. In this question, the issue was the truth of Ginsburg's testimony, not the accuracy of the writing (transcript). Bork's testimony, although partly hearsay, may be admissible under the "admission against interest" exception. Neither (A) nor (B) are correct, because it is not clear from these facts whether the declarant is available. This hearsay exception requires that the declarant be unavailable.

14. (B)   Evidence must be relevant to be admitted. Relevancy will be established if an item tends to prove or disprove a fact at issue. The color of Tim's shirt was not related to the plane crash in any manner. The testimony was hearsay (Choice A), but the first test for the admissibility of any evidence is its relevancy, making (B) a better answer.

     (C) is not correct because the term *res gestae* refers to excited utterances or present sense impressions.

15. (C)   A leading question is a question that suggests its own answer. The question asked of Sandy was leading. Leading questions are generally not allowed on direct examination unless the witness is classified as hostile. Since Sandy was testifying on Jane's behalf, she could not be considered a hostile witness.

     (D) is incorrect because one does not have to be an expert to testify about car speed.

16. (D)   Isaac's testimony is hearsay because he is recounting Jacob's knowledge. It is admissible under the "statement against interest" exception to the Hearsay Rule. This exception requires that the declarant be absent. (A), (B), and (C) each fulfill the absence requirement.

17. (B)   Answering this question requires a mastery of the fine-line distinction between two hearsay concepts. Wally's statement to Wendy was not hearsay, because it is based on Wally's inspection, not on a statement Wally heard from another party. Wendy's testimony regarding Wally's statement was hearsay because she was recounting the words of Wally. Students must be able to make the distinction between the "admission" and "declaration against interest" exceptions to the Hearsay Rule. For the "admission" exception it is necessary that the declarant be a party to the action or in privity with such a party. Wally's statement did not meet this requirement, but it did qualify as a declaration against interest. Both these exceptions require that the declarant be unavailable.

18. (B)   When Executive testified on direct examination that he had never smoked pot, he opened the issue to cross-examination. The privilege against self-incrimination applies to testimonial, not demonstrative, evidence. Asking a defendant to smile is demonstrative evidence.

19. (C)   All four choices involve exceptions to the Hearsay Rule. Under (C), the "former testimony" exception requires that the declarant be unavailable and, in this choice, he was available. The declarant was unavailable in (A), satisfying the requirements to admit a "dying declaration." Had Witness recovered, the exception would still apply as long as he believed he was about to die at the time the statement was made and he was unavailable to testify. The declarant must also be unavailable for the "statement of pedigree" exception (Choice B) to the Hearsay Rule. Under the "family record" (Choice D) exception, the availability of the declarant is immaterial.

20. (D)   The testimony concerning where Black lived, along with White's mother's mail, are admissible because Green had personal knowledge.

    (A) is not correct because the Best Evidence Rule applies when the terms of a writing are at issue, which is not the case in this question.

    Green's testimony of Black's statement is hearsay but it is admissible under the "pedigree" exception that provides, "Reputation among members of his family by blood, adoption, or marriage, or among his associates, or in the community, concerning a person's birth, adoption, marriage, divorce, death, legitimacy, relationship by blood, adoption or marriage, ancestry, or other similar fact of his personal or family history, are not excluded by the Hearsay Rule even though the declarant is available as a witness" [FRE 803(19)].

21. (A)   All four cases involve exceptions to the Hearsay Rule. Under the "former testimony" (I) and "dying declaration" exceptions (III), the declarant must be unavailable. The availability of the declarant is immaterial under the "present sense impression" (II) and "family records" (IV) exceptions.

22. (D)   The transcripts are hearsay, but may be admissible under the "former testimony" exception to the Hearsay Rule. This exception is only invoked when the declarant is not available. (A), (B), and (C) fulfill this requirement.

23. (D)   Ellen's testimony is not hearsay because it is not set forth to prove the truth of the statement. The testimony seeks to establish that Ellen was lacking the requisite *mens rea* to commit embezzlement.

24. (D)   At common law, agnostics (Choice A), persons convicted of treason (Choice B), and persons with a pecuniary interest in the case's outcome (Choice C) were incompetent to testify.

25. (C)   Freeloader's testimony about Hitcher's statement is hearsay, but will be admissible under the "present sense impression" exception. This exception allows statements made while, or immediately following when, a declarant was perceiving an event or condition that describe or explain that event or condition [FRE 803(1)].
        (D) is incorrect. To be a declaration against interest the statement would have to adversely affect a pecuniary or penal interest of Hitcher, the declarant. None of Hitcher's interests were affected because Hitcher was merely a passenger and not the driver.

26. (A)   Crosser's testimony is relevant and, therefore, admissible. (C) is incorrect because the common law rule against impeaching one's own witness has been abandoned. (D) is incorrect because a lay person is deemed capable of judging whether another person is intoxicated.

27. (D)   A failure to correct or deny the veracity of a statement when being accused may have probative value to confirm the existence of a fact. The test is whether a reasonable man would respond to such an accusation. Note: There is no "Double Hearsay" rule. It is a frequent incorrect choice on Multistate exams. There is a rule called "Hearsay within Hearsay" [FRE 805].

28.   (D)   On cross-examination, a witness may not be impeached on a collateral issue. In this question, Speeder was cross-examining Crosser, and the issue of how long Crosser was abstaining from alcohol is collateral to whether Crosser was a credible witness to the accident. Note: Addiction to alcohol is not relevant to the issue of veracity.

29.   (B)   Speeder's testimony would not be admissible to prove that his arm was broken. It is admissible to prove that he suffered pain.

(D) is incorrect because the testimony is not hearsay. Speeder is testifying about his own statements. If Freeloader attempted to testify about the statement and Speeder was unavailable, the testimony would be hearsay.

(C) is incorrect because one is free to make self-serving testimony. Of course, the party's opponent is free to impeach.

(A) is incorrect. "Present sense impression" is an exception to the Hearsay Rule, but this statement is not hearsay.

30.   (A)   Frank's testimony to Mrs. Tommy's statements is hearsay, but admissible as an "admission against interest" since she is Tommy's business partner.

In the absence of voice recognition, a witness can authenticate a speaker's voice by showing that he called the person's home phone number and the speaker identified herself.

31.   (A)   Frank's testimony is once again hearsay, but allowable within the "admission against interest" exception.

If a witness testifies that he recognized the voice of a speaker, that will fulfill the requirement of authentication [FRE 901(B)(6)(A)].

32.   (B)   Nick's statement was within the "admission against interest" exception to the Hearsay Rule, because Nick was an agent of Tommy's Trucking.

In the absence of voice recognition, the witness can authenticate the speaker's voice by showing that he (the witness) dialed the number assigned, and if the number is a business number, that the speaker identified himself and purported to act for the company called. It will be presumed that the speaker was allowed to act on behalf of the company [FRE 901(B)(6)(A)].

33.   (A)   Any witness, not only the person who took the picture, may authenticate a photograph by testifying that it is a correct and accurate representation of the relevant facts.

34.   (D)   Seatcover is testifying from her memory. She is not attempting to testify as to the content of Trucker's notes. Therefore, the Best Evidence Rule does not apply. The rule requires that the terms of a writing be proved by producing the document. Seatcover is not concerned with the writing. (C) is inapplicable to this question because it is a hearsay exception.

35.   (D)   If one remains silent when accused, the silence may constitute an admission. The test is whether the reasonable man would have felt compelled to answer in a similar situation. When confronted with a "reasonable man" standard, use your common sense. Although, on the Multistate, reasonable students may choose different answers.
    (A) might also be correct, but (D) is a more complete answer.

36.   (C)   Prior testimony of a witness may be used for impeachment and as substantive evidence. Remember: Lori is in court and can be examined and cross-examined on the statements and their subject matter.

37.   (B)   A party may mention the failure of her opponent to offer favorable evidence or testimony.

38.   (C)   (A), (B), and (D) are exceptions to FRE 611(C), the rule stating that leading questions should not be used.

39.   (C)   Leading questions can be asked on direct examination to further a child's testimony. FRE 611 provides the court with control over the permissibility of leading questions to further ascertain the truth.

40.   (C)   A lay witness may not form an opinion as to the mental health of another. Only a qualified expert may form such an opinion. The mental health of a witness is relevant to his veracity.

41.   (D)   FRE 608(2) states that evidence of truthful character is admissible only after the character of the witness for truthfulness has been attacked by opinion or reputational evidence or otherwise. Since Charles was not cross-examined and his truthfulness was never questioned by the prosecutor, the defense may not introduce what is essentially a new issue.

42.   (A)   FRE 609 provides that a conviction for a crime involving dishonesty or false statements is admissible for the purpose of impeaching a witness regardless of the actual punishment.

(B) is incorrect because, in most cases, the admission of a conviction for a similar or identical crime will be highly prejudicial. If the prejudice outweighs the probative value, this evidence may not be admitted.

(D) is incorrect because evidence of a felony — where a period of ten or more years elapsed since the date of conviction or release from prison, whichever is longer — is only admissible when the judge determines that the probative value outweighs possible prejudice. No such determination has been made here.

43.   (D)   The question is relevant to show the witness has bias — she may be hoping to get favorable treatment in her own case. (A) is incorrect because leading questions are permitted on cross-examination.

44.   (D)   A statement of the declarant's then existing state of mind or emotion is an exception to the Hearsay Rule. The statement is probative as to the mental state of the deceased, not necessarily as to her actions [FRE 803(3)].

A dying declaration (C) applies only to an implication of one's murderer and is not applicable here.

45.   (D)   Relatives are competent as witnesses, although their bias may be raised by the opposing party.

46.   (D)   Evidence of a pertinent trait of his character may be offered by the accused [FRE 404(a)(1)].

47.   (B)   FRE 901(b)(2) permits a non-expert opinion as to the genuineness of handwriting based upon familiarity not acquired for the purposes of litigation. In this case, Zack would have sufficient familiarity with Jeff's handwriting.

(C) is incorrect because Zack never had actual knowledge of the contents of the letter itself. He is only called to testify as to the authenticity of the handwriting.

(D) is not a correct statement of fact.

48.   (C)   Jeff's perjury conviction can be brought into evidence under FRE 609(a)(2) since the crime of perjury involves dishonesty or a false statement, regardless of the punishment. Generally, specific instances of a witness's conduct may not be proved by extrinsic evidence unless the specific conduct was a crime [FRE 609] or unless the

conduct is directly probative of the witness's truthfulness or lack thereof [FRE 608(b)].

(D) is incorrect because the crime of perjury is relevant to Jeff's veracity and not to the issue of whether he actually murdered Debby.

49. (C)   Janitor's testimony of Stan's statements was hearsay. All hearsay is admissible when trying to determine the state of mind of a declarant. In addition, Stan's statement that "the hotel value has tripled" would amount to an "admission against interest," when determining damages.

50. (B)   The Best Evidence Rule requires that a litigant prove the terms or contents of a material by introducing the original document, unless the document is shown to be unavailable. There is no indication in this question that the original lease is unavailable.

51. (A)   Anyone familiar with a person's handwriting may authenticate that person's signature. It does not matter that a substantial time has elapsed since the person seeking to authenticate has seen the other's writing.

52. (B)   "A duplicate is admissible to the same extent as an original unless (1) a genuine question as to the authenticity of the original is raised or (2) in the circumstances, it would be unfair to admit the duplicate in lieu of the original" [FRE 1003]. Since these exceptions do not apply to this question, the photocopy is admissible.

53. (B)   Mary's testimony is hearsay, because she has no personal knowledge of which side of the street Lazy was driving on, but is merely repeating Nervous's statement. However, the testimony is admissible as an "excited utterance" [FRE 803(2)]. It is not necessary to show that the declarant is unavailable under the exceptions set forth in FRE 803.

54. (A)   The statement is admissible despite being hearsay, because it is an admission against interest.

(D) is not correct. The physician-patient privilege does not apply, because the statement was not made in the course of treatment.

55. (D)   FRE 803(1) provides, "A statement describing or explaining an event or condition, made while the declarant was perceiving the event or condition, or immediately thereafter" is an exception to the Hearsay Rule as a "present sense impression."

56.   (D)   "A statement is not hearsay if the declarant testifies at the trial or hearing and is subject to cross-examination...and the statement is inconsistent with his [prior] testimony" [FRE 801(d)(1)(A)]. One may impeach his own witness.

57.   (C)   "When after an event measures are taken, which if taken previously would have made the event less likely to occur, evidence of the subsequent measures is not admissible to prove negligence or culpable conduct in connection with the event" [FRE 407]. Evidence of subsequent remedial measures is generally excluded on the grounds that the possible use of the evidence to prove relevancy or negligence is outweighed by the public interest in the implementation of such measures.

58.   (D)   Although FRE 408 excludes David's $10,000 settlement offer from being admitted, the rule does not require the exclusion of other evidence that would otherwise be discoverable. Therefore, David's statement about the "fifteen-year-old kid" is admissible under FRE 801(D)(2) as an "admission by party-opponent."

59.   (C)   FRE 404 makes it clear that evidence of Sean's bad reputation in the neighborhood cannot be introduced to show that he was acting in conformity with it at the time of his altercation with Shaheid.

60.   (A)   An accused may offer evidence of a pertinent trait of his character for the purpose of proving he acted in conformity therewith on a particular occasion [FRE 404(a)(1)].

61.   (B)   A character witness may be asked about the reputation of one on whose behalf he has testified in order to test the witness's knowledge of that person.

62.   (B)   FRE 404(a)(2) allows a trait in evidence if the trait is pertinent to the character of the victim (Shaheid) of the crime offered by an accused (Sean). If Shaheid was indeed a sick and violent man, then Sean's defense is supported by this relevant evidence.

63.   (C)   Prior crimes may be entered into evidence only if punishable by death, one year or more imprisonment, or if they involve dishonesty [FRE 609(A)]. Since ignoring a stop sign was not relevant to the issue of the case and was not admissible as a prior crime, the court should rule Nellie's testimony inadmissible.

(D) is incorrect because a witness's character is never an issue in determining admissibility. The other party may attempt to impeach the witness by bringing her character into issue.

64. (D)   In order to admit a photograph, the witness must know about the facts that are portrayed in the photo. The witness need not have taken the actual photographs.

(A) is incorrect because then existing physical condition applies to a statement made by the declarant regarding his physical or mental condition.

(C) is incorrect because the witness can testify that the photos are accurate representations of the scene, notwithstanding the time element involved.

65. (A)   Larry's statement is introduced to prove a fact he does not claim knowledge of — the car's speed. The statement is therefore hearsay, because Harry is the one with the knowledge. It will be ruled admissible under an exception to the Hearsay Rule, as an excited utterance [FRE 803(2)]. The testimony was not "against interest" (Choice B) because the declarant was not a party to the suit.

66. (C)   Offering a bribe does not prove negligence; therefore, it would not be admissible on the negligence issue. If Ernie was criminally prosecuted for attempted bribery, the statement would be admissible because it was not hearsay; Vincent is testifying about his own knowledge.

67. (C)   FRE 408 provides that evidence of offers to compromise are not admissible, because the law seeks to encourage settlements.

68. (D)   FRE 404 states that evidence of a person's character or trait, such as safe driving, is not admissible to prove that he acted in conformity therewith. Ernie's reputation will not be admissible to show that he did not act in a negligent manner in this instance, unless provided for through the exceptions in FRE 404 and 607, 608 and 609.

69. (B)   Although Croker's testimony is hearsay, since it is admitted to determine negligence of which Croker has no personal knowledge, it is admissible under FRE 804(b)(3), as a "statement against interest."

(A) is not correct because the position of the person or relationship of the person to the declarant is immaterial.

(C) is incorrect because a statement against one's interest can be made after the event that triggered it.

70.   (D)   Tim testified about another's statement. That is a classic example of hearsay. The statement does not qualify under the "statement against interest" and "admission of party opponent" exceptions to the Hearsay Rule, because the witness was not a party to the suit and had no interest in the outcome.

71.   (B)   Tim's testimony is introduced to prove that the windshield wipers were actually not working. Tim has no such firsthand knowledge; therefore, Tim's testimony is hearsay. It will be admissible under the "present sense impression" exception to the Hearsay Rule [FRE 803(1)]. The availability of the declarant (Choice A) is immaterial under all 803 exceptions.

72.   (D)   FRE 609(a)(2) allows evidence of a witness's past crimes to be admitted if they involve dishonesty or false statements. Since embezzlement is such a crime, it is admissible regardless of the punishment. This exception applies to criminal as well as civil trials.

73.   (D)   Extrinsic evidence of a collateral matter is not allowed for impeachment of an issue raised on cross-examination.

74.   (D)   Witness's recollection of Patti's statement is hearsay. The exceptions of "admission of party" and "declaration against interest" do not apply, because Patti was not a party to the suit.

75.   (D)   FRE 406 allows evidence of habit to be admitted in order to prove the conduct was in conformity with the habit or routine practice.
              (C) is incorrect because the evidence is admissible regardless of the presence of eyewitnesses.

76.   (B)   Billy is not attempting to admit the painting into evidence; it is hearsay. It is permissible to use the painting to jar the witness' memory, under the doctrine of "present recollection refreshed." The key to answering this question is to understand that the painting is used only for the purpose of refreshing the witness' memory. The memory is what is to be admitted, not the painting.

77.   (B)   The court in *U.S. v. Napier*, 518 F2d 316 (9th cir.), cert. denied, 96 S.Ct. 196 (1975), ruled that a startling event satisfying the exception to the Hearsay Rule may occur weeks after the actual crime. In that particular case, the declarant was startled

by seeing a photograph of the perpetrator. Availability of the declarant is immaterial under the "excited utterance" exception to the Hearsay Rule.

78.   (D)   FRE 804(b)(2) states that a statement made by a declarant (Mike) is admissible if it was made while believing that his death was imminent and concerned the cause of what he believed to be his own (Mike's) impending death.

         (A) is incorrect because the dying declaration exception does not permit Mike's statement to be admitted as evidence that Duran killed Sal.

79.   (B)   Evan may not be impeached on a collateral matter; however, Spider's testimony would be admissible to prove Duran had a motive to steal (to repay the loan), as provided for under FRE 404(b).

80.   (B)   The accused, in all criminal cases, may produce evidence of his good character as substantive evidence of his innocence. It is merely circumstantial evidence bearing on the probability that the accused did or did not commit the act with the required intent (McCormick, 191).

         (C) is incorrect because the rule stated in this choice applies only to negligence cases.

81.   (A)   A cross-examiner may ask a character witness whether he has "heard" or "knows" of other particular crimes of the accused, provided the question is asked in good faith.

82.   (B)   Henry's testimony was relevant to determine if Ron was unnecessarily aggressive. Such testimony is permissible under FRE 404(a)(2).

83.   (C)   It is true that the attorney-client privilege belongs to the client. In this question we have another problem: hearsay. Judy has no personal knowledge, she is merely being asked to repeat what Abe told her, and there is no evidence that any of the exceptions apply.

84.   (B)   FRE 411 allows evidence of whether or not a person was insured to be admitted to prove agency, ownership, control, or bias, but not to prove that the person acted negligently.

         (A) is not the correct choice because this exchange between Lilly and Harry does not resemble a startling event that would trigger the "excited utterance" exception [FRE 803(2)].

85.   (A)   The tape is relevant to determine the defendant's physical condition at the time of the accident. Videotapes, fingerprints, etc., may be taken without violating a defendant's right against self-incrimination.

86.   (A)   A criminal conviction is admissible in a civil suit arising from the same action in order to prove the defendant's behavior during the occurrence in dispute.

87.   (D)   "When, after an event, measures are taken which, if taken previously, would have made the event less likely to occur, evidence of the subsequent measures is not admissible to prove negligence or culpable conduct" [FRE 407].

88.   (D)   The trial judge will exclude the discussion if it falls under the physician-patient privilege. This privilege includes discussions before a contractual agreement exists, whether or not the physician is hired. The privilege does not extend to casual conversations where no treatment is intended. Jagger's conversation at a party is not assumed to be for purposes of treatment (Choice D) unless they already had a physician-patient relationship (Choice C).

89.   (A)   Since Ryan is unavailable, statements he made implicating a murderer are hearsay. The statement will be admissible only to impeach Ryan.

90.   (A)   FRE 901(b)(2) allows anyone familiar with the handwriting of a given person to supply authentication testimony, in the form of an opinion that a writing or signature is the handwriting of that person.

91.   (B)   The statement made by Joyce is an example of an exception to the Hearsay Rule under FRE 801(d)(2)(b). It is a statement in which the party (Gary) has manifested an adoption or belief of its truth. Gary's failure to reply accepts the suggestion implicit in Joyce's statement. Gary has in effect made an assertion that could be used against him. See *U.S. v. Hoosier*, 542 F.2d 687 (1976).

92.   (A)   Prior crimes are admissible for the purpose of determining length of sentence.

93.   (B)   Any person who has acquired sufficient familiarity with a voice may identify that person. The rules requiring the other person to identify herself, etc., only apply when the voice is not familiar [FRE 901].

94.   (B)   The statement is hearsay, but is admissible as a statement against interest under FRE 804(b)(3).

(A) is incorrect because the then-existing mental condition exception, FRE 803(3), is generally applicable when the declarant made the statement while perceiving the event or immediately thereafter.

95.   (D)   "Evidence of the beliefs or opinions of a witness, on matters of religion, is not admissible for the purpose of showing that by reason of their nature, his credibility is impaired or enhanced" [FRE 610].

96.   (B)   Although religious beliefs are not admissible to prove veracity, they may be admitted for another purpose, if relevant.

97.   (B)   (B) is the only correct answer because the report does not fit within any hearsay exception. It is not admissible under FRE 803(6) as a business record, because the facts indicate that the source of the report could have been biased (in favor of the fellow employee), making the record untrustworthy.

(C) is not correct, because a recorded recollection is used only to enable a witness, who has sufficient recollection, to testify fully and accurately.

98.   (D)   Evidence of a guilty plea, later withdrawn, or of statements made in connection with the plea, are not admissible either in a civil or criminal proceeding against the person who made the plea [FRE 410].

99.   (C)   Trucker's conduct in attempting to bribe Joseph is probative as to Trucker's negligence. Do not confuse this with an offer to settle. A settlement offer is also probative, but is not admissible due to public policy to encourage settlements.

100.   (A)   Dreamer's recounting of the statements of Mac and Peter is hearsay. Since Mac and Peter were not parties to the suit, their statements cannot be "party admissions" or "declarations against interest" to qualify as exceptions to the Hearsay Rule.

101.   (B)   Evidence of negotiations or offers in settlement negotiations are not admissible [FRE 408].

102. (D)   Dreamer is not attempting to submit the diary as evidence — it is hearsay. He is merely attempting to use the diary to help Joseph's memory. Since Joseph will be testifying from memory, the Hearsay Rule will be inapplicable.

103. (A)   "Evidence of subsequent measures is not admissible to prove negligence" [FRE 407]. The purpose of this rule is to encourage people to take necessary steps to remedy a dangerous situation in order to ensure public safety.

104. (D)   A reasonable person would not feel obligated to answer such a comment. Tony's non-response does not fit under FRE 801(d)(2)(b). Compare this problem to question #91 above.

105. (B)   The attorney-client privilege includes preliminary discussions, even if the attorney is never retained. The privilege belongs to the client, not the attorney.

106. (C)   Evidence of a person's character or a trait of character is generally not admissible except, under FRE 404(a)(1), if the evidence is offered by an accused, i.e., Tony, or as otherwise provided for under FRE 404.

107. (B)   The chance of misleading the trier of fact by allowing the prosecution to bring up a prior acquittal is extremely high in comparison to the probative value.

108. (C)   Since burglary is a felony, it is admissible under FRE 609(a) if the court determines it will not prejudice the defendant.

        (A) is too narrow. (B) is inapplicable since no writing is being offered into evidence.

109. (C)   Since Sophie is testifying based on firsthand knowledge, her testimony is admissible, even though the same information is written down.

        (A) is incorrect because the Best Evidence Rule only applies where the contents of the writing are being directly proved from the writing itself.

        (D) is not correct because Sophie is available to testify, and there is not an out-of-court statement at issue here.

110. (C)   Relatives are competent as witnesses, although their bias may be raised by opposing counsel.

111. (D)   An excited utterance must be made "while the declarant was under the stress of excitement caused by the event or condition" [FRE 803(2)]. Since Senile did not tell Kojack about the accident until an hour later, the law assumes he had time to plan his outburst and does not fit this into an exception to the Hearsay Rule.

    A present sense impression must be made "while the declarant was perceiving the event or condition, or immediately thereafter" [FRE 803(1)].

112. (C)   Evidence of negotiations or offers in settlement negotiations is not admissible [FRE 408]. An offer to compromise a disputed claim is a settlement offer.

113. (A)   A statement is not hearsay if the statement offered against a party is his own [FRE 801(d)(2)(A)].

114. (D)   Evidence of a person's character cannot be used to prove his actions were in conformity on a particular occasion [FRE 404(a)].

115. (A)   The doctor's testimony is relevant to determine if the calaloo soup was contaminated. Breadnut is relating the statements of others, which would ordinarily be hearsay, but in these facts, the statements qualify under the "statements for purposes of medical diagnosis or treatment" exception to the Hearsay Rule [FRE 803(4)].

116. (D)   FRE 803(4) permits statements to be admitted if they were for purposes of medical diagnosis or treatment, but such statements should not include statements as to cause.

    (B) is incorrect because statements as to fault are not admissible under FRE 803(4).

117. (C)   FRE(d)(2)(A) provides, "A statement is not hearsay if the statement is offered against a party and is his own statement."

118. (B)   A statement contained in a document, establishing an interest in property, is not hearsay unless "dealings with the property since the document was made have been inconsistent with the truth of the statement or the purport of the document" [FRE 803(15)]. A certified copy of a public document is admissible. The law does not want to burden the recorder's office by requiring court appearances of officials with records.

119.   (A)   Infants, interested persons, and incompetents are valid witnesses. Facts may be introduced as to matters of weight and credibility.

120.   (D)   Although evidence of subsequent remedial measures is not permitted to show negligence (FRE 407), such evidence may be admitted to rebut a claim that the precaution was impossible. The evidence is admissible here to controvert Cheepo's answer that it was impossible to design a trailer with proper equipment. Evidence of subsequent remedial measures can also be used for purposes of impeachment and to prove ownership or control.

121.   (D)   Extrinsic evidence of authenticity is not a condition precedent to admissibility with respect to books, pamphlets, or other publications purporting to be issued by public authority [FRE 603].

122.   (D)   "Before testifying, every witness shall be required to declare that he will testify truthfully" [FRE 603].

123.   (B)   "Although relevant, evidence may be excluded if its probative value is substantially outweighed by the danger of unfair prejudice" [FRE 402].
                   "Evidence of other crimes, wrongs, or acts is not admissible to prove the character of a person, in order to show that he acted in conformity therewith. It may, however, be admissible for other purposes, such as proof of motive, opportunity, intent . . ." [FRE 404(b)].
                   The probative value of Loser's gambling is small when compared to its prejudicial effect.

124.   (C)   The out-of-court statement is considered hearsay and not admissible if the declarant is unavailable [FRE 801(d)(1)(C)]. The reason is that the declarant must be available for cross-examination by the defense, even though the statement was one of identification of a person made after perceiving him and may be very reliable.

125.   (A)   A prior statement of a witness is generally only admissible if offered against the witness.

126.   (A)   "For the purpose of attacking the credibility of a witness, evidence that he has been convicted of a crime shall be admitted . . . if the court determines that the probative value of admitting this evidence outweighs its prejudicial effect" [FRE 609].

127. (C)   For the purpose of the attorney-client privilege, "client" is a person, public officer of a corporation, association, or other entity. The privilege extends to lower-echelon employees of a corporation [*Upjohn Co. v. U.S.*, 449 U.S. 383, 1981].

128. (A)   The propensity of an animal may be proved by specific instances.

129. (C)   A lay witness cannot be asked to form an opinion on what another person may have thought.

130. (C)   This is a classic example of hearsay.

131. (C)   An expert opinion may be offered in response to a hypothetical question where assumed facts have been previously offered into evidence.
              (D) is a generally correct statement, but is not as specific as (C).

132. (A)   "If a type is reasonably relied upon by experts in the particular field, in forming opinion or inferences upon the subject, the facts or data (i.e., the microscopic tissue) need not be admissible in evidence" [FRE 703].

133. (B)   Under the "former testimony" exception to the Hearsay Rule, a witness's testimony may be admitted, providing the witness is unavailable and the party against whom the testimony is being offered had an opportunity to cross-examine the witness [FRE 80(b)(1)].

134. (D)   "Evidence of subsequent measures is not admissible to prove negligence or culpable conduct in connection with the event. This rule does not require the exclusion of evidence . . . for another purpose, such as proving ownership" [FRE 407].

135. (B)   The fact that many others passed without injury does not prove the owner exercised due care in maintaining it.

136. (D)   A communication remains confidential and within the attorney-client privilege if a secretary, or other person necessary to assist the attorney in preparing the case, is present.

137. (B)   When a lawyer acts for two parties in a transaction, no privilege can be claimed in a suit between the two parties.

138. (A)   Erp's testimony of the witness's statement is hearsay and not admissible.
          (C) is incorrect because the witness had approximately one hour to reflect and plan her statement.
          (D) is incorrect because Erp's notes are a past recollection of the witness's statement, which is hearsay. Notes of hearsay remain hearsay.

139. (B)   Spify's truthfulness is not a collateral issue, and counsel may try to impeach Spify's truthfulness at any time.

140. (D)   Erp's recollection of Swifty's statement is hearsay but is admissible under the "statement against interest" exception [FRE 804(b)(3)].

141. (D)   The policy of the law is to encourage settlement negotiations; therefore, courts will not allow testimony of the actual negotiations.

142. (D)   (A), (B), and (C) are not correct because Suzie seeks to introduce the neighbor's testimony (i.e., the contents of the affidavits), not the documents themselves [FRE 801, 802, 803].

143. (B)   FRE 609 provides that any crime involving dishonesty or false statement is admissible to impeach a witness. Crimes punishable by more than one year in prison are admissible if the punishment was more than ten years ago, and the prejudicial effect is outweighed by the probative value. Since a conviction for a similar crime tends to be highly prejudicial, the court should rule the manslaughter conviction inadmissible.

144. (D)   The question is leading and, therefore, not permitted on cross-examination. Exceptions to this, under FRE 611(c), include when a party calls a hostile witness, an adverse party, or a witness identified with an adverse party.

145. (B)   Illegally obtained evidence may not be admitted as substantive proof of guilt, but may be used to impeach credibility [*U.S. v. Havens*, 100 S.CT. 1912(1980)]. Note: it does not matter whether the party is attempting to impeach testimony given on direct or cross.

146.   (D)   A witness does not need special qualifications to determine the speed of an automobile.

147.   (C)   The clergyman-penitent privilege operates in a manner similar to the physician-patient and attorney-client privileges. It may only be invoked by the penitent or his representative. The previous or subsequent relationship of clergyman and penitent is not material as long as there was a relationship, or discussion leading to a possible relationship, at the time they had a discussion.

148.   (C)   A witness may refer to collateral documents without producing the documents themselves.

149.   (D)   Redirect examination of a witness must be permitted only to reply to a new matter.

150.   (A)   This statement is classic hearsay.
        (D) is incorrect because Lou Weed is not a party to the action. Since Denise was not present when the statement was made, she could not have adopted it as an admission.
        (C) is incorrect because the facts do not tend to show that the statement was made by Weed in the excitement of the accident.

151.   (D)   The cost of a headlight is not relevant to liability or damages in the instant case.

152.   (A)   If an agent makes a statement within his agency, contrary to the principal's interest, this statement qualifies as a "statement against interest" exception to the Hearsay Rule [FRE 804(b)(3)].

153.   (D)   By blaming his agent, Johnson has in effect blamed himself and made an admission against his interest. The testimony is admissible as an admission against interest.

154.   (B)   Cane's secretary testified that she mailed something to Abel. Her testimony does not address the contents of the writing, and, therefore, the Best Evidence Rule does not apply. The Best Evidence Rule only applies when the contents of a writing are sought to be proved.

155. (B) Here, the secretary's testimony addresses the actual contents of the letter, invoking the Best Evidence Rule. The question of the availability of the original is decided by the judge, not the jury.

156. (C) FRE 610 prohibits the use of evidence of a witness's religious beliefs to prove the credibility of that witness.

157. (A) Although religious beliefs may not be introduced to prove credibility, they may be introduced for other reasons. Here, Debby's membership in the church is relevant to show possible bias in the church's favor.

158. (A) The standard to allow a defendant or witness to remain silent is a "reasonable possibility" that he may incriminate himself.

159. (D) One's reputation may not be offered to show he acted in a negligent manner in a specific situation [FRE 404].

160. (B) "Evidence of other crimes, wrongs, or acts is not admissible to prove a person acted in conformity therewith" [FRE 404(B)]. The testimony is, however, admissible to identify the driver of the car.

161. (D) The attorney-client privilege applies to written as well as oral communications, as long as it was intended by the parties to be confidential.

162. (B) FRE 1004(3) permits the contents of an original to be admitted if it is in the possession of the opponent.

163. (A) FRE 1004(4) permits an original writing, recording, or photograph to be admitted if it is not closely related to a controlling issue.

164. (A) An expert witness may base his opinion on facts not admitted into evidence. The opposing party may ask about these facts on cross-examination [FRE 704]. The questions may be leading and hypothetical in form.

165. (A) Leading questions are permitted when the witness needs aid due to immaturity.

166.   (D)   "Testimony in the form of an opinion or inference otherwise admissible is not objectionable, because it embraces an ultimate issue to be decided by the trier of fact" [FRE 704].

167.   (D)   One may not question a witness about his addiction to alcohol because it is not considered to have bearing on veracity. The relationship between witness and parties is relevant to veracity, as are prior crimes. The witness may be impeached by prior inconsistent statements.

168.   (B)   "Evidence of truthful character is admissible only after the character of the witness for truthfulness has been attacked" [FRE 608(a)(2)].
            (B) is the only choice where Woody is accused of not being truthful, and, therefore, Bo could introduce evidence of Woody's character.

169.   (D)   FRE 403 excludes evidence if it is unfairly prejudicial, but there is little danger of that here because the tape fairly shows the state of the defendant as being intoxicated.
            (A) is not correct because the tape does not seek to impeach the witness on a collateral matter as required by the rule against impeachment by use of extrinsic evidence regarding specific instances of conduct.
            (C) is not correct because it is unlikely his acts equal an admission, and there is not a hearsay problem in this question. An admission against a party opponent is a hearsay exception.

170.   (D)   In this choice, Nosey's testimony is hearsay because she does not have firsthand knowledge. The prosecution should call Talker's mother to the stand.

171.   (B)   Evidence that one is insured is not admissible to prove liability or damages, but is admissible to prove ownership or control [FRE 411].

172.   (B)   A foundation witness must attest that a photograph is faithful and accurate. The photographer need not testify.

173.   (A)   Evidence of the habit of a person is relevant to prove that the conduct on a particular occasion was in conformity with the habit of routine practice [FRE 406].

174.   (C)   Leading questions should be permitted on cross-examination and when a party calls a hostile witness or adverse party [FRE 611(C)].

175.   (A)   Convicted felons and relatives are competent witnesses. A conviction for a felony or a crime involving dishonesty or fraud is a basis for impeaching the witness [FRE 609], as is bias.

176.   (B)   The court, in *U.S. v. Mackay*, 405 F. Supp. 854, held that an attorney could be compelled to testify he was an incorporator because the attorney-client privilege does not apply to testimony concerning the general nature of legal services rendered.

PROPERTY CONTENTS

PROPERTY QUESTIONS

1. Alpha divided a plot of land he owned into two parts, Eastacre and Westacre. He then built a house on each. Beta purchased Westacre and Alpha kept Eastacre. In the course of construction, Alpha had run plumbing for Eastacre through Westacre. The pipes were underground and not apparent to the casual observer. One year later, Beta decided to put a swimming pool in his yard. Beta's contractor discovered Alpha's pipes, which obstructed the area for the pool. Beta asserted an action to force Alpha to remove his pipes from Westacre. Who most likely prevailed?

   (A) Beta, because Alpha's pipes trespassed on his land.

   (B) Alpha, because he owned an easement by implication.

   (C) Alpha, because he owned an easement by prescription.

   (D) Beta, because Alpha violated the covenant against encumbrances.

2. Which of the following conveyances would be altered by the Rule Against Perpetuities?

   (A) Errol conveyed his chain of video stores to his son, Errol Jr. "on the condition that he does not rent X-rated movies. Should Errol Jr. rent X-rated movies, Errol or his heirs have the right to reenter the premises."

   (B) Errol conveyed his chain of video stores to his son, Errol Jr. "for as long as X-rated movies are not rented from the stores."

   (C) Errol conveyed his chain of video stores "to my son, Errol Jr., then if my son Ernie is living at Errol Jr.'s death, to Ernie; upon Ernie's death to my grandchildren who have reached the age of twenty-five."

   (D) Errol conveyed his chain of video stores "to my son, Errol Jr., for life; remainder to Errol, Jr.'s children for life; remainder to Ernie's children and their heirs."

3. Alan owned Blackacre in fee simple. He wanted the land to eventually pass to his grandchildren, but he felt that the land would be put to better use by his hardworking friend, Jimmy. He devised the land as follows:

   "To Jimmy for as long as he shall live, then to the children of my children who reach the age of majority. Should none of my grandchildren reach the age of majority, then to my cousin Sharon."

   Alan had six grandchildren, all below the age of majority, when he

GO ON TO THE NEXT PAGE

died. Jimmy and Sharon were both alive.

Which of the following choices is correct?

(A)   The land will eventually pass to Sharon because the grandchildren's interest is void under the Rule Against Perpetuities.

(B)   Sharon owns a remainder in fee simple subject to defeasance by the grandchildren's interest.

(C)   The Rule Against Perpetuities was violated because one of Alan's children might die and be survived by a pregnant spouse.

(D)   Jimmy's life estate is determinable upon a grandchild reaching the age of majority.

4.   Alden granted Blackacre to Carlos in fee tail. Twenty-five years later Carlos was eighty-four years-old and had no issue. In a jurisdiction that completely recognizes fee tail, Carlos's interest in Blackacre can best be described as a

(A)   life estate by operation of law

(B)   life estate per autre vie

(C)   possibility of reverter

(D)   shifting executory interest

(alternative question) Alden's interest in Blackacre can best be described as a

(A)   possibility of reverter

(B)   shifting executory interest

(C)   life estate per autre vie

(D)   nullity

5.   Sidney, a retired physician without children, owned his former office, which was part of a professional condominium complex. Sidney rented out the office, but he wanted to give it to one of his nephews to ensure that someone would follow in his footsteps.

One of Sidney's nephews, Ernie, was in medical school and had chosen psychiatry as his specialty. As a proctologist, Sidney couldn't understand why Ernie wanted to waste all that good education to deal with nuts.

Sidney's other nephew, Peter, was a high school sophomore who did well in science class and seemed interested in proctology.

Sidney decided to convey his condominium "to Ernie for life, then if Peter should be awarded the degree 'Doctor of Medicine' and complete a residency, to Peter and his heirs as long as the office is used for the practice of medicine."

Which of the following choices is **NOT** correct?

(A)   While Peter is in college he holds a contingent remainder in fee simple determinable.

(B)   If Peter completes his residency in medicine he owns a fee simple determinable upon Ernie's death.

(C) Sidney's interest at the time of the conveyance is best described as a possibility of reverter.

(D) If Peter becomes a florist and never goes to medical school, possession will eventually return to Sidney without the fee simple determinable ever being invoked.

6. In 1916, Eric executed a deed conveying Blackacre "to my son George for life, upon George's death, to his children or their respective estates." George lived on Blackacre all his life. He had three children.

A creditor of his son Andy asserted an action to attach Andy's interest prior to George's death. Can the creditor succeed?

(A) Yes, because a remainder may be attached by creditors.

(B) Yes, because a vested remainder may be attached or sold by creditors.

(C) No, because neither a vested nor a contingent remainder may be attached or sold by creditors.

(D) No, because Andy's interest was a contingent remainder.

7. Morris owned a parking lot in fee simple. When Morris died his will provided, "I leave my wife a life estate in my parking lot. After my wife's death, the lot shall pass to my son Jacob, to use and manage in his lifetime. After Jacob's death the parking lot shall pass in fee simple to the heirs of Jacob's body."

Morris's wife died. Some years later, Jacob died intestate, married, and without issue. In a common law jurisdiction, the parking lot will pass

(A) to Jacob's wife in fee simple by the rules governing intestate succession

(B) to Jacob's long lost brother Joe

(C) to Morris's estate

(D) to Morris's wife's estate by reversion

8. Leslie conveyed three acres of his farm "to my son Tracey for his lifetime, then to the heirs of his body should he have any; if Tracey dies without heirs of his body, the land shall revert to myself or my estate." Leslie died one year before his only child Tracey.

Which of the following choices is **NOT** correct?

(A) In a jurisdiction recognizing the Rule in Shelley's Case, Tracey would have obtained the property in fee simple.

(B) A title taken via descent was considered worthier title at common law than title taken by purchase.

GO ON TO THE NEXT PAGE

(C) In a common law state, the Doctrine of Worthier Title would be applied and the land would pass to Leslie's heirs.

(D) Under the Doctrine of Worthier Title, one can give his own heirs a remainder of a life estate he grants to another.

9. Which of the following situations will be altered by the Rule Against Perpetuities?

I. Central donated 800 acres of land to the city of New York "on the condition that the land 1) be used in perpetuity for public recreation and 2) be called Central Park. Should the land be used for other purposes, it should revert to Frederick and Olmstead and their heirs."

II. Balboa conveyed 2,000 acres of land in San Diego to be used as a zoo "so long as alcohol and tobacco are not sold on the premises for the next 100 years. If alcohol or tobacco is sold, the land shall revert to my estate."

III. Biscayne conveyed his land in downtown Miami "to Suarez, remainder to his first child to reach the age of fifty." Suarez had one child, age thirty, at the time of the conveyance.

IV. Tim Mall, owner of land in central Washington, conveyed his land "to Jefferson for his life, remainder to Jefferson's children for their lives, remainder to Adams and his heirs."

(A) I and III

(B) II and IV

(C) I, II and III

(D) I only

10. Sidney sold his home to Roger with full covenants. The house, resting on a half acre of land, had three bedrooms and a two-car garage. Two years later, Roger conveyed the house to Eve by a quitclaim deed.
Which of the following choices is correct?

(A) Eve can successfully assert an action against Sidney if at the time Sidney sold the home a logging company owned the rights to all the timber on the property.

(B) Eve can force Sidney to take further action within his power to perfect title to the home when her next door neighbor argues that her fence is on his property.

(C) Eve can enforce Sidney's guarantee to Roger that the land is free from easements that diminish its value.

(D) Eve can enforce a covenant against encumbrances made by Sidney to Roger.

11.	Biscayne is a public utility that supplies the city of Coral Gables with water. Edward Flagler owned a large amount of vacant land in Coral Gables. Biscayne calculated that it could save $400,000 by running its pipes across some of Flagler's land rather than crossing a public highway. After months of negotiations Flagler granted Biscayne an eight-foot-wide strip of land under which to bury its pipes and use in perpetuity for consideration of $200,000.

Which of the following choices best describes the rights Biscayne acquired?

(A)	profit

(B)	easement in gross

(C)	easement appurtenant

(D)	real covenant

12.	In 1922, John, a Kentucky minister and strong supporter of Prohibition, conveyed a ten-acre farm he had inherited from his father "to my son, John Jr. and his heirs so long as this farm is not used to sell, produce, or warehouse alcohol or assist the alcohol industry in any manner." John Jr. died in 1925 whereupon the property passed to his children, John III and Jane. In 1965 they sold their interest in the property to Jake who sold the land to Frank in 1975. John III and Jane died in the early 1970s, each leaving three children and a spouse. Both spouses eventually remarried. Kentucky Fried Bourbon purchased five of the ten acres in 1990 and constructed a whiskey distillery.

What should the status of the land be now?

(A)	The land will remain in Kentucky Fried Bourbon's possession because the anti-alcohol clause violated the Rule Against Perpetuities.

(B)	The land will revert to John's heirs because the anti-alcohol clause created a valid fee simple subject to condition subsequent.

(C)	The land will revert to John's heirs because the anti-alcohol clause created an indestructible fee simple determinable.

(D)	The land will revert to John's heirs only in a minority of states that have not enacted statutes of limitations applicable to fee simple determinables.

13.	Ronny owned a lovely Pacific Palisades home, to which he had grown very attached, in fee simple. When he purchased a new and much larger house for his growing family, Ronny could not bear to part with his old home. So, he decided to grant a life estate in the house to his cousin Maurice, who had very little money and a family of his own to provide for. Ronny left himself the remainder of the life estate.

Maurice lived in the house for a little while, but then realized he

GO ON TO THE NEXT PAGE

could have a nice income if he rented it out. He decided to grant Aaron a ten-year lease on the house. Aaron, a yuppie attorney, agreed to pay $2,000 per month for the first year, with an increase each subsequent year tied to the local inflation rate.

Who can be said to have seisin after Aaron occupies the house?

(A)   Ronny

(B)   Maurice

(C)   Aaron

(D)   none of the above

14.   Ken was a lawyer besieged by friends, relatives, and acquaintances seeking free legal advice. Ken's cousin Doug, one of the cheapest men in North America, purchased a house without retaining counsel. He stopped by Ken's house on a Sunday, pretending to be in the neighborhood, and said, "Hey, I happen to have the contract to my house. Why don't you take a look at it as a refresher in contract law."

Ken looked at the contract and told Doug, "Your agreement provides for 'usual covenants.' You should have insisted on 'full covenants.'"

The difference will be important if Doug wants to assert an action against the person who sold him the house based on the covenant

(A)   for quiet enjoyment

(B)   of general warranty

(C)   for further assurances

(D)   for seisin

15.   In which of the following cases is the easement **NOT** valid and/or enforceable?

(A)   LBJ owned a 10,000-acre ranch that was divided by a river and a county highway into three distinct sections. One section had become known in the neighborhood as "Lady Bird Flats." Out of affection for his confidant, Kearns, LBJ signed a writing granting an easement to Kearns to "have full recreational use of, and all pleasure rights to, the part of my ranch known as Lady Bird Flats." Kearns recorded the easement pursuant to a local recording act.

(B)   Ira Gershwin owned a house with a large yard. After living in the house for twenty years, sky-rocketing real estate prices, followed by a large rise in taxes, began to deplete his bank account. Ira decided to sell one-half acre of his property to his brother George, who built a house on it. The only access from George's house to a public road was over Ira's property. George received no confirmation, written or otherwise, of an easement to drive over Ira's property, and he did not make any official recordings.

(C)   Runner jogged along a path on his neighbor Smoker's property every day for twenty-one years. Smoker, tired of hearing his wife nag him because Runner was active and healthy while he only sat around smoking and getting fat, asserted an action to prevent Runner from using the path. Runner claimed he had an easement by prescription. The statute of limitations was fifteen years.

(D)   Dicky, the owner of a three-story house with a view of the beach, paid Daffy, the owner of a neighboring parking lot, for a written easement assuring that "no structure blocking Dicky's light and air will be built on Daffy's property."

Questions 16-17 are based upon the following fact pattern.

Heir, a fifty-year-old bachelor, inherited a 200-acre estate that had been in his family's possession for more than a century. Since Heir did not have a family of his own, he decided he would be lonely living there. He had also never worked a day in his life and needed some cash. Heir decided half the land would be enough for his own use. He only needed sufficient acreage on which to ride his horses. Heir sold one-acre lots pursuant to a contract that contained the clause "Heir agrees to reserve ten acres of land to be used as a private park for the exclusive use of residents of the ninety one-acre plots. The purchaser of this lot agrees to erect no building taller than two stories. Such structures may be used for residential purposes only."

Heir kept two of the one-acre lots. He took a long trip to Rio with his new-

found money. While Heir was in Rio, Homeless moved into his mansion and remained in exclusive, open, notorious, continuous, and hostile possession for twenty-one years. Shortly before Heir returned from Rio, Homeless was granted title to the 100-acre estate in fee simple.

Frieda purchased a one-acre tract from Al, who had purchased from Heir. Frieda filed a building permit to construct a house three stories high.

16.   Will Homeless succeed in collecting damages from Frieda for constructing her house?

    (A)   Yes, because a common development scheme had been established for the entire subdivision.

    (B)   Yes, because the restrictive clause ran with the land.

    (C)   No, because Homeless received "new title" and should not be considered to have privity of estate with Frieda.

    (D)   No, because the restriction was not enforceable.

17.   Assume for this question only that Homeless had received title to Al's property, instead of Heir's, by adverse possession. Would Homeless survive a challenge by another plot owner to prevent his plans to build a hotel?

    (A)   Yes, because he received new title, and privity requirements

GO ON TO THE NEXT PAGE

are stricter for burdens than for benefits.

(B)   Yes, if the hotel was residential and within the height restriction.

(C)   No, if the court finds a common scheme of which Homeless had constructive notice.

(D)   No, because the covenant was valid and enforceable.

18.   On July 7, Alpha conveyed Rockacre to Beta. The deed provided for "usual covenants." Four years later on February 22, Beta conveyed Rockacre to Gamma. The deed contained the same language as the Alpha-Beta deed. In which of the following lawsuits will Gamma most likely prevail?

(A)   Six months after purchasing Rockacre, Gamma was notified by a neighbor that a real covenant prevented any construction on the property. After researching the relevant law, Gamma determined that he was bound by this covenant. Gamma sued Alpha for damages.

(B)   Six months after purchasing Rockacre, Gamma was notified by a neighbor that he was occupying her land. She had just been awarded title to Rockacre after a year of litigation. Gamma asserted an action against Alpha.

(C)   Six months after purchasing Rockacre, Gamma was

notified by the Bank of Bedrock that it held a mortgage on the property. Gamma was subsequently told that the mortgage was taken out eight years previously. He asserted an action against Alpha.

(D)   Gamma will not succeed in any of the above actions.

19.   Rachel had one year remaining on a twenty-four month, $400 per month, apartment lease. Hector and Rachel signed the following agreement on January 1:

"Hector agrees to sublease from Rachel apartment 13A in the building known as 'Lake View Manor,' 130-55 Lakeshore Drive for $420 per month. This sublease shall expire on December 31."

Hector paid his rent in a timely manner for six months. Rachel did not pay any rent to the landlord. Rachel and her husband were forced into bankruptcy by their creditors in November.

The landlord asserted an action against Hector to recover six month's rent. Is Hector likely to prevail?

(A)   Yes, because there is no privity of estate between a lessor and a sublessee.

(B)   Yes, because otherwise Hector would be paying his rent twice.

(C)   No, because a sublessee is liable to the landlord for rent.

(D)   No, because Rachel transferred to Hector the

rights for the complete
remainder of her tenancy.

20. Madisonacre was next to Parkacre
and to its west. Madison was granted
an easement by Park to cross his
property in order to reach the Grand
Train Station. Several years later,
Madison acquired Lexingtonacre,
which lay on Parkacre's east side.
May Madison use his easement to
pass between Madisonacre and
Lexingtonacre?

 (A) Yes, if the traffic is similar to
 the traffic passing to Grand
 Train Station.

 (B) Yes, if passage is the most
 economical means of
 transport.

 (C) No, because it is not an
 easement by necessity.

 (D) No, because Madison's
 easement limits use of the
 servient tenement to only the
 dominant tenement.

21. Ralph transferred an apartment
complex to Sidney and his heirs with
the proviso that "Sidney and his heirs
shall not have the right to convey or
transfer title to the complex." Sidney
conveyed the property to Grace "for
a period of thirty years, in exchange
for payment of $10,000 a month to
be increased by the greater of the
cost of living increase or prime
lending rate increase."
 Sidney then conveyed the
complex "in fee simple to Elyse or
her heirs upon termination of Grace's

interest and upon payment of
$1,000,000."
 Which of the following
choices is **NOT** correct?

 (A) Elyse's interest will still be
 valid despite Ralph's disabling
 restraint.

 (B) Ralph's conveyance to Sidney
 is void because the restriction
 was to last longer than a life
 in being plus twenty-one
 years.

 (C) Grace's heirs have a valid
 contingent remainder and
 their interest is not a
 violation of the Rule Against
 Perpetuities.

 (D) Sidney created a valid interest
 in Grace and a valid interest
 in Elyse and her heirs.

Questions 22-23 are based upon the
following fact pattern.

 Red owned a commercial fish pond.
Harvesting the pond became unprofitable
when demand and prices for catfish suffered
a prolonged slump. Stinky used the pond for
weekend recreational fishing.
 Curley owned a commercial fish pond
adjacent to Red's. One day, Curley told
Red, "I'm fed up with this pond. It's been
losing money for years, and it will always lose
money. You can fish in my pond from now
on."
 "Great, can you put that in writing so
the bank will finance me?" Red asked.
 Curley executed a proper writing
expressing his promise to Red. Since fishing
both ponds together was more economical

GO ON TO THE NEXT PAGE

than the cost of fishing both separately, Red was able to earn a healthy profit.

22.   Red's interest in Curley's fish pond can best be described as

(A)   an easement in gross

(B)   an easement appurtenant

(C)   a profit a prendre

(D)   a license

23.   Red sold his property to Kim. Will the right to fish in Curley's pond pass to her?

(A)   Yes, because there was privity between Red and Kim.

(B)   Yes, because the economic benefit of Curley's pond is tied to Kim's land.

(C)   No, because the benefit to Red was personal.

(D)   No, because the agreement between Red and Curley was an affirmative easement.

24.   Harold and Nathan owned abutting farms. Nathan's farm was adjacent to a public highway. Harold's farm was surrounded by water and dense woods wherever it did not border Nathan's farm. Harold's farm had two easements to cross Nathan's property when he first acquired it. One allowed passage to a public highway, and the other allowed passage between two of Harold's fields.

In 1922, Nathan granted Harold a written contract that expanded his previous easements with the right to use motorized vehicles on them. From 1922 to 1960, Harold drove his pick-up truck and tractor over the easements. In 1961, Harold decided to build a Formula One racetrack on his farm. One corner of the track ran across Nathan's property, but only on the easement that used to connect two of Harold's fields. The track was used for races every Friday night. The race cars were very noisy and emitted toxic fumes. Nathan asserted an action against Harold, hoping to enjoin all use of the easement. The court will most likely rule that

(A)   Harold has forfeited his right to one of the easements.

(B)   Harold could continue to use the easement for reasonable farm use, but not as a race track.

(C)   both easements were extinguished by blatant excessive use in an unintended manner.

(D)   use of the race track was proper, as long as it was within the guidelines of the original writing.

25.   Fran conveyed three acres of land to Karen, who intended to build twelve single-family homes on the land. The deed contained the clause "All usual covenants are included subject to deed restrictions and easements of record."

Several months later, Karen found out that Sigmond owned an easement to drain his property via a tiny stream that ran across Karen's land. The easement prevented the construction of two homes. Sigmond was able to enforce his easement despite never having recorded it.

If Karen asserts an action against Fran for breach of a covenant, she will most likely

(A)   prevail, because discovery of any easement is a breach of the covenant against encumbrances.

(B)   prevail, because this easement was unrecorded and an unknown defect in the title.

(C)   not prevail, because the language of the deed excludes easements that could be discovered.

(D)   not prevail, because it is a personal covenant.

Questions 26-27 are based on the following fact pattern.

Ann granted an easement for a right of way to Barbara. The grant, in the form of a deed, was properly recorded. Ann sold the property to Cory, who sold it to Denise, who then sold the property to Elaine. Cory, Denise, and Elaine recorded their deeds without mentioning the right of way.

Smith, Elaine's attorney, examined title to the property and told Elaine, "It's all yours." Two days later, Elaine conveyed the property to Francine with a covenant against encumbrances. Francine learned of Barbara's easement shortly thereafter.

26.   If Francine asserts an action against Smith to recover for the lower property value of the land due to the easement, is she likely to prevail?

(A)   Yes, as a third-party beneficiary, in states that recognize the duty of an attorney to the intended beneficiary of their services.

(B)   Yes, because the title was guaranteed.

(C)   No, because Smith did not owe a duty to Francine.

(D)   No, unless Francine can prove Smith was negligent.

27.   If Francine asserts an action against Elaine to recover for the lower property value of the land due to the easement, is Francine likely to prevail?

(A)   Yes, because Elaine did not satisfy her contractual agreement.

(B)   Yes, because Elaine was negligent.

(C)   No, because Elaine relied on Smith.

(D)   No, because a purchaser must conduct her own title search.

28.   Grandpa conveyed his land "to my grandson Archie, for the life of his wife Veronica, then to Betty." Archie's interest in the land can best be described as a

(A)   life estate

(B)   life estate per autre vie

GO ON TO THE NEXT PAGE

(C)   fee tail

(D)   term of years

29.   Craig owned Craigacre, an undeveloped tract of land, in fee simple. He conveyed a quitclaim deed to Rosalind in exchange for fair value. Rosalind never recorded the deed.

Two years later, Craig executed and delivered to Claudia, his niece, a warranty deed to Craigacre in exchange for Claudia's secretarial services. Claudia recorded the deed two years later. Neither Claudia nor Rosalind have occupied Craigacre. The jurisdiction has a pure notice recording act and requires that a junior claimant, to have priority, act in good faith and pay consideration of sufficient value. In an action between Rosalind and Claudia for title to Craigacre, which of the following is the best answer?

(A)   The outcome will be determined by whether Claudia gave consideration of sufficient value to Craig.

(B)   Rosalind will not prevail because she did not record the deed.

(C)   Rosalind will not prevail because she obtained a quitclaim deed.

(D)   The outcome will be determined by whether Rosalind gave consideration of sufficient value to Craig.

30.   Aquino contracted with Marcos to purchase a bullet-proof house. The contract stated that Marcos would provide a general warranty deed. The agreement had to be closed in a hurry because Marcos was rushing to get to Hawaii. Aquino did not notice that Marcos had given her a quitclaim deed.

In an action by Aquino against Marcos, Marcos should argue that

(A)   the quitclaim deed was not materially different from a warranty deed.

(B)   a deed is controlling when it conflicts with a contract.

(C)   Aquino does not have a cause of action until she actually loses title.

(D)   Aquino's only remedy is for damages.

Questions 31-32 are based upon the following fact pattern.

Wildacre and Overgrownacre are both undeveloped plots of land bordering Highway 007 in a remote area. Willie purchased Wildacre in 1967 and received permission to cross Overgrownacre from Ollie, its owner. By crossing Overgrownacre, Willie could more easily reach the Highway from certain parts of Wildacre. In 1977 Ollie purchased Wildacre from Willie. In 1990, Willie purchased Overgrownacre from Ollie.

31.   Did Willie own an easement to cross Overgrownacre in 1991?

(A)   Yes, because the original easement was still in effect.

(B)   Yes, because it should be inferred that the easement was sold back with the property.

(C)   No, because the easement had been extinguished.

(D)   No, because the Statute of Frauds was not satisfied.

32.   Assume for this question only that Willie owned an easement to cross over Ollie's land with a pick-up truck. What will be the legal effect if Willie builds a fence around the border between his and Ollie's property?

(A)   There will not be any change.

(B)   Ollie will have an action for partition.

(C)   Ollie will be able, at his own option, to sue for partition.

(D)   Willie's easement can be extinguished.

33.   Jill and Bill obtained title to Blackacre as tenants in common in 1960. Jill began constructing a house on Blackacre in 1963 and has occupied the house continuously since it was completed in 1966. Bill has never seen Blackacre. In 1985, Jill asserted an action to obtain title to Blackacre in fee simple. A local ordinance provides that the period to satisfy adverse possession is twenty years. Is Jill likely to prevail in her action?

(A)   Yes, because Jill's occupation of the land for the purpose of adverse possession began in 1963.

(B)   Yes, because building a house establishes a claim of right.

(C)   No, because Jill did not occupy her house until 1966.

(D)   No, because Jill's occupation of Blackacre was probably not adverse.

Questions 34-36 are based upon the following fact situation.

Lee purchased a house from Steve by signing a valid written contract. The contract did not specify the kind of title to be transferred.

34.   Lee paid the contractual price and accepted the deed from Steve. Rich came along and filed a successful suit to claim the title. In a suit between Lee and Steve, which of the following factors will **LEAST** influence who prevails in the suit?

(A)   the terms of the deed

(B)   the intent of the various parties

(C)   the good faith of each party

(D)   the remedies available

35.   Assume for this question only that the original contract between Lee

GO ON TO THE NEXT PAGE

and Steve called for Steve to convey an "effective title." Assume further that Lee received a deed, in exchange for the contractual purchase price, that did not contain any covenant of title. If Lee brings an action against Steve after he is evicted by Rich, is Lee likely to prevail?

(A)   Yes, because he did not receive good title.

(B)   Yes, because the terms of the written contract were not satisfied.

(C)   No, because the terms of the deed are controlling.

(D)   No, because Lee's rights against Steve, if any, were lost to Rich.

36.   If the house is destroyed by an "act of God" after the contract was signed but before the parties closed, which of the following doctrines will be most applicable?

(A)   equitable reformation

(B)   equitable conversion

(C)   equitable distribution

(D)   equitable servitude

(E)   risk follows dispossession

Questions 37-38 are based upon the following fact situation.

Francine and Joanne signed a valid agreement whereby Francine agreed to sell Whiteacre to Joanne. Two weeks before the scheduled closing, Francine died. Francine's will provided that Whiteacre should pass on to her son Rich and all other property should pass to her son Rob. Neither Francine nor Joanne breached their contract.

37.   Which of the following choices is the best answer?

(A)   Unless the contract specified otherwise, Francine's death terminated the agreement.

(B)   Rich is entitled to the property.

(C)   After closing, Rob will receive the proceeds of the property.

(D)   Rich and Rob will each own a share in the property.

38.   Assume for this question only that Joanne died before the parties closed on the contract. Which of the following choices is the best?

(A)   Joanne's heirs may enforce the contract.

(B)   The agreement was terminated.

(C)   Joanne's heirs have the option to terminate the contract.

(D)   Francine's heirs have the option to terminate the contract.

39.   Beverly owned 2,000 acres of mountain land that she named Beverly Hills. Blanche paid Beverly a yearly fee for the right to build and use a road that crossed Beverly Hills.

Blanche built a small wooden bridge to cross a small stream as part of the road. The parties did not specify who was to be responsible for maintenance of the road or river. One day, Beverly went jogging across Beverly Hills. Beverly passed over the bridge Blanche built. The bridge collapsed, causing damage to a garden that belonged to Beverly. An expert determined that improper maintenance caused the bridge to collapse. If Beverly asserts an action against Blanche for damage to her garden should Beverly prevail?

(A)   Yes, because the possessor of an easement is strictly liable to a servient estate.

(B)   Yes, because the owner of an easement is obligated to maintain the easement.

(C)   No, because the parties did not delegate duties.

(D)   No, because Beverly should have known the condition of the bridge, so she was contributorily negligent.

40.   Kandel's will provided that "in gratitude for twenty years of past service as my personal housekeeper, I leave $100,000 to Nadler." Kandel did not leave any property except for the Mott Avenue Motel he owned with Silver as tenants in common.
      Will Nadler's service constitute sufficient consideration to bind Kandel?

(A)   Yes, if Nadler performed services beyond his contractual duty before the will was written.

(B)   Yes, because Kandel received material benefit.

(C)   No, because Nadler was a paid employee.

(D)   No, because the bequest was made after the services were performed.

41.   Bettina conveyed Huronacre to Eastern Michigan University "so long as the University uses Huronacre as a practice field for its football team, then to Jerry and his heirs." The local jurisdiction has adopted the common law Rule Against Perpetuities. What is Bettina's interest in Huronacre after the above conveyance?

(A)   a fee simple absolute

(B)   a reversion

(C)   a possibility of a reverter

(D)   she has no interest

42.   Bertha executed a will whereby she left a life estate in an apartment building to her daughter. The will further provided that the building pass to Bertha's daughter's children in joint tenancy upon the daughter's death. A clause prevented any of Bertha's grandchildren from

GO ON TO THE NEXT PAGE

mortgaging, selling, or otherwise alienating their interest.

If challenged, what will be the status of Bertha's attempt to devise the apartment in her will?

(A)   The devise is wholly valid and enforceable.

(B)   The devise will be void due to the Rule Against Perpetuities.

(C)   The devise will be void as a restraint on alienation.

(D)   The clause against sale or mortgage will be held invalid, but the grandchildren's remainder will be held valid.

43.   Myron conveyed his farm "to Loretta for so long as Loretta does not grow tobacco or marijuana on the farm."
        Which of the following choices best describes Loretta's interest in the house if she does not grow tobacco or marijuana?

(A)   fee simple subject to a condition subsequent

(B)   fee simple determinable

(C)   fee simple subject to an executory interest

(D)   fee simple determinable subject to an executory interest

Questions 44-45 are based upon the following fact situation.

Judith executed a will that said, in part, "I hereby devise the house on Elm Street that I own in fee simple to be shared by any of my grandchildren that reach the age of twenty-one. If none of my grandchildren reach the age of twenty-one, the house should revert to my estate." Judith's only child, at the time the will was written, was Burt, age twenty-nine. Burt had a six-year-old daughter named Ruth.

44.   Will Judith's conveyance be held valid?

(A)   Yes, because Judith had a grandchild at the time the will was executed.

(B)   Yes, because Burt (or any other child born to Judith) can be the measuring life.

(C)   No, because of the Rule Against Perpetuities.

(D)   No, because the will is too uncertain.

45.   The clause will be held invalid under which of the following circumstances?

(A)   Judith changed the will into an inter vivos conveyance.

(B)   Burt died without children.

(C)   Burt died with children.

(D)   Burt changed the will into an inter vivos conveyance.

46.   Landlord rented a two-bedroom apartment to tenant. The apartment was modern and in good condition, except that one of the showers had spewed scalding hot water from its handle on two previous occasions. Landlord forgot to tell tenant about the shower. Two years after moving into the apartment, Tenant was

severely burned by hot water spewing from the handle. If Tenant asserts an action against Landlord for damages sustained in the shower, judgment should be for

(A)   Landlord, because a landlord is under no duty to deliver the premises to a tenant in a good state of repair

(B)   Landlord, because Tenant had ample opportunity to inspect the apartment

(C)   Tenant, because a landlord is strictly liable for injuries sustained on the premises

(D)   Tenant, because Landlord did not disclose the defect

Questions 47-49 are based upon the following fact situation.

Furst purchased a house from Secund in 1919 that was completely surrounded by property owned by Secund. Furst's only access to a public highway was via a dirt path that ran across Secund's property. Furst used the path from 1920 to 1960. In 1960, Furst sold his house to Thurd. In 1966, Thurd sold the house to Secund. Secund sold the property he purchased from Thurd to Furth in 1990. Twenty years is the time required to satisfy adverse possession in the jurisdiction.

47.   If Secund asserted an action in 1925 seeking an injunction ordering Furst not to enter upon his land, judgment should have been for

(A)   Secund, because Furst was using the path less than twenty years.

(B)   Secund, because he revoked an express or implied grant.

(C)   Furst, because Secund had impliedly given him a license to use the path.

(D)   Furst, because his land was entirely surrounded by Secund's property.

48.   If Secund asserted an action in 1965 against Thurd, seeking an injunction ordering Thurd not to enter upon his land, judgment should have been for

(A)   Secund, because his revocation of any express or implied grant was valid

(B)   Secund, because Furst's rights have been extinguished

(C)   Thurd, because he purchased the land from Furst

(D)   Thurd, because Secund had impliedly granted him an easement

49.   Secund's purchase of Furst's house and subsequent sale to Furth had which of the following effects?

(A)   Furst's easement was extinguished.

(B)   Tacking for an easement by prescription was stopped.

GO ON TO THE NEXT PAGE

(C)   Furth will not own an easement to his land.

(D)   None of the above.

50.   Prince, owner of Purpleacre, granted Jackson an easement to cross Purpleacre in 1981. Jackson did not record the easement. Prince conveyed Purpleacre to Vanity in 1982. Vanity promptly recorded the deed, which contained a reference to the easement. In 1983, Vanity conveyed Purpleacre to Madonna, who paid value but had no knowledge of the easement. May Jackson force Madonna to honor his easement?

(A)   Yes, because an easement may not be defeated by lack of notice.

(B)   Yes, because Madonna is considered to have notice.

(C)   No, because Jackson did not record.

(D)   No, because Madonna did not have knowledge of the easement.

51.   King owned a 200-year-old castle built on a mountaintop. King often enjoyed the spectacular view of a valley, river, and sea of mountains beyond. Unfortunately for King, many insects entered his castle through the windows. In 1980, King had screens installed on the windows. The screens had to be custom made because of the unusual shape of the windows. They were then soldered to the window frames. Duke purchased the castle from King in

1986. Must King leave the screens for Duke?

(A)   Yes, because the screens were custom made.

(B)   Yes, because these screens are fixtures.

(C)   No, because screens are generally not part of a building.

(D)   No, because the screens are not permanently attached to the building.

52.   Lilly, an elderly widow, owned a small house and several personal possessions. Lilly had trouble supporting herself, but desperately wanted to remain in her home. Lilly orally contracted with her neighbor Monique that if Monique took care of her, Monique would inherit her house. Monique quit law school and diligently cared for Lilly until she died seven years later. Jean, Lilly's daughter, showed up at the funeral. Lilly had not seen Jean since the 1960s when Jean ran away to join a hippie commune. Jean, Lilly's only heir, demanded Lilly's entire estate, since Lilly died without a will.
       Monique will most likely receive title to Lilly's house under which of the following legal theories?

(A)   A state statute provides that the Statute of Frauds is inapplicable where part performance has made the party's intentions obvious.

(B)   Monique's action of quitting law school will support her claim to the house.

(C)   A state statute provides that the Statute of Frauds is inapplicable where part performance will result in irreparable hardship.

(D)   Lilly's obvious break with her daughter will prevent Jean from recovering.

Questions 53-56 are based upon the following fact situation.

Jason owned eighty acres of land in fee simple. In 1976, he sold forty acres to thirty-five corporations that intended to build industrial buildings. Jason called the development "Bicentennial Park." Jason sold thirty acres of the land to sixty individuals in 1980, calling the land "Jimmy Carter Estates." All the lots in "Jimmy Carter Estates" were conveyed via a deed that stated that the grantee, his heirs, and his assigns agree to use their land only for single-family residences. This provision may be enforced by any person owning an interest in any part of "Jimmy Carter Estates."

Local zoning ordinances provided that "Bicentennial Park" may be used for light industry and "Jimmy Carter Estates" for residences only.

53.   If an owner seeks to build a two-family house in "Jimmy Carter Estates," other owners seeking to prevent such construction should assert an action based on

(A)   equitable estoppel

(B)   an easement

(C)   the covenant

(D)   privity of estate

54.   In a suit between an owner seeking to build a two-family home and owners seeking to prevent such construction, should the courts allow construction of the two-family home?

(A)   Yes, because the zoning laws allowed such construction.

(B)   Yes, because not allowing the two-family home would constitute an unlawful "taking."

(C)   No, because the two-family home would violate an express provision in the deed.

(D)   No, because a two-family home would not fit the character of "Jimmy Carter Estates."

55.   In 1986, Jason decided to sell the remaining ten acres of land for commercial development. Rosalie, a resident and homeowner in "Jimmy Carter Estates," asserted an action to limit development of this additional land to single-family residences. The court should rule

(A)   in favor of Rosalie if the ten acres were part of the common development scheme of "Jimmy Carter Estates"

(B)   in favor of Jason because he was the common grantor

(C)   in favor of Jason, because Jason may designate the land for any use although he may be liable for damages

(D)   in favor of Rosalie, because the other use of the land will be a nuisance

56.   If Jason decides to sell the entire ten acres to David, David will obtain

(A)   title free of encumbrances

(B)   title affected by a zoning ordinance limiting use to light industry

(C)   title affected by a covenant limiting use to single-family residences

(D)   title that will be decided by litigation

57.   Keith and Clinton signed a written valid agreement with Lauren to lease Lauren's seventy-acre farm. Lauren delivered possession of the premises. The lease provided that Keith and Clinton were to use the farm to grow corn. Lauren was to receive half of the profits earned by the farm. The lease further provided that "any attempted assignment, subletting, or transfer by Keith or Clinton without Lauren's written permission is null and void."

With Rick, Clinton signed a written agreement to sublet his share of the farm and to take his profits, without consulting Lauren. If Keith asserts an action to prevent Clinton's assignment, should Keith prevail?

(A)   Yes, because one may not assign an interest in real

property without the consent of all parties involved.

(B)   Yes, because of the clause prohibiting assignment.

(C)   No, unless Keith can show he will suffer pecuniary loss or other damage from the assignment.

(D)   No, because he may not enforce the clause restricting assignments.

58.   Alumnus conveyed a three-acre tract to his alma mater, University, by a deed specifying that "University shall own this land in fee simple provided a theater for University's Music Department is erected by 1980." University constructed a theater on the land conveyed by Alumnus, and this theater was used by the Music Department from 1979 to 1989. In 1989, a "theater in the round" was built for the Music Department, and the old theater on the land donated by Alumnus was transferred to the University Ballet Department.

If Alumnus asserts an action demanding the return of the three acres, will Alumnus succeed?

(A)   Yes, because the deed had the effect of creating a remainder in Alumnus.

(B)   Yes, because University's change in the use of the building violated a condition subsequent.

(C)   No, because University fulfilled the requirements of the deed.

(D)   No, because use of the
       building for ballet
       substantially fulfilled the
       requirement.

Questions 59-60 are based upon the
following fact situation.

       Smith was a life tenant of a large
house. A substantial mortgage had been
owed by the grantor on the house.

59.   Which of the following choices is
       correct?

       (A)   Smith will be liable to pay the
              principal owed on the
              mortgage but not the interest.

       (B)   Smith will be liable to pay the
              interest on the mortgage but
              not the principal.

       (C)   Smith will be liable for both
              the interest and principal on
              the mortgage.

       (D)   Smith will be liable for
              neither the interest nor the
              principal on the mortgage.

60.   Which of the following choices is
       correct?

       (A)   Smith will be liable to pay
              taxes on the house but not
              insurance.

       (B)   Smith will be liable to pay
              insurance on the house but
              not taxes.

(C)   Smith will be liable to pay
       both insurance and taxes on
       the house.

(D)   Smith will be liable for
       neither insurance nor taxes
       on the house.

61.   On April 1, Dennis conveyed title to
       Blackacre to Jim, who paid full value.
       Jim did not know that Blackacre was
       still owned by Bob on April 1. On
       May 1, Bob conveyed Blackacre to
       Dennis for full value. Dennis then
       conveyed Blackacre to Kathleen, on
       June 1, for full value. In a suit
       between Jim and Kathleen to obtain
       title to Blackacre, Kathleen's most
       persuasive argument is

       (A)   one cannot purchase an
              interest from someone who
              doesn't possess the interest

       (B)   Jim was never in the chain of
              title

       (C)   Kathleen could not have
              discovered Dennis's recording

       (D)   equitable estoppel should
              control

Questions 62-64 are based upon the
following fact situation.

       Stauber owned 2,000 acres of
undeveloped land in an isolated and remote
area. Stauber decided to develop the land
into a retirement village called "Everglades
Estates" and built 6,000 residential
apartments. Due to the remoteness of the
village, Stauber also built a health club,

GO ON TO THE NEXT PAGE

medical offices, a golf course, and retail stores. The remaining undeveloped land was left available for the use and enjoyment of the residents.

Frosty purchased an apartment from Stauber. The contract provided that Frosty could occupy the apartment indefinitely but would not own the apartment. Frosty was given a share in a corporation that owned the 6,000 apartments. He was obligated to pay a fee of $62,000 and a share of maintenance costs. Frosty's share was freely transferable. The contract further provided that the offices, sports facilities, and stores would continue to be used for their current purposes.

62.   Frosty's interest could be best described as a(n)

    (A)   leasehold

    (B)   easement

    (C)   covenant

    (D)   fee simple

63.   Which of the following best describes the clause guaranteeing that the stores and sports facilities will be maintained?

    (A)   leasehold

    (B)   covenant

    (C)   zoning law

    (D)   easement

64.   Which of the following devices will best guarantee that the open areas of "Everglades Estates" will remain undeveloped?

    (A)   leasehold

    (B)   covenant

    (C)   zoning law

    (D)   easement

Questions 65-67 are based upon the following fact situation.

Kinney owned a 5,000-car parking lot outside a sports arena. The jurisdiction's Recording Act provided: "Every conveyance of real property must be recorded in the county recorder's office. In the case of a conveyance not recorded, the conveyance is void as to a subsequent bona fide purchaser for value who does not have notice of the first conveyance."

On April 1, 1985, Kinney conveyed the parking lot to Meyers Brothers, Inc., at fair value. Meyers Brothers, Inc., did not record the deed until May 1, 1985. Kinney then mortgaged the lot on April 5 to Park N' Lock, Inc., who had no notice of the April 1 transaction. Park N' Lock promptly recorded the mortgage. Kinney then conveyed a warranty deed on April 13 to his son Kinney Jr. without consideration.

Kinney Jr. promptly recorded the deed. Kinney Jr. conveyed by general warranty deed his interest in the parking lot to Dollar Park on May 15. Dollar Park paid full value and promptly recorded.

65.   If Dollar Park loses in a suit brought by Meyers Brothers, Inc., it will be because

    (A)   Kinney Jr. recorded before Meyers Brothers, Inc.

    (B)   the first deed prevails in a dispute among deeds

(C)   Kinney Jr. did not have constructive or actual notice of Meyers Brothers' rights

(D)   Kinney Jr. was not a purchaser for value

66.   If Meyers Brothers asserts a suit against Park N' Lock to quiet title, who should prevail?

(A)   Meyers Brothers, because the consideration furnished by Park N' Lock was not sufficient to be considered "full value."

(B)   Meyers Brothers, because mortgagee and purchaser are not the same.

(C)   Park N' Lock, because Park N' Lock's transactions were without actual or constructive notice of Kinney's conveyance to Meyers Brothers.

(D)   Park N' Lock, because Park N' Lock recorded first.

67.   If, after Meyers Brothers had recorded its deed, but before Kinney Jr. conveyed the parking lot to Dollar, Meyers Brothers asserted an action against Kinney Jr. to recover title, who should prevail?

(A)   Meyers Brothers, because Kinney Jr. did not pay value.

(B)   Meyers Brothers, because they paid value.

(C)   Kinney Jr., because he obtained the property without notice of any claim of Meyers Brothers.

(D)   Kinney Jr., because he recorded before Meyers Brothers.

68.   Denise and George purchased a house as tenants by the entirety. They used the home, located near a ski resort, as a weekend retreat.

       Denise conveyed her right in the house to Heidi. The conveyance will be effective

(A)   because Denise and George were tenants in common

(B)   because George was never in the chain of title

(C)   if Denise and George were not married

(D)   because Denise was the sole owner

69.   Arlene conveyed Andyacre, a beachfront condominium, to "Paul for the remainder of his life, remainder to Mark and Michelle as tenants in common." The condominium had a substantial unpaid mortgage held by Holly. Which of the following choices will describe the mortgage obligations of the various parties if Andyacre is occupied by Paul?

(A)   Paul must pay the interest, but Mark and Michelle must pay the principal.

GO ON TO THE NEXT PAGE

(B)   Mark and Michelle must pay the interest, but Paul must pay the principal.

(C)   Paul must pay both the principal and interest.

(D)   Mark and Michelle must pay both the principal and interest.

70.   Gil agreed, in writing, to maintain the road between his property and Casey's property. Casey gave Gil his car in return for Gil's promise to maintain the road for Gil, his heirs, his successors, and his assigns. Gil sold his property to Wes. Casey sold his land to Joe. Wes refused to maintain the road. Joe asserted an action for damages against Wes for failure to maintain the road. The court should rule in favor of

(A)   Joe, because burdens run with the land

(B)   Joe, because the properties of Gil and Casey shared a common border

(C)   Wes, if Gil did not buy his land from Casey and Casey did not buy his land from Gil.

(D)   Wes, because he was not a party to the original agreement

71.   On March 1, Abraham sold Whitehouse to George for value. George did not record the deed until March 4. Abraham sold Whitehouse to Teddy, on March 3, for value. Teddy did not record the deed until March 5. Under which of the

following statutes will the court award title to Teddy?

(A)   pure notice recording act

(B)   race-notice recording act

(C)   race-race recording act

(D)   pure race recording act

Questions 72-73 are based upon the following fact situation.

Isaac owned 100 acres of undeveloped land. Isaac decided to subdivide the land into 200 plots of land. One hundred twenty plots were sold pursuant to a deed providing that "all parties, their successors, and heirs agree to construct no more than one single-family home on each lot. The land may not be occupied by trailers or other temporary structures."

The remaining eighty lots were unsold for many years. Isaac finally sold all the remaining lots to Speculator without any restrictions. Speculator then also sold the remaining lots without any restrictions.

72.   Suppose Speculator decided to build two homes on each lot. If an owner of one of the original lots asserts an action to prevent the building of more than one home on a lot, which of the following factors will be most crucial?

(A)   Whether the local government can provide services for housing of such density.

(B)   The local zoning ordinances.

(C)   Whether a common scheme of development had been established.

(D) Whether a contract takes precedence over a deed.

73. If a successor to an owner of one of the original lots asserts an action against a successor of Speculator to prevent installation of a mobile home, Speculator's successor should assert which of the following defenses?

(A) Time has made the two developments separate and independent entities.

(B) The totality of the facts presented establish that a common development scheme was not used for all the land.

(C) Speculator did not have notice of the restrictions.

(D) The plaintiff has not established pecuniary damages.

Questions 74-75 are based upon the following fact situation.

Alex granted a right of way to Waterco to run a pipe across the yard behind his house. The grant was in the form of a written deed that was properly recorded by Waterco. Alex sold his house to Richard, who sold it to William, who sold the house to Edward. Richard, William, and Edward recorded their interests without mentioning the right of way.

Edward asked Ralph, his attorney, to examine the title to the house. Ralph researched the title and told Edward, "It's all yours, clean as the Denver air." Relying on

his attorney's title search, Edward conveyed the house to Laurie with a covenant of warranty and a covenant against encumbrances. Laurie, who paid full value, learned of Waterco's rights and was furious.

74. If Laurie asserts an action against Ralph for damages, should Laurie prevail?

(A) Yes, because Ralph guaranteed the title was good.

(B) Probably, because she was a third-party beneficiary of Ralph's contract with Edward.

(C) No, because Ralph owed a duty only to Edward.

(D) Probably not, unless she can show Ralph was negligent.

75. If Laurie asserts an action against Edward for damages, should Laurie prevail?

(A) Yes, because Edward was negligent in hiring Ralph.

(B) Yes, because Edward did not fulfill his obligations to Laurie.

(C) No, because Laurie should have searched the title on her own.

(D) No, because Edward relied on Ralph.

76. Andy and Dandy owned adjacent plots of land. Andy agreed to allow

Dandy to cross his property. The property of both Andy and Dandy bordered on public highways. After crossing Andy's property for a month, Dandy was told by Andy, "I don't like you anymore, so stay off my land." Will Andy be able to prevent Dandy from entering his land?

(A)   Yes, because the permission to enter Andy's land was revocable at will.

(B)   Yes, because there was not an implied easement.

(C)   Yes, regardless of whether Dandy paid any consideration.

(D)   No, because Dandy had relied on Andy's promise.

77.   Ricky leased his store for thirty years to Betty. The parties orally agreed that if Betty made all of her payments, Ricky would give her title to the store at the end of the thirty years. Betty kept the premises in immaculate condition and was never a day late in making her payments. After twenty years, Betty spent $100,000 to redecorate the store. At the end of thirty years, Ricky notified Betty that her lease was being terminated because Ricky was leasing the building to Whitney Houston Discos, Inc. "What about our agreement that I get title after thirty years?" asked Betty. "I don't recall any agreement," said Ricky, an octogenarian suffering from Alzheimer's disease. Betty asserted an action for specific performance and brought two witnesses to her oral agreement with Ricky. Ricky asserted the Statute of Frauds as a defense. Which of the following statements will help Ricky most?

(A)   Although Ricky knew about it, he never approved the $100,000 remodeling.

(B)   Ricky will not benefit in an unconscionable manner when his relationship with Betty is looked at as a whole.

(C)   Betty's expenditures were not unusual for a tenant during a long-term lease.

(D)   Ricky should have been excused due to his age and mental state.

78.   Carl conveyed his home "to the Town of Smallville to be used as a community center; however, if the premises shall ever cease to be used as a community center, title shall pass to the First Church of Smallville." Which of the following choices best describes the interest owned by the Town of Smallville as long as Carl's house is used for a community center?

(A)   None, the conveyance should be held void due to the Rule Against Perpetuities.

(B)   Fee simple subject to a condition subsequent.

(C)   Fee simple subject to an executory interest.

(D)   Fee simple determinable.

79.   Belinda rented a house from Thomas for five years. Belinda, a professional

photographer, installed dark room equipment and studio lights. Toward the end of the fifth year, Thomas sold the house to Constance. Belinda was not notified of the sale of the house, but Thomas promptly recorded the transaction. At the end of the lease, Constance declined to renew and would not allow Belinda to remove the dark room equipment and studio lights. Which of the following choices will be Belinda's best argument if she asserts an action to be allowed to remove the equipment?

(A)   A tenant may remove anything she installs in rented premises.

(B)   None of the installed equipment could be considered fixtures.

(C)   The nature of the equipment shows it was installed for Belinda's benefit in the conduct of her trade.

(D)   There was a lack of privity between Constance and Belinda.

80.   Terry conveyed his house to his daughter, Eve, on March 1 as a birthday present. He did not tell Eve that, the same day, he had conveyed the house to Sherri for value. Eve recorded on March 2. Sherri did not record until March 5. In an action between Eve and Sherri for title of the home, Eve will prevail under which of the following statues?

(A)   pure notice recording act

(B)   race-notice recording act

(C)   pure race recording act

(D)   more than one of the above statutes

81.   Seattle owned several thousand acres of land used for logging. His will provided, "I leave all of my land to my son, Tacoma, for his life, then to Spokane." Tacoma took possession of the land and proceeded to remove many trees for his lumber business. If Spokane asserts an action against Tacoma to enjoin removal of the timber

(A)   Spokane will prevail, because Tacoma is exploiting the land's natural resources

(B)   Spokane will prevail, because Tacoma is committing waste

(C)   Tacoma will prevail, because he is committing ameliorative waste

(D)   Tacoma will prevail, because Seattle used the land for logging

Questions 82-85 are based upon the following fact situation.

Felicity purchased a house from Esther. Esther conveyed a deed to Felicity that contained a warranty of title and a right to quiet enjoyment. Felicity received

GO ON TO THE NEXT PAGE

physical possession of the deed, but did not record.

Coalcorp owned an easement behind Felicity's new house. The easement allowed access to a mine two miles away. The mine has been abandoned for some time and could not be detected by visual inspection.

82. Which of the following choices is the best answer?

    (A) The house was not legally transferred to Felicity because of the easement.

    (B) The house was not legally transferred to Felicity because she did not record.

    (C) The house was not legally transferred to Felicity because the warranty was not satisfied.

    (D) The house was legally transferred to Felicity.

83. Felicity later learned of the easement. Could Felicity recover damages for the easement from Esther?

    (A) No.

    (B) Yes, for breach of the covenant of quiet enjoyment.

    (C) Yes, for breach of the covenant of quiet enjoyment if Coalcorp begins using the easement.

    (D) Yes, for breaching the right to convey.

84. If Coalcorp uses the easement to store coal, which of the following choices is the most accurate?

    (A) The coal may be stored on a temporary basis only.

    (B) Felicity will recover from Esther for breach of a covenant.

    (C) Felicity may sue Coalcorp for damages only.

    (D) Felicity may obtain an injunction requiring removal of the coal.

85. Assume for this question only that Esther had originally purchased the house from Nelson pursuant to a written contract that contained the clause "Esther agrees not to sell the house to anyone whose name begins with the letter *F*." After Esther's transaction with Felicity, which of the following choices will be the best answer?

    (A) Nelson may be able to recover damages from Esther.

    (B) Nelson may set aside the conveyance.

    (C) The clause prevented Felicity from obtaining a valid title.

    (D) The clause was not enforceable in any jurisdiction.

Questions 86-87 are based upon the following fact situation.

Levit owned 2,000 acres of land just outside the corporate limits of a city. He decided to divide the land into two parcels. The southern 900 acres bordered the city he called Levitcity. Levit named the northern portion, also 900 acres, which was located further from the city, Levitown. Levitcity and Levitown were subdivided into many small lots. Purchasers of lots in Levitcity and Levitown signed deeds containing express provisions binding their grantees, heirs, and assigns. The Levitcity deeds provided that the land was to be used for residential purposes only. The Levitown deeds also provided that the land was to be used only for residential purposes, that only one house could be built on each plot, and that twenty feet of open space must remain between every two houses.

86. Traitor purchased three lots in Levitown and decided to build a row of attached houses. An outraged Levitown homeowner was filled with fright that the neighborhood would deteriorate and filed suit against Traitor. Will the contractual restriction be enforceable?

  (A) Yes, because any present owner of a lot in Levitown may enforce the restriction.

  (B) Yes, if the local zoning laws restrict the land use to detached, single-family homes.

  (C) No, if Traitor was not the original owner.

  (D) No, because limiting the use to detached houses is the equivalent of a "taking."

87. If the land not originally designated as part of Levitown is sold, will the owners be obligated to limit construction to detached houses?

  (A) Yes.

  (B) Only if the zoning laws so provide.

  (C) Yes, if the new land is deemed part of this common development scheme.

  (D) It cannot be determined from the above fact situation.

88. Seller agreed in writing to convey title to his sixty-acre farm to buyer. The farm was properly identified, as was the price. The contract was valid and complete except for the lack of any agreement regarding the quality of title to be conveyed. Will the contract be enforceable?

  (A) No.

  (B) Yes, and seller will be required to convey whatever interest in the farm he owns.

  (C) Yes, and seller will be required to convey marketable title.

  (D) Yes, and seller will be required to convey a warranty title.

Questions 89-90 are based upon the following fact situation.

GO ON TO THE NEXT PAGE

In 1952, Farmer granted an easement to Northamerican Rail to build and operate railroad tracks through a specific twenty-foot strip at the north end of a 2,000-acre farm that he owned in fee simple. Northamerican promptly recorded the easement.

In 1982, the farm was subdivided and several houses were built. Lawrence purchased the lot with the easement. His deed was properly recorded but did not refer to the easement. Lawrence built a house and swimming pool on the lot. In 1985, Northamerican notified Lawrence that it intended to run railroad tracks across the part of his property where his pool was located.

89.   If Lawrence attempts to secure an injunction to prevent the rail line from crossing his property, might he succeed?

(A)   Yes, because the statute of limitations extinguished Northamerican's rights.

(B)   Yes, because his deed did not mention the easement.

(C)   No, because Northamerican is entitled to use its easement.

(D)   No, because a railroad is more important than a swimming pool.

90.   If Lawrence seeks monetary compensation from Northamerican, might he succeed?

(A)   Yes, because Northamerican possessed an easement, not title in fee simple.

(B)   Yes, because the statute of limitations extinguished Northamerican's rights.

(C)   No, because a railroad is more important than a swimming pool.

(D)   No, because Northamerican is entitled to use its easement.

91.   Estelle, the owner of Blackacre in fee simple, executed a gift to her daughter, Karen, of a section of the property. The section was described in the conveyance as "one-eighth of my interest in Blackacre, the western half of the northeast corner of the property." The description of the land to be conveyed

(A)   is not sufficient, because the transfer was gratuitous

(B)   is not sufficient, because it is vague

(C)   is sufficient because it satisfied the requirements of seisin

(D)   is sufficient because it can be located

92.   The eleven homeowners on Elm Street in the resort area of Redondo Beach signed an agreement, in 1910, stating that "all homeowners agree that no stables are to be erected on their premises. The homes may not be occupied or owned by persons less than the age of eighteen. The homes may not be sold without including the terms of this agreement on the purchase agreements." Elaine, one of the original parties to the agreement, had two of her great-grandchildren spend the summer of 1985 with her. Both great-grandchildren were below the age of eighteen. Leslie, who

owned a house on Elm Street since 1905, brought suit to enjoin further occupancy by the children. Elaine's best argument will be

(A) one may use her own property as she sees fit

(B) the terms of the agreement are obviously obsolete

(C) enforcement would violate the Equal Protection Clause of the Fourteenth Amendment to the U.S. Constitution

(D) the agreement is unconscionable

93. Elvis executed a gift to his girlfriend, Presila. The gift was described as "The property I own in fee simple on Route 8, which was known as Ford Motor Company plant before I purchased it. This conveyance is to include the abandoned factory and the twelve acres of land surrounding it."
Elvis owned only eleven acres of land on Route 8. The description of the real property is

(A) sufficient despite the inconsistency

(B) insufficient because of the inconsistency

(C) insufficient because of the absence of metes and bounds

(D) insufficient because the description does not satisfy the Statute of Frauds

Questions 94-95 are based upon the following fact situation.

Ronald owned an entire square block of vacant land. He orally agreed to sell the northeast corner of the land to Vincent for $85,000. Ronald's counsel prepared the contract. Ronald signed it and mailed it to Vincent. Vincent called Ronald because the size of the lot was not stated. "Just write 150 x 85," said Ronald. Vincent wrote 150 x 100 and recorded the deed. Three weeks later, Vincent sold the land at slightly below its market value to Joan.

94. Assume for this question only that Ronald sought to rescind the contract the day after Vincent recorded it. Vincent's most persuasive argument will be that

(A) a recorded deed cannot be questioned

(B) Ronald should bear the consequences of his carelessness

(C) the difference is not material

(D) an oral agreement cannot alter the written contract

95. Assume for this question only that Vincent sold the land to Joan before Ronald learned of the terms Vincent wrote into the contract. If Ronald seeks to prevent Joan from obtaining title, Joan's best argument will be that

GO ON TO THE NEXT PAGE

(A)   Ronald should be estopped from asserting an action against a bona fide purchaser

(B)   a recorded deed may not be challenged

(C)   the Statute of Frauds is not satisfied

(D)   public policy demands the respect of all recorded deeds

96.   Ted and Bob signed a lease whereby Bob agreed to pay monthly rent to Ted until March 1988. Ted and his wife Alice owned the land concurrently in fee simple. Bob and Carol later signed a valid instrument whereby Carol agreed that she would occupy the premises until March 1988 in exchange for paying Bob's rent. Bob retained the right to re-enter the premises if Carol did not pay rent. Bob and Carol have created a(n)

(A)   assignment

(B)   sublease

(C)   sublease because Bob did not convey his entire interest

(D)   reversion

97.   In 1981, Jerome conveyed title to a large tract of land on Jerome Avenue to his daughter Mildred "in consideration of Mildred's love and affection." Jerome delivered the land's deed to Mildred, but neither Jerome nor Mildred recorded the transaction. In 1986, Mildred and Jerome became involved in a heated argument. Mildred took the deed to the Jerome Avenue land and burned it in her fireplace. Mildred then ran out of her house and was struck by a car. Mildred's heirs asserted an action demanding title to the Jerome Avenue property. Which of the following choices is the best answer?

(A)   Jerome's original conveyance to Mildred was effective, and Mildred never relinquished her title.

(B)   Jerome's conveyance was void due to the failure of the parties to record.

(C)   Jerome's conveyance to Mildred was effective as was Mildred's abandonment of the title.

(D)   Jerome's conveyance to Mildred can be retracted due to a lack of consideration.

98.   In 1955, Rob granted a life estate in his farm to Carl, "provided Carl continues to grow corn on the land." Rob's conveyance provided that the land pass to Jill in fee simple upon Carl's death or upon Carl's failure to grow corn, whichever came first.

Carl planted, grew, and harvested corn from 1955 to 1985. In 1979, the price of oil skyrocketed and Carl decided to drill for oil on the land. A large oil deposit was discovered, and Carl pumped 500 barrels a day from the ground.

Jill asserted an action seeking damages for removal of the oil and an injunction against future removal. Which of the following choices is the best answer?

(A) Jill will prevail because Carl's life estate was terminated when he drilled for oil.

(B) Carl will be enjoined and forced to pay damages.

(C) Carl will be liable for damages, but an injunction will not be granted.

(D) The injunction will not be granted, and Jill will not recover damages.

99. Playboy left a will providing that "my assets shall be divided among my children in equal shares." Playboy was survived by Helen, a daughter by his marriage that ended in divorce, Diane, a daughter from the wife to whom Playboy was married to at the time of his death; Linda, a step-daughter; Ellen, a granddaughter; Jean, an illegitimate daughter; and Rosanne, a legally adopted daughter. Which of Playboy's descendants might **NOT** receive a share of his estate?

(A) Ellen, Rosanne, Jean

(B) Ellen, Linda

(C) Ellen, Jean, Linda

(D) Ellen, Jean, Linda, Helen

100. James went to Europe for a month. He agreed to let Jeffrey use his apartment while he was away. When James returned from Europe, Jeffrey refused to vacate the apartment.

James asserted an action to evict Jeffrey; whereupon Jeffrey claimed protection under a local ordinance that required a landlord to give ten-working-days notice before evicting a tenant. James's best argument to prove the statute is not applicable is that Jeffrey is a

(A) periodic tenant

(B) tenant at will

(C) trespasser

(D) licensee

101. Which of the following clauses in the real estate laws of the local jurisdiction will help most buyers in assuring that title to real estate be as definite as possible?

(A) "Deeds may be executed without witnesses."

(B) "Value must be exchanged for real estate."

(C) "Title will be granted to the party who has recorded first in time."

(D) "It will be assumed that consideration has been paid in exchange for every deed."

102. Henrietta entered into a valid written agreement to sell her house to Henry. The parties agreed to close thirty days later, but did not specify who was to bear the risk of loss in the interim. After Henrietta and

GO ON TO THE NEXT PAGE

Henry signed the agreement, but before closing, the house was struck by lightning, causing a fire and explosion. The house was totally destroyed. There is no local statute that specifies which party shall bear the risk of loss in the interim. If Henrietta prevails in a suit against Henry for specific performance, the most likely reason will be

(A)   Henry should have taken out insurance on the property

(B)   the risk of loss follows possession

(C)   the doctrine of equitable conversion

(D)   the law will leave the parties where it finds them

Questions 103-104 are based upon the following fact situation.

Phyllis purchased two tracts of land in an industrial park still in its planning stages. Phyllis planned to build a hub for her air-freight business. She began construction of an airstrip on one tract of land and a warehouse on the other tract. The two tracts were to be linked by a road designated by the industrial park's developer, but not yet approved by the local authorities, as a public highway.

Phyllis sought to use the designated road immediately because the road was imperative to her ongoing construction. The developer refused to grant permission to use the land.

103.   The developer should advance which of the following arguments?

(A)   The Statute of Frauds.

(B)   The developer would be forced to incur insurance costs without reimbursement.

(C)   Phyllis must wait for the local governmental authorities to designate a road because an easement by implication has not yet arisen.

(D)   Phyllis would receive something for nothing.

104.   Phyllis should advance which of the following arguments?

(A)   The act of designating the streets is a dedication of a public road.

(B)   She has an implied right to use the road.

(C)   She obtained a constructive easement.

(D)   She possesses an easement by right.

Questions 105-106 are based upon the following fact situation.

Stacey and Karen inherited property, which they divided and designated as Northacre and Southacre, as joint tenants. Stacey and Karen orally agreed that Stacey would own Northacre in fee simple and Karen would own Southacre in fee simple. Stacey sold Northacre, took the proceeds to Atlantic City, and lost it all at the blackjack tables. Karen built a house on Southacre.

Stacey asserted an action to determine ownership of Southacre.

105.   If Karen is adjudged to be the owner in fee simple of Southacre, the most likely reason will be that

    (A)   Stacey's conduct estops her from claiming an interest in Southacre

    (B)   the logical division was more important than any formalities

    (C)   the oral agreement immediately terminated the previous ownership terms

    (D)   Stacey terminated the joint tenancy by selling Northacre.

106.   If Stacey and Karen are adjudged to be joint tenants, the most likely reason will be that

    (A)   the joint tenancy could not be terminated

    (B)   Northacre was smaller and worth much less than Southacre

    (C)   the agreement failed due to a lack of consideration

    (D)   the Statute of Frauds will cause the oral agreement to be ineffective

Questions 107-108 are based upon the following fact situation.

Tycoon owned an 800-acre peninsula in fee simple. Tycoon decided to divide the land and develop the area for single family homes. Realizing the houses would need access roads, Tycoon set aside some of the land for roads. He also set aside land on the part of the peninsula bordering a public highway to build a guardhouse and gate.

Tycoon sold all the lots with a clause providing that the property may be used only for residential purposes. Another clause provided that the residents agree to pay annual dues for maintenance of roads and for hiring a security guard.

107.   Cheepo purchased a lot and built a house. Cheepo refuses to pay the annual dues. Under which of the following theories will his neighbors be most likely to compel Cheepo to pay dues?

    (A)   easement

    (B)   personal contract

    (C)   covenant

    (D)   equitable servitude

108.   If the owners of the subdivisions seek to establish a common scheme, which of the following will hurt their case most?

    (A)   Cheepo had a right to contest the expenses.

    (B)   The agreement amounted to an unlawful "taking."

    (C)   The agreement to pay an indefinite sum for an indefinite time is oppressive, especially when future owners are bound.

GO ON TO THE NEXT PAGE

(D)   The agreement resulted in a restraint on alienation.

109.   Vic conveyed title to his house, which he owned in fee simple, to Sandy, who paid full value. Sandy never recorded the transaction.

Several months later, Vic conveyed title to the same house to his daughter, Doris "in consideration for services provided by Doris." Doris promptly recorded.

Vic was retired and living in Arizona and had not occupied the house for several years. Neither Sandy nor Doris attempted to occupy the house.

The jurisdiction has a pure race recording statute requiring "good faith" and "value" in order for a junior claimant to obtain priority.

In an action between Sandy and Doris for title to the house, which of the following choices is the best answer?

(A)   Doris will prevail because Sandy did not record.

(B)   Doris will prevail only if Sandy obtained a quitclaim deed.

(C)   The outcome will be determined by whether Sandy gave consideration of sufficient value.

(D)   The outcome will be determined by whether Doris gave consideration of sufficient value.

110.   Donald and Marla lived as husband and wife although they never formally married. They held themselves out to the community as husband and wife, signed contracts together, and had several children. They purchased a house together as tenants by the entirety and made payments on the house for twelve years. One day, Donald told Marla he was leaving her. The jurisdiction does not recognize common law marriage. If Donald seeks to partition the house will he be successful?

(A)   Yes, because this tenancy is terminated by operation of law when Donald and Marla separate.

(B)   Yes, because a tenancy by the entirety was never created.

(C)   No, because a tenancy by the entirety may not be partitioned.

(D)   No, because both parties must agree in order to partition a tenancy by the entirety.

111.   Jason purchased a twelve-acre farm from Patty. Which of the following statutes will require that Jason pay full value for the land and be the first to record in order to prevail over a subsequent purchaser from Patty?

(A)   pure notice recording act

(B)   race-notice recording act

(C)   pure race recording act

(D)   race-race recording act

112.   Cliff and Joe purchased bordering lots from Barry, who owned a country

club and had subdivided the club's land. A tennis court, left over from the country club, remained between Cliff's and Joe's houses. Half the court was on Joe's property, half was on Cliff's. Cliff and Joe would like to sign an agreement whereby successor owners would be prohibited from partitioning or limiting access to the tennis court. Cliff and Joe should agree to

(A)   each grant the other an express easement

(B)   a restrictive covenant against partition

(C)   a trust in perpetuity

(D)   a renewable lease

113.   Skipper leased 400 acres of land from Mr. Long Shoreman. The land bordered on a deep-water bay, and Skipper leased the land to dock his fleet of vessels. Skipper and Shoreman enjoyed cordial relations for several years, each fulfilling his respective contractual obligations.

      Both parties were notified that the government decided to build a super-highway and was going to take all 200 of Shoreman's acres bordering the water. The government reimbursed Skipper for the value of these 200 acres over the balance of the lease. Shoreman was reimbursed for the value of the land. Skipper notified Shoreman that the remaining land was of no value to him and refused further payments.

      If Shoreman asserts an action against Skipper, Shoreman should

(A)   prevail, unless he knew that Skipper's intended use was related to the water

(B)   prevail, because the contract between Skipper and Shoreman was not affected

(C)   not prevail, because the contract was void due to impossibility

(D)   not prevail, because the lease was breached

114.   Ford devised his collection of antique cars to "my former trusted employee, Iacocca, remainder to Iacocca's children and their heirs and assigns." Iacocca, who was divorced three times, had only a forty-year-old childless son. The remainder "to Iacocca's children" is

(A)   a possibility of a reverter

(B)   indefeasibly vested

(C)   vested and subject to a condition subsequent

(D)   vested, but subject to open

115.   In 1908, James and John decided to build a stable between their houses. They also erected a fence around a field, half of which was owned by James, the other half by John. Each kept a horse in the stable and allowed it to graze in the fenced-in area. James and John exchanged written easements allowing each to use the land surrounded by the fence

GO ON TO THE NEXT PAGE

and stable in perpetuity. The easements were properly recorded.

In the 1920s, John and James no longer used the stable or field because they replaced their horses with cars. The stable and fence remained standing. In 1982, James notified John that he could no longer use the field.

John objected because his grandchildren liked to occasionally play football there. If James asserts an action to prevent John from using the field, should James prevail?

(A) Yes, because the purpose of the easement had terminated.

(B) Yes, because an easement may be terminated at the option of a party in interest when use becomes sporadic.

(C) No, because an end to the necessity for an express easement does not terminate it.

(D) No, because the fence and stable were still erect.

116. Grace rented an apartment from Frank. Her lease provided that she pay $250 by the fifth of every month. Grace, who was compulsive, always paid her rent at least a week before it was due. Frank made a sexual advance that Grace refused. Frank decided to punish Grace by circulating a rumor in the apartment complex that Grace was "loose."

Frank maintained the apartments very poorly, and Grace circulated a petition among the tenants that enumerated the poor maintenance of the apartment building. When Frank learned Grace

was forwarding the petition to the housing authority, Frank moved to evict Grace. Of the following choices, which will be Grace's best argument?

(A) A tenant may not be evicted prior to the completion of the term of a lease.

(B) Grace possessed a periodic tenancy.

(C) Grace had an implied right to remain in her apartment.

(D) The doctrine prohibiting retaliatory eviction.

Questions 117-118 are based upon the following fact situation.

In 1985, Empire conveyed the State Building, which he owned in fee simple, to Art Museum "as long as they use the building to promote the arts. If the building is used for other purposes, then to Claire, her heirs, and assigns." Empire died in 1988. His valid will said, "I leave all my property to my daughter, World Trade."

117. In 1991, Art Museum contracted to sell the building to Ron in fee simple. After a title search, Ron refused to perform. If Art Museum asserts an action based on breach of contract against Ron, should Art Museum prevail?

(A) Yes, because the agreement with Ron was valid and enforceable.

(B) Yes, because the building was owned in fee simple by Art Museum.

(C)   No, because Claire had an interest in State Building.

(D)   No, because of World Trade's interest in State Building.

118.   Which of the following best describes Claire's interest in State Building in 1987?

(A)   fee simple

(B)   void executory interest

(C)   possibility of remainder

(D)   remainder subject to condition subsequent

119.   Leatrice signed a valid written contract to purchase a house from Irving. The parties agreed that Irving would provide a general warranty deed. At closing, Leatrice did not notice that Irving gave her a quitclaim deed. If Leatrice asserts an action against Irving, Irving should argue

(A)   when a deed conflicts with a contract, the deed is controlling

(B)   a quitclaim deed is not materially different from a warranty deed

(C)   Leatrice's only action is for damages

(D)   Leatrice may assert an action only when she actually loses title

120.   Seller owned Officeacre, a luxury downtown office building, subject to a $3,000,000 mortgage held by the First Downtown Bank. Seller and Buyer entered into a written agreement stating that Buyer was to pay $10,000,000 on April 1, 1986, in exchange for clear title to Officeacre.

On April 1, Seller offered to tender title, but Buyer refused to make the agreed upon payment, citing the bank's mortgage as an imperfection in the title. Seller claimed he would use part of the $10,000,000 to pay the remainder of the mortgage. Seller's best argument to compel Buyer to perform will be that

(A)   Buyer signed the agreement with full knowledge of the bank's mortgage

(B)   Seller has not breached the contract

(C)   Seller has an implied right to clear the title with proceeds from the building's sale

(D)   the contract implied that Buyer would assume the mortgage

121.   Tase-Tee Biscuit Company owned a large warehouse. Tase-Tee installed air conditioning units in several offices in the buildings. Large holes were made in the walls so vents could run between offices. Tase-Tee sold the building to Taste-Less. The air conditioning units were not mentioned in the contract. If Taste-Less asserts an action to include the

GO ON TO THE NEXT PAGE

air conditioners as part of the sale, judgment should be for

(A)   Tase-Tee, because the units were not attached to the building

(B)   Tase-Tee, because an air conditioner is not part of a building

(C)   Taste-Less, because Tase-Tee planned to permanently improve the building with the system

(D)   Taste-Less, because air conditioning units are fixtures

122.   Gertrude conveyed Hilltopacre to Western Kentucky University "for so long as the University uses the area for agricultural research, then to Rosalie and her heirs." The common law Rule Against Perpetuities has been adopted by the local jurisdiction. What is Gertrude's interest in Hilltopacre after the above conveyance?

(A)   no interest

(B)   a fee simple absolute

(C)   possibility of reverter

(D)   a reversion

123.   William conveyed three acres of land "to the Foundation for AIDS Research; however, if the premises shall ever cease to be used for medical research, title shall pass to the American Cancer Society." Which of the following choices best

describes the interest owned by the Foundation for AIDS Research?

(A)   fee simple absolute

(B)   fee simple subject to a condition subsequent

(C)   fee simple subject to an executory interest

(D)   fee simple determinable

Questions 124-125 are based upon the following fact situation.

Dawkins conveyed his home "to Richardson, but if Richardson should ever sell drugs on the premises, then Dawkins or his successors shall have the right to retake the home."

124.   Which of the following choices best describes the interest in the house owned by Richardson if he hasn't sold drugs?

(A)   fee simple subject to a condition subsequent

(B)   fee simple determinable

(C)   fee simple subject to an executory interest

(D)   fee simple determinable subject to an executory interest

125.   Which of the following choices best describes Dawkin's interest in the house, as long as Richardson does not consume cocaine?

(A)   reversion

(B) right of entry for condition broken

(C) possibility of reversion

(D) executory interest

Questions 126-128 are based upon the following fact situation.

Paul, the owner of a large tract of land, decided to develop the "Paul Industrial Mall." The land, which was undeveloped, did not have any roads running through it, but it did border on a major state road.

Paul subdivided the land into twenty parcels and recorded it as such, leaving a strip of land large enough to build a four-lane highway in the middle of the property.

Seven corporations each purchased a parcel from Paul, relying on the availability of the proposed highway. Each company signed a covenant providing, "No building taller than forty feet may be constructed in Paul Mall." Paul sold the remaining thirteen parcels of land to Homebuilder. Coalco purchased the land Paul promised to reserve for a road. It planned to build a coal burning facility.

126. If a corporation that purchased one of the original seven lots is able to prevent Coalco from building its coal burning plant, it will be because

(A) the corporation must have a road to its lot

(B) the corporation is a creditor beneficiary

(C) Coalco has not paid value

(D) the corporation owns an equitable servitude to the land

127. If Homebuilder attempts to build an 80-foot condominium apartment building, will the landowners in Paul Mall be able to stop him?

(A) Probably, because the real estate value will be lower due to the tall building.

(B) Probably, because the covenant it violates can be ruled to apply to all of Paul Mall.

(C) No, because Homebuilder's deed did not contain the covenant.

(D) No, because Homebuilder purchased several lots.

128. If the county decided to build a road on Coalco's plot and Coalco seeks to prevent the construction by the county, which party should prevail?

(A) Coalco, because it is the owner of the land.

(B) Coalco, because it purchased the land without reference to a covenant.

(C) The county, if it has made a dedication and acceptance.

(D) The county, because otherwise the other

GO ON TO THE NEXT PAGE

corporations will not be able to use their lands.

129. Seymour relinquished control of Alligatoracre by executing a deed in favor of Sylvia. Seymour gave the deed to Mr. Trust Worthy on March 1. Trust delivered the deed to Sylvia on March 15. On March 10, Poacher lost his leg to a hungry alligator while driving across Alligatoracre. If Poacher decides to assert an action for the loss of his leg, against whom should he file suit?

(A)   Seymour, because Trust delivered the deed after the accident.

(B)   Seymour, unless he can prove his intent was to extinguish ownership on March 1.

(C)   Trust, because he held the deed.

(D)   Sylvia, if Seymour released all control over Alligatoracre on March 1.

130. Rosemarie owned 500 acres of undeveloped land. She decided to subdivide the land into 1,000 plots of land, one-half acre each. Six hundred plots were sold with a provision that "all parties and their successors agree to construct only one single family house on each half-acre lot." The contract for the sale of the lots further provided that the land may not be occupied by trailers or other temporary structures.

Rosemarie was unable to sell the remaining 400 plots, and they remained idle for twenty years. Six hundred houses had been built on the lots Rosemarie sold previously. Many residents built white picket fences, had two cars, a dog, and children that aggravated them. Real estate values in the area suddenly skyrocketed, thanks in part to the booming nearby Silicon Hills high-tech area. Rosemarie sold the remaining lots to Developer without any restrictions.

If a successor to an owner of one of the original lots asserted an action against a successor of Developer to prevent installation of a mobile home, Developer's successor should **NOT** assert which of the following defenses?

(A)   The passage of twenty years made the two developments separate and independent entities.

(B)   The totality of the facts presented establish that there was no common development scheme for all 500 acres.

(C)   Plaintiffs must establish pecuniary or other tangible damages.

(D)   Developer did not have notice of the development.

131. Tenant first rented an apartment from Slumlord twenty years ago. Nineteen years later, Slumlord refused to keep the apartment in habitable condition. Tenant may **NOT**

(A)   move out, terminate the lease, and sue for damages

(B)   reduce his rental payments to equal the fair market value of the apartment with the defects

(C)   remain in possession without paying rent

(D)   all of the above

132.   Uncle devised his collection of antique cars "to the children of my favorite niece, Rachel." At the time of Uncle's death, Rachel had two children. A third child, Casper, was born three years after Uncle's death. Is Casper entitled to a share in Uncle's estate?

(A)   Yes, because Casper became a member of the class entitled to receive the estate.

(B)   Yes, because Uncle's intent is clear and obvious.

(C)   No, because the class was closed.

(D)   No, because Uncle may not have liked Casper.

133.   Rochelle owned 2,000 acres of land in fee simple. She had inherited the land in 1920 and had never visited the property. In 1923, Carlos asked Rochelle if he could use the land to hunt and fish. Rochelle assented, so Carlos hunted and fished on the land at least five times a week. In 1960, Carlos sought to acquire title to the land, claiming an easement by prescription. Carlos should be

(A)   successful, because he did not renew permission to use the land

(B)   successful, because the use was adverse for the necessary amount of time

(C)   unsuccessful, because the type of use Carlos enjoyed was not of sufficient quality to satisfy the requirements for adverse possession

(D)   unsuccessful, because of Carlos's request in 1923.

134.   Julius purchased a home at fair market value from Donald but did not record his deed. Julius moved into the house shortly after closing and has lived there ever since. Two years later, Donald conveyed the same house to Florence. Florence recorded her deed almost immediately. In an action between Florence and Julius for title to the house, judgment should be for

(A)   Julius, because he was the first purchaser

(B)   Julius, because Florence was on inquiry notice of Donald's conveyance to Julius

(C)   Florence, because she was the first to record

(D)   Florence, but only if she paid fair value

GO ON TO THE NEXT PAGE

135. Tenant leased a house from Landlord for twenty years in 1964. The house was located along a major highway. The area had been a sparsely populated farming and residential area, but in 1979 an interstate highway was completed, with an exit near Landlord's house. The area became inundated with fast food restaurants and gas stations. Tenant invested $75,000 to remodel the home and convert it into a tourist shop in 1980. If, in 1984, Landlord opts not to renew the lease and asserts an action against Tenant for the cost of restoring the house to a residence, judgment should be for

(A)   Landlord, because a tenant may not substantially alter a tenancy

(B)   Landlord, because Tenant has committed ameliorative waste

(C)   Tenant, because the character of the area changed

(D)   Tenant, because he has not violated any housing code

136. Esquire was given power of attorney by Ernestine to "sell or convey" all of her interest in Emptyacre, a large abandoned coal mine. Fred was granted a deed by Esquire that included a covenant of title. If Fred asserts an action based on breach of the covenant of title, he must prove

(A)   the deed was necessary to convey title

(B)   "sell and convey" includes granting a deed

(C)   he purchased for value

(D)   the sale per autre vie

137. Ned owned a very small farm. Waterco paid him ten dollars a year for the right to run a water pipe across Ned's farm. The pipe was ignored by both parties for many years. The parties never agreed who was responsible for the maintenance of the pipe. One day the pipe burst, causing a major flood, and several of Ned's pigs drowned. An expert determined that the pipe burst because it had not been maintained properly. If Ned sues Waterco for his damages, should Ned prevail?

(A)   Yes, because one who possesses an easement is held strictly liable to the servient estate.

(B)   Yes, because the owner of an easement is obligated to maintain the easement.

(C)   No, because the parties did not delegate duties.

(D)   No, because Ned knew the pipe's location and condition.

Questions 138-139 are based upon the following fact situation.

Trump owned Trump Tower, an office and apartment building, in fee simple. Trump conveyed the property to "Donald, his heirs, and assigns, but if Donald should be found guilty of any felony, to Ed Koch, if Koch has no less than three children by the time he is seventy years old. If Donald is convicted of a felony and Koch has less than three children, then to me and my heirs in fee simple." Trump's only heir is a son, Baby Trump.

138. The clause "to Ed Koch, if Koch has no less than three children by the time he is seventy years old" is

   (A)   not valid

   (B)   valid, because if it vests, it will vest within a life in being

   (C)   valid only if Donald has already been convicted of a felony

   (D)   valid, because Koch's interest has already vested although it may later divest

139. Which of the following best describes Baby Trump's interest upon Trumps death?

   (A)   fee simple

   (B)   possibility of a reverter

   (C)   condition subsequent

   (D)   none of the above

140. Alice and Eva owned homes built on adjacent lots. Both had scenic views of a lake from their living room windows. Eva often sat and knitted in the afternoons, enjoying the view and waiting for her children to come home from school. From her living room perch, Eva could see her children get off the school bus at the corner and walk home.

   Alice decided to erect a billboard in front of her house to provide the family with extra income. The billboard would block Eva's view of both the lake and the school bus stop. There are no applicable local zoning laws. If Eva asserts an action against Alice to enjoin building the billboard, should Eva prevail?

   (A)   Yes, because the billboard will block Eva's natural rights to an easement for light and air.

   (B)   Yes, because the neighborhood's lack of billboards created a reciprocal negative servitude prohibiting them.

   (C)   No, unless Eva used the view for a period long enough to create an easement by prescription.

   (D)   No, because Eva did not have a covenant to protect her view.

141. Pamela built a barn on her farm knowing that the barn extended two inches onto her neighbor Elaine's property. Pamela thought the infringement would go unnoticed because Elaine owned 2,000 acres of undeveloped land, which she had not visited for several years. The land was very hilly and rocky and had no economic value since it was in the boondocks and unfarmable. If Elaine asserts an action against Pamela based on trespass and praying for damages, should Elaine prevail?

   (A)   Yes.

GO ON TO THE NEXT PAGE

(B)   No, because she has not suffered pecuniary damages.

(C)   No, because no use of the land was affected.

(D)   No, because the trespass was not material.

142.   Ace owned a house with a very large back yard. Property values skyrocketed throughout Ace's neighborhood, and Ace decided to sell his back yard to Deuce. Ace forgot to tell Deuce that several pipes ran from the house to municipal pipes across the yard. If Deuce demands that Ace remove the pipes, Ace should argue that he owns an

(A)   easement by prescription

(B)   easement by implication

(C)   easement by reservation

(D)   easement by solicitation

Questions 143-145 are based upon the following fact situation.

Goldco dug a mine on its property that was adjacent to Homeowner's house. The mine was operated in compliance with all local ordinances and was built in a careful and prudent manner. The mine came up to, but not over, the boundary between Goldco and Homeowner's property. Homeowner's house settled and was severely damaged due to Goldco's mine. The property is in a common law jurisdiction.

143.   If Homeowner asserts an action against Goldco for damages to his house, is he likely to prevail?

(A)   Yes, because the support to his land was damaged by Goldco.

(B)   Yes, because the structural damage is evidence of Goldco's negligence.

(C)   No, because a house is an artificial structure.

(D)   No, because Goldco acted in a careful and prudent manner.

144.   Assume for this question only that an oak tree in Homeowner's yard collapsed due to Goldco's digging on its own property. If Homeowner asserts an action, should he prevail?

(A)   Yes, if he can prove Goldco was negligent.

(B)   Yes, regardless of Goldco's negligence.

(C)   No, because one is not liable for damaging a tree.

(D)   No, because Goldco acted in good faith.

145.   Assume for this question only that a stream that ran through Homeowner's property changed its course due to Goldco's mine. Despite careful and proper planning by Goldco, Homeowner's garage was ruined by the change in the stream's course. If Homeowner asserts an action against Goldco, is Homeowner likely to prevail?

(A)   Yes, because Goldco's actions were the legal cause of Homeowner's damages.

(B)   Yes, if Goldco was negligent.

(C)   No, because Goldco was using his land for its intended use.

(D)   No, because Goldco has drained only water.

146.   Carl Deal purchased a large tract of land from Hank Vastown. Carl Deal's land was completely surrounded by land owned by Vastown, and Carl Deal's only access to a public highway was across Vastown's land. Carl Deal will be allowed to pass across Vastown's land under a(n)

(A)   easement by implication

(B)   easement by prescription

(C)   easement by reservation

(D)   negative easement

Questions 147-148 are based upon the following fact situation.

Madison owned an apartment building called "Square Gardens" in fee simple. Madison conveyed the property to "Meadow Land, his heirs, and assigns, but if Meadow Land should not provide heat to his tenants then Phil Spectrum shall have a right of entry, if Phil Spectrum has two or more children before he reaches the age of sixty. If Meadow Land does not provide heat and Phil Spectrum does not have children, then to myself and my heirs in fee simple."

147.   The provision "to Phil Spectrum if Phil Spectrum has two or more children before he reaches the age of sixty" is

(A)   valid, only if Meadow Land has not provided heat

(B)   valid, because Phil Spectrum's interest has already vested even though it may divest at a later date

(C)   valid, because if it vests, it will vest within a life in being

(D)   not valid

148.   Which of the following best describes the interest held by Madison's children after his death as long as Meadow Land provides heat and Phil Spectrum has no children?

(A)   possibility of a reverter

(B)   fee simple

(C)   condition subsequent

(D)   none

PROPERTY ANSWERS

1. (B)   Alpha impliedly reserved himself an easement when he granted Westacre to Beta because he 1) owned a whole tract of land, one part of which was used to serve another (quasi-easement); 2) he conveyed part of the property and retained a portion; 3) the use was apparent, i.e., readily discoverable by investigation; 4) the use was continuous; and 5) the use was reasonably necessary. These are the five requirements for an easement by implication.

An easement by prescription (Choice C) is similar to adverse possession; the use must be open and notorious and continuous for the statutory time period (which is certain to exceed one year).

The covenant against encumbrances wasn't violated (Choice D) by Alpha's implied easement. We don't know from the facts that the land was conveyed with such a covenant, and the overall point is that Beta is charged with knowledge of Alpha's easement. There is also no trespass (Choice A) because Alpha's easement gave him the right to maintain his pipes on Beta's land.

2. (C)   The Rule against Perpetuities cannot defeat a vested remainder or a reversionary interest in the grantor. Therefore, (A), (B), and (D) are unaffected by the rule. (C) is correct because the remainder in the grandchildren is contingent upon their reaching the age of twenty-five. The very fact that the grandchildren must reach an age over twenty-one should put you on notice that the Rule has probably been violated. Ernie is the measuring life (because his life has a causal effect on the existence of the remainder), and twenty-one years after Ernie's death the class won't necessarily have vested or failed. To satisfy the Rule Against Perpetuities, the remainder must definitely vest or fail within a (measuring) life in being (at the conveyance or devise) plus twenty-one years.

These days, some states use the doctrine of equitable reformation to fulfill the testator's intention despite the Rule Against Perpetuities. This doctrine allows the court to reduce the age for the grandchildren's remainder to vest to twenty-one.

3. (B)   Under the Rule Against Perpetuities an interest must definitely vest or fail no later than twenty-one years after the death of some life in being at the creation of the interest. The longest living of Alan's children is the measuring life. All the living grandchildren necessarily will or will not reach majority within twenty-one years after that child's death. (The Rule allows a grace period for gestation — a person is alive upon conception for the purposes of the Rule.) Therefore, the Rule is satisfied.

When Alan died, Jimmy took possession of his life estate. Sharon owned the remainder subject to defeasance upon any of the grandchildren reaching majority. The interest of the grandchildren was still contingent on reaching the age of majority.

4.   (A)   At common law a fee tail was formed by language such as "to C and the heirs of his body." This meant that only the grantee's lineal heirs could inherit, i.e., if the holder has no children, the estate reverts to the grantor. The purpose of the fee tail was to keep land within the upper classes. It operates as a restriction on alienability and inheritability. Most states no longer recognize this estate.

Since Carlos most likely will not have children, Blackacre will revert to Alden upon Carlos's death, thus, by operation of law, his fee tail became a life estate.

A life estate per autre vie (Choice B) is created when a life estate is granted to A, but the duration is measured by B's life. In other words, it is a life estate that lasts for the life of a person other than the grantee. A possibility of reverter (Choice C) arises when the grantor transfers a determinable estate. A shifting executory interest (Choice D) divests one grantee of her interest in favor of another grantee. It is illustrated by a grant "to A and his heirs, but if A has no issue then to B and his heirs." In this example, B owns the shifting executory interest.

5.   (C)   Before Peter fulfills the conveyance's requirements, Sidney holds the remainder of Ernie's life estate (he really holds a reversion upon Ernie's death). After the requirements are met, then Sidney's interest becomes a possibility of reverter if the office is no longer used for the practice of medicine.

6.   (B)   A remainder vests when its holder is alive and any conditions precedent have been met. Andy's interest had vested as soon as he was born since he was one of George's children and there were no conditions precedent in the conveyance. Only a vested remainder may be attached or sold by a creditor, a contingent remainder may not be. A remainder is contingent if it is subject to a condition precedent or if it is in an unascertainable person. The vesting of Andy's interest might have seemed contingent upon his outliving George if Eric's will had not provided that a deceased child's portion should go to the respective estate. Therefore, Andy now owns a remainder even if he is deceased at the time he would have come into possession of Blackacre.

7.   (A)   The Rule in Shelley's Case applies in a state following the common law. It provides that when a grantor conveys a limited estate to a grantee and in the same instrument creates a remainder in the grantee's heirs (grantor must use the word heirs), the grantee takes the estate in fee simple. Under the Rule, Jacob had acquired the lot in fee simple and it will pass to his wife upon his death.

8.   (D)   The Doctrine of Worthier Title does not allow a grantor to make an inter vivos conveyance with a remainder in his heirs. If the grantor attempts to do so, as Leslie did with the words, "the land shall revert to myself or my estate," the remainder is void and the grantor holds a reversion instead. Since Leslie has died, the reversion goes to his estate anyway.

9.   (A)   The Rule Against Perpetuities will effect some but not all kinds of future interests. Interests effected by the Rule must vest or fail within a life in being plus twenty-one years. If something might happen to prevent this, the interest is void. In Example I, Frederick and Olmstead are given a shifting executory interest. Executory interests do not vest until they become possessory. Since Frederick and Olmstead will not either definitely come into possession or come into possession within a life in being plus twenty-one years, their interests are automatically void. In Example III, Suarez is the measuring life in being, he could possibly have another child after the conveyance, who would be the first of his children to reach the age of fifty, but not within twenty-one years after his death.

A reversionary interest in the grantor (Example II, after the doctrine of Worthier Title is applied) doesn't fall within the Rule. The life estate remainder in Example IV satisfies the Rule because Jefferson is the measuring life and all of his children will be ascertainable when he dies. The remainder in fee simple to Adams is vested because Adams is an ascertainable person.

10.   (B)   There are six covenants for title to real property, which are divided into "personal" (or present) covenants and "real" (or future) covenants. Personal covenants are usually breached (if at all) as of the time the deed was delivered. They may not be enforced by a remote grantee (Eve) against a grantor (Sidney). These are 1) for quiet enjoyment, 2) of the right to convey, and 3) against encumbrances. In contrast, real covenants may be enforced by a remote grantee. These are 1) for seisin, 2) of general warranty, and 3) for further assurance. (B) is correct because it is an example of the covenant for further assurances.

Profits (Choice A) and easements (Choice C) fall under the covenant against encumbrances, which is personal and unenforceable by a remote grantee.

Eve has no legal rights against Roger to perfect title because a quitclaim deed makes no guarantees. Roger only purported to pass on to Eve whatever interest he actually possessed.

11.   (B)   An easement is the right of one to make specific use of the land of another. An easement in gross benefits its owner in the conduct of its business, general affairs, etc., and not for the sole benefit of an adjacent parcel of land. This easement benefits Biscayne in its business of supplying water to the city of Coral Gables.

An easement appurtenant benefits its owner's adjacent parcel of land at the expense of the land owned by another. The land that is benefited is called the dominant tenement, and the land used is called the servient tenement. For an easement appurtenant to exist, you must be able to identify a dominant and a servient tenement. With an easement in gross, there is a servient tenement but no dominant tenement. Once created, an easement automatically runs with its tenements and binds successors to the land.

If Biscayne were to buy the rights to use a strip of land adjacent to its own land in order to run an electric cable that will power its water plant, that would be an easement appurtenant because the use of the adjacent land benefits Biscayne in the use of its own land.

A profit (Choice C) is the right to enter another's land to remove natural resources. A covenant (Choice D) is a promise or a contract between landowners that binds their successors.

12.   (D)   In 1922, John granted John Jr. a fee simple determinable with a possibility of reverter in himself. The key is in the use of the words "so long as" modifying the condition of the grant. As soon as this condition is broken the land automatically reverts to John, or his estate if he is deceased. John Jr. cannot convey any more than he owns; therefore, anyone who follows John Jr. in interest takes a determinable estate. At common law, the determinable status could last in perpetuity, but most American states have enacted valid statutes of limitations on the number of years for which such a possibility of reverter will be effective.

If this had been a fee simple subject to condition subsequent, language such as "but if this farm is used for alcohol production, I will have a right to re-enter" would have been used. The condition subsequent gives only a right of re-entry. The previous estate does not divest automatically, but the grantor holding the possibility of reverter must exercise her right to re-enter for the estate to divest.

13.   (B)   One has seisin of real property if he 1) has legal possession of that property and 2) has a freehold estate (fee simple, fee tail, or life estate). One does not have seisin when he holds a non-freehold estate, such as the various types of tenancies: a tenancy for years, periodic tenancy, tenancy at will, or a tenancy at sufferance. Since Aaron is a tenant with a tenancy for years, he has the right to actual possession, but he does not hold legal possession of the land or a freehold estate. Maurice, as the owner of life estate, has legal possession of the land until his death; therefore, he has seisin of the property despite the fact that Aaron is occupying the house. Ronny does not currently hold a freehold estate or legal possession, he owns only a future interest in the property.

14.   (C)   The six covenants for title to real property are 1) of the right to convey, 2) for seisin, 3) against encumbrances, 4) for quiet enjoyment, 5) of general warranty, and 6) for further assurances.

The first three covenants are "personal" and the second three are "real." If a deed provides for "usual covenants," the first five will be included. A deed that provides for "full covenants" will include all six. Under the covenant for further assurances, the grantor must take any action within his power to perfect the grantee's title.

15.   (A)   This easement is not enforceable due to the vagueness of its terms. The description of the usage granted and the area Kearns may use is too broad. (B) is a valid easement by necessity. Ira owned both parcels of land and granted one part

with no access to a road; therefore, it is implied that George will have the right to travel over Ira's land. (C) is most likely a valid easement by prescription, especially because Runner jogged on a specified path. Runner could not acquire an easement to run all over Smoker's land. If Smoker had given Runner permission to use the path in the past, he might try to argue that Runner had a license that was revocable at will. (D) is a valid negative easement. The number of negative easements is limited, but they are valid for light and air. Usually a real covenant can be used more effectively to achieve the same purpose as a negative easement.

16.   (C)   This clause was a valid restrictive negative covenant that "runs with the land." To be an enforceable covenant, the following conditions must, at the time of the covenant's creation, be present: 1) a writing, 2) the covenant touches and concerns the land, 3) privity between the covenantor and the covenantee, and 4) the parties intend that the covenant run with the land. All of these conditions were satisfied until Homeless acquired title by adverse possession. He cannot enforce the covenant because he was never in privity with Al.

17.   (C)   Although it is true that this restriction on land use is considered a burden as applied to Homeless and that privity requirements tend to be strict for burdens to be enforced, Homeless will most likely be charged with constructive notice of a common development scheme. Courts will enforce such a scheme against a person not in privity through the doctrine of implied negative servitudes. Since all the other deeds in the subdivision come from a common grantor and have this restriction, Homeless should have been on notice that it applied to him as well. Some jurisdictions will adhere to a stricter standard for enforcement and allow Homeless to build the hotel unless the restriction was in his chain of title.

18.   (B)   Gamma cannot enforce a personal covenant against Alpha. He may only enforce a real covenant that runs with the land. The covenant against encumbrances [(A) and (C)] is a personal covenant, which he may only enforce against Beta. However, (B), the covenant for quiet enjoyment, may be enforced by a remote grantee. When the neighbor asserted paramount title to Rockacre and effectively "evicted" Gamma, the covenant for quiet enjoyment was breached.

19.   (D)   This question examines the fine line distinguishing a sublease from an assignment. A transfer by a tenant of all of her interest in a leasehold is an assignment, despite any words to the contrary. A tenant who has transferred less than all of her interest has created a sublease. In this example, Rachel could have given Hector the remainder of her tenancy less one day. This is a loophole used to avoid an assignment, but will not be effective in all jurisdictions. An assignment creates privity of estate between the landlord and the assignee. Therefore, Hector is liable to Rachel's

landlord for rent, although Rachel was also liable as a surety. But now that Rachel is bankrupt, she's off the hook for her old debts.

A sublessee is not in privity of estate with the landlord and, therefore, may not be held liable for the lessee's failure to pay the rent or fulfill other obligations.

20.   (D)   An easement that is tied to the use of adjacent land is a very specific right. The owner of a dominant tenement receives the benefit of an easement over the servient tenement for use by the dominant tenement only. Madison cannot add another dominant tenement (Lexingtonacre) to this arrangement, because no party may unilaterally alter an easement. This answer does not need to address the intensity of Madison's use or the efficiency and the necessity involved. These considerations are irrelevant.

21.   (B)   Ralph's attempt to limit the fee simple is called a "disabling restraint," and the clause is void. Any provision that puts an undue restraint on the alienation of property will be deemed invalid by the courts. This usually applies when there is a penalty for conveying the property, such as when a person's interest is forfeited if she tries to convey it.

The transfer itself is valid and will be construed as if it were written without the restriction. The net effect is a fee simple transfer. The Rule Against Perpetuities does not come into consideration because the clause is already void.

22.   (C)   A "profit a prendre" (better known as just a "profit") is the right to go onto the land of another to remove a natural resource. Distinctions between a profit and an easement have virtually disappeared in practice, and the two seem identical as far as the law is concerned. A license (Choice D) is a privilege given to a licensee to enter or use another's land, but they usually may not remove anything.

23.   (C)   Just as with easements, profits may be in gross (benefits the holder without a dominant tenement) or appurtenant (tied to the land and passing only with the land).

For a profit or an easement to be appurtenant it must be intimately tied to that land. In this instance, the profit was a business arrangement and the right to use Curley's land was personal to Red. Profits are usually in gross and freely alienable by their owners. Red could sell Kim his profit, but it must be done separately from the sale of his land.

The majority of easements are affirmative; only a minimum of negative easements, i.e., for light and air, exist.

24.   (B)   One does not forfeit an easement due to excessive use. Although such use may exceed the use allowed by the easement, the original easement remains in force. Nathan can prevent car racing but not normal use of the easement.

(D) is false, which can be inferred from the facts of the question. (C) is simply incorrect. There is no reason for both easements to be extinguished.

25.   (B)   The easement was not readily discoverable and breached the covenant against encumbrances; therefore, it constituted a defect in the title. Had the easement been obvious, such as a paved road, the result might be different. (A) is a correct rule of law, but in the present case the deed disclaimed liability for recorded easements.

26.   (A)   Francine was a third-party beneficiary to the agreement between Smith and Elaine and she may, therefore, recover for a breach in this agreement. It is important that Smith knew that Francine wanted the title examined in order to sell it. However, this knowledge can easily be seen as implied in the request. (B) is incorrect because the facts make no mention of title insurance. (C) and (D) are false.

27.   (A)   Elaine executed a warranty deed and a covenant against encumbrances. Since the covenant was not satisfied, she will be liable to Francine.

28.   (B)   A life estate per autre vie is a life estate measured by the life of another person. (A) is also correct, but (B) is the best answer.

29.   (A)   Craigacre will be awarded to Claudia because she bought the land without notice of Rosalind's prior purchase, but only if she paid value for the land as required by the statute. Claudia is the junior claimant because she was the second purchaser although the first to record.

(B) is not the best answer because Rosalind's failure to record will only cause her to lose the land if Claudia qualifies for priority under the statute. A quitclaim deed (Choice C) is one given without any warranties to title. This choice is irrelevant because it does not affect the validity of Rosalind's purchase. (D) is incorrect because the statute only requires that a junior claimant pay value.

30.   (B)   The general rule is that when a deed and contract contain contradicting clauses, the deed is controlling. (A) is incorrect because a quitclaim and a warranty deed are materially different, in fact they can be considered opposites. (C) and (D) are false.

31.   (C)   The easement bought by Willie from Ollie was for his benefit in the use of Wildacre. This makes it an easement appurtenant to the land. Wildacre was the dominant tenement, and Overgrownacre was the servient tenement. Normally, when the dominant tenement is sold the new owner also gets the easement. You can think of it as Wildacre owning the easement. However, when the dominant and servient

tenement are both owned by the same person, merger occurs and the easement automatically extinguishes. You cannot own an easement over your own property. Therefore, no easement existed over Wildacre once Ollie owned both Wildacre and Overgrownacre.

32.   (D)   When an owner demonstrates an intention to permanently abandon an easement, the easement can be extinguished.

The extinction operates in a manner similar to adverse possession. Usually the abandonment must last for a statutory time period. A partition action, (B) and (C), is inappropriate in this case. Partition is used to divide a parcel of land that is owned jointly.

33.   (D)   The fact that one owner has maintained actual possession of a concurrent estate for the statutory time period will not be sufficient to give that owner sole title to the entire estate, because adverse possession must be hostile. A concurrent estate gives all its owners the right to possession, although they are not required to exercise that right. For the possession to be hostile the one owner must unequivocally notify all others that she intends to acquire sole possession. This requires more than simply an ouster. Since adverse possession is not applicable here, the other choices are irrelevant.

34.   (D)   (A) is the most important factor in determining the quality of the title conveyed. The parties' intent and good faith, (B) and (C), will also be influential factors in determining which party would prevail. Only (D) would be relatively unimportant.

35.   (C)   If the terms of the deed conflict with the terms of the contract, the deed will control. Since Lee accepted the deed, he is bound by it. Thus, (A) and (B) are false. (D) is also an incorrect statement of law.

36.   (B)   Under the doctrine of equitable conversion, the risk of loss is on the buyer once title passes, regardless of who is in possession. A modern doctrine that the risk of loss will follow possession of the property is now in effect in some states. Equitable reformation (Choice A) is a process where a court will reform the terms of a conveyance to prevent an interest from being invalidated by the Rule Against Perpetuities. Equitable distribution (Choice C) is a method to divide marital property upon divorce.

37.   (C)   The death of a seller will not terminate a contract (thus rendering (A) incorrect). Since the contract will be enforced, the proceeds will enter the estate and pass to Rob. (B) is clearly incorrect, as is (D), due to the terms of Francine's will.

38.   (B)   The death of a buyer automatically terminates an agreement.

39.   (B)   The owner of an easement has the obligation to maintain the easement and avoid unreasonable interference with the servient tenement. Strict liability, (A), is not imposed. (D) assumes facts not in the question.

40.   (D)   "Past consideration is no consideration" and will not satisfy the requirement to render a contract binding on the parties. Nadler had not relied on the terms of Kandel's will when he performed the services; therefore, he cannot enforce Kandel's promise.

41.   (C)   Jerry's future interest will be held void because it is too remote and because it violates the Rule Against Perpetuities. What remains is land held by the University as long as it is used for the football team. If it is not used for such purpose, it will revert to Bettina. Thus, Bettina's interest is a possibility of a reverter. This should be distinguished from a reversion (Choice B), which is created if the grantor transfers an estate of shorter duration than the one she holds. Keep in mind that the effects of the Rule Against Perpetuities differ in respect to determinable fees and fees subject to a condition subsequent. If Bettina had transferred a fee simple subject to a condition subsequent with an executory interest that was invalidated by the Rule, then Eastern Michigan U. would have a fee simple absolute.

42.   (D)   As a general rule, any restriction of a legal interest in property that prevents its free alienability is void. A disabling restraint provides that the grantee has no power to transfer her interest, and it will be voided. The property will then pass in fee simple. Hence, the grandchildren will obtain a fee simple interest. The Rule Against Perpetuities has not been violated because possession has vested within the required life in being (Bertha's daughter) plus twenty-one years.

43.   (B)   A fee simple determinable automatically terminates upon the happening of a certain even. Look for the key words, "for as long as," "while," "during," or "until." In contrast, a fee simple subject to a condition subsequent gives the grantor the potential power to terminate a grantee's estate upon occurrence of a condition. The key words indicating the estate is subject to a condition are, "but if" and "shall have the right to re-enter." An executory interest is one that divests a fee simple in favor of another grantee and not the original grantor. There is no such interest here, because Myron did not name any other parties capable of taking the estate.

44.   (B)   The "life in being plus twenty-one years" requirement was met. As it seems now, Burt is the life in being and all his children will turn twenty-one, if they reach that age

at all, within twenty-one years after his death. If Judith has more children, the one who lives the longest will be the measuring life in being. The fact that a grandchild exists (Choice A) is irrelevant because Burt could have additional children.

45. (A)   If the house is transferred as an inter vivos gift, the Rule Against Perpetuities may be violated because Judith could have more children. These children could not be the measuring lives, because they were not "lives in being" at the time of the conveyance. In contrast, once Judith has died all of her children will be ascertainable. Burt does not have the power to change Judith's will into an inter vivos conveyance (Choice D).

46. (D)   Ordinarily, a landlord is under no obligation to deliver premises to a tenant in good condition (Choice A). However, a landlord is obligated to disclose the existence of defects the tenant could not discover upon reasonable inspection if the landlord had actual knowledge or reason to know of such defects. Landlords will not be held strictly liable, in most jurisdictions, for conditions within an apartment.

47. (D)   Furst owned an easement by implication due to absolute necessity. When a grantor conveys a parcel of land that is surrounded by land retained by the grantor, the grantee is impliedly given an easement for access and utilities over the grantor's land. In this instance there was a path in existence to demarcate the location of the easement. If there hadn't been a path, Secund would have the right to locate the easement (since it is on his land) within reason. Since the elements of an easement by implication were satisfied, whether the elements of an easement by prescription were fulfilled is not material.

48. (C)   Thurd obtained Furst's easement upon purchasing his house; thus, he had the right to use the easement in a manner consistent with the scope of the easement. This is an easement appurtenant and will run with the land. Even if there had been no action between Furst and Secund firmly establishing the existence of an easement, Thurd would have the right to the easement impliedly created when Secund granted the landlocked parcel to Furst.

49. (A)   If ownership of the dominant and servient estate come together (this is called merger), the easement is extinguished because it is impossible to own an easement over your own land. Furth, however, will be the owner of a new easement by implication, since he purchased a landlocked parcel from Secund.

50. (B)   If a recorded instrument makes reference to an unrecorded transaction, a subsequent purchaser is bound to inquire into the nature of the unrecorded

transaction. In the instant case, the court should rule Madonna had "inquiry notice" of Jackson's easement because she could have found record of it in a thorough title search.

51.   (B)   A fixture is a chattel that has been annexed to real property. It becomes part of the real property and passes with the property. Most courts will examine whether it was intended that the chattel be permanently attached to the building. A custom-made screen does not automatically become a fixture, but since these screens were not easily removable it seems that it was intended that they be permanent.

52.   (C)   The contract between Lilly and Monique would ordinarily be void due to the Statute of Frauds because it is an oral contract for an interest in land. Monique's best chance will be under the facts enumerated in this choice.

        (A) seems like a good alternative, but it's not so clear that Monique's actions in caring for Lilly will make the intentions of their contract obvious.

53.   (C)   The clause written in each deed is a valid and enforceable real covenant. This covenant will obligate all successors in interest and may be enforced by any owner of land in the subdivision. (A), estoppel, is an equitable method of enforcing an agreement because one party has detrimentally relied on it although the agreement may otherwise be invalid. An easement is a non-possessory interest in another's land that gives the holder the right to use the land. A covenant is very similar to an easement. It is a device that can be used to enforce negative restrictions on land use, whereas easements are agreements that allow affirmative use. Privity of estate (Choice D) is defined, literally, as the "mutual or successive relationship to the same rights of property." In order to enforce a covenant, there must be privity of estate between the parties, but it is not the theory on which to bring the action.

54.   (C)   The covenant is valid and enforceable. Construction of a two-family home would violate a clear restriction in the deed. The other choices would be relevant only if the deed was ambiguous.

55.   (A)   A covenant will be extended to include a new development if the new and old developments were part of a common scheme. To be enforceable, the common scheme (1) must have existed at the time of the subdivision, (2) those seeking to enforce it must have purchased in reliance on the scheme, and (3) the person against whom enforcement is sought must have had some form of notice of the covenant. For example, this land would have been considered part of the common scheme if Jason had included it as part of "Jimmy Carter Estates" on a plot that he showed to purchasers in 1980.

56. (A)   Under the facts given, there is no evidence to show that the title would be hindered in any way. The existence of a common scheme was not in the fact pattern, but only an assumption in (A) of the previous question.

57. (D)   The assignment clause was not written to benefit Keith. Only Lauren may assert an action based on the clause. The lease simply prohibited an assignment without Lauren's permission; it did not prohibit assignments in general. Keith's interests are irrelevant since Lauren was the beneficiary of the restriction.

58. (C)   The requirement of the deed was to construct a theater for music within a certain time period. This requirement was met, and University obtained the land in fee simple. Use of the building for music in perpetuity was not a condition of the conveyance.

59. (B)   A life tenant is liable for interest that accrues on the mortgage of a tenancy but is not liable for the principal

60. (A)   A life tenant must pay the taxes on the property but will not be required to insure it.

61. (B)   Kathleen's argument that Jim was not in the chain of title is the view in the majority of jurisdictions. Jim's interest might have been discoverable, but it would put a tremendous burden on the title searcher. Therefore, Kathleen cannot be charged with notice of Jim's interest, and she will most likely be awarded possession. This is her most persuasive argument, although the other choices might be valid.

62. (A)   Frosty does not own a freehold estate; he has an indefinite leasehold for his apartment. Although the fact pattern says he "purchased" an apartment, what he really bought was a share in the corporation and the right to lease his apartment. This is an example of a cooperative apartment complex.

63. (B)   This is a covenant that is part of a development scheme. The covenant will be enforceable. An easement is a non-possessory interest to use another's land, such as a right of way.

64. (D)   An easement is the best method to secure the use of land. Easements bind the owners of land regardless of notice, touching and concerning the land, privity, etc. A covenant that runs with the land can remain in effect in perpetuity, but its

enforcement will not be as secure as an easement's. A zoning law is not the best device because it can be legislatively changed.

65. (D)   In this question it is important to examine the terms of the relevant statute. The statute clearly provides that one who records first without notice of a prior conveyance and pays value owns the land. Since Kinney Jr. hadn't paid value it didn't matter that he recorded his interest first.

66. (C)   The consideration furnished by Park N' Lock was sufficient to obtain title. They should be viewed as any other in the chain of title. Under most Recording Statutes, the status of mortgagee and purchaser are the same.

67. (A)   Kinney Jr. was not a bonafide purchaser for value as required by the statute. (B) is correct, but (A) is better since it explains why Meyers would prevail. The statute doesn't require the first purchaser, who failed to record promptly, to have paid value.

68. (C)   A tenancy by the entirety may only be created between a husband and wife. A co-tenant by the entirety may not unilaterally convey his interest; it can only be done jointly. Therefore, Denise and George would have a true tenancy in the entirety with this restriction on alienability only if they were married. It is also effective if they have a common law marriage.

69. (A)   A life tenant is obligated to pay only the interest on a loan owed for the tenancy. The remainderman is liable for the principal. Further, a life tenant is liable to pay taxes on the property but not insurance.

70. (C)   To be an enforceable covenant, the following conditions must, at the time of creation, be present: 1) a writing, 2) the covenant touches and concerns the land, 3) privity of estate between the covenantor and the covenantee, and 4) the parties intend that the covenant run with the land. This agreement resembles a covenant running with the land which benefits or burdens successors in interest to the original parties, but it will only be enforceable against Wes by Joe if Casey and Gil were in privity of estate, i.e., one of them had purchased his land from the other.

71. (A)   A pure notice recording act protects a subsequent bona fide purchaser for value, regardless of whether he was the first to record. To qualify as a bona fide purchaser for value, the purchaser must not have had actual or record notice of a prior conveyance at the time of buying the property and must pay value. A race-notice act would protect Teddy only if he recorded prior to George. A pure-race act would

protect Teddy if he recorded first — even if he had knowledge of the prior conveyance. (C) is nonsense.

72.   (C)   The courts will enforce a covenant against a buyer whose deed does not contain the restriction only if evidence shows that, when the sale of property began, the developer had a common scheme of development that included the lots in question. This is justified under the doctrine of reciprocal or implied negative servitudes. Most states assume that the unrestricted buyer had constructive notice of the restrictions on the other deeds. However, some states will refuse to enforce any covenants without actual notice.

73.   (B)   The above rule applies to this question. If Speculator was bound under the doctrine of reciprocal negative servitudes, his successors in interest will be as well. Therefore, the best defense is to argue that there was not a common development scheme.

74.   (B)   Laurie will most likely be considered a third-party beneficiary to the agreement between Edward and Ralph and she could therefore recover against Ralph for breaching his duty to Edward. See Answer 26. (D) is incorrect because Laurie can bring suit regardless of whether Ralph was negligent.

75.   (B)   Edward executed a covenant of warranty and a covenant against encumbrances. Since the covenant against encumbrances was not satisfied, Edward will be liable to Laurie.

76.   (A)   The Statute of Frauds requires that every conveyance of an interest in land must be evidenced by a writing. Since there was no writing and no consideration paid, Dandy only had Andy's permission, i.e., a license, to enter his land which was revocable at will. For an easement to be created there must also be an evident intention to create one. While it is true that Dandy had no rights to an easement by implication, it is irrelevant to the answer.

77.   (C)   A contract not satisfying the Statute of Frauds may sometimes be enforceable due to the doctrine of part performance. Under this doctrine, there must be part performance by one party in detrimental reliance on the invalid contract, while the other party has notice and sits idly by. This part performance should also clearly demonstrate the intentions of the parties to the contract. Since Betty did not take any actions that a person with a long-term lease would not take, the elements of this doctrine were not present. (D) may be correct but would be very difficult to prove. (B) is wordy nonsense.

78. (C)   Fee simple subject to an executory interest is an estate subject to divestment upon occurrence of a condition subsequent, and when the condition occurs the title will be given to another grantee rather than the original grantor. (D) is correct, the fee simple is determinable, but it's not the best answer because this fee simple is also subject to an executory interest. Although executory interests are rarely valid due to the Rule Against Perpetuities, in this case the "charity to charity" exception will apply. The "charity to charity" exception provides that the Rule Against Perpetuities will not void the executory interest of a charitable organization when it succeeds another charitable organization.

79. (C)   If the fixtures were by their nature installed to benefit the tenant in the conduct of her business, she may remove them. This is an exception to the rules of fixtures to prevent a businessperson from losing an investment. (A) is an incorrect statement of landlord-tenant law. Proving (B) would be difficult. The general darkroom equipment may be easily removable, but the lights could be regarded as permanent attachments. (D) is false.

80. (C)   Under a pure race recording act, a subsequent purchaser will prevail if she is the first to record, regardless of whether she paid value. Under pure notice (Choice A) and race-notice (Choice B) statutes, only a bona fide purchaser for value will prevail.

81. (D)   A life tenant may not commit waste on the tenancy. When land has been previously used to exploit natural resources, it is assumed that the grantor expected the life tenant to do the same. However Tacoma may not remove an inordinate amount of the timber, because a life tenant does not have the right to impair the interest of the remainderman. Ameliorative waste (Choice C) is that which changes the nature of the premises in a "good" way, i.e., one that increases its value.

82. (D)   Title to real property is transferred when a deed is conveyed, despite the purchaser's failure to record. The purchaser may not be protected against subsequent bona fide purchasers for value who recorded first. The existence of an easement will not negate the transfer.

83. (C)   Felicity would be entitled to damages if the easement was used. If the easement remained dormant, Felicity will not be able to prove damages.

84. (D)   The easement is for a right of way and not for storage. When an easement is granted, the holder may not exceed its "boundaries."

85.   (A)   In some states, the covenant will be deemed valid and run with the land. Breach of the covenant will then give rise to an action for damages. However, it cannot be enforced injunctively; so the conveyance is not void, and Felicity's title is valid. Most states will consider this covenant to be an unreasonable partial restraint on alienation and invalidate it.

86.   (A)   The covenant was valid and runs with the land. (B) and (D) are incorrect because they deal with zoning laws that aren't of concern in this case.

87.   (C)   If the court determines that the land was part of a common development scheme, the newly developed land must be used in conformity with that scheme. Another method to have construction limited to detached houses is to enact a zoning ordinance (Choice B), but zoning ordinances are less secure than common schemes because they may be changed.

88.   (C)   Under a contract for the sale of real property where the kind of title has not been specified, delivery of "marketable title" is implied.

89.   (C)   An easement is a non-possessory right one holds to use the land of another. An easement is of perpetual duration unless otherwise stated. (A) is incorrect because traditionally easements were granted in perpetuity. However, an easement can be extinguished by hostilely cutting off access for the statutory time period or when abandoned by the owner. (B) is incorrect because failure to mention an easement does not negate it. Lawrence will most likely be charged with constructive notice of the easement.

90.   (D)   For the reasons stated in the answer above, monetary damages will not be available to Lawrence. However, he might be able to collect monetary damages from Farmer if his purchase was accompanied by a covenant against encumbrances.

91.   (D)   To be a proper conveyance, the deed and contract must identify the land precisely enough for anyone to locate it. Although this description is not given in metes and bounds, it is exact enough for "Joe Shmoe" to figure out where the plot of land lies.

92.   (C)   The agreement can be viewed as an equitable servitude, which is a type of covenant that binds the successors of land. It is a subset of real covenants, but privity of estate is not a requirement to enforce it. An equitable servitude is enforceable through injunction only and will not give rise to monetary damages. However, this equitable servitude will not be enforced, because it violates the equal protection clause. The servitude will not be invalidated, but no court will enforce it against

homeowners with children. Although unenforceable in regard to children, the rest of the agreement remains valid.

93.   (A)   The nature of the property and the description are sufficient to identify the property. The mistake in acreage will not affect the conveyance, it will simply be reformed to represent what Elvis actually possessed.

94.   (D)   The Parole Evidence Rule will prevent testimony of oral understandings to alter a written contract. (A) is incorrect because recording a deed does not make it immune to attack, particularly since the error is merely computational.

95.   (A)   Joan is a bona fide purchaser who properly recorded. She will be able to obtain valid title to the land. However, the computational mistake that Vincent made will most likely be rectified.

96.   (A)   A transfer by a lessee of his entire interest is an assignment, and a transfer of less than his entire interest is a sublease. Under the majority view, a right of re-entry is not a true reversion; therefore, Bob's transfer was an assignment. Also see Answer 19.

97.   (D)   (D) is correct because a court of equity will look into the adequacy of consideration when determining the ownership of land. The transfer to Mildred will most likely be considered a gift, which is not binding on the donor. Even at law, "love and affection" is not usually considered adequate consideration. (A) would be correct if Mildred had furnished consideration for the land.

98.   (B)   Carl has committed waste, which is using a life estate to the full estate's detriment. A life tenant is not allowed to impair the interests of the remainder. By pumping this oil, Carl has reduced the value of the land. Jill will succeed in recovering the value of the waste and preventing future waste. Carl's life estate was not terminated (Choice A), since he satisfied the condition of growing corn through 1985.

99.   (C)   A person's "children" are defined as children by all marriages and adopted children. The following are generally not defined as children: 1) step-children, 2) grandchildren, and 3) illegitimate children. But some states have enacted statutes that will include illegitimate children in the definition.

100.   (D)   License is merely permission. James can argue that he gave Jeffrey permission to live in his apartment but did not give him an interest in the apartment. A licensee is one with formal permission or authority to do something on the land of another. A licensor may terminate a license at will.

                    (A) and (B) are incorrect since any type of tenancy will subject James to landlord-tenant laws. Jeffrey is not a trespasser, since he initially occupied the apartment with James's permission.

101.   (C)   This is a common sense question and is not to be worried about. (C) simply makes the title of he who records first unassailable.

102.   (C)   Under the doctrine of equitable conversion, the risk of loss is on the buyer when damage is caused by neither the buyer nor seller. The original contract is valid and enforceable. (D) is incorrect since such a remedy would effectively "undo" the contract. Though Henry should have taken out insurance (Choice A), the reason for doing so is that equitable conversion will place the risk of loss on him. Some states have abandoned this doctrine and determined that the risk of loss follows possession. If this standard had been applied, Henrietta would have been unsuccessful in her bid for specific performance.

103.   (C)   The developer must argue that he cannot manifest the granting of an easement prior to handing the property to governmental authorities.

104.   (A)   This is the best of four bad arguments. Her only hope is to argue that the street was already dedicated. Proving that she already had an easement [Choices (B), (C), and (D)] would be exceedingly difficult.

105.   (D)   When two parties share a joint tenancy, they each own a one-half undivided interest in the whole. When Stacey conveyed Northacre, the court might find that she terminated the joint tenancy by selling her entire interest in the estate. Unlike a tenancy by the entirety, a joint tenancy can be severed by one party acting alone. Therefore, the estate has effectively been partitioned, and Southacre is Karen's alone in fee simple.

106.   (D)   If Stacey transferred less than her entire interest in the joint tenancy, she still has rights to Southacre. Since we are assuming she did not sell a complete one-half interest and under the Statute of Frauds the oral agreement to partition the land is invalid, the joint tenancy has not been severed.

107. (C)   The agreement to share expenses was an affirmative covenant. It can be enforced in a court of law for damages. An easement is a non-possessory interest allowing use of another's land, and an equitable servitude is a subset of real covenants that can be enforced by an injunction. (B) is wrong because Cheepo did not contract with his neighbors.

108. (C)   Courts are reluctant to enforce such agreements on public policy grounds. The owners would have a better chance of enforcing it if it were for a limited amount and a limited duration. (B) is incorrect because this is not an eminent domain problem. (D) is incorrect because the contested provision does not restrain the sale of the land, but only adds a condition to ownership. Although (A) is true, it does not, as (C) does, hurt the owner's case.

109. (D)   The house will be awarded to Doris, who was first to record, only if she satisfied the statute by providing consideration of sufficient value. This depends on the worth of the services she performed compared to the fair market value of the house.

110. (B)   A tenancy by the entirety may only be created between a husband and wife. It requires five unities: time, title, interest, possession, and marriage. Since the local jurisdiction did not recognize common law marriage, a tenancy by the entirety was never created. Therefore, the property may be partitioned.
      Jurisdictions differ in interpretation of what type of tenancy is actually created when an unmarried couple attempts to obtain property through a tenancy by the entirety. Some will say that they have a tenancy in common and others will give them a joint tenancy because it better approximates their intention. All the unities necessary for a joint tenancy are already present. Both of these alternative estates are capable of partition.

111. (B)   Race-notice recording acts provide that a subsequent bona fide purchaser will prevail only if he was the first to record. Under a pure notice act (Choice A) Jason would not have to record. Under a pure race act (Choice C), Jason would not have to be a bona fide purchaser for value. There is no such thing as race-race act (Choice D).

112. (A)   Since each party owns part of the tennis court, all they have to do is grant the other party an easement in writing. This option is the most secure. All of the other choices are contestable and must conform to specific requirements, such as privity for enforcement.

113.   (B)   When the government obtains title to part of a leasehold through eminent domain or condemnation, the tenant will take part of the award and then be held to the full contract. If Skipper wants out of the lease his only redress is against the government. He can also sublet the land. If any other party had obtained paramount title to part of the land by purchasing it from Shoreman and evicted Skipper from that portion, the covenant of quiet enjoyment within the lease would be breached. Quiet enjoyment is a dependent covenant; if the landlord breaches it the tenant is not required to pay rent. Most leases currently contain a condemnation clause which provides that the agreement will be terminated and the landlord will receive all compensation from the government.

114.   (D)   The correct choice, "vested, but subject to open," means the same as vested and subject to a partial defeasance. Until Iacocca should have another child, the son owns the remainder alone in fee simple. If Iacocca has more children, the estate will be shared. Iacocca's son will still own a partial interest, but not the whole. Therefore, it is subject to open if Iacocca has additional children.

115.   (C)   An easement created in writing to last in perpetuity will not be terminated due to a lack of necessity. Although, if it were an implied easement due to necessity, it would be terminated. Abandonment would be one way to terminate this easement, but John still used the field. If James had first told John to keep off the land in the 1940s and John then stayed away for the statutory period, James could claim that the easement was extinguished adversely.

116.   (D)   In many jurisdictions, under the doctrine that prevents retaliatory evictions, a landlord may not raise rents or otherwise harass a tenant because she has sought to enforce her rights.

117.   (D)   The Rule Against Perpetuities will void the clause creating Claire's interest because it may not vest or fail to vest within twenty-one years. World Trade inherited Empire's possibility of reverter and will own State Building in fee simple if it is not used for promoting the arts.

118.   (B)   Since the clause was invalidated by the Rule Against Perpetuities, Claire's interest was voided.

119.   (A)   When a deed and contract contain contradicting clauses, the deed is generally controlling. Since a quitclaim deed is one that makes no warranties, (B) is clearly false.

120. (C)   A promise to deliver good title will be satisfied by clearing title of a previous mortgage shortly after the sale with the proceeds from the sale. (A) and (C) are not evidenced by the stated facts. In general, when the defect in title is easily curable, the buyer must give the seller a fair opportunity to remedy it. Seller will not be in breach for failing to pay off the mortgage before receiving payment, but Buyer will be in breach for refusing to comply with the contract.

121. (C)   A fixture is a chattel that has been permanently annexed to real property. It becomes part of the real property and passes with the sale of the property. To determine if a chattel becomes a fixture, the courts look at the manifest intent of the owner at the time of installation. The greater the degree of annexation of the chattel to realty, the stronger the inference of its being a fixture. Since these air conditioning units required a significant alteration of the building, it seems that they were meant to be permanent. (D) is incorrect because air conditioners are not fixtures by nature, it depends on the relative circumstances.

122. (C)   Gertrude tried to create a future interest for Rosalie, called a shifting executory interest, but it will be invalidated because it is too remote and violates the Rule Against Perpetuities. However, the University still holds the land in fee simple on the condition that it be used for agricultural research. If not used for research, the fee divests in favor of Gertrude. This is called a possibility of reverter because there is a possibility that the land will revert to the original grantor.

123. (C)   Fee simple subject to an executory interest is an estate subject to a divesting condition subsequent, which, if the condition occurs, will vest title in a third person rather than the grantor. Although executory interests are subject to the Rule Against Perpetuities, the "charity to charity" exception to the Rule will apply in this question and allow the American Cancer Society's interest to remain valid indefinitely. This fee simple is also determinable (Choice D), but (D) is less specific and not the best answer.

124. (A)   A fee simple subject to a condition subsequent is an estate where the grantor has the power to terminate a grantee's estate on the happening of a specified condition subsequent (i.e., the sale of drugs). This estate differs from a fee simple determinable in that it does not revert until the grantor exercises his right of re-entry, whereas under a fee simple determinable the estate automatically reverts.

125. (B)   The right of a grantor under a fee simple subject to a condition subsequent is called "right of entry for condition broken." (C) is incorrect in the most part because the proper term is "possibility of reverter."

126.   (D)   Under the law of equitable servitudes, one who takes property with notice of a restriction on that property is subject to that restriction. The subdivision serves as constructive notice to Coalco. (B) is incorrect because the corporation is not an intended beneficiary of the Paul-Coalco contract. (C) is incorrect ("Coalco purchased the land..."). (D) is the best answer presented, but remember that equitable servitudes require a written agreement.

127.   (B)   Under a subdivision plan deemed a common development scheme, most courts will enforce the provisions of a covenant even though it is not contained in the violator's deed. The court will assume Homebuilder has "inquiry notice" of the restriction.

128.   (C)   The act of recording a designation for the road will cause the property to vest in the county. (B) is incorrect because the court will probably assume that Coalco had constructive notice of the covenant.

129.   (D)   When a grantor delivers the deed to a third person as an intermediary, the conveyance will be effective if he has surrendered all control over the property conveyed.

130.   (C)   The courts will enforce a reciprocal negative servitude or covenant if the evidence shows that when the sales began, the developer had a common scheme of development that included the lots in question. Whether there are resultant damages is irrelevant.

131.   (C)   A tenant — if he remains in possession — must pay the fair market value of the defective apartment.

132.   (C)   Under the rule of convenience, a class closes when some member of the class can call for a distribution of his share of a class gift. Upon Uncle's death, Rachel's children have the right to receive their distribution. (B) is incorrect because, if Uncle intended to benefit Casper, he would have used more explicit language.

133.   (D)   An easement by prescription is acquired through a process similar to adverse possession and has many of the same requirements. The main distinction lies in that exclusive use of the easement is usually not required.
        Since Rochelle had knowledge and granted permission to use the land, Carlos's use wasn't "hostile to the rights of the true owner"; therefore, a necessary element for adverse acquisition of an easement was absent.

134. (B)   A title search is incomplete until the possession of the land has been examined. If the record does not explain who is in possession, the purchaser must inquire further. Since it is presumed that the buyer conducted a diligent title search, Florence will be charged with inquiry notice that Julius owned the home. The fact that Julius occupied the house for two years simply furthers his rights.

135. (B)   Ameliorative waste is usually an improvement in the character and nature of the premises. Courts will not allow recovery for ameliorative waste if the change increases the value of the premises, the tenant was in possession of the premises for a long time, and the change reflects a change in the character of the neighborhood. In this instance, Tenant may have increased the value of the house for someone who wants to sell souvenirs, but he has reduced the value for residential purposes; therefore Landlord will be able to recover. (A) is generally correct since waste usually lessens a property's value. (C) alone does not entitle a tenant to change the character of the premises.

136. (B)   Esquire could not have exceeded his authority by granting a deed.

137. (B)   The owner of an easement has the obligation to maintain the easement and to avoid unreasonable interference with the servient estate. Strict liability (Choice A) is not imposed.

138. (B)   This clause is valid in all respects. It does not violate the Rule Against Perpetuities, because all conditions will or will not be fulfilled during a life in being.

139. (B)   "Possibility of a reverter" is a future interest left in a grantor who conveys a fee simple determinable. Trump has conveyed a determinable fee because the estate will divest in his favor upon the happening of certain events. If these conditions are not satisfied at some point subsequent to Trump's death, the estate will revert to Trump's heirs.

140. (D)   Eva's use of the view did not provide her with an easement or any other rights to prevent the construction of the billboard. Negative easements have traditionally existed only for rights to light and air and must be in writing. If she had anticipated a neighbor blocking her view, she could have attempted to enter into a valid covenant that would have prohibited the erection of billboards and the like, but since she hadn't, she had no enforceable rights.

141. (A)   Construction on the property of another gives rise to a cause of action regardless of the magnitude of the transgression or condition of the land. Trespass gives rise

to liability regardless of actual damage. Pamela's only defense would be a bona fide boundary dispute or that she had acquired the strip through adverse possession.

142.   (B)   When an owner sells a portion of his property, the existence of a prior use over that portion may give rise to an easement by implication, even though no reference is made to the continuation of that use. (C) is not correct because an easement by reservation can only be created with an express clause in the deed.

143.   (C)   A landowner has no obligation to provide support to artificial structures on his neighbor's land; however, he will be liable for negligence. Structural damage alone (Choice B) does not prove Coalco acted negligently.

144.   (B)   A landowner may bring an action for damage to the natural condition of his property caused by the removal of the lateral support of his land.

145.   (D)   Homeowner could have recovered if Goldco had caused the damage by removal of rocks or soil.

146.   (A)   An easement by implication, which allows a grantee to use the land of a grantor for access to the grantee's own land, arises when the grantor sells a part of his land that has no outlet to a public road except over the remaining portions of his property.

147.   (D)   This clause violates the Rule Against Perpetuities because Phil Spectrum was given an executory interest, which does not technically vest until it becomes possessory. The intention of Madison was to give Spectrum the right to re-enter Square Garden if Meadow Land should fail to provide heat for the tenants, but since Meadow Land and his heirs and assigns might fulfill this condition for longer than a life in being plus twenty-one years, Spectrum's interest is voided by the Rule. The portion of the clause requiring that Spectrum have at least two children before he turns sixty is valid on its own, because it must vest or fail within a life in being.

148.   (A)   Possibility of a reverter is a future interest left in a grantor who conveys a defeasible fee simple estate. Madison conveyed a fee simple subject to an executory interest to Meadow Land when he attempted to give Phil Spectrum the right to re-enter upon the happening of certain events. Unlike fee simple determinables, when an executory interest following a fee simple subject to condition subsequent is invalidated by the Rule Against Perpetuities, it will usually transform the grantee's (Meadow Land's) interest to a fee simple absolute. But in this instance, Madison's last clause granted himself and his heirs a possibility of reverter and maintained the estate's defeasibility.

TORTS CONTENTS

TORTS QUESTIONS

1. The Keystone College of Podiatric Medicine operated a clinic where students under the supervision of the school's faculty examined and treated patients with foot problems without charge. The school included in its clinic's advertisements that "appointments are recommended but not necessary." Eli saw the advertisement on a public bus one morning and decided to go to the clinic to have his bunion treated. Since he didn't have an appointment, Eli sat in the waiting room for two hours. As he stood up to get another magazine from the coffee table, a piece of plaster fell from the ceiling and landed on his foot. He immediately sat down because he was in so much pain. The falling plaster severely aggravated his bunion. Eli sued the school. Is he likely to prevail?

   (A) Yes, if the school knew or should have known about the possibility of falling plaster.

   (B) Yes, but only if an agent of the school knew the plaster was a hazard.

   (C) No, because Eli did not have an appointment.

   (D) No, because the school's treatment was to be gratuitous.

2. Katherine purchased a jar of Chunky Nutty Peanut Butter at the local Food Mart grocery store. She made a sandwich for her son, whose mouth began to bleed profusely after the first bite. After carefully examining the product, she discovered several shards of glass and peanut shells in the peanut butter. The peanut butter was manufactured by the Nutty Butter Co. and placed in jars supplied by a local glass factory. The peanut butter was then sold to a wholesaler from whom Food Mart purchased it. In a product liability suit brought by Katherine, on behalf of her son, against the Nutty Butter Co., which of the following will Katherine **NOT** need to prove for Nutty Butter to be held strictly liable for the injuries?

   (A) The product was not altered from the time it left the defendant's control until it reached the plaintiff.

   (B) Privity between the plaintiff and defendant.

   (C) The defendant was a commercial supplier.

   (D) The product's defect was the actual and proximate cause of the plaintiff's injuries.

3. Kenny, a security officer at Burke Lakefront Airport, was on his way home from a wild evening at the

GO ON TO THE NEXT PAGE

Flats, a local watering hole on Cedar Road. Realizing he was drunk, Kenny drove home in his Ford Bronco truck well within the city-wide speed limit of twenty-five miles per hour. Kenny relaxed at the wheel once he was within a mile of his home. He made a left turn onto Warrensville Center Road northbound where he mistakenly drove on the wrong side of the double yellow line.

Frank was a mechanic who worked for a nearby garage. After work, he customized cars for profit and pleasure. He decided to "see what his latest project could do." This latest project was a hot-pink Chevy Nova that was not yet completed and had only two out of its four brakes installed, but Frank assumed he would be safe because the roads were usually deserted at 2 a.m. He drove the car southbound on Warrensville Center Road at eighty miles per hour.

Just as Frank approached Cedar Road, Kenny turned his Ford Bronco and came straight at him. Frank could have stopped had his car been equipped with four brakes. The cars collided. Frank suffered $4,000 in damages. Kenny's damages were $3,000. After a full and fair civil litigation, both Kenny and Frank were judged to be negligent by a jury of their peers, Frank 60 percent and Kenny 40 percent. Which of the following choices best represents their respective liability?

(A)   If the jurisdiction has a pure comparative negligence statute, Frank will have to pay Kenny $200.

(B)   If the jurisdiction follows the last clear chance doctrine, Kenny will recover $1,800.

(C)   Frank assumed the risk and will not recover in any jurisdiction.

(D)   Frank will recover $1,600 in a contributory negligence jurisdiction.

4.   Dr. Craig was a world-famous heart surgeon who pioneered a life-saving heart bypass treatment. Throughout his distinguished career, he performed hundreds of operations, almost all of them successful. His bedside manner, on the other hand, was less than pleasant, and he frequently alienated patients.

Mrs. Huffenpuff, a cantankerous, sixty-three-year-old widow, was referred to Dr. Craig, who recommended the now routine bypass surgery. Although she sailed through the operation, Mrs. Huffenpuff felt that the scar on her chest was "more unsightly than average." Dr. Craig responded by telling her, not so tactfully, that if she lost 100 pounds, the scar would fade. Mrs. Huffenpuff, after conducting extensive research on the subject, found that the average scar in such a case was a half-inch shorter than hers. She sued for malpractice. The jury found for Dr. Craig. However, the doctor felt that his brilliant reputation was seriously tarnished. Several patients unexplainably canceled their scheduled surgeries a few days after Mrs. Huffenpuff instituted the malpractice suit. If Dr. Craig brings a common law suit against Mrs. Huffenpuff for malicious prosecution, which of the following is the best answer?

(A) Dr. Craig will win the action if he can prove that Mrs. Huffenpuff's suit was lacking probable cause and resulted in damages.

(B) Dr. Craig will win his action if he can prove that Mrs. Huffenpuff was motivated by an improper purpose in bringing her action, and the suit resulted in actual damages to him.

(C) Dr. Craig will win his action if he can prove Mrs. Huffenpuff's action lacked probable cause, she asserted the action for an improper purpose, and the suit resulted in damages to him.

(D) Dr. Craig will not prevail.

5. In which of the following situations has the court erred?

(A) Plaintiff became severely ill after eating popcorn flavored with rancid butter. Plaintiff, who purchased the popcorn at a multiplex theater, brought a product liability action against the theater alleging strict liability. The trial judge ruled in favor of the multiplex theater on the grounds that since the sale of popcorn was subsidiary to the theater's primary business activity of showing movies, it was not a commercial supplier.

(B) Plaintiff, while on a tour of Cole Pineapple's Hawaii cannery, is injured by an exploding boiler and brings a product liability action against the owner alleging strict liability. The trial judge dismissed the action because Cole cans pineapples and does not supply boilers.

(C) Plaintiff, injured in a plane crash, brought a product liability action alleging strict liability against the airline. The trial judge dismissed the case.

(D) Plaintiff, injured in a plane crash, brought a product liability action alleging strict liability against the airplane manufacturer. The trial judge instructed the jury that Plaintiff need not prove negligence.

6. In which of the following four cases will "Plaintiff" most likely not prevail?

(A) Defendant's convertible stalled on an isolated highway. Sensing an imminent thunderstorm, he broke the window of a nearby shack that appeared abandoned and climbed through for shelter from the dangerous storm. Plaintiff, owner of the shack, asserted an action to recover for the damage to his shack.

(B) Defendant loaned $1,000 to Plaintiff, who did not repay the loan when it was due.

GO ON TO THE NEXT PAGE

Defendant complained to Plaintiff one day, when they happened to meet on Main Street. Plaintiff had his toy poodle with him on a leash. Defendant's tone was so hostile that Plaintiff's dog became upset, growled, and barked at Defendant. Defendant struck Plaintiff's dog with his newspaper, causing a slight cut. Plaintiff brought an action against Defendant based on trespass to chattels.

(C)   Plaintiff's employee took home a stereo system from Plaintiff's warehouse without paying for it, used it for a week, and then sold it to Defendant. Defendant, the owner of Wizard Discount Electronics, was unaware that Plaintiff's employee did not rightfully own the stereo system. Defendant sold the system at 20 percent less than his usual price for comparable equipment, during his "After-Christmas Sale." Plaintiff brought an action against Defendant based on conversion.

(D)   Defendant assaulted Robby in Plaintiff's full sight. Defendant thought Plaintiff was a mere passerby, while Plaintiff was, in fact, Robby's brother. Plaintiff brought an action against Defendant based on intentional infliction of emotional distress.

7.   Terry Liar was the editor of the Liar Letter, a high-priced weekly investment letter. The Liar Letter of December 1, 1987, advised, "I have absolutely reliable information from both labor leaders and government officials in South Africa that the long strike of the diamond miners will end this week. South Africa is the world's largest producer of raw diamonds, and the worldwide price of raw diamonds is always affected by occurrences in that country. For example, South African racial unrest has had a substantial effect on the international price of diamonds. The currently inflated price is primarily due to the strike. When the strike is settled, prices will plummet. I cannot overemphasize the certainty with which I make the following recommendations: (1) sell all diamonds held for investment purposes, (2) sell all stock in industry companies that have mines outside South Africa, (3) buy stock in companies with mines in South Africa, (4) buy puts in non-South African mining companies, and (5) for highest return on your investment, purchase options for South African mining companies."

On December 3, having read the Liar Letter, retired accountant Ernest Whinney invested $140,000, his life savings, in South Africa Mining, Ltd., options. On December 7, labor negotiators for the Association of South African Mining Companies announced that they were breaking off negotiations with the miner's labor union because of the union's unreasonable demands. Union members responded with violent rioting, resulting in massive destruction. Due to these events, Whinney's options became worthless less than one week after their acquisition.

If Whinney brings an action against Liar based on deceit, will he prevail?

(A) Yes, because Liar gave erroneous advice that he represented as certain.

(B) Yes, if Liar did not honestly believe his own advice.

(C) No, because investment letters are considered advisory.

(D) No, because there is no implied warranty in a newsletter.

8. Saul, a 110-pound weakling from Tallahassee, Florida, was in New York visiting a friend. Saul went drinking at several of New York's lower-priced establishments, where he succeeded in getting drunk for less than $20, not a small accomplishment in Manhattan.

Saul then went for a stroll north on Sixth Avenue, turning right when he came to Central Park South. Upon passing the Plaza Hotel, Saul noticed former World Heavyweight Champion Michael Spinks leaving the hotel accompanied by three armed bodyguards. All three bodyguards were former offensive linemen at Division I-A colleges. Saul, suffering from an alcohol-induced momentary delusion of grandeur, decided he was going to "scare the living daylights out of Spinks."

Saul walked over to Spinks and said, "I think you are ugly and a coward. To punish you, I am going to knock out your only remaining tooth." Spinks laughed and walked away.

Saul has committed

(A) assault.

(B) assault, if Spinks had an apprehension of being hit by Saul.

(C) assault, if Spinks was afraid of Saul.

(D) none of the above.

9. Hoosier Trucking (HT), a cargo hauler, owned and operated trucks out of its Bloomington offices and depot.

A state civil statute, enacted to ensure that large vehicles would be visible at night, required that "lights must be placed along any moving vehicle at intervals no greater than ten feet and turned on at dusk."

HT owned a twenty-two-foot-long trailer, which by law should have had at least two working lights on each of its sides.

Boilermaker was driving his car south, down a dark West Lafayette road. He approached an intersection, stopped at a stop sign, and saw HT's truck heading west. Since HT's truck lights were out, Boilermaker did not realize that a long trailer was attached to the truck, and he entered the intersection before the truck had cleared it, crashing into the trailer.

Boilermaker should assert an action against HT based on

(A)   strict liability because driving without lights is an ultra-hazardous activity.

(B)   negligence because absence of the working lights can be considered negligence per se.

(C)   negligence per se because absence of working lights is conclusive evidence of negligence.

(D)   negligence per se because violation of a statute automatically creates an irrebuttable presumption of negligence.

10.   Defendant, a driver, will be most likely to succeed in his appeal of which of the following four verdicts?

(A)   Victim was injured in a traffic accident caused by Defendant's negligence. Victim was in excruciating pain due to a compound fracture of his right leg. Idiot, driver of the ambulance, did not properly set Victim's leg before rushing him to the hospital. Debby, a doctor in charge of the emergency room, was also negligent in her treatment of Victim. The leg became gangrenous and had to be amputated at the hip. The jury found that Idiot's negligence alone would have resulted in Victim's leg being amputated at the knee. The amputation at the hip was due to Debby's negligence. The trial judge ruled Defendant must compensate Victim for the loss of his entire leg.

(B)   Victim's car was immobilized after a collision with Defendant's car caused by Defendant's negligence. Victim could have walked away to safety, but instead she stood in front of her car on the well-lit road and waved a flag to prevent further damage to her car. Victim was struck by a car while waving the flag. After three weeks in the hospital, doctors concluded that Victim, steadily recovering, would not suffer any permanent disability. Several days later, Victim contracted pneumonia because of her weakened condition. She died several weeks later of pneumonia-related complications. The jury found that Victim had acted completely without negligence, and the trial judge ruled Defendant should be held civilly liable for Victim's death.

(C)   Roger, a hunter holding a gun and walking along a country road, was so startled when a car, negligently driven by Defendant, crashed into a nearby tree that he accidentally fired his rifle. A bullet from the rifle struck Victim, Roger's son, in the leg. Two weeks later, Victim fell while walking with the help of crutches and broke his other leg. The trial judge ruled Defendant was liable for the damage to both of Victim's legs.

(D) Defendant struck and knocked down a telephone pole due to his negligent driving. Victim was forced to sit in traffic with his car because the pole had blocked the state highway on which he was driving. Victim's car was struck by lightning while waiting, and Victim was electrocuted. Victim was rushed to the hospital, where he received an emergency blood transfusion. Victim recovered from the electrocution, but died ten years later of AIDS contracted from the transfusion. The trial judge ruled Defendant civilly liable for Victim's death.

11. On October 1, 1981, Ronny had his appendix removed by Dr. Iacocca at Pontiac General Hospital. Three days after the operation, Dr. Iacocca told Ronny to rest, drink plenty of water, eat lots of ice cream, and go home. On October 1, 1982, Ronny visited Dr. Iacocca and complained that ever since the operation he felt a sharp pain in his stomach.

"Oh, I wouldn't worry about it," said Dr. Iacocca.

Ronny moved 100 miles away and never saw Dr. Iacocca again. The pain did subside, and he completely forgot about it until October 15, 1986. That was the date when Ronny went to another doctor for a routine check-up. An X-ray showed that Ronny had been carrying a surgical tool in his abdominal cavity. Ronny brought an action against Dr. Iacocca, who moved to dismiss the case due to the statute of limitations. The jurisdiction where the surgery was performed allows five years to commence a malpractice action and follows the majority position as to when the statute begins to run. Which of the following statements is the best answer?

(A) The case should not be heard because the statute begins when the malpractice occurs.

(B) The case should be heard because the statute begins when the doctor-patient relationship terminates.

(C) The case should be heard because the statute begins to run when the malpractice is discovered.

(D) The case should be heard because the statute begins to run at the time the object left inside the body is discovered.

12. Leonard, a truck driver, had thirty years' experience and had been awarded several company commendations for safe driving. Leonard drove down East 5th Street, passing a sign that warned him to take a detour due to demolition work in the area. Leonard did not take the detour and was injured by debris falling from a building in the process of being demolished. If Leonard brings an action against the demolition company, which of the following is most accurate?

GO ON TO THE NEXT PAGE

(A)   Leonard will recover because demolition is an ultra-hazardous activity.

(B)   Leonard will recover under strict liability.

(C)   If Leonard's ignoring the warning sign is considered negligent, he will not recover.

(D)   If Leonard read the sign, he may be found to have assumed the risk of injury.

13.   Henry knew Friday, June 22, was going to be a rough day, but it was even rougher than he expected. At 3 p.m., Henry waited apprehensively behind the steering wheel of his school bus as the young students chanted, "No more pencils, no more books, no more teachers ugly looks" and sang Alice Cooper's "School's Out Forever."

   Henry drove off, realizing it was useless to ask the students to be seated or to be quiet. The celebrations began relatively innocently with the emptying of loose-leafs out the windows of the bus into the dry and warm June breeze, but then progressed further, culminating with many students breaking windows and lights, ripping seats, and causing whatever damage their juvenile strength could muster and their minds could conjure up. After destroying everything that they could get their hands on, the contented children returned to singing. Henry decided to pass three scheduled stops and take the children to a nearby police station.

   Mallisa, a passenger seated in the rear of the bus, was so engrossed in reading Tolstoy's *War and Peace*

that she did not even notice the commotion. Mallisa sued for false imprisonment.

   Henry's best defense will be

(A)   public necessity

(B)   private necessity

(C)   self-defense

(D)   justification

14.   Billy dictated a letter to his secretary that contained the following sentence: "In sum, Mr. Johnson, it seems quite obvious to me that Jerry's dealings have been consistently dishonest and certainly unethical, and his character makes him a bad risk for a loan from your bank."

   After dictating the letter, Billy thought for a moment and then told his secretary, "Do me a favor. Destroy the letter I just dictated. There's no reason to type it. Why should I help out the bank? They charge me eight dollars to certify a check."

   The letter was never typed, and no one other than Jerry found out about the letter's contents. If Jerry asserts a defamation action against Billy

(A)   the action will fail because of the absence of publication.

(B)   the action will fail because Jerry has not suffered damages.

(C)   an action based on slander will succeed, but a similar action based on libel will fail.

(D)   an action based on libel will most likely succeed, but a similar action based on slander will probably fail.

15.   Gabby Pressman, a homeless middle-aged woman, lived on a sidewalk heating vent on Second Avenue in Manhattan's exclusive Upper East Side. Formerly a secretary for ten years, she became homeless when she decided that she preferred the outdoor life to the comfort of having four walls and a roof. Gabby consistently refused offers of assistance and shelter from city officials. Late at night, she found plenty of good hot food to eat by sorting through the garbage of the area's fine restaurants. Gabby decided to spend the night at the Manhattan Women's Shelter one evening after word had spread among East Side street people that the police were about to go out with psychiatrists to pick up deranged homeless people and take them to Bellevue Hospital for psychiatric testing.

The Manhattan Women's Shelter was owned and operated by New York Charities (NYC), a nonprofit corporation. It relied on private donations and federal grants. As she waited to speak to a social worker, a scaffold, used to change light bulbs, collapsed on top of Pressman, causing her serious injury. Sky High, Inc., was an independent contractor engaged in the business of changing the light bulbs in all NYC shelters. Sky High had a reputation in New York as a dangerously sloppy company. NYC knew of this reputation but was politically motivated to retain Sky High because the company president had once been homeless.

If Gabby Pressman asserted an action against NYC for injuries sustained, which of the following choices is the best?

(A)   The trial judge should dismiss the action because NYC is a nonprofit organization.

(B)   NYC will prevail if it could not have known of the danger through reasonable inspection.

(C)   NYC will prevail because an employer is not responsible for the negligence of an independent contractor.

(D)   Gabby Pressman will prevail because she was an invitee.

16.   Yossi was employed as a laborer by Clayton Landscapers, a firm that maintained the lawns and gardens of homeowners residing in the affluent St. Louis suburbs. Yossi resented his employers. He felt his work was extremely difficult even for a man as talented as he. He was especially bitter that Clayton Landscapers paid only the minimum wage without a health plan or any other perquisites. Yossi found this to be insufficient compensation when he had to endure a daily commute from East St. Louis and support a family. He also believed that Clayton Landscapers operated at a high profit margin. They required their clients to sign yearly contracts, but did not provide any services in the winter months.

GO ON TO THE NEXT PAGE

One day, Yossi decided he would make sure that he received his due share. Instead of reporting to work that day, Yossi knocked on the doors of Clayton Landscapers' clients and explained that, as an added convenience, they could pay him in cash instead of mailing a check to Clayton Landscapers. The company found out about Yossi's activities after failing to receive $22,000 worth of checks from their customers. Which of the following choices is the best answer?

(A)   Yossi cannot be charged with conversion, because intangibles may not form the basis for a conversion suit.

(B)   Embezzlement is the offense that Yossi has committed.

(C)   Yossi will be liable to Clayton for conversion.

(D)   Yossi will be liable to Clayton for interference with contractual advantage.

17.   Chelm Bank was chartered to operate in the state of Nebraska in 1869. Deposits were insured by the Federal Savings and Loan Insurance Corp. Corcoran was the president of the bank, which had assets of five billion dollars. Chelm was poorly managed, but its banks were all nicely maintained, and its slick advertising campaigns helped the bank keep a favorable public image.

Entrepreneur owned seven video stores in the Omaha metropolitan area. In 1978, she borrowed $3,000 from her spinster aunt to buy some movies and rent them from a six-foot counter located in a candy store. The counter was leased to Entrepreneur for fifty dollars per month. Business was so brisk she rolled over her receipts to buy more tapes. Within six months, she needed much more space and rented her own store. The store performed extremely well, and because it was Omaha's first video store, she was able to rent tapes for five dollars per night. She opened one store at a time, filling new stores with tapes that no longer rented at other locations because they had been on the shelves for months or years.

By 1984, Entrepreneur had a total of 13,200 movies in the inventories of her seven stores. The movies had cost Entrepreneur a total of $686,400 and had an estimated wholesale market value of $377,520. Used tapes were in great demand because video stores were opening all over the country and new store owners tried to stock their inventories with used movies to save costs. Entrepreneur was acutely aware of the value of her movies. She made a practice of selling copies of tapes she no longer needed to used tape dealers. These dealers, who brokered used tapes, had surfaced with the video boom. When the movie *Terms of Endearment* was first issued, Entrepreneur purchased seventy copies of the movie that retailed for $79.95 per tape. During the two months after the movie was released, she rented virtually every copy of this movie nightly. After two months, many customers had seen the movie and its rental slowed to a trickle. Entrepreneur kept two copies per store and sold the remaining tapes to a used tape dealer for thirty dollars each. The dealer then sold them to newly opened stores for about forty-five dollars per tape.

In 1984, Entrepreneur decided to open four new "super stores," each stocking five thousand movies. She felt that consumers would prefer to rent from stores that had a wider selection. She was also convinced that these stores would intimidate competitors with less capital to lay out.

She requested a loan of $350,000 from several banks, deciding to use her personal savings for the balance of the investment. The banks wanted collateral, and Entrepreneur offered her inventory. Each banker she consulted checked a little book, and all the books stated that video movies were to be valued at three dollars per movie. Entrepreneur explained that her movies were worth much more, and she offered to prove their value, but all she received was sympathy.

Finally, Entrepreneur decided to put up $350,000 in bearer bonds to secure a loan from Chelm Bank. She handed the bonds to Corcoran to be held until she paid back the loan on January 2, 1988. On that date, Entrepreneur made her last payment and asked for her bonds. Corcoran could not find the bonds, for which no record of ownership is kept. Corcoran had, in fact, accidentally used the bonds to house train his puppy in 1984. If Entrepreneur brings a tort action against Chelm, the court should rule the bank, through Corcoran as its agent, is liable for

(A)   trespass to chattels

(B)   conversion

(C)   negligence

(D)   nothing that will give rise to liability

Questions 18-20 are based upon the following fact situation.

Elmo took his girlfriend to a comedy club where they saw several up-and-coming talents. It was a cold winter night toward the end of February. Elmo was bundled up in his new white fox fur coat and matching hat. Elmo and his date had such a good time that they stayed for hours and enjoyed several acts. The club showcased some known comedians, one of whom had recently appeared on many national talk shows, and two men Elmo recognized from a beer commercial. Both Elmo and his date consumed more than the club's minimum of two drinks. Elmo is a big guy; his blood alcohol level was below that which would seriously impair his judgment.

When he left the club, Elmo mistakenly took someone else's hat.

18.   Assume for this question only that Elmo did not realize the hat was not his own until three months later. After realizing his mistake, Elmo immediately returned the hat to the comedy club's "lost and found." Elmo will most likely be liable to the hat's owner for

(A)   trespass to chattels

(B)   conversion

(C)   neither trespass to chattels nor conversion, because the hat was returned to its rightful owner

GO ON TO THE NEXT PAGE

(D)   neither trespass to chattels
       nor conversion, because Elmo
       acted in good faith

19.   Assume for this question only that, as
       Elmo left the club, a strong wind
       blew the hat off his head and into a
       sewer. He tried to retrieve it from
       the sewer by dangling a string with a
       chewed piece of gum on the end into
       the dark abyss, but he had no luck.
       All he managed to retrieve was fifty-
       nine cents. Elmo will most likely be
       liable to the hat's owner for

       (A)   trespass to chattels

       (B)   conversion

       (C)   neither trespass to chattels
              nor conversion, because the
              wind was a superseding
              intervening cause

       (D)   neither trespass to chattels
              nor conversion, because Elmo
              acted in good faith

20.   Assume for this question only that
       Elmo knowingly took the wrong hat.
       As he crossed the street, he changed
       his mind and returned it. Elmo will
       most likely be liable to the hat's
       owner for

       (A)   trespass to chattels

       (B)   conversion

       (C)   neither trespass to chattels
              nor conversion, because he
              returned the hat right away

       (D)   both trespass to chattels and
              conversion

21.   Larry, a forty-five-year-old fading
       soap opera star, purchased a cigarette
       lighter manufactured by Acme
       Matches & Lighters. The package
       boldly stated that "this lighter is
       guaranteed to work problem-free for
       ten years or your money back."
       Three days later, it exploded and
       caused minor, but permanent,
       cosmetic damage to his face. If Larry
       brings a product liability action
       against the manufacturer to recover
       the lost economic value of his good
       looks, under which theory is he most
       likely to recover?

       (A)   Implied warranty of fitness

       (B)   Negligence

       (C)   Strict liability

       (D)   Express warranty

22.   Lenny owned a store on the
       boardwalk in Atlantic City that he
       had rented to Benny for twenty-three
       years under a tenancy at will. Benny
       ran a retail salt-water taffy operation
       in the space he leased. When New
       Jersey legalized gambling in Atlantic
       City, Lenny notified Benny that he
       was going to triple the store's rent.
       Benny was happy to pay the
       increased rent because the added
       traffic more than tripled his volume
       and the new breed of tourist paid for
       taffy without looking at the price.
           Lenny received many offers
       from developers interested in
       purchasing his store, but he refused
       to sell. Lenny's wife begged him to
       accept the offers, some of which
       were for more money than Lenny
       ever dreamed he would have, but
       Lenny was convinced that the value

of the property would continue to increase.

Casinos International, a Nevada corporation, wanted Lenny's store because they had secretly acquired several nearby properties. After Lenny refused an offer of three million dollars in cash, Casinos sent Arnold Intimidator, one of their employees, to visit Benny. Intimidator, a huge man wearing a pinstripe suit, black shirt, and white tie, walked into the salt-water taffy store carrying a violin case. He told Benny about a retailer in Vegas who stayed longer than he was welcome when Casinos wanted his store: "The man died a slow, painful death." Benny called Lenny, as soon as Intimidator left, and told him he was retiring.

Lenny should assert an action against Casinos International based upon

(A)   interference with prospective advantage.

(B)   interference with existing contract.

(C)   interference with business relations.

(D)   intimidation.

23.   Dorothy bought a little house surrounded by a white picket fence in Topeka. Dorothy's house was not the kind of place that impressed her friends and family, but Dorothy loved it. After a hard day's work, she found it an ideal environment in which to relax with her puppy.

When she came home one day, a man named Mark introduced himself as her new neighbor. Mark asked Dorothy to go to dinner, and she agreed because she thought he was cute.

After that first date, Mark asked Dorothy to dinner again, but she refused. She decided that he was a creep. Dorothy had paid for the entire dinner because Mark forgot his wallet. Mark refused to accept Dorothy's rejection and kept calling her. At first, he called every few days, but later the calls became more frequent, often several times a day until long past midnight, and they were often threatening. Dorothy was extremely disturbed by these calls. They also prevented her from getting eight hours of sleep each night. She lost her job one day when she fell asleep at her desk. Dorothy has grounds to assert an action based on

(A)   private nuisance.

(B)   intentional infliction of emotional distress.

(C)   invasion of privacy.

(D)   all of the above.

24.   Farmer Jack hated the railroad. Several times a day, he stopped his tractor, took a cigarette break, and watched a noisy train spewing black smoke as it passed his farm. Farmer Jack was convinced that the noise, vibrations, and especially the smoke from the train damaged his organic crops.

On November 1, a strike idled all trains passing Farmer Jack's

GO ON TO THE NEXT PAGE

property, and Jack was in ecstasy. Farmer Jim was not pleased. He had ten thousand bushels of apples loaded on an idled train, and the apples had begun to rot. On December 6, the strike was settled. Farmer Jack, having become accustomed to the peace and quiet, hated the trains more than ever, and, out of anger and desperation, blocked the railroad tracks with an old car. The train carrying Farmer Jim's apples struck the car and derailed. The accident caused Farmer Jim's apples to be delayed an additional six days.

In a suit asserted by Farmer Jim against Farmer Jack, Farmer Jim should

(A)   not recover, because Farmer Jack is not responsible for the strike.

(B)   not recover, because of the alternative causes doctrine.

(C)   recover the part of the loss due to Farmer Jack's actions.

(D)   recover the difference between the value of the apples when delivered and the value had the apples not been spoiled.

25.   Emile could not find a parking spot in his grocer's lot. He decided to park his car in a nearby driveway because he was in a hurry. A car was already in the driveway that Emile pulled into, but Emile simply left his car at the beginning of the driveway, blocking the sidewalk. He didn't think anyone would be inconvenienced. Since all he needed was a container of orange juice, he planned to be gone for less than a minute.

While Emile was in the store, Tyke, a small boy, rode toward Emile's car on his tricycle. He could not pass, because the sidewalk was blocked. Tyke rode into the street to get around the car and was struck by an automobile negligently driven by Joe. Tyke received nothing more than bruises and cuts, but he was rushed to General Hospital, where an intern confused him with another patient who was named Spike and brought him into surgery to have his spleen removed. While recovering from the surgery, Tyke died from an overdose of a sedative administered by the attending anesthesiologist. Which of the following choices is **NOT** correct?

(A)   Emile's parked car was a cause in fact and a legal cause of the car's striking Tyke.

(B)   If Tyke's estate asserts an action against Emile for the death of Tyke, the estate will prevail.

(C)   The anesthesiologist's mistake was a superseding cause.

(D)   The Joe-Tyke accident was a foreseeable consequence of Emile's actions.

Questions 26-27 are based upon the following fact situation.

Bubba, a seven-year-old boy, was nervous and full of aggression. Bubba's father, a psychiatrist, encouraged Bubba to vent his anger. "If someone or something bothers you, let them have it," Bubba was told by his father. Bubba followed his father's advice, wrecking property and bruising his friends on several occasions. One day, Bubba was in an especially bad mood because he had struck out four times in his little league baseball game. He smashed two large window panes of the First National Bank while walking home. "Why did you do that?" asked Bones, Bubba's best friend. Bubba proceeded to break four of Bones's front teeth.

26. If First National Bank asserts a claim against Bubba's parents, is the bank likely to prevail?

    (A) Yes, because parents of a minor are strictly liable for the torts of their minor child.

    (B) Yes, because Bubba was encouraged to vent his anger.

    (C) No, because a parent is not liable for the torts of his child.

    (D) No, because Bubba was too young to form the requisite intent.

27. If Bones brings suit against Bubba, is he likely to prevail?

    (A) Yes, because Bubba was of sufficient age to understand that his actions were wrong.

    (B) Yes, because Bubba intentionally harmed Bones.

    (C) No, because Bubba's parents were solely responsible for his action.

    (D) No, because a child Bubba's age cannot be liable in tort.

Questions 28-31 are based upon the following fact situation.

Shikker was severely inebriated. He walked into a store and asked questions in a loud and abrasive manner. Salesman, an employee of Storekeeper, told Storekeeper, "This guy is drunk as a skunk." Shikker was insulted and said to Salesman, "If I wasn't in such a good mood, I would flatten your face." Shikker then prodded Salesman's shoulder with his index finger. Storekeeper called over two other employees and told them to "take care of this bum." The employees shoved Shikker into Storekeeper's car over Shikker's protests and dropped him off on a state road. Shikker wandered into the middle of the road and was hit by a bus just five minutes after having been thrown out of the car.

28. If Salesman brings an action against Shikker, his best cause of action will be for

    (A) assault

    (B) battery

    (C) defamation

    (D) intentional infliction of emotional distress

29. If Shikker sues Salesman for defamation, is he likely to prevail?

    (A) Yes, because Shikker's reputation was damaged.

    (B) Yes, because Shikker was insulted.

(C)   Yes, because the statements were slander per se.

(D)   No, because the statement did not cause him special damages.

30.   Shikker is most likely to recover from Storekeeper in which of the following claims?

(A)   violation of the Civil Rights Act

(B)   strict liability for ejectment

(C)   negligence because he should have known Shikker was drunk

(D)   false imprisonment for having him thrown in the car

31.   Shikker is most likely to recover from Storekeeper in a suit for damages suffered when he was hit by the car by arguing that

(A)   Storekeeper is liable for his employee's, in the course of their employment, negligently placing a drunk in peril

(B)   Shikker was an invitee

(C)   Storekeeper guarantees the safety of his customers

(D)   Storekeeper was not privileged to eject Shikker

Questions 32-35 are based upon the following fact situation.

Stroh, a fifteen-year-old girl, was staying at a neighbor's house for a week while her parents were away on vacation. She went back to her own house after school one day and took the keys to her father's car. The minimum legal driving age of the state in which Stroh lives is sixteen. Stroh opened the garage door, got behind the wheel of her father's new sports car, started the engine, and cruised over to a local strip of road perfect for drag racing. Stroh revved her engine, floored the accelerator, and within seconds reached a speed of ninety miles per hour. She watched with amazement as the speedometer's needle disappeared. Stroh's town had enacted a statute prohibiting people from driving in excess of sixty miles per hour on any of its roads.

Stroh did not slow down as she approached a railroad crossing. She knew that the crossing was equipped with flashing lights that signaled whenever a train was passing. No lights were flashing as Stroh approached the tracks. The lights had malfunctioned. Stroh drove across the tracks while a train was rapidly plowing through. The train struck the back of Stroh's car. The tiny sports car flipped over three times. Stroh emerged remarkably with only minor cuts and bruises, but she was a hemophiliac and bled to death from her apparently minor cuts. Her estate filed suit against Detroit Railroad, owners of the train, track, and signal lights. Subsequent investigation showed that the signal had been malfunctioning for three weeks.

32.   What effect will Stroh's age and lack of a driver's license have on her estate's action?

(A)   It proves she was contributorily negligent.

(B)   It makes her a trespasser on the state roads; therefore, Detroit Railroad's only duty was to refrain from willful and wanton conduct.

(C)   It does not release Detroit Railroad from any liability.

(D)   It prevents Stroh from invoking the doctrine of last clear chance.

33.   Will the fact that Stroh was speeding defeat her cause of action?

(A)   Yes, because she was contributorily negligent.

(B)   Yes, because had Stroh been driving below the speed limit she would not have been on the tracks when the train passed.

(C)   No, because the accident was not caused by her speeding.

(D)   No, because Detroit Railroad is liable on the theory of *res ipsa loquitur*.

34.   Assume for this question only that Detroit Railroad is found liable for Stroh's injuries. Will Detroit also be held responsible for Stroh's death?

(A)   Yes, because Detroit should have known that fatalities are the foreseeable result of the broken signals.

(B)   Yes, despite the fact that death is not a common result of an accident that causes minor cuts and bruises.

(C)   No, because hemophilia is a rare disease.

(D)   No, because an ordinary person would have suffered minor injuries.

35.   The trial judge should not allow the jury to consider the fact that Stroh violated the city speeding ordinance because

(A)   the jury would be forced to conclude that Stroh was the cause of her own harm.

(B)   Stroh's estate has not denied the fact.

(C)   the injury to Stroh was not the type of harm that the statute was designed to protect.

(D)   Detroit's negligence was a superseding intervening cause.

Questions 36-37 are based upon the following fact situation.

Homeowner purchased a lawnmower from E.J. Corvairs. The mower, manufactured by Green Thumb, had the following cautionary statement printed on it in large red letters: "Warning, this lawnmower has exposed blades. Keep children away. It can be very dangerous." Homeowner left his mower outside on the lawn. He was about to mow the grass, but first he went inside his house to refresh himself with a drink of lemonade. Junior, Homeowner's five-year-old son, was curious about the inner workings of a lawn mower and stuck his hand inside the mower. The

GO ON TO THE NEXT PAGE

blades were whirring. Two fingers on Junior's right hand were severed and chopped up so badly that no surgeon could attempt to save them. A small piece of one bone was shot out of the mower, striking Junior in his left eye and causing him a permanent partial loss of vision.

36.   If a product liability suit is brought on Junior's behalf based on Green Thumb's strict liability, Junior must establish that

   (A)   the blades' shield conformed with the design standard prevalent in the community.

   (B)   the mower was negligently constructed.

   (C)   the mower had a design defect that made it unreasonably dangerous.

   (D)   the warning was insufficient.

37.   If Junior brings a strict liability action against E.J. Corvairs, he must establish that

   (A)   the mower had not been substantially altered after purchase

   (B)   his parents were in privity with E.J. Corvairs

   (C)   E.J. Corvairs was involved in the design

   (D)   E.J. Corvairs was aware, or should have been aware, of the hazardous design

Questions 38-40 are based upon the following fact situation.

Jeff thanked Quick at Quick's Repair Garage for repairing his car's steering column, paid him, and drove away. Quick forgot to tell Jeff that he had not found time to repair the car. Jeff saw Employee, one of Quick's mechanics, walking home, and offered him a ride. Employee knew that Jeff's car had not been repaired. He also knew that Jeff thought it had been fixed, but he kept this information to himself because Employee and Jeff were good friends, and Employee didn't want to ruin Jeff's day.

It was a beautiful spring day. Jeff was driving with his windows open, well within the speed limit, casually appreciating the smell of the early evening air, when Wendy opened the door of her parked car. She had seen Jeff's car approaching, but reasoned that, if she moved quickly, she could close her door in plenty of time. Jeff tried to swerve out of the way of the open door, but his wheel locked because of the malfunctioning steering column. Both Employee and Jeff were seriously injured. Had the steering column been repaired, the collision could have been avoided.

38.   If Employee asserts a claim against Wendy in a pure comparative negligence jurisdiction, will Employee recover?

   (A)   Yes, but only a percentage of his damages as calculated from the relative negligence of himself and Wendy.

   (B)   Yes, if Employee's negligence is determined to be less than 50 percent.

   (C)   No, because the collision was caused by the defective steering column.

(D)   No, because Employee had the last clear chance.

39.   If Jeff brings suit against Wendy, is he likely to prevail?

(A)   Yes, because Jeff reasonably believed the car was repaired, and Wendy was negligent in opening her door.

(B)   Yes, but the amount of the recovery will be reduced because Employee was also negligent.

(C)   No, because the negligence of Quick's Repair and Employee superseded Wendy's negligence.

(D)   No, because Wendy did not assume the risk that his steering column would malfunction.

40.   If Jeff asserts a claim against Quick's Repair, he will most likely

(A)   recover under the theory of strict liability

(B)   recover under the theory of negligence

(C)   not recover, because Quick's Repair did not attempt to repair the vehicle

(D)   not recover, because Employee's failure to warn Jeff was a superseding cause relieving Quick of negligence

Questions 41-48 are based upon the following fact situation.

Constructor, a construction worker, was in a designated hard hat area. According to state statute, construction workers must wear protective helmets in designated hard hat areas. Constructor was eating his lunch and took his helmet off to use it as a seat.

Careless decided to sneak into the City Club located next door to the construction site. Careless was not a member of this Club and was technically not permitted to be in the building. A city ordinance established that to enter a private club without proper authorization was a misdemeanor. Careless took an elevator up to the Club's rooftop lounge, sat down on a lounge chair by the pool, sipped a can of soda pop that the porter brought him, and enjoyed the spectacular view of the city from 400 feet above the street.

After Careless drank half the can of soda pop, he had quenched his thirst. Careless nonchalantly tossed the can over the protective gate that ran along the roof's perimeter. The can plummeted 400 feet to the street by the construction site, grazing Constructor's shoulder. The impact was so slight that a typical person would not have been seriously injured, but Constructor was in the midst of recovery from a serious bone fracture. The bones of his shoulder were held together by surgical pins. The can shattered the surgical work in Constructor's shoulder. The pain was so great that Constructor lost consciousness, toppled into a heap on the ground, and smashed a watch that he kept in his pocket. It was a precious family heirloom worth five thousand dollars. A city ordinance provides that it is illegal to throw objects from a rooftop. Another ordinance makes it illegal to litter. Constructor brought an action against Careless.

GO ON TO THE NEXT PAGE

41. To determine negligence, Careless's conduct will be judged by the standard

    (A) of a reasonable person of Careless's age and gender

    (B) set by the city ordinance forbidding the throwing of objects from rooftops

    (C) of a reasonable person and by the relevant city ordinance

    (D) of a *situs inversus*

42. Constructor's violation of the hard hat statute

    (A) was the sole cause of his injury

    (B) was not a cause of his injury

    (C) was a superseding cause of the injury

    (D) was a concurring factual cause of the injury

43. Careless might try to assert the defense of

    (A) *respondeat superior*

    (B) *res ipsa loquitur*

    (C) negligence per se

    (D) contributory negligence

44. The fact that Careless violated the city ordinance policing illegal entry to a club

    (A) will disqualify him as a witness

    (B) will not affect his liability to Constructor

    (C) makes Careless absolutely liable

    (D) makes Careless liable as a trespasser

45. Assume for this question only that Careless is found liable for throwing the can of soda pop that grazed Constructor's shoulder. Is Careless liable for injuries sustained by Constructor because his shoulder was especially sensitive?

    (A) No, unless a nonsensitive person occasionally had a similar reaction.

    (B) No, because shoulders held together with pins are unforeseeable.

    (C) Yes, because Careless could have predicted the results of his actions.

    (D) Yes, regardless of the injury's foreseeability.

46. The violation of the hard hat statute by Constructor should not defeat his cause of action because

    (A) the last clear chance doctrine applies

    (B) Careless was more negligent than Constructor

(C)   this is not the type of injury the statute intends to prevent

(D)   Constructor did not assume the risk of Careless's littering

47.   If Careless is found liable for Constructor's physical injuries, he will

(A)   also be held liable for the cost Constructor's family paid for the watch

(B)   also be held liable for the fair market value of the watch

(C)   also be held liable for the sentimental value of the watch

(D)   not be held liable for the watch, because Constructor was negligent to keep it in his pocket

48.   The jury should not be allowed to consider the hard hat statute, because

(A)   Careless's conduct was a superseding cause as a matter of law

(B)   the injury was not of the type the statute was designed to prevent

(C)   the actual cause is not disputed

(D)   Careless acted without malice

Questions 49-53 are based upon the following fact situation.

Hensly's Auto Collision buys wrecked cars, disassembles them for their parts, and rebuilds them. Hensly obtains most of his additional parts from junkyards, but he occasionally needs to buy new parts.

Miss Margaret, owner of Housing Scheme Transport, purchased a van that Hensly rebuilt from a wreck. Miss Margaret informed Hensly that the van's snow tires were acceptable for her purposes because, though the treads were almost bare, the van was to be driven in a warm climate where it does not snow.

Hensly agreed to install four brand new radial tires purchased from Bobby's Tyre Mart and manufactured by Carenage Tyres. Carenage Tyres had recently received an award from the St. George's Manufacturing Association for its exemplary inspection procedures.

Two days after putting the van into service, Crispin, an employee of Miss Margaret, was involved in an accident with the van during which he sprained his right ankle. The van was fixed within two hours, but Crispin was unable to drive for three days. Miss Margaret could not find another driver.

49.   Assume for this question only that the trier of fact concluded that the accident was caused by the van's front axle falling out. Miss Margaret brought a product liability action based on strict liability in tort against Hensly for her loss of income due to Crispin's injury. Will Miss Margaret prevail?

(A)   Yes, because Hensly was aware that the van was to be used in the transport business.

(B)   Yes, because Hensly was in effect the manufacturer and,

GO ON TO THE NEXT PAGE

therefore, was the legal cause of the accident.

(C)   No, because there was no privity of contract between Hensly and Crispin.

(D)   No, because the compensable damages will not include loss of income due to an employee's injury.

50.   Assume for this question only that the trier of fact determined that the accident was caused when the front axle fell out. This was due to faulty installation of the tires which had dangerously loosened the front axle. The van struck Mellow, who was standing on the sidewalk at the time. If Mellow brings an action against Hensly based on strict liability in tort, which of the following is **incorrect**?

(A)   He will prevail because his injuries were a direct result of defective installation of the tires.

(B)   He will prevail even though the van was rebuilt.

(C)   He will prevail even though he was a bystander.

(D)   He will not prevail, because there is no privity between Hensly and Mellow.

51.   Assume for this question only that the trier of fact concluded that the accident was caused by the van's axle falling out of the front end, but could not attribute the fault for the axle's falling. If Crispin brings an action based on strict liability in tort against

Grenville Motors, the original manufacturer of the van, will he prevail?

(A)   Yes, if the axle had not been altered since it left the Grenville Motor Company showroom.

(B)   Yes, because the accident was a foreseeable result of a faulty axle.

(C)   No, because Hensly had rebuilt the van.

(D)   No, because there was no privity of contract between Crispin and Grenville.

52.   Assume for this question only that the trier of fact concluded that the accident was caused by a manufacturing defect in the left front tire. In an action brought by Crispin against Hensly, Crispin's cause of action would be under the theory of

(A)   negligence, arguing *res ipsa loquitur*

(B)   express warranty

(C)   negligence in dealing with an ultra-hazardous product

(D)   strict liability

53.   Assume for this question only that the trier of fact determined that the accident was caused by a slow leak in the front left tire incurred when Crispin stopped to visit his girlfriend in a junkyard full of broken glass. Carenage Tyre's best defense to an

action based in strict liability in tort brought by Crispin is

(A)   lack of privity of contract

(B)   contributory negligence

(C)   Carenage inspected the tire for defects with its award-winning inspection team

(D)   the tires were subjected to an improper use

54.   Dr. Mun E. Grubber was vacationing on lovely Grand Anse Beach. Grand Anse is located in a jurisdiction that has a Good Samaritan statute. Several feet away from where Dr. Grubber stood, another vacationer was surrounded by a crowd. Grubber casually walked over and asked another bystander what was happening. "A big insect bit Denise, and, all of a sudden, Denise was grabbing her neck and choking," replied the bystander.

   No one in the very confused and hysterical crowd knew what to do for Denise. They stood gawking at her. Dr. Grubber calmly said, "She is suffering from anaphylactic shock. All she needs is some medication." Dr. Grubber had the medication in his hotel room, seventy-five yards away, but he chose to enjoy the suddenly desolate adjacent portion of the beach. He lay down his towel, made himself comfortable, and certainly did not wish to walk all the way back to his hotel. Denise was rushed to the nearest hospital, Grenada General, but the ride took almost a half-hour. By the time the ambulance arrived at the hospital, it was too late. Denise had already passed away.

   If Denise's estate asserts a claim against Dr. Mun E. Grubber for wrongful death, is the estate likely to prevail?

(A)   Yes, because a physician is required to provide assistance in a Good Samaritan jurisdiction.

(B)   Yes, because Dr. Grubber was the proximate cause of Denise's death.

(C)   No, because Dr. Grubber assumed the hospital would easily cure Denise.

(D)   No, because Dr. Grubber did not place Denise in peril.

55.   Redhead was scheduled to fly on Trans Wreck Airlines. She was leaving home for a year to study abroad and had many valuables in a bag that she was planning to carry onto the plane. Jerko, an employee of Trans Wreck, decided to hassle Redhead out of a demented hatred for people with red hair. Jerko alerted Redhead that she was suspected of carrying explosives in her bag and asked her several brief questions at the check-in counter. Jerko told Redhead that her bag would have to be searched at a nearby office and she could watch if she wanted, or she could leave and pick the bag up before boarding the plane. Redhead decided to watch the bag being searched. Jerko searched the bag and then put it aside. Redhead politely reminded

GO ON TO THE NEXT PAGE

him that her flight was scheduled to leave in five minutes. "Go on the plane, we'll send the bag to you," he replied. Redhead decided to stay with the bag and missed the flight.

If Redhead asserts an action for false imprisonment against Trans Wreck Airlines, will Redhead prevail?

(A)   Yes, if Jerko held the bag with the intent of forcing Redhead to stay.

(B)   No, because Redhead was free to leave at any time.

(C)   No, because Redhead was never confined.

(D)   No, because only Redhead's bag was inspected.

Questions 56-60 are based upon the following fact situation.

Feeder owns an exclusive restaurant set in a tranquil wooded area along the Trout River. The restaurant offers views of the river, and Feeder sets up tables outdoors in the summer. Nukeco is a privately owned utility that owns Two Mile Island, a nuclear reactor a mile upstream from Feeder's restaurant. Nukeco uses the river to cool its reactors. The water temperature further upstream from the reactor averages 65 degrees in the summer; below the reactor, the water temperature sometimes reaches 95 degrees because of the heat generated by the power plant. Thousands of trout and other fish swimming downstream were killed by the heat. Many of the dead fish floated behind Feeder's restaurant. Feeder tried cleaning them up, but to no avail. His restaurant smelled like dead fish, and his business dropped so quickly that he was forced to close down. Feeder lives with his wife and eleven children in an apartment above the restaurant. He must keep his windows closed all year round to partially eliminate the smell.

56.   If Feeder asserts an action based on private nuisance against Nukeco, Feeder will

(A)   prevail, if he can prove that Nukeco's actions unreasonably interfere with Feeder's use and enjoyment of his property

(B)   prevail, if he can prove that the powerplant interferes with Feeder's business and restaurant

(C)   not prevail, because the plant was so far away that the damages must have been unintentional

(D)   not prevail, because the value of a restaurant is inconsequential when compared to a billion dollar power plant

57.   Feeder's chances of having Nukeco found liable for nuisance would be helped **LEAST** by which of the following arguments?

(A)   Nukeco had prior knowledge of the effects on the stream.

(B)   Nukeco would be able to afford a settlement without undue hardship.

(C)   The dead fish are also disturbing local wildlife.

(D)   Feeder tried to insulate his restaurant to keep out the smell.

58.   Assume for this question only that Feeder wins his action against Nukeco for private nuisance. Feeder has prayed for injunctive relief. Most likely, the remedy granted will be

    (A)   injunctive relief

    (B)   specific performance

    (C)   monetary compensation

    (D)   nominal damages

59.   Nukeco had a very large work of modern art in front of the reactor. Feederette, Feeder's nine-year-old daughter, walked around the reactor's grounds looking for flowers to pick. Upon discovering the art, she climbed on it to play. On her way down, Feederette slipped, fell, and broke her neck. In a suit against Nukeco, may Feederette invoke the attractive nuisance doctrine?

    (A)   Yes, if Nukeco knew the art might attract children and that it would be dangerous to them.

    (B)   Yes, under strict liability.

    (C)   No, because artwork is a public amenity, not a nuisance.

    (D)   No, because Feederette was not attracted to the area by the art work.

60.   In discussing private nuisance, which of the following choices is most accurate?

    (A)   The prevention of dangerous activities of a party are of paramount importance.

    (B)   It is enforceable under strict liability.

    (C)   It is a doctrine that requires the balancing of competing interests.

    (D)   One must show he was damaged in a way others were not.

Questions 61-62 are based upon the following fact situation.

Harvey drove a 1967 Chevy without a third brake light in the rear window. Harvey's left rear brake light was not functioning, and a police officer pulled him over and warned him to fix the light. A week later Cynthia, Harvey's neighbor, who owns an identical car, stole Harvey's right rear brake light to replace a broken light of her own. Harvey was completely unaware that the light was stolen since Cynthia had carefully replaced the light's red encasement. He still had not fixed the left light. Later in the day Harvey stopped short in the middle of a highway to prevent hitting a grasshopper. Since neither of Harvey's taillights worked properly, Tailgator, who was driving behind Harvey, did not realize he should stop until it was too late. He collided with Harvey. Both sides agree that the collision would not have occurred if either of the lights were properly functioning.

GO ON TO THE NEXT PAGE

61. If Tailgator asserts a civil claim against Cynthia, the likely result is that Cynthia's actions will be found to be

   (A)   neither the legal nor actual cause of Tailgator's injuries

   (B)   the legal but not actual cause of Tailgator's injuries

   (C)   the actual but not legal cause of Tailgator's injuries

   (D)   both the actual and legal causes of Tailgator's injuries

62. If Harvey brings an action against Tailgator and Tailgator argues that Harvey was contributorily negligent for driving without taillights, Tailgator's best argument is that

   (A)   Harvey had an absolute duty to maintain his taillights in good repair

   (B)   Harvey is strictly liable for harm caused by defective taillights

   (C)   Harvey was negligent for driving with a light out for a week

   (D)   Harvey is the legal cause of the injuries

Questions 63-65 are based upon the following fact situation.

Wake Up, Inc., manufactures Mr. Caffeine, a home coffee maker. Retailer purchased several hundred Mr. Caffeines under an arrangement whereby Retailer was responsible for shipping the merchandise from Wake Up's factory to his stores.

While loaded with Mr. Caffeines, one of Retailer's trucks skidded on a highway and careened into a guardrail. The appliances were thrown about the truck, toward the front of the cargo area.

Hyper purchased a Mr. Caffeine from Retailer at a reduced price because the box was damaged. Hyper had no reason to assume the appliance inside was damaged as well. Innocent, a guest at Hyper's home, turned on the Mr. Caffeine to make a cup of coffee in the morning. The machine exploded. Innocent suffered third-degree burns on his face. The explosion was caused by a defect created in the truck's accident.

63. If Innocent asserts an action against Wake Up, Inc., based on negligence, may she assert the doctrine of *res ipsa loquitur*?

   (A)   Yes, because there is privity of contract between the ultimate user and the manufacturer.

   (B)   Yes, because the manufacturer is strictly liable.

   (C)   No, because the purchaser assumed all risks.

   (D)   No, because of the truck accident.

64. Will Innocent prevail in an action for her injuries against Hyper?

   (A)   Yes, because Hyper was the owner of the appliance.

   (B)   Yes, but only if Hyper's conduct was malicious and wanton.

(C) Yes, if Hyper was negligent.

(D) No, because Innocent was a social guest.

65. Will Innocent recover in an action against Retailer?

(A) Yes, under strict liability in tort.

(B) Yes, under *res ipsa loquitur*.

(C) No, because there was no privity of contract.

(D) No, because Retailer did not imply any warranty.

Questions 66-69 are based upon the following fact situation.

Nerdo wanted to join a fraternity at school, so he went to a party sponsored by Delta House. Nerdo overheard Flounder whisper to Blutarsky, "That Nerdo guy seems like a real jerk." Nerdo picked up a cake knife and said to Flounder, "If I was a little more angry, I would slice your throat with this." Nerdo put the knife down, while pinching Flounder's neck with his fingers. Flounder ordered two pledges (younger students that must follow orders given by older fraternity members) to take Nerdo and drop him off in the woods. Nerdo was taken to a spot ten miles from the nearest house. The temperature was less than eight degrees Fahrenheit. Nerdo lost eight fingers and two toes from frostbite and exposure.

66. If Flounder brings suit against Nerdo, his best cause of action will be

(A) assault

(B) battery

(C) defamation

(D) intentional infliction of emotion distress

67. If Nerdo sues Flounder for defamation, is he likely to prevail?

(A) Yes, because Nerdo's reputation was damaged.

(B) Yes, because Nerdo was insulted.

(C) No, because the statements were slander per se.

(D) No, because the statements were neither broadly disseminated nor premeditated.

68. Nerdo wants to bring an action against Flounder and the two pledges. Nerdo will be most likely to succeed if the action is for

(A) violating a civil rights statute

(B) strict liability

(C) negligence by aggravating Nerdo

(D) false imprisonment

69. Nerdo is most likely to recover for frostbite injuries by arguing that

(A) Flounder and his friends acted negligently by placing Nerdo in peril

(B)   he had a right to be at the party

(C)   the fraternity ensures the safety of all those present at its parties

(D)   Flounder did not have a right to eject him from the party

Questions 70-71 are based upon the following fact situation.

Tabak, Gruner, and Kahan, all minors, stood on the edge of the Bayswater Dock, watching boats enter and depart from Jamaica Bay. They decided it would be fun to throw rocks at passing vessels. To show off his superior rock-throwing skills, Gruner picked up a large rock and tossed it. The rock smashed through the windshield of a yacht. Shards of broken glass entered Skipper's left eye, causing a permanent loss of vision.

70.   If Skipper asserts a claim against Gruner's parents, Skipper will

(A)   prevail, because Gruner's parents are strictly liable for any tort he commits

(B)   prevail, if they encouraged him to throw rocks

(C)   not prevail, because, as a minor, Gruner was not able to commit a tort

(D)   not prevail, because parents are generally not liable for their children's torts

71.   If Skipper brings an action against Gruner, Skipper will

(A)   prevail, because Gruner committed all the elements of a tort

(B)   not prevail, because Gruner's actions could not be malicious since he did not know Skipper

(C)   not prevail, because Gruner is a minor

(D)   not prevail, because Skipper's only chance at recovery would be to bring an action against Gruner's parents.

72.   Ellen and Bob had been close friends since elementary school. Bob was constantly finding himself in dangerous situations from which Ellen would save him. Frequently, when Bob would yell for Ellen to come help him, she would faithfully run to his rescue. Finally, she got fed up and told Bob that, from now on, he was on his own. Several days later, Bob went swimming in a pond near school. He had just eaten lunch. Bob got a cramp and was struggling to keep his head above the water. Ellen was standing on a bridge above him with a rope she was carrying home. Ellen would be obligated to throw the rope if

(A)   she heard him ask for her help

(B)   she could save Bob without risking harm to herself

(C)   she caused Bob's perilous situation

(D)   Bob's own negligence did not place him in his perilous situation

Questions 73-74 are based upon the following fact situation.

Grouch was a childless widower who owned a small house in a neighborhood with many young children. The house was surrounded by a three-foot-high picket fence. A large cashew tree grew in Grouch's front yard. One day Maria, an eight-year-old girl, climbed up over the fence, then climbed the tree and plucked a few cashews. When she jumped from the tree, she landed on a broken beer bottle, severely lacerating her foot. Grouch was aware that children played on the tree. Maria's parents asserted a claim against Grouch.

73.   Which of the following is **NOT** an element Maria must prove?

(A)   Grouch was aware there was broken glass in the yard.

(B)   The fence was easy to climb.

(C)   The broken glass and the tree were a private nuisance.

(D)   The glass could have been cleaned up for less than fifty dollars.

74.   Which of the following is the most significant in Maria's suit against Grouch?

(A)   The tree was visible from the street.

(B)   The tree and glass were a public nuisance.

(C)   The tree and glass were a private nuisance.

(D)   The children could have been kept out of the yard at a minimal expense by raising the height of the fence.

75.   Sneeky passed the bar exam and filed an application to be admitted to the state bar. He was required to submit a letter of good conduct from every firm that had ever employed him. Dependable Egg Company wrote a letter stating that Sneeky occasionally stole eggs from them when he had been employed as a truck driver. The allegations turned out to be false, but Sneeky's application was delayed for more than a year while the investigation was pending.

If Sneeky brings a defamation suit against Dependable Egg Company, will Sneeky prevail?

(A)   Yes, because he has proved the statements were false.

(B)   Yes, because the statements caused Sneeky real and actual harm.

(C)   No, if Dependable reasonably believed that Sneeky had stolen the eggs.

(D)   No, if eggs were actually stolen while Sneeky was on duty.

Questions 76-77 are based upon the following fact situation.

GO ON TO THE NEXT PAGE

The state motor vehicle code provides that it is illegal to cross a double yellow line under any circumstances. Rusher, on her way to her sister's wedding in which she was the maid of honor, was driving westbound on a street divided by a double yellow line. The entire westbound lane was blocked by Thoughtless's illegally double parked bus. Rusher looked to see if there was any oncoming traffic, then very carefully passed the bus by crossing the double yellow line and entering the eastbound lane. Cruiser, driving negligently in the eastbound lane, struck Rusher's car.

76.   Rusher asserted a claim against Thoughtless in a state that does not follow a comparative negligence doctrine. Will Rusher be successful?

(A)   Yes, because the accident that followed was exactly the type the state intended to prevent when it passed an ordinance barring double parking.

(B)   Yes, because Thoughtless is strictly liable for all injuries arising from his violations.

(C)   No, because Cruiser's negligence was an intervening cause.

(D)   No, because Rusher assumed the risk when she passed the truck.

77.   In a suit between Rusher and Cruiser in a jurisdiction that follows a modified comparative negligence doctrine, the fact that Rusher crossed a double yellow line

(A)   will, as a matter of law, prevent Rusher from any recovery since she assumed the risk

(B)   will, as a matter of law, prevent Rusher from any recovery, unless she can prove Cruiser had the last clear chance to avoid the accident

(C)   will not, as a matter of law, prevent Rusher from any recovery if she was less negligent than Cruiser

(D)   will not, as a matter of law, prevent Rusher from any recovery since her actions resulted from an emergency situation

Questions 78-82 are based upon the following fact situation.

Daredevil took Hysterical for a ride in his private plane. A dense fog set in just before the plane took off, and the airport had been closed. Daredevil took off anyway. Daredevil was unmoved by Hysterical's high-pitched screams. Daredevil flew the plane, which was manufactured by Going, at speeds twice as fast as those at which the plane was designed to fly. Hysterical pointed out that the gauges indicated the plane was overheating, but Daredevil called her a "party-pooper" and ignored her.

"The engine's on fire," screamed Hysterical. "Relax," said Daredevil, looking over his shoulder at the flaming engine. Daredevil proceeded to make a perfect landing in the ocean, one mile from shore. The two climbed out of the cockpit and grabbed the two lifeboats, manufactured by Savers and sold with the plane, that automatically inflated. Daredevil and Hysterical climbed into the lifeboats and paddled away from the sinking plane. Hysterical's boat had a manufacturing defect and, all of a sudden, sank. As Daredevil was rowing over to let Hysterical climb into his lifeboat, a shark ripped off Hysterical's left leg.

78. If Hysterical brings an action against Going, how will negligence on the part of Daredevil affect the action?

    (A) It will prevent Hysterical from recovering from Going because Daredevil's dangerous flying was a superseding cause.

    (B) It will prevent Hysterical from recovering from Going if Daredevil's actions contributed to Hysterical's injuries.

    (C) It is irrelevant because Hysterical was not injured in the crash landing.

    (D) It is irrelevant since Going is strictly liable for any defects causing the lifeboat to sink.

79. If Hysterical brings an action against Going based on strict liability in tort, Hysterical must prove

    (A) only that the lifeboat was defective when the plane was sold

    (B) that the lifeboat was defective and had not been inspected by Going

    (C) that the lifeboat was defective and that Going had inspected the boat but did not discover the defect

    (D) that the lifeboat was defective and the cause of Hysterical's injuries

80. If Hysterical sues Going, claiming negligence, Going will be most likely to prevail by asserting that

    (A) Daredevil's negligence was the proximate cause of Hysterical's injuries

    (B) Hysterical assumed the risk by flying with Daredevil

    (C) Going exercised due care in testing the lifeboat

    (D) Savers is solely responsible for the lifeboat's safety

81. Hysterical asserted a claim against Savers based on negligence. Savers was able to prove that Daredevil never properly tested the lifeboats. This proof will

    (A) relieve Savers of liability, because of the intervening cause

    (B) limit Savers' liability, because of the contributory negligence doctrine

    (C) cause Savers to be liable, because of the *respondeat superior* doctrine

    (D) be irrelevant as to whether or not Savers is liable

GO ON TO THE NEXT PAGE

Questions 82-83 are based upon the following fact situation.

In 1972, Sugar Mill Disco, Inc., bought an abandoned sugar mill and converted it into a discotheque. The surrounding area consisted of abandoned fields that had previously been used to grow sugar. In 1975, Rocky founded a sheep farm in the nearby town of Mourne Rouge. Sugar Mill routinely played very loud music from early evening to dawn. The vibrations and noise prevented Rocky's sheep from sleeping. After several months, the stress prevented the sheep from growing wool.

82.   If Rocky brings suit based on the theory of public nuisance, does he have a chance of prevailing?

   (A)   Yes, if the noise adversely affected the sheep.

   (B)   Yes, if Rocky's damages are different from the harm to the public at large.

   (C)   No, because a public nuisance action may be asserted only when the general public suffers harm.

   (D)   No, if Rocky purchased the property with knowledge of the disco.

83.   If Rocky brings a suit based on the theory of private nuisance, does he have a chance of prevailing?

   (A)   Yes, because the noise reduced the value of Rocky's land.

   (B)   Yes, because the noise unreasonably interfered with

Rocky's use and enjoyment of his land.

   (C)   No, because the Sugar Mill disco was being operated before Rocky purchased the property.

   (D)   No, if he has not adduced evidence to distinguish his harm from that to the general public.

Questions 84-85 are based upon the following fact situation.

Nervous was enjoying a camping trip sponsored by Wild Wilderness Tours, Inc. The trip was scheduled to last seven days and cover 400 miles of Alaskan wilderness. The tourists were transported in a large luxury bus. At night, they set up tents to sleep in. On the third day of the trip, the bus driver came to a fork in the road. He paused for a moment, but was embarrassed to say he was unsure of which road to take, so he guessed and ended up choosing incorrectly. The driver drove hours out of the way into a very remote area. Several hours after the bus passed the fork, it ran out of fuel. The nearest gas station was seventy-five miles away.

After six hours of sitting in the parked bus, Nervous began to panic. He was worried that he would either starve or freeze to death. Nervous decided to get out of the bus and try to walk to the nearest town. The other passengers decided to wait in hope that another vehicle would pass. Approximately one hour after he left the bus, a bear came along and ate Nervous's entire left leg.

84.   Nervous filed a suit against Wild Wilderness, Inc., based on negligence. If Wild Wilderness raises the defense

of assumption of the risk, who is most likely to prevail?

(A) Wilderness, because the other passengers did not venture out.

(B) Wilderness, because Nervous should have recognized the danger of leaving.

(C) Nervous, because the group was stranded due to the negligence of Wilderness's driver.

(D) Nervous, if a reasonably prudent person would have ventured outside in search of assistance.

85. If Sitter, another passenger, brings an action under false imprisonment, is he likely to prevail?

(A) Yes, because being confined to the bus is the equivalent of being imprisoned.

(B) Yes, if he can prove mental anguish.

(C) Yes, because the driver was negligent.

(D) Yes, unless the driver's mistakes were not made with the intention of sequestering the passengers.

Questions 86-87 are based upon the following fact situation.

On a cold rainy day, Leslie was riding a bus to her home. The bus was owned by Expressco, a private company. The windshield fogged up, limiting the driver's visibility. Expressco had provided the driver with an extra-quick defogger, a new product it purchased from Retailco. The product, which contained a defogging chemical in an aerosol can, was manufactured by Defogco. The driver carefully read the instructions, which said, "Danger, this product contains isopentanol, a chemical that is extremely toxic if swallowed. Keep out of the reach of children."

Moments after the driver sprayed the defogger, the passengers began coughing. Many of them, including Leslie, suffered severe burns of the internal respiratory tract.

Isopentanol is a dangerous chemical extremely caustic to the outside layer of internal human membranes.

86. If Leslie asserts a claim against Retailco for injuries sustained, will she recover?

(A) Yes, unless she entered the bus without paying the fare.

(B) Yes, if she can recover against Defogco.

(C) Yes, unless Retailco altered the spray in any way.

(D) No, unless she can prove Retailco was negligent.

87. If Leslie asserts a claim against Expressco, based on negligence, will she prevail?

(A) Yes, if she can recover against Defogco.

(B)   Yes, because the driver, an agent of Expressco acting within the scope of his employment, sprayed the chemical.

(C)   No, because the driver and Expressco did not know that product was so dangerous.

(D)   No, because the purpose of the spray was to defog windows.

Questions 88-89 are based upon the following fact situation.

Singh was a professional snake charmer who toured the country, performing at county fairs. Singh took several precautions to ensure the safety of his act. All of his snakes were operated on by Dr. Careless so that they would not be able to secrete poisonous venom. Each time he performed, Singh built a fence around himself and posted signs that said, "Warning: these snakes are dangerous."

Brainless, a spectator at one of Singh's performances, bragged to his girlfriend, "It's easy. I could do the same thing." Brainless jumped the fence and grabbed the flute. The snake bit Brainless's leg, causing a localized permanent paralysis. It turns out that the snake was capable of producing venom.

88.   If Brainless brings suit against Singh, is he likely to prevail?

(A)   Yes, because a professional snake charmer should have control of the snake at all times.

(B)   Yes, because snakes are not domesticated animals.

(C)   No, because Singh took reasonable precautions to prevent injury.

(D)   No, because Brainless was a trespasser.

89.   If Brainless asserts a claim against Dr. Careless, does he have a chance of prevailing?

(A)   Yes, under strict liability.

(B)   Yes, if Dr. Careless was negligent.

(C)   No, because there is no privity between Brainless and Careless.

(D)   No, because Brainless was guilty of contributory negligence.

Questions 90-94 are based upon the following fact situation.

Exploiter owned a very large meat packing plant. One day, Exploiter summoned Exploited, a longtime employee, to her office. Exploiter accused Exploited of being infected with hepatitis and demanded that Exploited resign from her job. Exploited did not, in fact, have the disease, nor did Exploiter have any reason to suspect that Exploited was ill. In fact, Exploiter wanted Exploited to leave the job so she could hire a recent immigrant from Haiti, at a fraction of the cost.

Several of Exploited's co-workers overheard Exploiter's charges against Exploited, and they told Exploited they did not believe the statements.

90. In an action brought by Exploited against Exploiter, based on defamation, Exploited

    (A)   must prove she could not find comparable employment

    (B)   must prove special damages

    (C)   must prove the statements adversely affected her social life

    (D)   need not prove special damages

91. Assume for this question only that Exploited was the only person to hear Exploiter's statements. Which of the following statements is most correct?

    (A)   Exploited will win an action based on defamation if she can prove she suffered severe emotional distress.

    (B)   Exploited will win an action based on defamation if she can prove Exploiter's statements were made so that she could hire cheap labor.

    (C)   Exploited should base her action on intentional infliction of emotional distress.

    (D)   Exploited will have no cause of action.

92. If Exploited's fellow employees heard Exploiter accuse Exploited of having hepatitis, but they did not believe the statements,

    (A)   Exploited will not have suffered special damages

    (B)   Exploiter will have a complete defense to defamation

    (C)   it proves the statements were not believable

    (D)   it shows that Exploited most likely suffered no damages

93. Assume Exploiter brought a civil action, demanding Exploited leave her job and vacate the premises, alleging Exploited's infection with hepatitis. The allegation that Exploited has hepatitis will be privileged

    (A)   only if Exploited did in fact have hepatitis

    (B)   only if Exploiter has reasonable grounds to believe the truth of the statements

    (C)   only if Exploiter believed the statements

    (D)   absolutely

94. To recover under intentional infliction of emotional distress, Exploited will prevail if she can prove that

    (A)   she was extremely sensitive to allegations that she carried diseases

    (B)   she was extremely sensitive to allegations that she carried

GO ON TO THE NEXT PAGE

diseases, and Exploiter was careless in not realizing this

(C)   accusing one of having hepatitis is reasonably likely to cause emotional distress

(D)   accusing one of having hepatitis is substantially certain to cause severe emotional distress in a person of average sensibility

Questions 95-99 are based upon the following fact situation.

Roberts is in the business of installing and reconditioning elevators. A statute, enacted for safety reasons, provides that elevators must have a safety device to absorb the impact caused when an elevator travels too fast toward the bottom of a shaft. Roberts regularly purchases this safety device from Silvestri. Roberts conducts its own tests on the safety devices.

Jimmy Corp. contracted with Roberts to install six new elevators in Trevor Tower, a building at 115th Fifth Avenue that Jimmy recently purchased and refurbished.

Avelleta, an employee of Jimmy Corp., operated Trevor Tower's freight elevator, which was also installed by Roberts and is identical to the other elevators in the building, except that it must be manually operated.

On one occasion, Avelleta negligently let the elevator drop to the basement at high speed. The safety device, which should have prevented the passengers from being injured, failed. The passengers, Gus and Shakedown, suffered serious injuries, as did Avelleta. Avelleta would have suffered the same injuries even if the safety device had worked properly, because he had been leaning on the drive shaft. Subsequent tests showed that the metal in the safety device was

defective. Roberts had performed these same tests before installing the elevator.

95.   If Gus and Shakedown bring a tort action based on product liability against Silvestri, which of the following will be most relevant?

(A)   privity of contract

(B)   warranty

(C)   *res ipsa loquitur*

(D)   the tests proving that the safety device was defective

96.   If Gus and Shakedown bring a negligence action against Roberts, to establish a *prima facie* case it is necessary that they prove that

(A)   the safety device failed

(B)   the safety device failed and had not been inspected by Roberts

(C)   the safety device failed and Roberts inspected it, but did not discover the defect

(D)   the safety device was defective and would have been discovered had Roberts exercised reasonable care

97.   If Gus and Shakedown bring a negligence action against Roberts, Avelleta's negligence will be considered

(A)   the proximate cause of Gus's and Shakedown's injuries

(B) a concurrent cause of Gus's and Shakedown's injuries

(C) irrelevant to Roberts's negligence

(D) an intervening act after Gus's and Shakedown's injuries

98. An argument by the defense that would probably prevail in a negligence action by Gus and Shakedown against Roberts is that

(A) Avelleta's negligence caused the accident

(B) Roberts properly performed tests on the safety device

(C) Silvestri, not Roberts, is responsible for the failure of the safety device

(D) Trevor Corp. proximately caused the injuries

99. In a negligence action by Gus and Shakedown against Roberts, a guest statute will

(A) compel the judge to dismiss the case before the merits are heard

(B) prevent recovery

(C) not affect the outcome of the case

(D) prevent recovery, unless Roberts was extremely negligent

100. Tim borrowed Jim's electric razor. Jim forgot to warn Tim to ground the razor since the razor had some bare wires inside of it that were not visible to the casual user. Tim received a severe shock while shaving, causing permanent paralysis in his right arm. If Tim asserts a claim against Jim, he will most likely

(A) prevail under strict liability in tort, because the shaver was defective when lent by Jim

(B) prevail in negligence, because Jim knew the razor was defective and likely to cause injury and did not warn Tim of the danger

(C) not prevail, because Jim fulfilled the duty of a gratuitous lender

(D) not prevail, because Jim was a gratuitous lender

Questions 101-103 are based upon the following fact situation.

Stienbruner owns a baseball team. At times, the team's fans throw objects out of the stands onto the playing area. During one game against their archrival, the Mudhens, the players engaged in a fight that inspired the fans to throw all sorts of objects from the stands. When the Mudhens came to town again, Stienbruner ordered that extra precautions be taken. Fans were searched for cans and bottles as they entered the stadium. Beer was not sold at the stadium concessions. Leo managed to smuggle a can of beer into the stadium by hiding it in the lining of his jacket. He threw the full can at a Mudhen fan in the back row. The can

GO ON TO THE NEXT PAGE

missed the fan, sailed out of the stadium, and landed on Policeman, who was patrolling the parking area.

101.   If Policeman sues Stienbruner for damage, he will most likely

(A)   prevail, because an owner is strictly liable to licensees for any hazardous conditions on his property that result in injury

(B)   prevail, because Stienbruner was on notice that violence may occur

(C)   not prevail, because Stienbruner was on notice of danger to players only

(D)   not prevail, if the trier of fact determines that Stienbruner took reasonable actions to prevent injuries

102.   If Policeman asserts a claim against Leo based on battery, is Policeman likely to prevail?

(A)   Yes, because the doctrine of *res ipsa loquitur* would apply.

(B)   Yes, because of the doctrine of transferred intent.

(C)   No, because Leo was lacking the requisite intent.

(D)   No, because Policeman was never under any apprehension or fear.

103.   Assume for this question only that Policeman was successful in his suit against Stienbruner. If Stienbruner

brings an action against Leo, is he likely to prevail?

(A)   Yes, because Stienbruner should be entitled to indemnity from Leo.

(B)   Yes, because Stienbruner should be entitled to contribution from Leo.

(C)   No, because Stienbruner assumed liability by instituting security procedures.

(D)   No, because it is impossible to identify the degree of fault.

104.   On a snowy New Year's eve, Cowboy was driving his pickup truck down a state road. He happened to notice a car parked strangely on the side of the road and decided to investigate. Five severely inebriated people were sleeping in the car. Cowboy opened an unlocked door and tried unsuccessfully to wake the car's occupants. Fearing they would die of exposure, Cowboy locked his own truck, which was too small to transport the drunks, and started the parked car. He shifted the car into reverse. Cowboy was unaware that the car's transmission was not working and the car lurched forward instead of going backward, causing it to slide down a ravine. All the occupants suffered serious injuries.

If the passengers assert a claim against Cowboy, they will most likely

(A)   recover, because they were placed in greater peril when the car was moved

(B)   recover, because Cowboy did not have any right to move the car

(C)   not recover, because they were inebriated at the time of the accident

(D)   not recover, if Cowboy acted reasonably

105.   Mugger walked over to Tiny, who was standing at a bus stop, and stared at him for a while. Mugger then told Tiny, "I am going to slice your throat and then cut you up limb by limb." Tiny was afraid for his life and used his talents as an Olympic sprinter to run away.

    If Tiny asserts a claim against Mugger, based on assault, is Tiny likely to prevail?

(A)   Yes, if Tiny was under a reasonable apprehension of harmful or offensive contact.

(B)   Yes, because Mugger had the requisite intent to bring about Tiny's apprehension.

(C)   No, because Tiny should have known a sprinter could outrun almost anyone.

(D)   No, because Mugger did nothing more than talk big.

Questions 106-110 are based upon the following fact situation.

    D. Lerious placed an advertisement in the Boom Town Gazette that stated he was looking for a waitress, fifteen to seventeen years of age. Nah Eve, fifteen years old, called D. Lerious and expressed interest in the job. Eve hesitated when Lerious told her she would have to make deliveries atop the many construction sites in downtown Boom Town. Eve met Lerious at the foot of a forty-story office building under construction. "I am scared to death, but I need the money for my baby," said Eve. Lerious said, "Don't worry, my restaurant always coaches people on how to do this." He then ordered Eve to walk along a steel beam, four hundred feet above the street, and hand a man a can of soda pop. Eve was afraid for her life, but she made it.

    On the way down in the elevator, Nah Eve asked, "Did I get the job?" Lerious answered, "I was only kidding. There's no job. I am a construction worker. I do this all the time for kicks." Eve had a nervous reaction that required a six-month hospital stay.

106.   If D. Lerious pleads insanity, the insanity plea will not be accepted

(A)   if he is above the age of minority and a court has not appointed a guardian

(B)   if he had the state of mind required for the tort at issue

(C)   if D. Lerious did not conform to the actions of the "reasonable incompetent."

(D)   if he is in possession of assets to cover a possible judgment

107.   If Lerious argues that Eve consented, Eve's best argument would be that

(A)   she is a minor

GO ON TO THE NEXT PAGE

(B)   Lerious did not have a restaurant that coached people on how to walk on steel beams

(C)   her consent was obtained by duress

(D)   one cannot consent to a life-threatening activity

108.   If Eve sues Lerious for assault, which of the following will be the most relevant evidence of his intent?

(A)   Lerious knew the walk was dangerous.

(B)   Lerious had intended for Eve to fall.

(C)   Lerious wanted to fool Eve.

(D)   Lerious knew that Eve thought she might fall.

109.   Which of the following is **incorrect**?

(A)   Lerious lacked any intent to inflict emotional distress

(B)   Eve might recover for her emotional distress even though she suffered no physical injuries.

(C)   Lerious's actions might fall within the bounds of "extreme and outrageous" conduct.

(D)   An action for mental suffering may arise from an act intended as a joke.

110.   If Eve brings an action based on false imprisonment for the time she spent

in the elevator, Lerious might assert which of the following defenses?

(A)   Eve did not try to leave the elevator.

(B)   Eve could have stopped the elevator on the way up.

(C)   Lerious was not asked to stop the elevator.

(D)   Eve entered and stayed in the elevator of her own volition.

Questions 111-113 are based upon the following fact situation.

Thoughtless parked his car at a bus stop, in violation of a city ordinance, because he had to use a nearby restroom. He had planned on leaving the car for less than two minutes and turned on his hazard lights to warn approaching vehicles. Thoughtless admits he violated a city ordinance that makes it unlawful to park at a bus stop or at any curb painted with a yellow line. Martin was driving at a safe speed along the same street when a dog ran in front of his car. Martin managed to avoid the dog by veering right and crashed into Thoughtless's car. Lilly, who was standing on the sidewalk waiting for a bus, was hit by the front of the car, which also knocked down a "No Standing" sign.

111.   If Lilly asserts a claim against Thoughtless for injuries sustained from the collision, she will most likely

(A)   prevail, because Thoughtless violated a statute

(B)   prevail, because Thoughtless's actions were negligent per se

(C) not prevail, because her injuries were not of the type the statute sought to prevent

(D) not prevail, because the statute gives rise to a criminal, not a civil, action

112. Assume for this question only that Martin was negligent in swerving the car. If the city asserts a claim against Martin for damage to the "No Standing" sign, Martin's negligence should be ruled

(A) neither the legal cause, nor the cause in fact, of the city's damages

(B) the legal cause, but not the cause in fact of the city's damages

(C) the cause in fact, but not the legal cause, of the city's damages

(D) the legal cause and the cause in fact of the city's damages

113. If Thoughtless brings an action against Martin for damages to his car, Thoughtless should

(A) prevail, because of the last clear chance doctrine

(B) prevail, because Martin should have seen his car and avoided it

(C) not recover, because Thoughtless's actions were

the proximate cause of the accident

(D) not recover, because Thoughtless assumed the risk

Questions 114-116 are based upon the following fact situation.

Olympia was the developer of a seventy-story luxury condominium complex in Metropolis City. She hired York, an independent contractor, to build the steel frame of the building. York was given carte blanche from Olympia to handle all technical matters concerning the construction of this frame.

A week after the frame was completed and Olympia had paid York, a steel girder fell from the top floor. The end of the girder fell on Reichman, a building inspector, and caused him severe leg injuries.

Reichman brought suit against both Olympia and York, who both admit that the girder fell because York had not followed the standard procedures of the construction industry in building the frame.

114. In the suit brought by Reichman against York, York's best argument is that

(A) Olympia's architect provided the specifications for the frame

(B) Olympia assumed all liabilities upon tendering payment

(C) the structural failure was not due to any lack of care of York

(D) the work was performed on behalf of Olympia

GO ON TO THE NEXT PAGE

115. Reichman is most likely to recover against Olympia on the theory that

    (A)   Olympia assumed the liability by paying York

    (B)   Olympia is strictly liable

    (C)   Olympia is liable for York's negligence, if York was her employee and not an independent contractor

    (D)   Olympia is liable under *respondeat superior*

116. Assume that Reichman recovers against Olympia. In a suit by Olympia against York, Olympia will most likely

    (A)   recover, because Olympia's conduct did not in fact cause the injury

    (B)   recover, if Reichman's judgment against Olympia was based on vicarious liability

    (C)   not recover, because Olympia's payment for the work implied acceptance of liability

    (D)   not recover, because by selecting York to do the construction, Olympia has admitted to York's competence

Questions 117-118 are based upon the following fact situation.

    Dr. Blind is a surgeon in Grenville, a very small town. In a routine operation, Blind removed Victem's gallbladder, but left a pair of scissors in Victem's abdomen. Blind admitted he left the scissors in and offered to remove them for free. Victem filed suit against Blind for negligence.

117. To establish a breach of the duty to exercise care by Blind, Victem

    (A)   must provide an expert from Grenville to testify that Blind's conduct was negligent

    (B)   must provide an expert in abdominal surgery to testify that Blind's conduct was negligent

    (C)   can rely on the common knowledge of the jurors to decide whether there was negligence

    (D)   can rely on the judge to advise the jury if there was negligence

118. Besides proving negligence, to recover Victem must also prove that

    (A)   she would have recovered fully and rapidly had the scissors not been left in her abdomen

    (B)   she suffered a loss or detriment due to the scissors

    (C)   she suffered permanent injuries due to Dr. Blind's negligence

    (D)   she was not guilty of contributory negligence

119. Mechanic repaired Cynthia's car pursuant to a written contract and

drove the car to her home. Mechanic rang the front doorbell, but Cynthia did not answer. Assuming Cynthia had an extra set of keys to the car, Mechanic left his set of keys in the ignition and locked the car's doors. An hour later, a thief broke the car's window and drove away. If Cynthia brings a claim against Mechanic for damages for the loss of the car, is she likely to prevail?

(A) Yes, because the repair was pursuant to a written contract.

(B) Yes, because by leaving the keys in the ignition, Mechanic created a substantial risk of theft.

(C) No, if Cynthia told Mechanic that she would be home when Mechanic brought the car.

(D) No, because the act of the thief was a superseding cause.

Questions 120-121 are based upon the following fact situation.

Crazy Teddy shopped around for the lowest price on a new compact-disc player. He decided to buy a Lazerpro player from Antar, a very large dealer. Lazerpro is manufactured by Lazertone, a very reputable electronics manufacturer. Excited with his purchase, Crazy Teddy rushed home to play his new disc player. On the way home, the bus Teddy had taken was stuck in a terrible traffic jam for more than two hours. Luckily, Crazy Teddy had something to read, the Lazerpro's instruction manual, which he read carefully seven times. When he finally got home, Crazy Teddy carefully connected the Lazerpro to his stereo. When he turned it on, he received severe burns on his right hand. The manufacturer had pointed the laser beams in the wrong direction, and this mistake caused the burns.

120. If Crazy Teddy brings an action against Antar based on negligence, is Crazy Teddy likely to prevail?

(A) Yes, because there is privity of contract between the two.

(B) Yes, because Antar is responsible for the negligence of Lazertone.

(C) No, because only a manufacturer can be liable in negligence.

(D) No, because there is no evidence that Antar did not exercise due care.

121. If Crazy Teddy brings suit against Lazertone based on strict liability in tort, will Crazy Teddy probably recover?

(A) Yes, because the product was defective.

(B) Yes, because Crazy Teddy would not have an action against Antar.

(C) No, because there is no evidence that Lazertone failed to exercise due care.

(D) No, because there was a lack of privity.

GO ON TO THE NEXT PAGE

122. Brakeless knew his car's brakes were in poor condition, yet he drove the car anyway. He was driving toward an intersection and did not see the stop sign. By the time he noticed the sign it was too late to stop. Had his brakes been in proper order, he could have stopped in time. Teacher was also driving toward the intersection and saw Brakeless. Teacher could have stopped, but did not. They had a minor collision. If Brakeless asserts a claim against Teacher, Brakeless will most likely

    (A)   prevail, for all his damages, if he can prove that Teacher had told a bystander, "I could have stopped, but I wanted to teach that dude a lesson"

    (B)   prevail, for all his damages, if a comparative negligence statute is in effect

    (C)   prevail in full, if a last clear chance statute is in effect

    (D)   not prevail, if the motor vehicle code requires that brakes be inspected once a year

123. Adam is under a legal duty to rescue Eve if

    (A)   Eve is Adam's aunt

    (B)   Eve was placed in peril by a stranger

    (C)   Eve was placed in peril by Adam's negligent actions

    (D)   Eve was placed in peril by her own negligent conduct

124. While walking home from work, Igor had been assaulted by Allan on three separate occasions. Allan always wore boots, jeans, a leather coat, and a wool cap. Igor had managed to get a look at Allan's face, although it was dark out on each occasion. Allan usually had two or three day's worth of beard growth on his face. One night, as Igor was walking home from work, he spotted Reverend Richard walking toward him from about a block away. When Igor crossed the street so did Reverend Richard and the two men continued to approach each other. Reverend Richard was wearing boots, jeans, a leather jacket, and a wool cap. He had been bedridden with the flu for three days and had not shaved. When the two came within six feet of each other, Richard raised his hand. Igor then lurched forward and punched Reverend Richard across the chin, injuring his jaw. Reverend sued Igor for battery. Igor claimed self-defense. Judgment should be in favor of

    (A)   Reverend Richard, because to sustain a claim of self-defense there must be an overt action to defend against

    (B)   Reverend Richard, because he did nothing extraordinary

    (C)   Igor, if he honestly believed he was about to be attacked

    (D)   Igor, if a reasonable person would believe he was being attacked under the circumstances

125. Shakedown, an art dealer, went to a public tag sale conducted by Heiress,

who was disposing of the furniture and belongings of her late parents. When Heiress saw Shakedown staring at a painting above a fireplace, she walked over to him. "We just had this painting appraised; it is a very old Italian oil. Its value is six thousand dollars. We'll sell it for five," Heiress said to Shakedown. Shakedown recognized the painting as a genuine Da Vinci, worth at least a million dollars. He wrote out a check for five thousand dollars and took the painting to his gallery.

If Heiress seeks to recover the painting and asserts an action based on misrepresentation, will she prevail?

(A)   Yes, because Shakedown's silence in the face of Heiress's statements amounted to fraud.

(B)   Yes, because failure to disclose material facts can also be a misrepresentation.

(C)   No, because Heiress was negligent in selecting a bad appraiser.

(D)   No, unless Shakedown told Heiress the painting was worth six thousand dollars.

126.   Metropolis Transit Corp., a private company, owns and operates the Metropolis Subway System. Metropolis has a staff of safety engineers who examine the system to ensure the passengers' safety. For the past seven years, the system has been using the X-1, an air-conditioned subway car complete with the latest technological advances.

Capable, a forty-year-old blind woman, has been riding the subway to work for almost twenty years. When the train pulls into her station she waits for the doors to open and then pokes for the opening with her walking cane. Upon feeling an opening, she steps onto the train. One morning, a train made of X-1 cars pulled into Capable's station. As always, Capable felt with her cane. The design of the X-1 left a space as large as an open door between the cars. Capable mistook the space for an open door and stepped forward. She fell to the tracks and received severe electrical burns from the third rail. A subsequent investigation revealed that twelve blind people had made the same mistake and fallen to the tracks.

If Capable asserts a claim against Metropolis Transit Corp., she will most likely

(A)   prevail, because, as a common carrier, Metropolis Transit insured Capable's safety while she was on its property

(B)   recover, if Metropolis could have taken reasonable steps to prevent blind persons from walking onto the tracks

(C)   not recover, because Capable assumed the risk

(D)   not recover, because Metropolis does not insure the safety of its passengers

GO ON TO THE NEXT PAGE

Questions 127-128 are based upon the following fact situation.

Weirdo, a world-famous rock star, was constantly followed by Opportunist, a free-lance photographer. Weirdo brought several unsuccessful actions to prevent what he called harassment by Opportunist. Weirdo went jogging every morning, and Opportunist followed him on a bicycle. One morning, a sudden rainstorm interrupted Weirdo's run. He hailed a cab to get back home. Opportunist took a photo of Weirdo getting into the cab. A large advertisement for Yellow Guitars rested on top of the taxi. Opportunist sold the photo to Middleman, Inc., who sold it to Yellow Guitars, Inc. Yellow used the photo in a major advertising campaign without determining whether Weirdo had given consent. As a result of the ads, Slick Guitars, Inc., canceled its million-dollar-a-year fee to Weirdo to endorse its guitars.

127.   In an action by Weirdo against Yellow Guitars for invasion of privacy, Weirdo will most likely

(A)   prevail, because he is a public figure

(B)   prevail, because Yellow Guitars accepted the photo without making any attempt to determine if Weirdo had granted permission

(C)   not prevail, if Yellow Guitars determined that the photo was not defamatory

(D)   not prevail, if a reasonable person would conclude the photo was not defamatory

128.   In an action for invasion of privacy by Weirdo against Opportunist, Weirdo will most likely

(A)   prevail, because the photograph was taken without Weirdo's authorization

(B)   prevail, because the photograph was used for profit

(C)   not prevail, because Weirdo was on a public street

(D)   not prevail, because he is a public figure

Questions 129-130 are based upon the following fact situation.

Spitz, a former all-state swimmer, was walking over a bridge when he heard screams from below. Spitz looked over the side of the bridge and saw Gross, who screamed, "Help! I have a cramp, and I may not make it to the shore." Spitz shouted some words of encouragement and walked away. A few moments later, Knieval, driving his motorcycle at more than twice the speed limit, crashed over the side of the bridge, landed on Gross, and killed him.

129.   In a suit by Gross's estate against Spitz, the estate will probably

(A)   prevail, because Spitz was an expert swimmer, and a reasonable man with such skills would have saved Gross

(B)   prevail, because Spitz's skills created an obligation to save Gross

(C) not prevail, because Spitz did not in any way affect Gross's struggle

(D) not prevail, because Gross assumed all liability by swimming in unsupervised waters

130. In a suit by Gross's estate against Knieval, the estate will probably

(A) prevail, if Knieval is known to be a reckless driver

(B) prevail, because the accident was due to Knieval's negligence

(C) not prevail, because it was not possible for Knieval to realize the consequences of his speeding

(D) not prevail, because Gross's actions were a proximate cause of his death

131. Sucker purchased a brand new car, manufactured by Tokyo Motor Company, from Nakasoni Tokyo, Inc. The car was sold as part of a year-end promotion that excluded dealer preparation. Sucker took the car to Flying Aces Gas, who performed the preparation. The sales contract provided a thirty-day warranty for parts and labor. Thirty-seven days after purchasing the car, Sucker and Jill were driving along a freeway when the car stalled. Sucker managed to push the car to the side of the road. Since Sucker had no

knowledge of car mechanics and Jill did, Jill checked under the hood.

Flying Aces had forgotten to install a gas filter and the gas line was clogged up. Jill repaired the car. She left the hood open while Sucker started the car to make sure all was well. The car started, but a blade from the fan flew out and hit Jill in the face. The blade was defectively manufactured by Tokyo Motor Co. If Jill makes a claim against Tokyo Motor Co. for damages based on strict liability, she will probably

(A) recover, because Tokyo Motor Co. is responsible for proper dealer preparation

(B) recover, because Tokyo Motor Co. did not properly manufacture the car

(C) not recover, because she assumed the risk

(D) not recover, because there was no privity of contract

132. Water Commissioner Samo testified before the City Council Corruption Committee. "Plumber has bilked the city out of two billion dollars. This man's business is corrupt in every aspect. No one should ever do business with Plumber," said Samo. If Plumber asserts a claim against Samo for defamation, is Plumber likely to prevail?

(A) Yes, if the statements were false, and Samo knew the statements were false.

GO ON TO THE NEXT PAGE

(B)   Yes, if the statements were false, and Samo would have discovered the falsity had he exercised reasonable care to investigate the charges.

(C)   No, if the statements were true.

(D)   No, regardless of the truth of the statements.

Questions 133-134 are based upon the following fact situation.

Susan was struck by an automobile driven negligently by Darter. Susan suffered a fractured right hip and required two weeks hospitalization. Three months later, her hip apparently cured, Susan resumed her daily five-mile run. One day, approximately one month after resuming jogging, Susan ran across a busy street at the crosswalk. Ordinarily, she would have made it across with plenty of time to spare, except, this time, her hip froze, an after-effect of being hit by Darter. Susan could not move once her hip froze, and she was hit by a car.

133.   If Susan is able to bring a successful action based on negligence against Darter, will she be able to recover for injuries from the second accident?

(A)   Yes, if Darter's negligence is found to be a proximate cause of the second accident.

(B)   No, because the second accident was not a foreseeable result of Darter's negligent action.

(C)   No, because Susan decided to jog and assumed the risk that her hip would freeze.

(D)   No, if Susan's physicians pronounced her in good health.

134.   If Darter asserts the defense of contributory negligence to the claim arising from the second accident, is it likely to be accepted?

(A)   No, because Susan was not negligent.

(B)   No, but only if Darter's conduct in the first accident is deemed reckless and wanton.

(C)   Yes, because Darter will be able to assert the defense of contributory negligence only with respect to the first accident.

(D)   Yes, because in her condition Susan should not have been jogging.

135.   Sally Sleeze, a famous Hollywood actress, was the subject of a cover story in the *National Yenta*, a weekly tabloid. Sleeze had recently called a press conference to announce that she had AIDS and had been an intravenous drug user for many years. The *National Yenta* wrote that Sleeze's mother, Suzy, an octogenarian residing in a Los Angeles nursing home, became sexually active at the age of fourteen and was hospitalized for alcoholism more than twenty-seven times.
    If Sally Sleeze asserts a claim against the *National Yenta,* based on invasion of privacy, for the statements about her mother, Sally will

(A) not prevail, if the *National Yenta* can prove that the statements about Suzy are true and that the newspaper acted without malice

(B) not prevail, because Sally is a public figure and invited inquiry into her personal life by making the announcement

(C) not prevail, because the right to privacy is personal

(D) prevail, because the statements hold Sally up to ridicule and contempt

136. As part of a promotion, Hubbard's Department Store had its employees stuff chocolate bars in the pockets of pedestrians passing the store. Wilson, a passerby, was surrounded by four employees who stuffed chocolate in his jacket pockets. Wilson testified, "I saw them coming at me from across the street, and I thought they were going to mug me. When they reached toward me, I tried pulling out my wallet to give it to them." Wilson desires to bring suit against the employees. The best action for him to bring should be

(A) battery

(B) assault

(C) false imprisonment

(D) none of the above

Questions 137-139 are based upon the following fact situation.

Mel was driving along a two-lane road with Lloyd in the passenger seat. In the lane going in the opposite direction a car was passing a truck and did not see Mel's car. Facing a potential head-on collision, Mel drove his car off the road, through a barbed wire fence, and into Farmer Tom's tomato patch.

Farmer Tom was furious and drove his tractor as fast as he could toward Mel and Lloyd to scare them. He was planning to swerve out of the way at the last moment, but his tire went flat, the tractor went out of control, and it hit Lloyd.

137. In an action by Farmer Tom against Mel for the damaged tomatoes, Farmer Tom should

(A) prevail, because Mel did not have any privilege to enter Farmer Tom's land

(B) prevail, because Mel damaged the tomatoes.

(C) not prevail, because Mel entered Farmer Tom's property to avoid serious injury

(D) not prevail, because Farmer Tom threatened Mel with injury

138. If Lloyd brings suit against Farmer Tom for battery, he should

(A) prevail, because Farmer Tom would be liable under strict liability

(B) prevail, because Farmer Tom tried to scare Lloyd

(C)   not prevail, because Farmer Tom did not authorize Lloyd to enter his property

(D)   not prevail, because Farmer Tom intended to scare, not injure, Lloyd

139.   If Mel brings suit against Farmer Tom for assault, he should

(A)   prevail, if he reasonably believed he was about to be injured by the tractor

(B)   prevail, because Farmer Tom did not have any right to threaten Mel with force

(C)   not prevail, because Mel was not injured

(D)   not prevail, because Mel was a trespasser

140.   Sue E. Seidel decided she was going to become a Hollywood stunt driver. She needed some cars to practice jumping, so she asked Don and Juan if they would lend her their cars. Sue told Don that she had been a Hollywood stunt driver for twenty years and had jumped over hundreds of cars. After hearing Sue's claims, Don agreed to lend her his car. Sue, in fact, had never attempted to do any kind of jump with her car. Sue subsequently asked Juan if she could borrow his car to jump over without any assurances of her ability. Juan said yes. He intended to give her the keys to an old jalopy but gave her the keys to his Rolls Royce by mistake. Sue took Don's and Juan's cars. Both had been previously owned by

famous people and were very valuable. Sue attempted the jump, but crashed into both cars. The cars caught fire and burned beyond repair.

Don and Juan brought suit against Sue. If Sue asserts the defense of express consent against Don, will she likely prevail?

(A)   Yes, because Don expressly told Sue that she could jump over the car.

(B)   Yes, because Don realized the activity was very dangerous.

(C)   No, because Sue had never jumped before.

(D)   No, because Sue did not know the value of the car.

141.   Ray and Ballard were sitting quietly in a bar on Exchange Street. Ray casually mentioned that he thought the Zips Football team was lousy. Ballard stood up and threatened to knock Ray's teeth out. Ray responded by punching Ballard. Ray continued to beat Ballard until Dennison happened to walk into the bar. Dennison pulled out a knife, held it to Ray's neck, and said, "Let go of him or you are a dead man." In a suit for assault against Dennison, Ray is likely to

(A)   prevail, because the threat was real and imminent

(B)   prevail, unless the knife had a dull blade

(C)   not prevail, because Ballard was the first aggressor

(D) not prevail, because Dennison was just trying to prevent Ray from injuring Ballard

142. Trespasser often jogged on a golf course near his house. He ignored repeated warnings by the groundskeepers to leave the area. In fact, he taunted the employees when they fertilized the golf course each month. Trespasser would jog alongside the tractor that was spraying fertilizer, forcing the workers to turn the machine off. One day, one of the workers said, "Let's teach this jerk a lesson and leave the machine on." Trespasser was sprayed with toxic chemicals and was severely burned. To prevail in a suit based on battery, Trespasser must establish that

(A) the toxic chemicals caused severe emotional distress

(B) his taunting was not the cause in fact of his injuries

(C) the toxic chemicals constituted a harmful or offensive contact

(D) he suffered severe injuries

Questions 143-145 are based upon the following fact situation.

Felon broke into Rich's garage, opened the hood of Rich's Ferrari, and tried to start the engine. He managed to start the engine, but also caused the car to lunge forward. Felon was pinned between the car and the wall. The gas tank ruptured and gas spilled all over the garage floor. Passerby heard Felon screaming for help and ran to assist him. Passerby grabbed a crowbar and managed to free Felon. The crowbar caused severe cuts in Passerby's hand. "Thanks, you saved my life," said Felon. "You're welcome," Passerby replied, as he lit a cigarette and threw the match on the floor. The match ignited the spilled gas. Both Felon and Passerby suffered severe burns.

143. If Passerby asserts a claim against Felon for injuries sustained, Passerby may

(A) not prevail, because he voluntarily rescued Felon from peril

(B) prevail, for injuries from the crowbar but not from the fire

(C) prevail, for injuries from the fire, but not the crowbar

(D) not prevail, because Passerby assumed the risk

144. If Felon asserts a claim against Passerby for injuries sustained in the fire, Felon may

(A) prevail, because Passerby was negligent

(B) prevail, because Passerby assumed the risk

(C) not prevail, because Passerby acted gratuitously and was under no duty to rescue Felon

(D) not prevail, because Felon assumed the risk of Passerby's competence by calling him for help

GO ON TO THE NEXT PAGE

145.   If Passerby asserts a claim against Rich for personal injuries, Passerby will recover for injuries arising from

(A)   both the fire and crowbar injuries

(B)   the fire, but not the crowbar injury

(C)   the crowbar, but not the fire

(D)   neither the crowbar nor the fire

Questions 146-147 are based upon the following fact situation.

Alfred, a traveling salesman, was driving through a coastal community five hundred miles from his home during the beginning of a hurricane. While approaching a flooded intersection, Alfred decided it would be best to abandon his car and seek refuge in a nearby public library. He parked his car on top of a hill to reduce the chances of the car being flooded. The hill belonged to Selfish, who came out screaming as soon as Alfred parked his car. Selfish demanded that Alfred remove his car, but Alfred refused, explaining that the car would likely be damaged by the storm if parked elsewhere. Selfish jumped into Alfred's car, put it in neutral, and rolled it down the hill, causing four thousand dollars worth of damages.

146.   In a suit by Selfish against Alfred for trespass, a necessary element to determine whether Alfred is liable is

(A)   whether a reasonable person would have known the land belonged to Selfish

(B)   whether Alfred knew the land belonged to Selfish

(C)   whether Alfred had a reasonable fear his car would be damaged by the storm

(D)   whether Alfred was on notice to inquire regarding the ownership of the land

147.   In a suit by Alfred against Selfish for damages to his car, should Alfred prevail?

(A)   Yes.

(B)   No, because he became a trespasser as soon as he entered Selfish's property.

(C)   No, because he became a trespasser the moment he refused Selfish's demand that he remove his car.

(D)   No, if Selfish proves that the car would have damaged his property.

Questions 148-150 are based upon the following fact situation.

Constructor was building a single-family home on a previously empty lot in a middle-class area. Constructor had a fence built around the lot, but it was often left open after construction hours.
Early one evening, Herby, a six year-old, walked through the unlocked fence and played in the house. Intrigued by a strange noise, Herby went up to the top floor and discovered Carpenter cutting wood with an electric buzz saw. Carpenter was unaware of Herby's presence because of the noise created by the saw. The blade of the saw broke loose and struck Herby in the eye. Carpenter had just repaired the saw the day before at Pete's Saw Repairs.

Herby's guardian filed claims against Constructor, Carpenter, and Pete's.

148. Carpenter's best defense to Herby's action is that

    (A)   his actions did not in fact cause Herby's injuries

    (B)   he was unaware of Herby's presence, and his presence was unforeseeable

    (C)   the saw was maintained in a reasonable manner

    (D)   the accident was free from any willful, malicious, or wanton actions

149. Concerning Herby's suit against Constructor, Herby should

    (A)   prevail, because Constructor should have made sure the gate was locked after hours

    (B)   prevail, because construction is an ultra-hazardous activity

    (C)   not prevail, because Pete's faulty repair acts as an intervening cause

    (D)   not prevail, because the duty owed to a trespasser is to merely refrain from inflicting willful and wanton injury

150. Who should prevail in Herby's action against Pete's?

    (A)   Herby, if Pete's was negligent.

    (B)   Herby, because Pete's is strictly liable.

    (C)   Pete's, because Constructor was an intervening cause.

    (D)   Pete's, because the duty owed to a trespasser is to merely refrain from willful and wanton injury.

151. Aycee and Deecee, attorneys at law, had their offices next door to Geebee Box Company. Aycee constantly complained that trucks making pickups and deliveries at Geebee's blocked the sidewalk. Virtually all of the trucks were owned by Geebee, who ignored Aycee's requests to keep the sidewalk clear. One day, Deecee was forced to back out of the Aycee-Deecee driveway without checking for oncoming traffic, because Geebee's trucks blocked the view. Geebee had been cited, on several occasions, for violating city ordinances.

    If Aycee brings suit against Geebee based on public nuisance, praying for injunctive relief and alleging that he is currently unable to walk past Geebee's store, Geebee will most likely prevail if he argues that

    (A)   monetary damages are the only remedy available at law

    (B)   Aycee consented to the trucks by allowing them over the years

    (C)   there was no claim of unique damage

GO ON TO THE NEXT PAGE

(D)   Aycee should have used abatement by self-help

(C)   Buckeye only

(D)   John Moosee only

Questions 152-153 are based upon the following fact situation.

Brown purchased a tractor from Buckeye Tractors. The tractor was manufactured by John Moosee. John Moosee purchased the blades and many other components from Cutless Corp. The day after the purchase, Brown was riding the tractor when, all of a sudden, the machine's blade flew off, striking Brown in the eye and causing severe damage. An investigation revealed that the blades had been properly manufactured, but improperly installed.

152.   If Brown asserts a claim based on negligence against Buckeye Tractors, to recover Brown must prove that the tractor

(A)   was defective

(B)   was defective, and Buckeye had not inspected the tractor

(C)   was defective, and Buckeye inspected the tractor but did not discover the defect

(D)   was defective, and Buckeye would have discovered the defect had it exercised reasonable care

153.   Under an action for strict liability in tort, Brown should recover from

(A)   Buckeye, John Moosee, and Cutless

(B)   Buckeye and John Moosee

Questions 154-156 are based upon the following fact situation.

John was hit by a car driven by Maurice. Both parties agree that John was in a crosswalk and Maurice drove past a red light. Mary, a bystander, tried to stop the bleeding in John's leg, but actually aggravated the injury. John was rushed to Charity Hospital, where he was treated by Dr. Death. Death, a graduate of Popa Doc University, an unaccredited medical school in Haiti, was a licensed doctor in the jurisdiction, yet forgot to put disinfectant on the wound. John's leg subsequently became infected, and John was forced to walk with a cane. Two months after the injury, while John was crossing the street, Vicious grabbed John's cane and hit John over the head with it. John asserted an action based on negligence against Maurice.

154.   Will John be able to recover the damages attributable to Mary's actions from Maurice?

(A)   Yes, because Mary's actions were a foreseeable intervening event.

(B)   Yes, because one who is negligent is responsible for all results of that negligence.

(C)   No, because Mary's actions were a superseding intervening cause of injury.

(D)   No, because Mary's actions were not foreseeable by Maurice.

155. Will John be able to recover damages due to Dr. Death's actions from Maurice?

    (A) Yes, because Dr. Death's actions were a foreseeable intervening event.

    (B) Yes, because one who is negligent is responsible for any and all results of that negligence.

    (C) No, because Dr. Death's actions were a superseding intervening force.

    (D) No, because Dr. Death's actions were not foreseeable by Maurice.

156. Will John be able to recover damages from Maurice due to Vicious's actions?

    (A) Yes, because Vicious's actions were a foreseeable intervening cause.

    (B) Yes, because one who is negligent is responsible for all results of that negligence.

    (C) No, because Vicious's actions were a superseding intervening cause.

    (D) No, because Vicious could have assaulted John with other weapons.

157. State Senator Bob Fatnose was the subject of a series of stories in the *Metropolis Press*. The newspaper reported that Fatnose was addicted to cocaine and that this addiction motivated his behavior in office.

    The newspaper further alleged that Fatnose used his influence to steer construction contracts to companies controlled by organized crime. The article claimed that "reliable sources" had provided the information. The reporter believed that the story was true.

    Fatnose lost his bid for re-election and suffered severe bouts of depression that caused him to be hospitalized. Fatnose brought suit against the Press based on defamation. Should he prevail?

    (A) Yes, because the sources cited are not sufficient for such allegations.

    (B) Yes, if he can prove the story was absolutely false.

    (C) No, because the Press was not aware that the story was false and it did not publish the story with malicious intent.

    (D) No, if the Press exercised ordinary care to determine the truth or falsity of the statements.

158. Mary was hosting a charity benefit for the local church. Thirty minutes before the guests were scheduled to arrive, she realized she would need much more ice. She sent Lunatic, her sixteen-year-old son, to get the ice from the local supermarket. Lunatic, a licensed driver, drove through the residential neighborhood

GO ON TO THE NEXT PAGE

at speeds over eighty miles per hour. He decided he would take his chances and keep going when he came upon a red light. Unfortunately, a car driven by Sane was legally entering the intersection at the same time. The cars collided, causing serious injuries.

If Sane asserts a claim against Mary for injuries suffered, Sane will most likely prevail because

(A)   parents are vicariously liable for torts of their children

(B)   of the doctrine *respondeat superior*

(C)   she was negligent

(D)   Lunatic was acting as an agent of Mary

159.   Mouth is a popular disk jockey on a local morning radio show. One morning, he said over the air, "Those of you running late in Kling County, hit the pedal to the floor. You can pay off any cop in the county for less than ten dollars." A class action based on defamation was brought by the Kling County Patrolmen's Benevolent Association on behalf of six hundred law enforcement officers. Mouth will probably

(A)   prevail, because it is obvious he was only joking

(B)   prevail, because a group of six hundred is too large to be collectively defamed

(C)   not prevail, because the language was defamatory and damaged the reputations of the plaintiffs

(D)   not prevail, unless his statements were read verbatim from a script

Questions 160-161 are based upon the following fact situation.

Hermit raised chickens on a remote farm. His nearest neighbors were twenty miles away. Stripper bought 20,000 acres of land approximately a half-mile from Hermit's farm and began removing the top layers of soil to recover coal.

Hermit filed written complaints on several occasions, demanding that Stripper use Whispertractors instead of the ordinary tractors being used. He claimed that Whispertractors were 80 percent quieter and made fewer vibrations. Hermit had evidence showing that his egg production had been cut in half since the mining began. He personally suffered migraine headaches from the noise.

Stripper responded with a letter stating that it would cost an extra fourteen million dollars per year to use Whispertractors and that the company did not feel that the expense could be justified.

In 1989, Hermit's egg sales amounted to thirteen thousand dollars, his best year ever.

160.   In an action by Hermit for personal injuries from Stripper based on nuisance, Hermit will most likely

(A)   prevail, if Hermit's injuries were caused by an unreasonable interference with the use of his land imposed by Stripper

(B)   prevail, because Stripper is engaged in ultra-hazardous activities

(C)   not prevail, because the expense involved in purchasing Whispertractors is prohibitive

(D)   not prevail, because the vibrations are a public nuisance

161.   In a suit based on negligence by Hermit· against Stripper for decreased production of eggs, should Hermit prevail?

(A)   Yes, because the mining was a private nuisance.

(B)   Yes, but only for the actual damages incurred.

(C)   No, because the mining constituted a public nuisance.

(D)   No, because Stripper was not negligent.

162.   Father received a stun gun for Christmas from Mother. The gun emitted an electric charge that could paralyze a person for up to ten minutes. Kid, Father's twelve-year-old son, begged his father for weeks to allow him to borrow the gun. Finally, Father relented. Kid brought the gun to school and shot a teacher whom he hated for giving too many homework assignments. The teacher fell down on his head and suffered severe neurological damage. If the teacher asserts a claim against Father for injuries sustained, he will most likely prevail because of the rule of

(A)   *respondeat superior*

(B)   negligence

(C)   non-delegable duties

(D)   caution

163.   Skinhead despised men with long hair. Hippie had shoulder-length hair. Every afternoon Hipness, Hippie's wife, would drive her car to the front gate of Radical University and wait to pick up her husband. One day, Skinhead ambushed Hippie while he was walking across Radical U's campus. Skinhead held a knife against Hippie's neck to instill some fear in him and proceeded to cut Hippie's hair with a pair of scissors. Hipness saw the entire incident while sitting in her car approximately 100 yards away. Ever since the incident, she has not been able to sleep, forcing her to quit her job.

If Hipness asserts a claim against Skinhead for intentional infliction of emotional distress, Hipness should

(A)   prevail, because Skinhead's actions were extreme and outrageous and would shock the person of average sensibility

(B)   prevail, because Skinhead's actions were the proximate cause of Hipness's injuries

(C)   not prevail, because Skinhead was unaware of Hipness's presence

(D)   not prevail, because Hipness was outside the zone of danger.

GO ON TO THE NEXT PAGE

164. Debra Slinger is a famous movie star. Slinger has starred in dozens of movies. She often appears on television shows. The *National Requirer* decided to capitalize on Slinger's popularity and placed her picture on the newspaper's cover. Research has shown that the newspaper's sales tripled after publication of the issue in which Slinger was featured on the cover. If Slinger asserts a claim against the *National Requirer*, based on invasion of privacy, Slinger will most likely

    (A)   prevail, because her picture was appropriated for the *National Requirer's* commercial advantage

    (B)   prevail, because a magazine cover story interferes with one's solitude

    (C)   not prevail, because commercial advantage may be taken of a public figure

    (D)   not prevail, because National Requirer may use Slinger's picture for profit in this manner

165. Don was depressed over not being offered a job at a prestigious Main Street law firm. His anger was fueled when he found out the job went to Wally. Don wrote a letter informing the law firm that Wally enjoyed having sexual relations with sheep and sent a copy of the letter to the State Bar Ethics Committee. Neither the law firm nor the committee made the contents of the letter public. Upon learning of the letter, Wally became clinically depressed. His condition required several months of hospitalization. Wally brought suit against Don based on defamation. Proof that the statement is true will

    (A)   not be a defense

    (B)   be a defense only if Don was sure his letter was true at the time he wrote it

    (C)   be a defense only against punitive damages

    (D)   be a defense

Questions 166-167 are based upon the following fact situation.

Fred purchased an auto from Heewanora Hiroshima Motors. The car was manufactured by Hiroshima Motor Company. Fred ordered an option called "ultimate cruise," which regulated the car's speed and was set by the driver. Ultimate cruise, manufactured by Hiroshima, works by automatically controlling the gas pedal and brakes to keep a constant speed. The brakes were manufactured by Tokyo Motor Company. The gas pedal system was manufactured by Japan Accelerate Co.

A week or two after Fred bought his car, he decided to go for a long drive with his family. He drove out to the country, where, for the first time, he was able to use the "ultimate cruise." Fred did not know that there was a malfunction in the system. The "ultimate cruise" signaled the gas pedal to the floor. To prevent the car from going too fast, the brakes were signaled to be used for three hours straight. When approaching a toll plaza, Fred turned the "ultimate cruise" off and stepped on his brake to stop. Since the linings were completely worn down, Fred could not stop the car in time, and he slammed into a toll-collecting machine. Fred, his wife, and his three children all suffered serious injuries. Fred's six-year-old son, Charlie, asserted claims against Heewanora, Hiroshima, Tokyo, and Japan Accelerate Co.

166. Charlie's claim against Heewanora is based upon negligence. To recover he must prove that the car

   (A) was defective

   (B) was defective, and Heewanora had not inspected the car

   (C) was defective, and Heewanora inspected the car, but did not discover the defect

   (D) was defective, and Heewanora would have discovered the defect had it exercised reasonable care

167. Charlie's claims against Hiroshima, Tokyo, and Japan Accelerate Co. are based on strict liability in tort. Charlie should prevail against

   (A) Tokyo, because the brakes failed

   (B) Hiroshima only, because the "ultimate cruise" was defective

   (C) Tokyo and Hiroshima, because the "ultimate cruise" and brakes combined to cause the injuries

   (D) Tokyo, Hiroshima, and Japan Accelerate Co., because the "ultimate cruise" system comprised all three systems

168. Deb and Beck, two sisters, have despised each other ever since their mother died and litigation concerning the estate began. Beck knew Deb had a pathological fear of burglars. One night Beck dressed up in black and walked, after gaining entry through an open door at Deb's house, across Deb's living room. Deb was in the shower at the time, but Bud, Deb's fiancee, saw Beck in the living room and chased her out. Bud ran upstairs to tell Deb what had just happened. Deb passed out and cracked her skull when Bud told her.

   If Deb asserts a claim against Beck based on intentional infliction of emotional distress, the fact that Bud told her of the "burglar" will

   (A) relieve Beck of liability, because Bud's actions made Deb's reaction foreseeable

   (B) relieve Beck of liability, because Bud was the immediate cause of the injury

   (C) relieve Beck of liability, because Bud acted as a mitigating circumstance

   (D) not relieve Beck of liability, because Beck intended to frighten her sister and her intent was achieved

169. Kojack was an inspector for the Department of Agriculture. Elsie owned a dairy farm. Elsie was notified that Kojack would be inspecting her farm. "Go right ahead, look around," said Elsie when Kojack arrived. Kojack walked to the area used to milk cows. He stood in the

GO ON TO THE NEXT PAGE

area specifically designed for the cows, and not for people. He put his hand inside the machine used for milking. The cows were all out to pasture, having already been milked that morning. Someone suddenly turned the machine on, and severed three of Kojack's fingers. Upon later inspection, it was found that the milking machines and their switches were all in proper working order. If Kojack brings suit against Elsie based on negligence, he will

(A)   recover, because Elsie or an employee was negligent

(B)   recover, because Elsie is strictly liable

(C)   not recover, because Kojack assumed the risk

(D)   not recover, because Kojack was a licensee

TORTS ANSWERS

1.   (A)   Eli was an invitee. An invitee is generally a patron of a business open to the public. The invitor has a special duty to an invitee because the invitee is considered to have entered the invitor's premises in response to an express or implied invitation. There is an affirmative duty to protect the invitee against all dangers of which the invitor is or should be aware. (B) is incorrect. Actual knowledge is not required; the school will be charged with constructive knowledge if it should have known about the hazard by reasonable inspection. (C) and (D) are irrelevant because Eli was an invitee.

2.   (B)   A manufacturer who sells a product in a defective condition that is unreasonably dangerous to the foreseeable user is strictly liable for injury if (1) the manufacturer is in the business of sales to the general public (Choice C), (2) the product reaches the consumer in substantially the same condition in which it was sold (Choice A), and (3) the product's defect was the actual and proximate cause of injuries (Choice D). (B) is incorrect because the requirement that the injured party be in privity with the manufacturer to sustain a product liability action has been abolished in all jurisdictions.

3.   (A)   Comparative negligence statutes allow recovery based on relative degrees of fault when both parties were negligent. The recovery of each party is based on the damages incurred. A pure comparative negligence statute requires that each party pay for the percentage of damage that he caused. Frank's $4,000 in damages will be reduced by his 60 percent of fault, to equal $1,600. Kenny's $3,000 damages are reduced by 40 percent to total $1,800. From these calculations, Kenny owes Frank $1,600 and Frank owes Kenny $1,800; Kenny has a net recovery of $200. A modified comparative negligence jurisdiction will not allow a party who was more than 50 percent at fault to recover. Frank would be liable to pay for Kenny's entire sum of damage ($3,000) in such a jurisdiction.
    The last clear chance doctrine (Choice B) provides that the person who had the last clear chance to avoid the accident, but failed to do so, is wholly liable. Last clear chance is used by the plaintiff as a defense to contributory negligence. It would not apportion the damages.
    A plaintiff may be denied recovery under the Assumption of Risk Doctrine (Choice C) on the theory that the plaintiff knew the situation contained a risk and then voluntarily assumed that risk. Since neither party in our case knew of the other's reckless driving, this doctrine does not apply. Comparative negligence statutes subsume the doctrine of assumption of risk by factoring each person's knowledge of the risk involved into his percentage of fault.
    Contributory negligence (Choice D) is a defense that completely bars the plaintiff from recovery if he is at all negligent. The inequitability of this doctrine led to the adoption of comparative negligence statutes.

4.   (D)   The suit will fail because malicious prosecution applies to criminal proceedings only. Medical malpractice is a civil action. The elements of malicious prosecution are (1) institution of criminal proceedings, (2) termination in favor of plaintiff, (3) absence of probable cause to prosecute, (4) prosecution for an improper cause, and (5) damages.

5.   (A)   The elements that must be present to support strict liability in a product liability tort case are (1) an absolute duty owed by a merchant or commercial supplier to the user, (2) a breach of this duty (a defect), (3) the defect actually and proximately causes injury, and (4) damages. The multiplex is a "popcorn merchant" because its business includes the regular sale of popcorn. This merchant-supplier requirement is meant to exclude a casual one-time seller from strict liability, such as one who sells his personal washing machine. There is no requirement that the sale of the particular good must be the defendant's primary business activity. The rancid butter constituted a defect in the product.

(B) is incorrect because Cole Pineapple is not a merchant or a supplier of boilers. The plaintiff may have prevailed on a theory that Cole owed its visitors a duty that the plant was free from hazards. (C) is incorrect because the airline uses planes, but does not make or sell them. The instructions given in (D) are appropriate, since strict liability does not depend on fault.

6.   (D)   The elements of intentional infliction of emotional distress are (1) an extreme and outrageous act by defendant, (2) intent by defendant to cause plaintiff severe emotional distress, (3) causation, and (4) damages. Plaintiff must establish that Defendant **intended** to cause Plaintiff emotional distress. Such intent requires, at the very least, that Defendant know that there is a very high probability that his actions will cause Plaintiff emotional distress. Defendant did not have the necessary intent, since he did not know that Plaintiff was Robby's brother.

Although Defendant in (A) could use the defense of private necessity to a trespass action, he is still liable for the actual damages he caused. In (B), Defendant's purposeful beating of Plaintiff's dog rendered him liable for trespass to chattels. Since the dog was on a leash, Defendant doesn't seem to have a valid claim of self-defense. Plaintiff will most likely prevail on his conversion suit in (C). Conversion is the intentional exercise of control over a chattel that interferes with the true owner's right to dominion over it. To establish liability, it is only necessary that Defendant intend to control the chattel, but Defendant need not know the chattel belongs to another.

7.   (B)   The elements of deceit are (1) a misrepresentation, (2) that is knowingly false, (3) with intent to induce reliance, (4) justifiable reliance by plaintiff, and (5) damages. Unless Liar knew his statements were false, he will not be held liable for deceit.

8.   (B)   Assault is the intentional causation of an apprehension of harmful or offensive contact. Apprehension is not the same as fear. Regardless of whether the plaintiff is afraid of the defendant, if the plaintiff **anticipates a battery** an assault has been committed.

9.   (B)   Courts attribute differing degrees of probative weight to the violation of a statute in a negligence action. First, to be admissible, the statute's purpose must be to prevent the type of injury that occurred. Once admitted, according to the respective jurisdiction, the violation might be considered 1) negligence per se (negligence established as a matter of law unless the defendant can provide a legally justifiable excuse), 2) *prima facie* negligence (in the absence of a response by the defendant, the plaintiff will have proved negligence), 3) a rebuttable presumption of negligence, 4) some evidence of negligence. Courts are loath to impose strict liability (Choice A) or to make the presumption of negligence irrebuttable (Choice D). Although the plaintiff may plead that the violation constituted negligence per se, the action itself is **based upon** negligence (Choice C).

10.   (D)   All four choices deal with the issue of intervening causes. An intervening cause occurs after the negligence of the defendant and adds to or causes the damage. The issue related to intervening causes is at what point the defendant should be relieved of liability. The rule is that the defendant will be liable for the entire damage if the intervening cause was foreseeable. This rule provides that if a defendant should have reasonably foreseen that the resultant injury might occur in the due course of events, the court will find that the defendant has proximately caused the injury and is liable. If the intervening action was unforeseeable, then the defendant's negligence will have been **superseded**, and the defendant will not be held liable for that damage attributed to the intervening cause.

          (A), (B), and (C) are generally considered foreseeable events by the courts and therefore are not superseding intervening causes. Driver will be liable for causation of the entire injury.

          Extraordinary acts of nature are generally considered unforeseeable, which makes them superseding causes of injury. In this case, Victim was no more likely to be hit by lightning while waiting on the highway than if he were driving five miles away.

11.   (D)   In a medical malpractice case, the majority rule is that when a foreign object is left in the body the statute begins to run at the time the injury is discovered. (B) and (C) are rules followed in other types of malpractice cases. (A) is the traditional rule, but is no longer followed in the majority of jurisdictions.

12.   (D)   If one knowingly, voluntarily, and unreasonably subjects himself to a risk, he has assumed the chance of injury. On this basis, Leonard's recovery may be limited or denied. Once Leonard read the sign, he knew that he was encountering a dangerous

environment. (C) differs from the assumption of risk. It refers to the doctrine of contributory negligence, which provides that if the plaintiff was at all negligent he will be barred from recovery. (C) is not the best answer, because most states abolished the contributory negligence defense in enacting comparative negligence statutes.

13.   (D)   Justification is a "catch-all" defense to intentional torts, including false imprisonment. Although all the elements of false imprisonment were present in this question, Henry's defense of justification contends that since his actions were justified, he had a privilege to take such action. A court allowed the defense of justification upon similar facts by finding that the driver had a duty to take reasonable safety measures [*Sindle v. New York City Transit Authority*, 307 N.E. 2nd 245 (NY 1973)]. Necessity is the privilege to harm a property interest during an emergency. The harm may be done for the public good (Choice A) or for the private individual (Choice B).

        A person is allowed to use self-defense when he believes he is in danger of imminent harm (Choice C). Since there is no evidence that the children were going to harm Henry, justification is his best defense.

14.   (B)   Defamation encompasses the doctrines of slander and libel. Although the two sometimes overlap, slander is oral defamation and libel is printed. For defamation to be actionable, there must be publication of the defamatory material, which is accomplished merely by communication to one person other than the plaintiff. Billy's dictation to his secretary will be treated by some courts as if he wrote the letter himself without an intermediary. However, most courts will consider it **libel** when the defamatory words are taken down. Restatement (Second) of Torts § 577 provides that dictation to a stenographer who takes notes is libel. Although these words were spoken, they would be treated as libel and not slander. An action for libel requires that Leonard suffer actual damages. From the facts of this question, it does not seem that Leonard has incurred any damages since the bank never received the letter. Therefore, his action will fail.

15.   (B)   The general rule is that an employer is not responsible for the negligence of an independent contractor (Choice C). However, this rule does not excuse the employer from its own negligence. In our case, NYC should have foreseen harm when it hired a contractor known to be incompetent. The knowledge of Sky High's incompetence created a duty in NYC to reasonably inspect the safety of Sky High's work site. (D) is partially correct because NYC also owed Gabby a duty as an invitee, but NYC has not breached this duty unless they had actual or constructive knowledge of the danger. NYC will not be held strictly liable for Gabby's injury.

        (A) is incorrect because Charitable Immunity has been abrogated in most jurisdictions and is filled with exceptions in where it remains in effect.

16.   (D)   The tort of interference with contractual advantage is committed by a person who induces someone to breach a contract he has entered with another. The clients

breached their contracts with Clayton Landscapers by paying Yossi instead of making their payments due to the company. Yossi has not committed conversion (Choice C). The taking of another's cash will not qualify as conversion, because money is not a chattel. (A) is incorrect because intangible rights closely linked to a document have been recognized as the subject of conversion, but no such document was present in Yossi's case. Embezzlement (Choice B) involves the conversion of property entrusted to an employee by the employer. Yossi was never entrusted with property by Clayton.

17. (C)   The elements of negligence are (1) a duty, (2) breach of this duty, (3) proximately causing injury, and (4) damages. Corcoran had a duty to hold the bonds in safekeeping. He breached this duty when he accidentally housetrained his puppy with them. The breach proximately caused injury to Entrepreneur and resulted in damages. He did not commit trespass to Entrepreneur's bonds (Choice A) because he had the right to their possession. Conversion requires intent (Choice B) to maintain dominion over the property. Corcoran had no such intent.

18. (B)   The owner of a chattel (personal property) may bring a tort action against someone who deprives him of use or possession of that chattel. Trespass to chattels and conversion only differ in the extent to which the plaintiff was deprived of property. The Multistate will often ask questions that require knowledge of the fine-line distinction between these two torts.

The elements of trespass to chattels are (1) an act interfering with plaintiff's right to possess his chattel, (2) intent to perform the act, (3) actual deprivation of property, and (4) damages.

The elements of conversion are (1) wrongful possession of chattel of such serious nature or consequence to warrant that the defendant pay the rightful owner its full value, (2) intent to control the chattel, and (3) causation.

To distinguish between trespass and conversion, the court will examine the time period of the deprivation, the extent of deprivation, the defendant's intent, the harm done to the chattel, the inconvenience to the plaintiff, and the expenses the plaintiff incurred as a result. The more significant the deprivation, the more likely it will be classified as conversion.

(B) is the correct answer because a three-month deprivation of property is sufficient interference to qualify as conversion (Restatement (second) § 222A, illus. 2). The rightful owner of the hat was deprived of the entire use of this expensive item for the rest of the winter and might have understandably replaced it.

19. (B)   Since the property was completely destroyed, this is a conversion despite Elmo's good faith (Restatement (second) § 222A, illus. 3).

20. (B)   Elmo's bad faith will present sufficient grounds for conversion despite the short period of deprivation (Restatement (second) § 222A, illus. 4).

21.   (D)   The express warranty is the best theory for his law suit. First, it will entitle Larry to the cost of the lighter, since the price of the defective product itself is not recoverable in the absence of a warranty. Second, Larry wants to sue for the loss of the intangible asset of his good looks. Generally, this is only recoverable under an express warranty. However, this warranty might not suffice, since it only guarantees the return of his money and does not unconditionally guarantee the product. He will still be able to hold Acme strictly liable (Choice C) for the harm proximately caused by the lighter. (A) would apply if the lighter had not been suitable for its intended purpose of igniting cigarettes. This choice is incorrect because the lighter fulfilled its purpose until it blew up.

22.   (A)   Interference with prospective advantage is a tort committed when a person unlawfully interferes to cause another the loss of future income. It differs from the tort of interference with contractual advantage (Choice B) in that it doesn't require deprivation of a contractual benefit, only the unlawful interference with a relatively certain economic return. (B) is not a basis for Lenny's action because a tenancy at will does not create a contract right.

        (C) and (D) are not names of torts.

23.   (D)   Private nuisance is the interference with one's use and enjoyment of land. Repeated telephone calls have been ruled private nuisance [*Wiggins v. Moskins Credit Clothing Store*, 137 F. Supp. 764 (EDSC. 1956)].

        The elements of a *prima facie* case for intentional infliction of emotional distress are (1) an extreme and outrageous act by a defendant, (2) intent to cause severe emotional distress, (3) causation, and (4) damages.

        Invasion of privacy can be based on one of four actions: (1) appropriation, (2) intrusion, (3) public disclosure of private facts, or (4) false light. Intrusion has been held to include persistent phone calls.

        Therefore, Dorothy may assert an action based on any of these three torts.

24.   (C)   When damages have been caused by two or more independent causes the plaintiff can recover from either or both. Pursuant to these facts, neither the railroad nor Jack will be liable for that portion of damage caused by the other. With respect to the railroad's liability, Jack's actions will be deemed a superseding cause of damage because intentional torts are not considered foreseeable. Since Jack's actions were subsequent to the railroad strike, Farmer Jim may only recover from Jack that damage he actually caused. Jim must prove the decrease in value of his apples caused by the derailment.

25.   (C)   A defendant will usually be liable for all harm caused directly by his negligence and for all harm caused by foreseeable intervening events that would not have occurred in the absence of his negligence. Such foreseeable events include medical malpractice and a plaintiff's subsequent actions. A defendant will not be held liable for those further consequences caused by unforeseeable intervening events, also called

superseding causes. (C) is the correct choice because medical malpractice has been ruled a foreseeable event, and not a superseding cause. (D) is an incorrect choice because Tyke was reacting in a reasonable manner to the situation Emile created, so his actions are considered foreseeable.

26. (B) As a general rule, a parent is not vicariously liable for the torts of a child. However, if a parent has knowledge of the child's proclivity to commit the specific tort, encouraged the behavior, or directed or ratified the child's tortious conduct, the parent will be liable. A young child is considered capable of forming the intent (Choice D) required for an intentional tort. All that is necessary is that the child have knowledge to a substantial degree of certainty that the prohibited results will follow.

27. (B) Minors are held liable for assault and battery, trespass, conversion, defamation, seduction, deceit, and negligence (Prosser Sec. 134). Prosser quoted Lord Kenyon, who said, "If an infant commits an assault or utters slander, God forbid that he should not be answerable for it in a court of justice." However, a child will not be held liable if incapable of forming the requisite intent. To prove intent, Bones only needs to show that Bubba knew to a substantial degree of certainty that by swinging his arm at Bones he would strike him and cause him harm. At age seven, and after having been encouraged by his father, Bubba knew what he was doing and is thus liable for his torts.

    (C) is incorrect. Parents are not solely responsible for their child's conduct.

28. (B) The elements of battery are (1) harmful or offensive contact, (2) intent, and (3) causation. The little shove that Shikker gave Salesman is enough to constitute a battery. Shikker's actions are not nearly outrageous enough to constitute an attempt to inflict emotional distress (Choice D).

29. (D) Slander is oral defamation. To be actionable, Shikker must prove that he suffered special damages, which is monetary loss. The only exception to the special damages rule is for slander per se, where the damages are presumed. Slander per se includes oral defamation in regard to 1) imputation of a major crime, 2) loathsome disease, 3) a person's business, trade, profession or office, and 4) serious sexual misconduct. Therefore, (C) is not correct. The mere fact that Shikker was insulted (Choice B) does not give rise to an action for defamation. Salesman may assert in his defense that the statement was true or even that it was pure nonsense because skunks do not truly get drunk.

30. (D) Storekeeper was not privileged to authorize that Shikker be thrown into his car. (A), (B), and (C) are incorrect because there was no evidence of a Civil Rights

violation from the facts of the question, strict liability will not arise from ejectment, and (C) is too vague.

31. (A)   Letting a severely inebriated person out on a major road constitutes negligence, because it breaches the common duty to act like a reasonable person. A reasonable person should recognize that Shikker was placed in danger. Storekeeper will be liable for the actions of his employees since they were acting as his agents.

(C) is incorrect, a store owner does not unconditionally guarantee the safety of his customers. A store owner is liable for an invitee's safety (Choice B) from hazardous conditions within his store.

32. (C)   The accident was caused by Detroit's negligence. A car driving at any speed could have been hit by the train. Stroh's age and lack of a driver's license were not factors in the accident and will not play a role in the case. "Last clear chance" (Choice D), the doctrine providing that the party with the last opportunity to avoid the accident is wholly liable for the ensuing damages, is completely unaffected by whether Stroh had a license to drive.

33. (C)   For the purpose of this action, Stroh was not negligent. One is not expected to stop and check oncoming trains before crossing railroad tracks unless signs and/or signals indicate to do so. (B) is incorrect because Stroh's speeding did not cause the accident. *Res Ipsa Loquitur* (Choice D) is a doctrine that will allow a plaintiff to create an inference of negligence without a precise showing of the defendant's negligent behavior when the cause of the injury was within the defendant's control. This doctrine is unrelated to the issue of Stroh's speeding.

34. (B)   One is liable for all consequences proximately caused by his negligence whether foreseeable or not. This is because "the defendant takes the plaintiff as he finds him" [*Watson v. Rinderknecht*, 84 NW 9798 (Minn. 1901)].

35. (C)   Evidence that a statute has been violated may only be introduced in a tort case when the injury is of the type the statute intends to prevent. Since speeding laws are not enacted to prevent cars from being hit by trains at railroad crossings, the statutory violation is not admissible. (D) is incorrect because Stroh's speeding was not a cause of the accident. (A) and (B) are not relevant legal factors.

36. (C)   To recover under strict liability in a product liability suit, a plaintiff must prove (1) an absolute duty owed to users by a commercial supplier or merchant, (2) breach of duty (a defect), (3) actual and proximate cause, and (4) damages. The breach of duty will be established by showing that the product is defective. There are two types of defects. They are the manufacturing defect and the design defect. Manufacturing

defects are easier to prove. They exist when the product deviates from its intended design in a manner that makes it unreasonably dangerous. Design defects exist when the product has been designed in an unreasonably dangerous manner. Restatement of Torts defines defective as "unreasonably dangerous" to users. (A) is an element that will help show the defective design, but it is not imperative that (A) be established. (B) is extraneous to a strict liability action. While an insufficient warning may be considered a design defect (Choice D), a warning will not absolve the defendant of liability for an unreasonably dangerous product.

37. (A)   To establish the strict liability of a retailer, a plaintiff needs to prove 1) sale by the defendant, 2) existence of the defect, 3) proximate cause, and 4) that the defect existed at the time the product left the defendant. Privity (Choice B), involvement in the product's design (Choice C), and knowledge of the hazard (Choice D) are not necessary elements.

38. (A)   Under a pure comparative negligence statute one recovers or pays damages based upon his percentage of fault, even if it is greater than 50 percent. Under a modified comparative negligence statute (adopted in a majority of jurisdictions), a plaintiff will recover only if he is less than 50 percent negligent (Choice B). (D) is incorrect. Employee did not have the last clear chance to avoid the accident.

39. (A)   Since Jeff was not aware, and did not have reason to be aware, of any defect, he was not negligent. Wendy was negligent in opening the car door and, therefore, will be liable. Employee's negligence (Choice B) is irrelevant in a suit between Jeff and Wendy. A superseding cause would potentially relieve Quick's Repair of liability, not Wendy (Choice C). (D) does not absolve Wendy of negligence. The mere fact that she did not assume a specific risk, does not excuse her otherwise negligent actions.

40. (B)   Quick's failure to warn Jeff that the car had not been repaired negligently created an unreasonable risk of harm to Jeff. Quick breached his duty to act as a reasonable person, and injury resulted. Employee's subsequent failure to warn Jeff will not supersede (Choice D) or negate Quick's Repair's liability for its own negligence. It is foreseeable that other people will act negligently.

41. (C)   The city ordinance that makes it illegal to throw objects from a rooftop was enacted to prevent injuries like the one to Constructor. Therefore, the statute is admissible to establish the appropriate standard of care in the jurisdiction (Choice B). However, the statute will not be the only standard by which Careless is judged. The statute will be part of the evidence regarding whether Careless acted in the manner of a reasonably prudent person. (D) is a rare medical condition in which the patient's internal organs are reversed. (A) is not a valid standard.

42. (B)   The absence of the hat did not affect Constructor's injuries. If he had been hit on the head, lack of a hard hat would have been a factor.

43. (D)   This is a question where clearly incorrect choices can easily be eliminated. (B) is a plaintiff's weapon; (A) is irrelevant because it deals with the liability of an employer for the torts of an employee. Negligence per se (Choice C) will most likely be alleged against Careless by Constructor for his violation of the ordinance. (D) is the only defense listed, and therefore the only potentially correct option.

44. (B)   The ordinance regarding trespassing is in no way related to the present action and will therefore not affect the outcome. Careless is not absolutely liable (Choice C) as a result of his trespassing; his negligence must still be proved. Careless trespassed (Choice D) on private property and will be civilly liable to the club's owners, but not liable under the criminal statute this question addresses. Violation of a statute will not prevent Careless from acting as a witness (Choice A).

45. (D)   As long as the defendant's negligent act is the proximate cause of injury, the defendant is liable for the entire extent of the plaintiff's injuries, no matter how bizarre. The fact that Constructor's shoulder was extra-sensitive is irrelevant. The defendant can't choose his plaintiff; he takes him as he finds him. (C) is incorrect because liability attaches regardless of whether Careless could foresee the potential consequences.

46. (C)   The hard hat statute was enacted to protect heads, not shoulders. (A) and (D) are defenses to negligence.

47. (B)   Damages are determined by the fair market value of an item, not the price paid (Choice A) or the subjective value to the owner (Choice C). Careless will be held liable for the watch due to the same reasoning that renders him liable for the added shoulder trauma. Once a person proximately causes injury, he is liable for the entire extent of the damage.

48. (B)   Since Constructor's violation of the statute was not the proximate cause of his injuries, the jury will not be allowed to consider the statute at all.

49. (D)   A plaintiff suing under strict liability in a tort action is not entitled to recover for pure economic loss. Crispin may sue for his lost income during his convalescence, but Margaret may not recover the loss her business incurred while she lacked a driver. She might recover this loss under an express warranty theory if the van had been expressly and unconditionally guaranteed. Hensly's knowledge of the intended use

of the van (Choice A) is irrelevant to a strict liability action. It will only be a factor in the determination of whether there exists an implied warranty of fitness for a particular purpose. (C) is irrelevant because privity is no longer a requirement in product liability cases. In a majority of jurisdictions, (B) is incorrect because a seller of used goods is not strictly liable for those defects not created by him. With used goods it is understood that the product has been altered between the time it left the manufacturer and the time it reached the salesman.

50. (D)   In a strict liability action, privity is no longer a requirement. The statement in (B) is correct, but (B) is not a correct answer to this question. Although in a majority of jurisdictions sellers of used goods are not held strictly liable for defects, a seller cannot escape liability for those defects he created.

51. (C)   When a manufactured item has been substantially altered, the manufacturer is freed from strict liability.

52. (D)   Crispin would win a suit brought under strict liability in tort. Although Hensly usually sells used cars, in this instance he can be considered the retailer of a new good. Sellers and retailers, in addition to manufacturers, may be held strictly liable. Since one element of a strict liability case is proving that the defect existed at the time the good left the defendant, it is easiest to prove in regard to the last person in the chain of sale — in this case, Hensly. The other choices are incorrect because 1) there was no express warranty (Choice B), 2) negligence (Choice A) will be more difficult to prove than strict liability, and 3) a van is not considered an ultra-hazardous product (Choice C).

53. (D)   Improper use is a defense to a strict liability tort action. However, it will not be a very effective defense, because it requires that there be **unforeseeable misuse**. If the manufacturer should have anticipated that the product will be used in such an improper manner, it has a duty to take precautions. Note that contributory negligence is not a defense to strict liability (Choice B). Lack of privity (Choice A) and due care (Choice C) are also not valid defenses to strict liability.

54. (D)   This is the best answer because a person is not usually under a duty to rescue another from peril. A duty may be established by 1) a special relationship between people, such as that of an invitor to an invitee, 2) the defendant's negligently causing the dangerous situation, or 3) the defendant's undertaking of a rescue attempt. Good Samaritan statutes limit the liability of a volunteer who makes a rescue attempt, but they do not obligate a potential rescuer (Choice A). If Dr. Grubber's assertion that he had the proper medication for Denise might be found to constitute the beginning of a rescue attempt, he can be found liable for her death.

55.   (A)   The elements of false imprisonment are (1) an act that unlawfully confines or restrains a person to a bounded area against her will, (2) awareness of the confinement by the plaintiff, (3) intent, and (4) causation. To satisfy the first element, the restraint may be by acts or words. False imprisonment has been found where the unlawful act was directed toward a person's property. Although Jerko said Redhead was free to go, she was restrained by his threat to deprive her of her property. Since she could only leave if she let Jerko hold onto her bag of valuables, Redhead should win her action based on false imprisonment.

56.   (A)   An action for private nuisance arises when one party causes substantial and unreasonable interference with the use or enjoyment of another's property.
    (C) is not correct, because intent is not an element of private nuisance. (D) is incorrect because, although the relative values of the restaurant and power plant are relevant in determining the form of the remedy, they are not relevant in determining whether Nukeco is liable for nuisance.
    (B) is incorrect because nuisance law protects a person's interest in the use and enjoyment of property. One use of property might be the conduct of business, but a business entity does not receive special protection in the absence of a property interest.

57.   (B)   The argument is irrelevant to the case. The financial resources of Nukeco might affect the remedy once nuisance has been established, but will not be factored into the determination of liability for nuisance.

58.   (C)   The usual remedy for a private nuisance is money damages. Injunctive relief may be granted when monetary damages would be insufficient, are unavailable, or for other reasons. The court will consider the relative hardships. In our example, it seems very unlikely that the court will force a public utility to move or shut down so that a popular restaurant can remain in business. Since the damage is rather substantial, Feeder will likely be awarded more than nominal damages (Choice D).

59.   (A)   Under the attractive nuisance doctrine, landowners have a duty to exercise ordinary care to avoid a reasonably foreseeable risk of injury caused by artificial conditions on their property where children are likely to trespass. The actual nuisance need not have attracted the child. Thus, even though the art did not cause Feederette to approach the reactor, Nukeco may still be liable for negligence. They have a responsibility to get rid of the attractive nuisance or to make it inaccessible.

60.   (C)   "Life in organized society and especially in populous communities involves an unavoidable clash of individual interests . . . the process of weighing the gravity and probability of the risk against the utility of its course" (Restatement (Second) of

Torts § 822). The initial determination of unreasonable interference represents a clash of individual interests. In the remedy stage of private nuisance, the court must weigh the interests of society, the plaintiff, and the defendant when it decides what type of relief to grant. Who bears the brunt of the nuisance through injunctions or monetary awards will inevitably impact society. (D) applies when an individual seeks a remedy under public, not private, nuisance theory.

61. (D) Causation in negligence cases requires that the act be both the actual and proximate cause of the injury. One's conduct is considered the cause in fact of an injury if "but for" the act of the defendant the injury would not have taken place. This is called the "but for" test and is easily satisfied. Another test for causation in fact is whether the defendant's action was a "substantial factor" in bringing about the injury. The substantial factor test is useful when there are concurrent causes of injury. To establish liability, the conduct must also be the legal or proximate cause of the injury. Proximate cause is more narrowly drawn than cause in fact and is largely driven by policy considerations that seek to limit the defendant from infinite liability for his actions. An act will generally be considered the proximate cause of injury if no "superseding" acts have intervened. Since Tailgator would have been able to stop if Harvey had a functioning brake light, Cynthia's action was a "substantial factor" in the chain of events causing the injury. "But for" Cynthia's actions the accident would not have occurred. There were also no superseding acts subsequent to Cynthia stealing the light. Therefore, she is an actual and proximate cause of the injury.

62. (C) Tailgator's best argument is that it is unreasonable to drive for a week without fixing a nonfunctional taillight. (D) may be correct, but it is not Tailgator's best argument. Harvey's role in causing the accident is a conclusion that must be drawn from the facts. Courts do not impose strict or absolute liability for driving with a broken taillight (Choices A and B).

63. (D) The doctrine of *res ipsa loquitur*, "the thing speaks for itself", will find a defendant liable for negligence in the absence of a sufficient explanation. It requires that 1) the injury be of a type that doesn't generally occur in the absence of negligence and 2) the defendant has complete control over the instrumentality causing the injury. If an unexplained accident can be attributed to any possible cause (such as the truck accident) that is not the responsibility of the defendant, the *res ipsa* argument will fail. Privity (Choice A) has nothing to do with *res ipsa loquitur*. (C) is inapplicable because Hyper never assumed the risk that the product was unreasonably dangerous.

64. (C) Hyper will be held liable if she was negligent. (B) is incorrect, Hyper would be liable not "only" for the malicious and wanton infliction of injuries, but also for

negligence, etc. The word "only" makes the choice incorrect. (D) is incorrect. Hosts do have a duty toward their social guests.

65.   (A)   A seller is liable under strict liability if 1) he is engaged in the business of selling such product, 2) the product travels from the seller to the consumer without substantial change, 3) the product is defective (unreasonably dangerous to the user or consumer), and 4) the defect causes injury. (B) might be an alternate avenue of liability, but strict liability in tort is much more certain of success. This seller can be liable even though the manufacturer was not, because the goods were damaged while in the seller's possession.

66.   (B)   The best cause of action is for battery. The elements of battery are (1) harmful or offensive contact, (2) intent, and (3) causation.

67.   (D)   Broad dissemination and premeditation are necessary elements of slander. Slander per se (Choice C) is a type of oral defamation that is actionable without proving special damages.

68.   (D)   Flounder and his boys had no right to throw Nerdo into their car. Nerdo was unlawfully confined to the car against his will. One important element of false imprisonment is awareness of the confinement. If Nerdo had been unconscious while he was in the car, he would be unlikely to succeed.

69.   (A)   Leaving someone out in the elements on a cold night constitutes negligence. A reasonable person would not act in such a manner.

70.   (B)   Parents are generally not vicariously liable for the torts of their children. However, there are exceptions to this rule. One of which is when the parent encouraged the tort. (C) is false; a minor can commit a tort. Note: This question illustrates a classic Multistate ploy. You may think that Skipper doesn't stand a chance, so you skip right to the "not prevail" choices. Watch out! Read each choice carefully!

71.   (A)   Infants can be held liable for their torts. The requisite intent will be established if Gruner knew to a substantial degree of certainty that the prohibited results would follow from his actions.

72.   (C)   As part of the cause of action for negligence, Bob must prove that Ellen had a duty to rescue him. Generally, no duty exists — even between friends — unless the

defendant either causes the peril or actually commences a rescue attempt (in which case she is obligated to use reasonable care in finishing the rescue).

73.   (C)   To find Grouch liable, Maria must prove that his tree and the broken glass were an attractive nuisance. (A), (B), and (D) are elements that must be proved to establish an attractive nuisance. (C) mentions "private nuisance," which is substantially different and irrelevant to this fact pattern. An attractive nuisance is an artificial condition on one's property where children are likely to trespass that may attract children and subsequently injure them.

74.   (D)   These questions involve knowledge of the elements of attractive nuisance. An attractive nuisance is an artificial condition on one's property that may attract children and subsequently injure them. The elements are (1) a dangerous condition on one's land of which one should be aware, (2) the knowledge that children frequent the area, (3) children are unable to appreciate the risk, and (4) the expense of remedying the danger is slight when compared to the risk. Dorothy is most likely to prevail if a cost-benefit analysis tips in her favor. (A) is related to the likelihood that children will trespass on Grouch's property, but will not be as significant as the cost of preventing the nuisance.

75.   (C)   The elements of defamation are (1) defamatory language, (2) concerning the plaintiff, (3) publication, (4) damage to the reputation, and (5) intent. If Dependable reasonably believed that Sneeky stole the eggs, it could not have intended to defame Sneeky and the action will fail.

76.   (D)   A plaintiff "assumes the risk" when she voluntarily decides to gamble that the harm associated with the activity will not occur. Under the common law, a plaintiff who assumes the risk is barred from recovery. Rusher assumed the risk of a collision by crossing the yellow line when she could have waited. Since this jurisdiction follows the common law and not the modern doctrine of comparative negligence, her actions render Thoughtless's violation irrelevant.

77.   (C)   Modified comparative negligence is a doctrine whereby a plaintiff may recover only if he carries less than 50 percent of the blame or, in other words, is less negligent than the defendant. (A) and (B) represent the "all or nothing" approach that comparative negligence was designed to avoid. This type of emergency is not likely to relieve Rusher from responsibility for her dangerous actions (Choice D).

78.   (D)   Regardless of the cause of the plane crash, Going may be held strictly liable as the retailer of a defective lifeboat that was an immediate and proximate cause of

Hysterical's injuries. (B) is incorrect because a plaintiff may collect from defendants who are jointly liable.

79.   (D)   The elements of product liability under strict liability are (1) an absolute duty owed by a commercial supplier, (2) breach of that duty (a defect), (3) actual and proximate cause, and (4) damages. Due care and diligent inspection (Choices B and C) are defenses to negligence, not to strict liability. A commercial supplier need not have created the defect in question; thus, Going may be liable for Savers' defective workmanship.

80.   (C)   Due care is an effective defense to negligence. If one can prove that she has exercised due care, she is not negligent. It's that simple. Although Daredevil's actions may have been a proximate cause of Hysterical's injuries, an effective defense to relieve Going of liability would need to contend that Daredevil's negligence was a superseding cause of Hysterical's injuries.

81.   (D)   Savers is liable of negligence if it did not perform a proper inspection. Savers cannot shift its duty to Daredevil, whose subsequent negligence is foreseeable. Daredevil's negligence is a foreseeable intervening event (Choice A) which will not relieve Savers of liability. (B) is incorrect because Hysterical was not contributorily negligent. *Respondeat superior* (Choice C) is a doctrine applied to employer-employee relationships.

82.   (B)   Although (C) is the general rule with regard to public nuisances, a private citizen may bring an action for public nuisance when he or she suffers damages different from those of the general public. The fact that Rocky knew about the disco when he purchased the land (Choice D) is relevant only at the remedy stage when the court "balances the equities" to arrive at the appropriate amount of damages or an injunction.

83.   (B)   A private nuisance affects one person's, or a few people's, use and enjoyment of property. (A), although correct, is only one element that will aid him in proving private nuisance. (B) better incorporates the "essence" of private nuisance. (C) illustrates what is considered "coming to the nuisance," which is a factor in the defendant's favor but not a complete defense, and (D) deals with the theory of public nuisance.

84.   (D)   The dilemma was caused by the driver. Nervous did not assume the risk of his injury as long as he acted reasonably in departing for help. Justice Cardozo has written "danger invites rescue." Since the driver led the bus into a dangerous situation, it is reasonable to expect someone to venture for assistance. (C) alone will

not support Nervous's claim if he was unreasonable to venture out of the bus. "Reasonable" does not mean that a majority of passengers have to think like Nervous (Choice A).

85.   (D)   Intent is an element of false imprisonment. Note: This is a classic example of a Multistate trick. At first glance the question looks like it says the passenger will prevail, but the answer changes later on. Read the entire choice. Words like "unless" change a "yes" to a "no," a "prevail" to a "not prevail," an "admissible" to a "not admissible." Mental anguish and negligence (Choices B and C) are not elements of false imprisonment.

86.   (B)   Under product liability based on strict liability in tort, a commercial supplier or merchant is held equally as liable as the manufacturer if the product is not altered. Therefore, Leslie can certainly recover against Retailco if she could have recovered against Defogco. (C) is incorrect because Leslie would still be able to recover against Retailco if Retailco had altered the spray.

87.   (C)   Since the action was brought under negligence, Leslie will not recover, because Expressco and its driver were not negligent. They had no reason to believe the product would cause such harm.

88.   (B)   An owner of an animal generally considered undomesticated is strictly liable for the harm that animal causes, even if the particular animal has been "tamed." The fact that Singh exercised reasonable care (Choice C) is not a defense to strict liability.

89.   (B)   The snake bite causing serious injury was a foreseeable consequence of the failure to properly perform the operation. Careless will only be held liable if he performed negligently; strict liability will not be imposed upon a physician in a medical malpractice action (Choice A).

90.   (B)   Slander is spoken or oral defamation. Its elements require that the defendant (1) make a defamatory statement (2) that identifies the plaintiff (3) that is published and (4) intended by defendant to (5) harm plaintiff's reputation. Ordinarily, a plaintiff must prove special damages (that actual monetary loss ensued) to sustain the action. Slander per se provides four exceptions to that rule. When the defamatory statement concerns (1) plaintiff's professional reputation, (2) loathsome disease, (3) crime, or (4) the sexual misconduct of a woman, special damages need not be proved. In the past, the loathsome disease exception rendered allegations of incurable communicable diseases, which carried a strong social stigma, slander per se. Hepatitis does not

qualify under this exception. This exception has also not been used successfully in the past century.

91.   (C)   An element of defamation is the publication of the defamatory language to a person other than the plaintiff. Since Exploiter communicated the allegation only to Exploited, Exploited will not be able to sustain a cause of action for defamation. She may be able to pursue an action for intentional infliction of emotional distress, the elements of which are (1) an act of extreme and outrageous conduct, (2) intent to cause severe emotional distress, (3) causation, and (4) damages.

92.   (D)   If the employees did not believe the statements, proof of damages will be limited. (A) is incorrect because it is too sweeping. (B) is incorrect because the defenses to defamation are only truth, consent, and privilege. Exploiter's statement was neither true nor privileged, and Exploited never consented to its publication.

93.   (D)   All statements made by the judge, jurors, counsel, witnesses, or parties in judicial proceedings are protected by absolute privilege. When statements are absolutely privileged, there is no liability for their content, even if defendant acted maliciously.

94.   (D)   The test for whether conduct is "outrageous" under the doctrine of intentional infliction of emotional distress is satisfied if the type of conduct will be substantially certain to cause severe distress to a person of average sensibility. People with extreme sensitivities should sue under negligent (not intentional) infliction of emotional distress.

95.   (D)   Gus and Shakedown should bring an action in strict liability because it is easier to prove than negligence; they must merely show that the device was defective and was the proximate cause of the injuries. (C) is incorrect because the *res ipsa loquitur* doctrine may not be applied against a manufacturer who is no longer in control of the product. Privity of contract (Choice A) is unnecessary for a strict liability action, as is warranty (Choice B).

96.   (D)   The elements of a *prima facie* case of negligence are (1) a duty, (2) a breach of the duty, (3) causation, and (4) damages. It should be clear that the installer of a safety device has a duty to diligently inspect it. Breach of this duty (Choice D) remains to be proved. The proximate cause of injury, for the purposes of this action, is the failure of the safety device (Choice A) which is not in dispute.

97.   (C)   The fact that Avelleta was speeding does not eliminate liability for the defective safety device. It was designed to protect a speeding elevator; therefore, its failure was

a proximate cause of the accident. Avelleta's negligence would be considered a concurrent cause of the injuries (Choice B) if proximate cause were to be determined by a "substantial factor" test. This case is determined instead by a "but for" test. (A) and (D) are false.

98.   (B)   Due care is a defense to negligence. Avelleta's negligence (Choice A) will not relieve Roberts of liability. (C) and (D) are false.

99.   (C)   Most states have enacted a guest statute that provides that the driver of a car is liable to her passenger only for gross or wanton and willful misconduct. This statute is inapplicable in the facts of this question because an elevator is not sufficiently analogous to a car.

100.   (B)   Although Jim was a gratuitous lender, he was obligated to warn Tim since he had knowledge of the defect and that it created an unreasonable risk of harm.

101.   (D)   A licensee is one who enters an owner's property for the owner's benefit or with the permission of the owner. The owner must exercise reasonable care in ensuring the safety of licensees. (A) is incorrect because an owner will not be held strictly liable.

102.   (B)   Battery is an intentional tort. However, Leo may not argue that he is not liable because he did not intend to hit Policeman. The important fact is that he intended to hit someone. Under the law, this intent will be transferred from his chosen victim to whomever was actually harmed. In other words, if one acts with the intention of unlawfully harming someone, he is liable for the resulting harm to another, unintended victim. (A) is a doctrine for proving negligence, and (D) is an element of battery.

103.   (A)   For Policeman to have been successful in his suit, Stienbruner must have been held vicariously liable for the actions of Leo. Vicarious liability renders one person liable for the actions of another. This liability arises due to the relationship between the individuals, i.e., employer to employee or invitor to invitee. Indemnification would force Leo to wholly reimburse Stienbruner for damages paid to Policeman. Vicarious liability provides the plaintiff with another "deep pocket" that may be sued, but it also gives the vicariously liable defendant a right to indemnification from the primarily liable party. Stienbruner may sue Leo to recoup his outlay to Policeman.

(B) is incorrect because contribution is an action to apportion liability among defendants. Indemnity involves all of the judgment; contribution involves only a percentage.

104. (D)   Cowboy was most likely correct in determining that the passengers were in danger. In general, one has no duty to take affirmative action to benefit others. However, one who does act is under the duty to act in the manner of a reasonably prudent person. Cowboy acted properly if he reasonably assumed he could drive the passengers to safety. (A) is incorrect because under ordinary circumstances Cowboy's actions would not have placed the passengers in any greater danger.

105. (A)   A threat coupled with the apparent present ability to carry it out is sufficient to create the reasonable apprehension of harmful or offensive contact necessary to legally establish assault. Although Mugger did not brandish a knife in Tiny's face, he may very well have had one available. Words alone are not enough (Choice D), but Mugger seems to have inspired a reasonable apprehension of an imminent battery in Tiny.

106. (B)   A mental incompetent is generally held liable for torts, as are children. If, however, intent is an element of the tort and the mental illness renders the individual incapable of forming the requisite intent, he will not be liable. (D) will be a substantial factor in the remedy stage, but will not be determinative of liability.

107. (B)   Eve could not have consented, because the assurance of safety she accepted was based on false pretenses. Consent is invalid if it was (1) obtained by duress, (2) induced by fraud (as in this question), (3) given by mistake, or (4) given by one without capacity to consent, e.g., a mentally incompetent person. Although children are generally not considered capable of consenting (Choice A), a fifteen-year-old would probably be deemed capable. (C) is incorrect, because Lerious did not unlawfully threaten Eve to obtain her consent.

108. (D)   Assault is the reasonable apprehension of imminent harmful or offensive contact inspired intentionally by the defendant. To prove assault, Eve must prove Lerious knew she was afraid of falling.

109. (A)   To prove intent, Eve must only establish that Lerious acted recklessly in regard to causing her distress. Intent can also be proved if Lerious had knowledge to a substantial degree of certainty that the prohibited result would follow. It is not necessary for the defendant to "wish" the consequences to occur, only that the defendant realize that they are very likely to occur. Intent seems easy to prove from these facts, because Lerious's actions were extreme and outrageous.

110. (D)   The elements of false imprisonment are (1) an unlawful act or omission of defendant that confines plaintiff to a bounded area, (2) plaintiff's awareness of the confinement, (3) intent, and (4) causation of confinement. Lerious's act of lying to

Eve was not enough to confine her to the elevator. Although he falsely induced her, he did not threaten her in any way. The fact that Eve could have stopped or gotten out of the elevator will not defeat an action for false imprisonment.

111. (C)   The purpose of the statute is to allow buses to stop without impeding the flow of traffic. This accident was totally unrelated to the purpose of the statute. It was caused by Martin's actions, not by Thoughtless's. The accident with Lilly could not have been foreseen by the reasonable person in Thoughtless's position, and he is not liable to Lilly.

112. (D)   To prove negligence, the city must prove that Martin's actions were the cause in fact and the legal (or proximate) cause of the damage. Cause in fact requires that "but for" Martin's actions the damage would not have occurred. This is easy, since Martin's swerving to avoid the dog began a chain reaction. Proximate cause requires that it be foreseeable that such actions might cause damage. The actual extent of the damage is irrelevant.

113. (B)   The accident was due to Martin's negligence. Thoughtless's violation of the statute is not relevant, because the parking statute was not enacted to prevent this type of accident. One does not assume the risk of a car being hit when parking along the curb (Choice D).

114. (C)   An independent contractor is liable for damages incurred due to negligence involved in his work. York's best argument is that he was not negligent and exercised due care. (A) is incorrect because the fact pattern specifically states that York made all the decisions concerning the frame.

115. (B)   An employer is vicariously liable for the negligence of her employees in the course of their employment.

116. (B)   If a judgment against Olympia was based on vicarious liability for York's negligence, it would provide Olympia with a cause of action against York. This action would be for indemnification for the damages she must pay to Reichman.

117. (C)   Traditionally, the plaintiff had to provide expert testimony from the same community to prove malpractice (Choice A). This would usually be shown by a deviation from the local custom or standard of care. Modern courts have modified this standard to make it national. However, it is considered apparent, even to the lay-person, that leaving an object inside a patient is a significant deviation from the

reasonable standard of care; therefore, expert testimony is unnecessary to establish negligence in this question.

118.   (B)   Mere breach of duty is not sufficient; actual damages must be proved before a recovery is allowed.

119.   (B)   It was foreseeable that the car would be stolen if the keys were left in the ignition; therefore, Mechanic is liable. The act of the thief is not a superseding cause. It is the foreseeable result of leaving one's keys in the ignition of a car. (A) and (C) are incorrect because they imply that Cynthia assumed the risk of having her car stolen — which she did not.

120.   (D)   The action will fail because the injury was not caused by any negligence on the part of Antar. Plaintiff has made a big mistake — he should have brought the action based on strict liability in tort. There was privity (Choice A), but that will not be enough to support this action. (C) is false; negligence claims are not limited to the manufacturer of the product.

121.   (A)   The elements of strict liability in tort were fulfilled. They are (1) a duty owed by a commercial supplier, (2) breach of the duty (i.e., a defect) (3) that caused the injury, and (4) damages. (D) is incorrect because privity does exist between the buyer and the manufacturer. (C) is irrelevant to strict liability, and (B) is incorrect. As a supplier in the chain of sale, Antar will be strictly liable for the damage caused by a defective product that he sold.

122.   (C)   Under the last clear chance doctrine, a plaintiff may recover despite his own negligence. The party who had the last clear chance to avoid the accident will be held liable for all damage.
        Under a comparative negligence statute, each party is able to recover based on his percentage of negligence. (B) is incorrect as written. Since Brakeless's actions were also a cause of the accident, he would not recover for all of his damages in a comparative negligence jurisdiction. (D) assumes more information than was in the fact pattern. We do not know the last time Brakeless's brakes were inspected.

123.   (C)   One is generally under no duty to rescue another. However, a duty to rescue will exist in someone who either intentionally or negligently places another person in danger.

124.   (D)   One who has reasonable grounds to believe he is being attacked or is about to be attacked has the privilege to defend himself by using that force necessary to repel the

attack. When a defendant is mistaken in the belief that force was necessary, she will not be held liable if the belief was formed reasonably. The honesty of the belief is not considered (Choice C).

125. (D)   The elements of intentional misrepresentation are (1) misrepresentation, (2) knowledge of falsity, (3) intent to induce reliance, (4) causation, (5) reliance, and (6) damages. Silence (non-disclosure) can be held to be a misrepresentation (Choice B), but in this fact pattern, Shakedown did not make any representations at all; either by his silence or by his actions.

126. (B)   If Metropolis had notice of the danger (by virtue of the past twelve occurrences) and could have taken reasonable steps to prevent the injury, Capable will most likely prevail in an action for negligence. Common carriers are generally held to a high standard of care, but they are not strictly liable and they are not insurers for all individuals on their premises (Choice A). Posting barriers between cars and/or warning blind commuters are examples of such measures. "Assuming the risk" (Choice C) is rarely the correct answer. Comparative negligence statutes have made assumption of the risk considerations largely unnecessary. If you have no idea as to what is going on in a question, do not assume the risk!

127. (B)   Use of a person's picture or name for commercial advantage, such as in an advertisement, requires consent. Unauthorized use will give rise to liability for invasion of privacy. Yellow Guitars was obligated to determine if Weirdo had consented to the use of the photograph. This is a separate cause of action from defamation. Defamation requires defamatory language and will not be satisfied by the publication of a picture (Choices C and D). Public figures may sustain an action for invasion of privacy (Choice A).

128. (C)   Opportunist may take anyone's picture he pleases if that person is out in public at the time. Although Opportunist sold the picture for a profit, the tort of invasion of privacy is generally limited to instances where the picture is used by the defendant in advertisements (Choice B).

129. (C)   There is generally no duty to aid one in peril. Spitz is not liable, despite his swimming skills, because he did not contribute to Gross's situation.

130. (B)   Knieval's negligence was the cause of Gross's death. Knieval's lack of knowledge of Gross's presence is irrelevant. But for Knieval's negligence Gross might have lived. Knieval's negligence was also a proximate cause of Gross's death.

131. (B)   Jill will recover in her product liability action against the manufacturer under strict liability. A manufacturer will be held strictly liable for an injury caused by a defect in its product if the product contained the defect when it was sold. This product had a manufacturing defect that caused her injury. The gas filter and dealer preparation were immaterial. (C) is incorrect because one does not assume the risk of such an accident by opening a car's hood. "Assuming the risk" is usually an incorrect choice. (D) is incorrect because privity is not required in product liability actions.

132. (D)   Governmental executive officials have an absolute defense to defamation actions. All statements reasonably related to an executive matter are privileged.

133. (A)   For Darter to be liable, he must have been the proximate cause and the cause in fact. (A) assumes that Darter was a proximate cause. The best approach to judge whether he was also the "cause in fact" is to apply the "but for" test. But for Darter's negligence, the second accident would not have occurred. Therefore, he may be held liable for the second accident.

134. (A)   Darter's defense of contributory negligence will fail because Susan was not at all negligent. As far as she knew, she was capable of jogging safely.

135. (C)   The right to privacy is personal and does not extend to family members. (A) is incorrect because truth and lack of malice are not defenses to invasion of privacy. (B) is incorrect because facts disclosed about a public figure that are so "intimate" that they outrage the average person are not privileged.

136. (D)   Assault is the apprehension of immediate physical harm (Choice B). It is not satisfied in this question, because it requires an intent on the part of the defendant to arouse apprehension. (A) is incorrect because there was no offensive touching. (C) is incorrect because its intent element is also missing. These are all intentional torts, and the employees had innocent intentions.

137. (B)   One is permitted to enter the land of another if necessary to avoid injury, i.e., in the case of private necessity (this makes (A) incorrect), but is liable for any damage he causes. (C) is incorrect for the same reason. (D) is irrelevant to this question.

138. (B)   Since Farmer Tom intended to scare Lloyd, he is liable for battery for all consequences of this action. Strict liability (Choice A) would not apply in this question, since Farmer Tom's actions would not be deemed ultra-hazardous. (D) incorrectly applies the "intent" element of battery. (C) is irrelevant; Tom's actions were not privileged by self-defense.

139. (A)   Assault is an intentional act that causes the apprehension of a battery. Farmer Tom acted intentionally, and if Mel reasonably feared a battery, he should prevail. The fact that Mel may have been a trespasser (Choice D) does not relieve Tom of liability.

140. (C)   Express consent that was induced by fraud will not constitute a defense. Therefore, (A) is incorrect. (B) implies that Don assumed any risk involved, which he did not. He merely assumed the risk of damage caused by an experienced driver. (D) is irrelevant.

141. (D)   The elements of assault are (1) an act, (2) intent to bring about apprehension, and (3) causation. Although Dennison's acts satisfied these requirements, Dennison might claim that he was acting in Ballard's defense. Someone who intervenes to save another may legally use the amount of force the other person was privileged to use in self-defense.

142. (C)   The elements of battery are (1) harmful or offensive contact, (2) intent, and (3) causation. (C) is one of the elements of battery. (A) and (D) are not necessary to establish battery. Trespasser need not prove (B), but may have to rebut the allegation that he instigated the action if it is introduced by the workers.

143. (B)   Felon was at fault in causing the accident; therefore, he is liable to a voluntary rescuer. "Danger invites rescue." The fire was caused by Passerby's negligence, and he may not recover from Felon for injuries suffered from it.

144. (A)   One has no legal duty to rescue another; but, if he does decide to volunteer in a rescue attempt, he must act in the manner of an ordinary, prudent person. In this question, Passerby did not act reasonably and is liable for the damage caused by his negligent behavior.

145. (D)   Rich was not at fault; therefore he is not liable. The fact that the injuries occurred on his property is irrelevant. Rich, on the other hand, can assert successful actions against both Felon and Passerby for the damages to his property and for trespass.

146. (C)   If Alfred's panic was reasonable, he had the right to protect his car from the storm by parking on the hill. Alfred had the right to assert the defense of "private necessity." A person may interfere with the property of another where it is necessary to avoid injury and the threatened injury is more serious than the injury to be caused

by the trespass. In such a case, a person asserting the defense of private necessity is liable for actual damages caused to the other party's property.

147.   (A)   Since Alfred was justified in parking on the hill (see discussion from previous question), Selfish will be liable for damages to the car.

148.   (C)   Carpenter's best defense is that his actions were free from any negligence since he properly maintained the saw. While (A) and (B) are correct, they are not the best answers due to the difficulty of proving them. (D), even if correct, would not relieve Carpenter of liability in a negligence action.

149.   (A)   With minimal effort and expense, Constructor could have made sure the gate was locked; therefore, his failure to do so constitutes negligence.

150.   (A)   Herby would be able to recover against Pete's if the trier of fact determines that Pete's negligence caused the blade to fly off the saw. Strict liability (Choice B) does not apply to a commercial repair shop. (C) is incorrect because Constructor's actions did not supersede any potential negligence of Pete's.

151.   (C)   One of the elements that the plaintiff must prove in a claim based on public nuisance is that he suffered a special or unique damage different from that of the general public. Aycee is suing to clear a sidewalk. Since every member of the public has a right to use the sidewalk, Aycee will not be able to show a special damage. Note: Abatement by self-help (Choice D) is the right of one to enter the property of another and use as little force as possible to end the nuisance. (B) is incorrect since Aycee repeatedly asked Geebee to move his trucks. (A) is not true; monetary damages in this case will be inadequate.

152.   (D)   The elements to establish a *prima facie* case for product liability on the theory of negligence are (1) a legal duty, (2) breach of duty, (3) actual and proximate cause, and (4) damages. In this question, elements (1), (3), and (4) are all obvious from the fact pattern. All that must be proved is (2), the breach of the duty. Such a breach is shown by lack of reasonable care. Plaintiff should sue under strict liability because it requires a lower burden of proof.

153.   (B)   Moosee is strictly liable as the manufacturer of the product. Buckeye is strictly liable as the retailer of a defective product. Cutless is not liable, because the blade was not defective.

154. (A)   A defendant will be held liable for damages incurred from foreseeable events that occurred subsequent to his negligent acts.   Negligent rescuers are foreseeable; therefore, Maurice will be held liable for Mary's negligent actions.

155. (A)   Subsequent medical malpractice causing aggravation of plaintiff's condition will be considered a foreseeable intervening cause.

156. (C)   Criminal acts and intentional acts of third persons, if not foreseeable, are superseding intervening causes that break the chain between the initial wrongful act and the ultimate injury.

157. (C)   Since Fatnose was a public figure, actual malice must be proved in addition to falsity.

158. (D)   Parents are generally not liable for the tortious conduct of their children.   One exception is when the child is acting as an agent for his parents.   *Respondeat Superior* (Choice B) is the doctrine whereby an employer is responsible for the negligence of his employees.

159. (B)   If a defamatory statement refers to an overly large group, no member of that group will fulfill the element that the defamation be "of or concerning" the plaintiff. (A) is inapplicable. (C) is irrelevant because of the size of the group.

160. (A)   Hermit has suffered a loss due to the unreasonable invasion of his rights by Stripper and is entitled to recovery.

161. (D)   Hermit made a mistake — he sued for negligence rather than intentional and unreasonable conduct.

162. (B)   A parent is not vicariously liable for the torts of a child. An exception is when a parent negligently allows the child to perform a dangerous act (for example shooting a stun gun). In such an instance, the parent may be liable for his own negligence in permitting the child to act in such a manner. (A) describes a doctrine regarding employers and employees. (C) is a term used in contract law, and (D) is not a legal rule.

163. (C) The elements of intentional infliction of emotional distress are (1) an act of extreme and outrageous conduct, (2) intent to cause severe emotional distress, (3) causation, and (4) damages. In the instant case Skinhead could not possibly have fulfilled the element of intent, because he was not aware of Hippness's presence. The answer to this question could be found with common sense. The name of the cause of action — intentional infliction of emotional distress — makes it evident that intent is one of the elements.

164. (D) Appropriation of one's picture or name for commercial advantage is actionable as an invasion of privacy. However, this action is limited to advertisement or promotion of product or goods. A one-time magazine cover will not qualify. The mere fact that the *National Requirer* used Slinger's picture to boost its sales will not make it liable under invasion of privacy.

165. (D) Truth is an absolute defense to defamation, no matter how damaging. Note: Defendant has the burden of proving the statement's truth.

166. (D) The elements required to establish a *prima facie* case for product liability on the theory of negligence are (1) a legal duty, (2) breach of duty, (3) actual and proximate cause, and (4) damages. In this question, elements (1), (3), and (4) are all obvious from the fact pattern. All that must be proved is (2). Plaintiff must show that the defendant breached a duty to take reasonable care in inspection of the product. Plaintiff should sue under strict liability because it requires a lower burden of proof.

167. (B) Hiroshima built the mechanism that sent the signals to the accelerating and braking systems. This mechanism was the only component to malfunction. The brakes wore out because of overuse. They were not defective; therefore, Tokyo will not be held liable.

168. (D) The elements of intentional infliction of emotional distress are (1) an act of extreme and outrageous conduct, (2) intent to cause severe emotional distress, (3) causation, and (4) damages. Deb's injuries were not only foreseeable, but were also the intended outcome of Beck's actions.

169. (A) The machine was operated under the exclusive control of Elsie. It should not have been turned on when the cows were not being milked and this was the cause of Kojack's injuries. Strict liability (Choice B) is inapplicable since this is a negligence action. (C) is incorrect because Kojack did not assume the risk of the machine's being turned on. (D) is inappropriate.